T0329806

DEMOCRATIC FEDERALISM

Democratic Federalism

THE ECONOMICS, POLITICS, AND
LAW OF FEDERAL GOVERNANCE

ROBERT P. INMAN

DANIEL L. RUBINFELD

PRINCETON UNIVERSITY PRESS

PRINCETON & OXFORD

Published by Princeton University Press
41 William Street, Princeton, New Jersey 08540
6 Oxford Street, Woodstock, Oxfordshire OX20 1TR

press.princeton.edu

Library of Congress Cataloging-in-Publication Data
Names: Inman, Robert P., author. | Rubinfeld, Daniel L., author.
Title: Democratic federalism : the economics, politics, and law of federal governance /
    Robert P. Inman and Daniel L. Rubinfeld.
Description: Princeton : Princeton University Press, 2020. | Includes bibliographical
    references and index.
Identifiers: LCCN 2019057550 (print) | LCCN 2019057551 (ebook) |
    ISBN 9780691202129 (hardback) | ISBN 9780691202136 (ebook)
Subjects: LCSH: Federal government. | Central-local government relations. |
    Intergovernmental fiscal relations. | Intergovernmental tax relations. |
    Revenue sharing.
Classification: LCC JC355 .I57 2020 (print) | LCC JC355 (ebook) |
    DDC 320.4/049—dc23
LC record available at https://lccn.loc.gov/2019057550
LC ebook record available at https://lccn.loc.gov/2019057551

British Library Cataloging-in-Publication Data is available

Editorial: Joe Jackson and Jacqueline Delaney
Production Editorial: Nathan Carr
Jacket/Cover Design: Layla Mac Rory
Production: Erin Suydam
Publicity: Kate Hensley and Kate Farquhar-Thomson
Copyeditor: Ashley Moore

This book has been composed in Arno Pro

Printed on acid-free paper. ∞

Printed in the United States of America

10 9 8 7 6 5 4 3 2 1

To our teachers

Martin Feldstein, Richard Musgrave, and Paul Samuelson

Healthy democratic states need strong institutions. Strong institutions are much more important than strong leaders.

—KOFI ANNAN, FORMER SECRETARY GENERAL,
THE UNITED NATIONS

CONTENTS

ACKNOWLEDGMENTS

OUR SCHOLARLY INTERESTS in matters of federal governance began in graduate school (Bob at Harvard, Dan at MIT); hence this book's dedication to our teachers who got us started. Our collaboration began soon thereafter. The division of our labors was defined early on as well. Dan followed his interests in law and economics to focus on the design of local regulations, initially zoning laws, while Bob followed his interests in political economy and economics to focus on the design of local tax and spending policies. Our first joint project, published in the *Harvard Law Review,* brought those interests together for an evaluation of then-recent judicial decisions whose goal was to ensure greater fairness in the provision of local government services. It has been a productive and rewarding collaboration ever since.

Perhaps most rewarding has been this book, for it has allowed us to both look back on and move forward with the application of our research interests in economics, political economy, and the law as they apply to the design of federal institutions and government policies. The specific motivation for this larger research agenda was South Africa's decision to adopt federal governance as the basis for its new democracy and our opportunity to observe firsthand the important deliberations defining its new constitution. The Interim Constitution agreed to in December 1993 by the leadership of the African National Congress, the National Party, and the Inkatha Freedom Party created the political institutions for a new federal democracy but left largely unsaid exactly which institutions should do what and how. To that end, President Nelson Mandela appointed six commissions and an overseeing constitutional committee to fill in the details that led to the drafting of the final constitution, which was approved unanimously by the newly elected National Assembly on May 8, 1996. One of the commissions, the Financial and Fiscal Commission, was to assign tax and spending responsibilities to the three new tiers of government—national, provincial, and municipal. Beginning in May 1994 and for the next six years, we served, along with our colleagues Richard Bird and Charles McLure, as advisers to this commission and to the government agencies responsible for the implementation of the commission's recommended policies. While certainly one of the most rewarding experiences of our professional lives, it left a deep impression on our scholarly lives as well. During our tenure, we attended many joint meetings with members and advisers to our own commission and the commissions charged with specifying a bill of rights, legislative and presidential responsibilities and powers, the role of the courts and administration of justice, and public administration. What became evident to us was how little we understood of others' agendas, and perhaps they of ours. As economists and financial advisers, political theorists and public administrators, and legal scholars and practitioners, we all had productive conversations within our own commissions, but rarely with each other. Yet we all had the same objective: create the institutions necessary for a sustainable federal democracy capable of improving the lives of all South Africans. In hindsight, we thought that our joint skills in economics, politics, and the law might help to facilitate this wider conversation. Thus this book.

The ideas that form the basis for our own contributions to this conversation were first developed during a year spent at the Center for Advanced Study in the Behavioral Sciences, located on the campus of Stanford University. The Smith Richardson Foundation provided funding for a seminar on federalism that allowed us, for the first time, to think systematically about how the different disciplines of economics, politics, and law address questions of institutional and policy design in federal governments. Seminar speakers included John Ferejohn, Peter Hall, and Barry Weingast from political science and Akil Reed Amar from the law. In addition, we presented our own work, which included the first public presentation for what now appears in this book as Chapter 6, "FIST: Having the Federal Dialogue." The impact of John's, Peter's, Barry's, and Akil's own presentations is apparent in this effort to facilitate productive conversations as to the relative strengths and weaknesses of federal institutions for democratic governance. Since then we have continued our own research and professional work, together and separately, on a wide range of applications: the political economy of fiscal policy, the impact on citizen welfare of spending and taxation in open economies, the regulation of market competition for efficiency and fairness within and across states, and the design of national policies for macroeconomic performance when states must implement those policies. Each finds a place within the chapters of this book.

It will be evident to our readers that much of our work, and all that is presented here, relies heavily on the outstanding research and thinking of earlier and contemporary scholars of federal governance. Along the way, we have sought to give full credit where credit is due. In the end we have been more than impressed, even stunned, with the length of the final list of references, and we thank Princeton University Press for never doubting the importance of each citation. The resulting bibliography is a clear testimony to how important federal institutions have become to the governance of contemporary affairs.

Special thanks are due to those colleagues, often cited in our work here, who have had the greatest impact on our thinking over the years, both in their writings and in our conversations. From economics we must mention, first, Wallace Oates. Like many of us, Wally got us started in our thinking on fiscal federalism and was a great supporter of both our economics research and our efforts to introduce the insights of political economy and law and economics into the study of federalism. Pranab Bardhan, Robin Boadway, Bob Cooter, Paul Courant, Dennis Epple, Ned Gramlich, Lewis Kornhauser, John Quigley, David Wildasin, and Jay Wilson have been important critics and supporters of our work over the years, and on several of the chapters presented here. From political science, we must first thank William Riker, the founder of the contemporary political analysis of federalism, if not all of modern political science. Riker read some of our early work, and was not discouraging—in hindsight we take that as praise. Geoff Brennan (also our host for a productive visit to the Australian National University), John Ferejohn, Geoff Garrett, Jonathan Rodden, Tom Romer, Jim Snyder, and Barry Weingast have been particularly important to our thinking on the issues studied here. From the law, we first thank Akil Amar, who presented at our Center for Advanced Study in the Behavioral Sciences seminar and exposed us to the importance of constitutional design—the legal rules—for understanding how governments perform. As economists we had been trained to treat rules as exogenous. We now appreciate that understanding how alternative rules affect citizen interactions must be the starting point for the study of institutional design. Much of what we do here is explore the implications of those rules that define what we call Democratic Federalism. In this effort, we have been fortunate to have outstanding law school colleagues to steer us along the way: particular thanks to Michael Fitts, Clay Gillette, Rick Hills, and Sam Issacharoff. Colleagues who have provided valuable comments on specific chapters, for which we are very grateful, include Gerald Carlino, Erwin Chemerinsky, Barry Eichengreen, Dennis Epple, Bill Ewald, Malcolm Feeley, Richard Herring, Simon Hix, Mattius Kum, Catherine Sharkey, and Richard Valelly.

The best test for our thinking on the issues here has been to participate in policy deliberations for the design of federal policies in environments other than the United States. We wish to thank our hosts for two such collaborations: Junaid Ahmad from the World Bank and Jørn Rattsø of the Norwegian University of Science and Technology. Junaid was our host for our work in South Africa and Jørn for our participation in the evaluation of, and subsequent decision to decentralize, the financing and provision of government services in Norway. Both have been become our close friends. An additional reality check was provided by the responses to Bob's presentation of our core arguments in Chapters 2–6 to his colleagues from the sciences, humanities, and arts during a very productive stay at the Rockefeller Foundation's Bellagio Center.

Princeton University Press has been extremely supportive of our efforts to bring this project to publication. Joe Jackson has been our editor. From our first conversation to acceptance of the manuscript to final publication, Joe's belief in the project has been an important source of confidence that we could get this done. As we had been thinking about this project for so long, the press's publication deadlines were a new experience but essential for reaching closure. Angela Piliouras handled all the details from manuscript to publication with great skill and good humor, for which we are most grateful. Special thanks to Dianne Hallowell, who did all the graphics for this project, as she has done for Bob for over thirty years. She has been a blessing.

For all those who have helped us along the way, none deserve more thanks than our families. Bob needs to thank (how inadequate that sounds!) his wife, Margie Linn, for her support over the course of this project as both a sounding board for and insightful critic of ideas both small and large. Her love and patience when all of this seemed too trivial to matter or too large to be completed were what was needed to keep pushing on. In a similar vein, Dan would not have had the patience and dedication to complete this project without the continuing strong support from his wife, Gail. At times, Gail's legal training and practical experience came in handy, but more often it was her willingness to listen and to discuss, any time of day or night, substantive issues that warranted immediate and valuable feedback.

Finally, it is an embarrassing confession to admit we had not carefully read *The Federalist Papers* until we began this project. But perhaps only from our perspective today can we now say we truly appreciate the depth and power of the *Papers'* arguments for Democratic Federalism. More humbling still is to recognize that the authors were, at the time, half our age and that their careful arguments and inspiring prose ensured the final passage of the U.S. Constitution. If this book encourages others to read or reread *The Federalist Papers*, our efforts here will have been successful.

1

Introduction

1. Introduction

The federal state, a federation of subnational self-governing units under a central national government, once the constitutional foundation for only a few Western governments, now seems to be the polity of choice, both for emerging democracies and for established states undergoing economic and democratic reforms. After long periods of military dictatorships, Argentina, Brazil, South Africa, and the democracies emerging from the old Soviet Union have each chosen to use a federal form of government. The once-dictatorial East Germany has been reconfigured as new democratic *länder* within the Federal Republic of Germany. Federal institutions have allowed Nepal to include previously discriminated minorities in a more inclusive political order. The European Union, first begun as simply a trading partnership for coal and steel and then reconfigured as a transnational federal union under the rules of the Maastricht Treaty, has now assumed central responsibility for economic and monetary policies of the twenty-eight (perhaps soon to be twenty-seven) member European nations. Centralized political systems as different as those of China, Norway, and Sweden are now finding a federal style of governance to be a potentially useful path for implementing needed economic reforms.

Even the original and perhaps still strongest of the modern federal unions—Australia, Canada, and the United States—are facing significant challenges to their current structure of federal governance: a redefinition of state financing in Australia, the ever-present question of Quebec's provincial status in Canada, and an invigorated U.S. Supreme Court seeking to limit the powers of Congress over U.S. states. Each of President Barack Obama's major policy accomplishments, from his economic stimulus to reinvigorate the U.S. economy to his health-care reform to his energy and climate regulations, has involved federal and state policy coordination and cooperation. President Donald J. Trump's effort to deregulate the U.S. economy will promote further decentralization of U.S. education, health care, and environmental policies.

What is it about federal governance that makes it so attractive? For political scientists, the attraction has always been the ability of small governments to foster political participation, democratic deliberation, and a commitment to the democratic process itself. Plato in *The Laws* and Aristotle in *The Politics* each argued that the optimal size of political jurisdictions was no more than 5,040, and ideally 1,000 citizens, as this would ensure personal representation of all residents.[1] John Milton and James Harrington saw the virtues of small government not just in its ability to encourage participation and to decide policies but also in its ability to tailor service delivery to the expressed needs of individual populations. Niccoló Machiavelli and Baron de Montesquieu favored small governments for all these reasons and then advocated a larger union with decisions made by unanimity, called a confederation, for the provision of a common defense. John Stuart Mill and Jean-Jacques Rousseau championed small governments too, but both preferred to use a majority-rule central government with representation from each small state, rather than unanimous decision-making by treaty, as the most effective means for setting the union's common course.[2] It was James Madison who provided the most complete theoretical foundation for modern federalism by joining Montesquieu's arguments for small government with David Hume's theory of representative government for conjoint, larger polities.[3] Madison's major fear was tyranny by the majority over minority democratic rights within the smaller states, but Hume's analysis of a representative central government eased his concerns. While political theorists quarreled over the relative importance of central and local governments in the ideal (here, democratic) state, most saw

---

1. Plato (1970, p. 205); Glotz (1929, p. 26); Aristotle (1958, p. 57:1265a).

2. Beer (1993, chaps. 1–3, 7) is the very best reference on the early political theories of federalism.

3. Hume took exception to the views of Machiavelli and Montesquieu that large governments could not reach consensus and function efficiently because of their "great variety of interests." Hume argued in his essay "The Ideal of a Perfect Commonwealth" that debate and discussion would not be dysfunctional but rather the means to reveal the "public interest." Madison embraced Hume's arguments as he made his own case for representative government in *Federalist* No. 39 and for the benefits of discussion and debate in *Federalist* Nos. 10 and 51. See Beer (1993, pp. 264–270) and Beer (1978), where Madison's theory of federalism is seen as combining the ideas of Montesquieu and Hume as "representational federalism."

both tiers as making important contributions to citizen participation and democratic stability.

Beginning with Adam Smith, economists too have appreciated the advantages of jointly using both large, central governments and smaller, local governments, now for the efficient provision of government services. When the benefits of an economic activity encompass a large number of individuals or a wide geographical area, a government of many people or wide reach will be needed for the cost-efficient provision of the public good or service. For Smith this included national defense, the administration of justice, protection of private property, and the provision of public works that benefit the whole society: "The expense of defending the society . . . of the administration of justice . . . [and] the expense of maintaining good roads and communications [are], no doubt, beneficial to the whole society, and may, therefore, without any injustice, be defrayed by the general contribution of the whole society" (bk. 5, chap. 1, pt. 4, pp. 814–815).[4] Conversely, when an activity benefits only a few people or the benefits are spatially concentrated, then a smaller government in numbers or geography will be preferred. Again, Smith had it right:

> Even those public works which are of such a nature that they cannot afford any revenue for maintaining themselves, but of which the convenience is confined to some particular place or district, are always better maintained by a local or provincial revenue, under the management of a local and provincial administration, than by general revenue of the state. . . . The abuses which sometimes creep into the administration of a local or provincial revenue, however enormous they may appear, are in reality almost always very trifling, in comparison with those which commonly take place in the administration and expenditure of the revenue of a great nation. They are, besides, much more easily corrected. (Bk. 5, chap. 1, pt. 3, pp. 730–731)

Larger governments are less expensive, but smaller governments are more likely to provide the right match of citizen preferences to service levels. Just as do their colleagues in political theory, economic theorists debate the relative virtues of central and local governments in the ideal (here, efficient) state, but again, most see both tiers as making valued contributions to the efficient provision of government services.

Political philosophers and legal scholars concerned primarily with protecting individual rights and liberties have found their guidance for the potential

---

4. Page numbering is for Smith (1976).

benefits of federal governance well summarized by Alexander Hamilton and James Madison in *The Federalist Papers*.[5] Madison's *Federalist* No. 10 makes the now-famous case for the virtues of a central democratic government as a protector of personal rights and liberties: "[A national legislature] make[s] it less probable that a majority of the whole will have a common motive to invade the rights of other citizens; or if such a common motive exists, it will be more difficult for all who feel it to discover their own strength, and to act in unison with each other" (Hamilton, Madison, and Jay, 1982, p. 48).

First, a national legislature of state-represented minorities provides protection by being able to check any state-level tyranny of one of the member states. A national bill of rights, a national court with the power to adjudicate state violations of those common rights, and a national army to enforce adherence to the common standards when violations do occur can be used by any aggrieved minority within a member state for relief and subsequent protection. But second, states are needed too, and particularly so in societies where one large ethnic, religious, or economic group constitutes a national majority or near majority. In *Federalist* No. 51 Madison argues that in such polities, state governments can provide protection against tyranny by a majority-controlled central government: "In the compound republic of America, the power surrendered by the people, is first divided between two distinct governments, and then the portion allotted to each, subdivided among distinct and separate departments. Hence a double security arises to the rights of the people. *The different governments will control each other*; at the same time that each will be controlled by itself" (Hamilton, Madison, and Jay, 1982, p. 264; italics added). States provide these protections through coordinated political, and perhaps military, action. Hamilton in *Federalist* No. 26 sees state legislatures using politics ("VOICE") and military powers ("ARM") to check the central government threats to the rights of citizens: "The state Legislature will always be not only vigilant but suspicious and jealous guardians of the rights of the citizens, against encroachments from the Federal government, will constantly have their attentions awake to the conduct of the national rulers and will be ready enough . . . to sound the alarm to the people and not only to be the VOICE but if necessary the ARM of their discontent" (Hamilton, Madison, and Jay, 1982, p. 129). For

5. Certainly this is so for America's leading legal theorists, such as Ackerman (1991, chap. 7), Amar (1987), Dworkin (1986, pp. 381–382), Ely (1980, chap. 4), Michelman (1977), and Sunstein (1987), and for leading jurists too—for example, Breyer (2005, chap. 2), McConnell (1987), and Scalia (1982).

Madison and Hamilton, the national and state governments are "but different agents and trustees of the people," as the common electorate uses national powers to check state abuses and conversely. Like political theorists seeking democracy and economists valuing efficiency, the task for those who champion "justice [a]s the end of government" will be to find that "judicious modification and mixture of the *federal principle*" most conducive to freedom's cause (Hamilton, Madison, and Jay, p. 265).

The federal form of governance offers those seeking a more democratic, efficient, and just society a credible alternative to the polar alternatives of a single, unitary state or a loose and often shifting network of small governments. It was the earlier experiences of the American colonies with these two alternatives, first the oppressive rule of unitary England and then the ineffectiveness of their own Articles of Confederation, that led their representatives to the 1787 Philadelphia Constitutional Convention to fashion, arguably, the first *modern* federal constitution for their new United States.[6] What was *modern* in the new constitution was a structure of two-tier representative government by majority rule designed explicitly to promote and protect a stable democracy, to provide for a common market and the efficient protection of the member states yet permit local choice for what were seen as important local public services, and to protect the rights and liberties of the citizens of the new republic.

If *The Federalist Papers* provided the intellectual arguments for this new form of governance, the state-by-state ratification process was its test as practical politics. The audiences were not always friendly, particularly so in Massachusetts, New Hampshire, Virginia, and New York. But the new constitution survived intact, with the promise to dissenters to approve a bill of rights (Amendments I–IX) and to provide explicit recognition that powers not delegated to the national government by the Constitution would remain with the states and their peoples (Amendment X). On May 29, 1790, the new constitution was approved and the federal union was formed.[7] Modern Democratic Federalism was now a political reality.

---

6. Supporting the view that the U.S. Constitution was the first truly federal constitution are three of the leading political and legal theorists of federalism, Martin Diamond (1961), Samuel Beer (1978, 1993), and Akhil Reed Amar (1987).

7. For a factual history of the ratification process, see Rossiter (1966, chaps. 14, 15) and Rakove (1996, chap. 5). For a survey of the ideological foundations of the ratification debates, see Beer (1993, chap. 10).

We set as our broad task here that of detailing and evaluating the contemporary arguments for the democratic federal state. In this introductory chapter, we first define what we see as the key institutional features of federal governance and provide evidence as to the relative importance of federal states among the nations of the world; see Table 1.1. We then provide a first (some might say speculative) empirical evaluation of the ability of Democratic Federalism to advance the three objectives embraced by its supporters: economic efficiency, political participation and democratic stability, and the protection of individual rights and liberties; see Table 1.2. Causation is always a question in such exercises, but the correlations are clear. Societies governed by the principles of Democratic Federalism are richer, safer for personal rights and liberties, and democratically more engaged. The stronger case for a causal connection from Democratic Federalism to valued outcomes will come in Part I, Chapters 2 (Economic Federalism) and 3 (Cooperative Federalism), and then in Chapters 4 and 5 (Democratic Federalism), where we present the theoretical arguments and direct evidence for how the democratic institutions of federal governance affect efficiency, participation, and rights.

From Part I we conclude that there is much to recommend Democratic Federalism as a way to organize national governance, but, perhaps like all political institutions, it is fragile and susceptible to what William Riker (1964) has called the "overawing" tendencies of centralized government. There are good reasons why the Founding Fathers hoped to preserve and protect state government responsibilities with the adoption of the Tenth Amendment to the U.S. Constitution and why the Maastricht Treaty establishing the European Union made the principle of "subsidiarity" so central to EU governance. Part II proposes our own version of these protections, which we call the Federalism Impact Statement, or FIST. Chapter 6 outlines our FIST proposal and stresses the importance of an independent judiciary for its enforcement. Chapters 7 and 8 implement FIST in two important policy areas: fiscal policy (Chapter 7) and regulatory policy (Chapter 8).

There will be many examples throughout the book illustrating how existing federal institutions might affect national policies and explaining how one might reform those institutions to improve performance, whether to enhance democratic participation, economic efficiency, or rights and fairness. But there is the prior question that we address in Part III: Do you want to be federal at all, and if so, what is the best way to facilitate the transition to federal governance? Chapter 9 provides a summary of the EU's path to federal governance and an evaluation of its current strengths (economic) and weaknesses (participation and rights). We suggest a modest reform path to what we have called Cooperative Federalism. Chapter 10 examines the central role of federal institutions in what at the time was, and hopefully can still be, the last century's most impressive transition from dictatorship to democracy—the creation of a fully free South Africa. We argue that the peaceful transition would not have been possible without the adoption of Democratic Federalism. Whether that constitution will survive the corrupting and centralizing influences of modern South African politics remains an open question, but one we address explicitly.

Chapter 11 summarizes our results and stresses the need for a companion volume, perhaps called *Unitary Democracy*. We hope we will have made a compelling case for Democratic Federalism, but to be called a "winner" with any certitude, it must be shown to outperform its major competitors on one or more of the valued outcomes.[8] In the end, we would expect Democratic Federalism to be best for some nations, unitary governance best for others, and finally, remaining as an independent state and negotiating treaties a third alternative. Chapter 11 concludes by offering some thoughts to begin this conversation.

2. What Is Federal?

The word *federalism* has its roots in the Latin *foedus*, meaning "league," "treaty," or "compact." In a broad sense, *federal* has come to represent any form of government that brings together, in an alliance, constituent governments each of which recognizes the legitimacy of an overarching central government to make decisions on matters once exclusively the responsibility of the individual member states. All definitions of the federal state begin from this point: two or more lower-tier governments joined together to form a single central government with both the lower-tier and central levels of government having responsibilities for policies benefiting the citizens of all member states.[9]

---

8. Two important recent studies have begun this comparison. First, Treisman (2007) provides a valuable critique of political decentralization and in the process begins the theoretical case for unitary governance. Second, Alesina and Spolaore (2005) present an economic framework for the comparison and provide valuable evidence that will be needed to make the choice.

9. Elazar (1968, p. 353), in his survey of federal governance, defines federalism "to describe the mode of political organization which unites separate polities within an overarching political system so as to allow each to maintain its fundamental political integrity, ... [accomplished] by

Typically, the specification of lower-tier governments is based on geography, and responsibilities are those formally assigned to them by the federal constitution.[10] Policy responsibilities need not be exclusive to one level of government or another. Responsibilities can be shared, and in this case assignment is called *concurrent*. More *decentralized* federal states will have more provincial or state governments or assign more policy responsibilities and revenues to those governments. Such constitutionally grounded definitions of federalism are overly restrictive, however. Kenneth Wheare (1964, p. 33), for example, rules out as federal Montesquieu's foundational analysis of informal unions of independent states and excludes from the analysis the United States when governed by the Articles of Confederation, the Union of Utrecht of 1579 (United Netherlands), the Austro-Hungarian Empire under the Compromise of 1867, Germany under the Imperial Constitution of 1871, and now the European Union.[11] By Wheare's definition, only the United States today, Canada, Switzerland, Germany, and Australia qualify as federal.

In his now-classic *Fiscal Federalism* (1972), Wallace Oates also found Wheare's narrowly legalistic definition too confining for his own study of how multitier, hierarchical governments might best provide public goods and services. For Oates, "What is crucial . . . is simply that different levels of decision-making do exist, each of which determines levels of provision of particular public services" (p. xvi). If Wheare's definition is too confining, we find that Oates's definition admits too much. For example, a single, unitary government that grants its lower-tier administrative agencies policy discretion would qualify as federal by Oates's definition. As Oates himself notes, "By this definition, practically any fiscal system is federal or at least possesses federal elements" (p. xvi).

We think William Riker, arguably political science's most careful and influential scholar of federalism, has found the productive middle ground. Riker specifies federal governance as a "political organization in which the activities of government are divided between regional governments and a central government in such a way that each kind of government has some activities on which it makes final decisions" (1975, p. 101). By Riker's definition, there are multiple tiers of *governments*, by which Riker means two or more coordinate political entities

---

distributing power among general and constituent governments in a manner designed to protect the existence and authority of all governments."

10. See Wheare (1964).

11. As well as states defined not by geography but by age, race, religion, or ethnic origin; see J. McGarry (2002, p. 425) and Sunstein (1988, p. 1586).

each with elected—not appointed—leadership and each with its own sphere of responsibilities. This distinguishes Riker from Wheare's tightly legalistic specification of federal governance and distinguishes him from Oates's overly inclusive economic specification by excluding as federal all unitary governments managing public policy with a hierarchical bureaucracy.

Under Riker's definition of federal governance, a federal state may arise because the independent local governments constitutionally empower an encompassing national government with its own sphere of responsibilities, as was the case for the original thirteen U.S. colonies.[12] Alternatively, a federal state may arise when the constitution of a new nation-state creates a group of provinces and assigns to them specific governmental responsibilities, leaving residual powers in the hands of the national government, as was true for the new South African constitution. In both cases, the number of provinces and the allocation of government responsibilities between the provincial and national tiers of governments are specified, though perhaps only vaguely, by a national constitution.

While the specification of multiple provincial governments and the domains for provincial and central government policy-making are the two necessary features of federal governance, they have not always been seen as sufficient. Certainly not so for the framers of the U.S. Constitution.[13] Motivated by the experience of the colonies under British rule, the concern was an overarching central government. The colonies' disagreements with England were not over what policies the colonies could or could not institute—the policy responsibilities of the colonies were sizeable by any measure—but rather over what the British Parliament could do without consulting the colonies. Indeed, at the time of the Revolutionary War, the level of taxes collected by the British from the colonies was almost trivial. The colonists' complaint was over process. The famous saying from the streets of Boston was quite precise on the point: "No taxation without representation." The concern was not policy; it was the democratic process.[14] George Mason, a representative to the

12. See Rakove (1996, chap. 7).

13. Even though the Constitution did require the states to directly elect the national executive through population-weighted voting in the Electoral College and gave the states the ultimate power to amend the Constitution with three-fourth's approval.

14. Early efforts by American pamphleteers, John Dickinson in particular, to justify the American position of "no taxation" sought to defend the colonial position as a disagreement over appropriate policy assignments, not one of representation. But William Knox, in *The Controversy between Great Britain and Her Colonies*, saw a policy debate as to whether the tax was

Constitutional Convention from Virginia and a champion of states' rights, expressed the concern directly: "The State Legislatures also ought to have some means of defending themselves against encroachments of the National Government" (Rakove, 1996, p. 62). The final compromise for the framers of the U.S. Constitution was a coequal chamber called the Senate with equal representation from each state government, chosen directly by the state legislatures (Rakove, 1996, pp. 57–79). Along with national and provincial or local governments and separately assigned responsibilities and powers, Martin Diamond argues, the direct representation of states within the national government should be added as a third essential feature of federal governance. Paraphrasing Madison from *Federalist* No. 39, Diamond states, "The House of Representatives is national because it derives from the whole people treated as a single body politic; the people will be represented in it, Madison says, exactly as they would be in any unitary state. Contrarily, the Senate is the *federal element* in the central government because it derives from, and represents equally, the states treated as 'political and coequal societies'" (1977, p. 1278; italics added). The role of this provincial chamber will be to provide a forum for expressing and coordinating provincial interests in the setting of national policies. By acting in concert, it was hoped that this chamber would protect the unique interests of provincial governments to set policies that may stand in conflict with national policies; see, for example, the arguments by legal scholar Herbert Wechsler (1954) and Jesse Choper (1980, chap. 4). For Wechsler and Choper, the provincial chamber was not just desirable but in fact foundational for a stable system of federal governance. Wechsler argues, "If this analysis is correct, the national political process in the United States—*and especially the role of the states in the composition and selection of the central government*—is intrinsically well adapted to retarding or restraining

---

trade policy (assigned to the Crown) or tax policy (assigned to the colonies) as hair-splitting: "Either the colonies are a part of the community of Great Britain or . . . [they are] in no case . . . subject to the jurisdiction of that legislative power . . . which is the British Parliament." So stated, the debate moved from theoretical arguments of what is or is not a compelling central government policy responsibility to matters of representation. Edmund Burke in his famous speech to Parliament "On American Taxation" clearly saw the consequences of British intransigence: "When you drive him hard the boar will turn upon the hunters. If that sovereignty and their freedom cannot be reconciled, which will they take? They will cast your sovereignty in your face, nobody will be argued into slavery." (MacLaughlin, 1918, p. 231) MacLaughlin presents this history and concludes, "It is the practices of English imperialism [to which] we owe the very essence of American federalism" (1918, p. 216).

new intrusions by the center on to domains of the state" (1954, p. 558; italics added). Choper elevates this argument to the status of an absolute requirement: "The major thesis of this chapter—hereafter referred to as the Federalism Proposal—may be briefly stated: The judiciary should not decide constitutional questions respecting the ultimate power of the national government vis-a-vis the states; rather [such issues] should be treated as nonjusticiable, final resolution being relegated to the political branches—that is, Congress (i.e., the Senate) and the President" (1980, p. 175).

To the requirements for federal governance that (1) there be both national and lower-tier (state, provincial, or local) governments, each recognized as a separate government, and that (2) both national and lower-tier governments have assigned policy responsibilities and the ability (typically revenue) to exercise those responsibilities, we now add the requirement that (3) lower-tier governments have direct representation in a central government chamber with veto powers over national legislation. When these three requirements are met, we will classify the government as federal. When both lower-tier and national government representatives are democratically elected, then the government is classified as Democratic Federalism.

Table 1.1 provides a list of the world's federal governments divided into two groups. The first we classify as governed by *constitutional federalism*, reflecting the fact that the country's constitution specifically creates lower-tier governments, assigns to those governments the responsibilities and the powers needed for their implementation, and finally, requires the direct representation of the provinces or lower-tier governments in the central government. This is the case for the United States and the new Republic of South Africa. A second group we classify as governed by *de facto federalism*. These countries allow for politically independent lower-tier governments and their assigned responsibilities but do not allow for their direct representation to the central government. This is the case for the Scandinavian democracies, Italy, and Japan. The list of countries satisfying our three requirements for federal governance includes all countries typically called "federal" by other scholars.[15] Finally,

---

15. See Riker (1964, chap. 2), Wheare (1964, chap. 1), Watts (1999, table 2), Bird (1986, pt. 1), Boix (2003, p. 161), and Griffiths and Nerenberg (2002). Within each federal category, we also indicate which countries have been primarily democratic or dictatorial governments for the period from 1950 to today. Those countries that have transitioned between democracy and dictatorship over the period are allocated to democracy's columns if they have been democratic by the Przeworski et al. (2000) criteria for at least half of the last seventy years and are also

TABLE 1.1. Federal Countries

Constitutional Federalism		De facto federalism
Democratic	Dictatorial	Democratic
Argentina (.47)	Comoros (NA)	Denmark (.43)
Australia (.21)	Ethiopia (.05)	Finland (.30)
Austria (.46)	Malaysia (.15)	France (.30)
Belgium (.15)	Mexico (.24)†	Italy (.20)
Bosnia-Herzegovina (NA)	Nigeria (.55)	Japan (.64)
Brazil (.39)	Pakistan (.25)	Netherlands (.21)
Canada (.51)	Russia (NA)	Norway (.26)
Colombia (.26)	Tanzania (NA)	Sweden (.37)
Germany (.50)	United Arab Emirates (NA)	Uruguay (.43)
India (.33)		
Kosovo-Serbia (NA)		
Nepal (NA)		
South Africa (.18)		
Spain (.15)		
Switzerland (.51)		
United States (.46)		
Venezuela (.05)*		

Notes: Countries qualifying as *constitutionally federal* states have the three qualifying features of the federal state—independent provincial, state, or local governments; own revenue and policy responsibility; representation in the national government—explicitly defined by the country's adopted constitution. Countries qualifying as *de facto federal* states have independently elected provincial, state, or local governments and, while not constitutionally required, those governments play an active role in the financing and provision of public services. In the case of de facto federal countries, the provincial, state, or local governments have locally elected representatives but do not have direct representation in the national legislature. Included within parentheses is the percentage of the country's government nondebt revenues that are raised by provincial, state, or local governments, averaged over the decades 1960–2005; NA indicates that the revenue shares could not be computed from available data.

*Venezuela is classified as dictatorial after 1999.

†Mexico is classified as democratically federal after 2000.

Table 1.1 separates the federal governments into those that are democratic and those that are dictatorial, with democratic governments defined by Przeworski et al. (2000) as those that have had contested elections and recognized transitions of power for more than half of the years since 1970 and are democratic today. Together the democratic and dictatorial federal states occupy 52 percent of the world's land area, govern 46 percent of the world's population, and account for 54 percent of the world's incomes. Adding the European Union as a

democratic today. South Africa and Nepal are new federal democracies and are listed in Table 1.1 as democratic.

new federal state to the list of federal countries increases the share of the world's land area to 53 percent, the share of the world's population to 53 percent, and the share of the world's income to 71 percent. The reach of these institutions over the world's people and incomes strongly suggests that a careful analysis of federal governance is in order.

3. Does Democratic Federalism Matter? A First Look

Table 1.2 provides a first look at the potential for the institutions of Democratic Federalism to promote the valued societal outcomes of economic efficiency, citizen participation and democratic stability, and the protection of individual rights and liberties.[16] The analysis compares the performance along each of seven valued outcomes for the seventeen countries listed in Table 1.1 as both constitutionally federal and democratic with a sample of fifty-six other countries, nine of which are federal dictatorships, twenty-five of which are either de facto federal or unitary democracies, and twenty-two of which are unitary dictatorships. The performance measure for each of the outcomes is an average of the annual performance measures for the sample period, 1965 to 2000.[17] The two measures for economic performance are an index of government efficiency (bureaucratic efficiency and lack of corruption) and market efficiency (the average product of workers). The three measures for participation and democratic stability are the rate of voter participation in national elections, the average annual rate of peaceful protests and demonstrations, and the percentage of years over our sample period (1965–2000) that the country has been democratic. The two measures for individual rights are indices based on the Freedom House measures for the protection of property rights and of political and civil rights. With the exception of five countries, all the constitutional institutions for the countries in the sample were in place before

16. Table 1.2 is an update of the results first reported in Inman (2007).

17. Many studies evaluating the contribution of democracy and federal institutions to economic outcomes—most often economic growth—relate the outcome to being democratic last year and to lagged levels in the share of government spending (or revenues) done by state and local governments. Such studies run the risk of conflating the consequences of temporary shocks to outcomes with the possible consequences of a more fundamental, institutional change. The appropriate approach for measuring the impact of institutions on outcomes is to relate the history of institutions to the long-run pattern in an outcome of interest; see Tavares and Wacziarg (2001). The results in Table 1.2 employ this historical approach.

TABLE 1.2. Democratic Federalism and Valued Outcomes

	Government efficiency	GDP per worker	Voter participation	Protests and demonstrations	Percentage of years democratic	Rights	
						Property rights	Political/civil rights
Absolute Latitude	.007	.010	.004	.069	.004	.007	.007
	(.001)*	(.001)*	(.001)*	(.026)*	(.002)*	(.001)*	(.002)*
Democracy	.083	.136	.065	.014	.513	.274	.231
	(.039)*	(.048)*	(.043)	(.920)	(.062)*	(.058)*	(.060)*
	.39	**.46**	**.41**	**.01**	**1.25**	**.84**	**.75**
Democratic Federalism	.100	.211	.038	-1.74	.201	.160	.120
	(.047)*	(.056)*	(.055)	(1.03)*	(.076)*	(.070)*	(.070)*
	.47	**.71**	**.24**	**-.68**	**.49**	**.49**	**.39**
R²(Adj)	.66	.75	.36	.21	.73	.67	.61

Notes: Standard errors for each regression coefficient are reported within parentheses. Reported below each regression coefficient and its standard error is the estimated effect size (shown in bold if statistically significant) as a measure of the magnitude of the difference between Democracy and Democratic Federalism and Dictatorships for each measure of a valued outcome. Effect size (also known as Cohen's d) is computed as the estimated coefficient divided by the standard error of each outcome measure as reported below.

*Statistical significance from zero at the 90 percent (or higher) confidence interval.

Measure of Valued Outcomes

Government efficiency: The Hall-Jones index of government antidiversion policies, created for the years 1986–1995 as a measure of government's enforcement of law and order and control of corruption, scaled from 0 to 1, with a higher score representing policies supportive of private economic activity. Mean = .664; SD = .214. *Source:* Hall and Jones (1999).

GDP per worker: Output per worker in 1988 as estimated by Hall-Jones, measured relative to the United States as a value equal to 1.00. Mean = 375; SD = 298. *Source:* Hall and Jones (1999).

Voter participation: Rate of voter participation in national elections measured as the number of voters as a share of registered voters. Mean = .652; S.D. =.159. *Source: World Handbook of Political and Social Indicators, Various Years.*

Protests and demonstrations: The sum of peaceful protests, demonstrations, and political strikes within the country in a year, averaged over the period 1962–1977. Mean = 1.47, S.D. 2.57. *Source: World Handbook of Political and Social Indicators, Various Years.*

Percentage of years democratic: Percent of years from 1965 to 2000 that the country is classified as democratic. Mean = .520; S.D. = .410. Source: Adam Przeworski, et. al. (1990) supplemented by *Freedom in the World: Annual Survey of Political Rights and Civil Liberties,* Freedom House, 1991–2000.

Property rights: The inverse of the Freedom House's measure of property rights protection (scaled as 1–7, with higher values representing weaker property rights), averaged over the period 1965–1995. The inverse is used so that higher values represent stronger property rights protection. Mean = .458; S.D. = .327. *Source:* Freedom House: *Freedom in the World: Annual Survey of Political Rights and Civil Liberties,* Various Years.

Political/civil rights: The inverse of the Freedom House's measure of civil and political rights protection (scaled as 1–7, with higher values representing weaker civil or political rights), averaged over the period 1965–1995. The inverse is used so that higher values represent stronger civil and political rights protection. Mean = .427; S.D. = .306. *Source: Freedom House: Freedom in the World: Annual Survey of Political Rights and Civil Liberties, Various Years.*

1960, and most before 1950.[18] Together the full sample includes 76 percent of the world's population and 85 percent of the world's income.

Table 1.2 reports the estimated difference and associated effect sizes from being a democratic nation (democracy = 1, 0 otherwise) and then having federal institutions beyond being democratic (Democratic Federalism = 1, if both democratic and federal, 0 otherwise) when compared with being governed as a dictatorship. A positive coefficient represents an improvement in performance over that observed under dictatorships; a negative coefficient represents a reduction in the measured outcome (e.g., protests and demonstrations) in democracies and federal democracies when compared with dictatorships. The reported effect sizes (when statistically significant, reported in bold) compare the estimated differences in performance with the standard deviation of the performance outcome and are a measure of the relative importance of being democratic and federal rather than a dictatorship.[19] The joint impact on each of the outcomes of being both democratic *and* federal will be the summation of the marginal effects of both democracy and Democratic Federalism. Finally, for each performance outcome, the contributions of democracy and federalism are measured conditional on the country's distance from the equator (absolute latitude), shown in previous research to be an important "all-purpose" control for a broad list of a country's cultural, political, legal, and economic institutions.[20]

Both governance by democracy and governance using democratic federal institutions show statistically significant and positive advantages over dictatorships for all of the valued outcomes, with the exception of voter participation in national elections (even after controlling for compulsory voting). Statistically significant effect sizes for each estimated difference between democracy

18. The exceptions were the newly independent countries of Bangladesh (unitary dictatorship, 1971), Mauritius (unitary dictatorship, 1968), Comoros (federal dictatorship, 1975), the United Arab Emirates (federal dictatorship, 1971), and Zimbabwe (unitary dictatorship, 1980). Omitting these countries from the analysis has no effect on the estimated effects.

19. Effect sizes, also known as Cohen's *d*, are a common metric used in psychology and educational research to evaluate the potential importance of an intervention between treatments (Democracy and Democratic Federalism) and control groups (Dictatorships); see Ferguson (2009).

20. See Bloom and Sachs (1998) and Acemoglu, Johnson, and Robinson (2001). Including an expanded list of controls in the core specifications of Table 1.2 (to include ethnic, religious, and language fractionalization, natural resource endowments; a country's colonial and legal origins; and whether national governance is presidential or parliamentary) does not meaningfully affect the results for Democracy and Democratic Federalism.

and then federal democracies with dictatorships are shown in bold. Effect sizes greater than 0.2 are generally considered "large enough" to encourage a deeper examination for why outcomes differ between the groups.[21] First, being a democracy and adopting federal institutions to become a federal democracy both show large differences in performance over dictatorships, particularly so for economic efficiency and the protection of property, civil, and political rights. Not surprisingly, being democratic in 1960 or earlier has a strong impact on remaining democratic over the sample period, 1965–2000, although there are exceptions (Brazil, Argentina, and Greece). What is also important is the additional impact that being both democratic and federal has on democratic stability. The statistically significant added contribution of federal institutions to stability above democracy alone may come from the ability of Democratic Federalism to significantly reduce the average annual rate of political protests and demonstrations, as in Table 1.2, just what we might hope for by allowing politically independent local governance and citizen choice.

Figure 1.1 provides one plausible—but certainly not the only—explanation for how democracy and federal institutions might affect the valued outcomes in Table 1.2. First, the path from a federal constitution to democracy represents the possibility that the federal constitution itself may allow agreements between competing minorities, and thus a transition to democracy that would not have been possible without the constitutional protections provided by politically independent local or state governments. This was certainly the case for South Africa as it negotiated its new democracy.[22] Second, the path from federal constitution to Democratic Federalism creates the two key institutions defining a federal democracy: (1) independent state or provincial governments (N = number of state governments) and (2) the direct representation of those governments in the national legislature (R = 1 if representation, 0 otherwise), shown in Figure 1.1. Third, Democratic Federalism links back to democracy as federal governance contributes directly to democratic stability by providing a peaceful outlet for minority disagreements with the national government. Fourth, democracy is foundational for the protection of individual rights and liberties. This is shown in Figure 1.1 by the two direct paths from democracy to our measures of property rights and civil and political rights. Fifth, the two institutions specific to Democratic Federalism (N, R) add to the protection of rights through their creation and political protection of

21. Interventions with effect sizes greater than .2 are typically considered "promising," while effect sizes greater than .5 are "recommended" for intervention; see Ferguson (2009).

22. See Waldmeir (1997) and our Chapter 10.

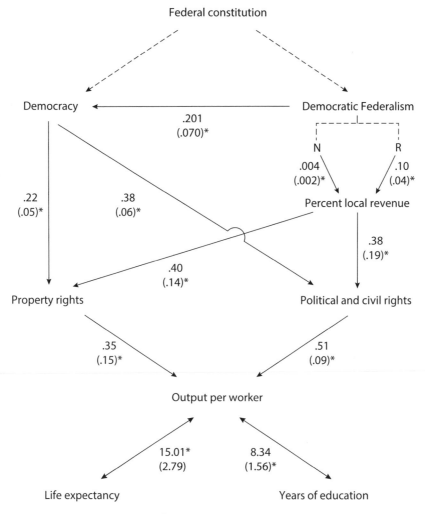

FIGURE 1.1. Federal Institutions and Valued Outcomes

Note: All estimated effects reported along the pathways are for the political institutions before 1960 and for the average of annual performance outcomes for the sample period, 1965–2000. The estimated effects also control for the absolute latitude of the country. An asterisk indicates statistical significance at the 90 percent level of confidence or higher. See Inman (2007).

policy-independent state and local governments. They do so by increasing the share of national revenues raised and controlled by these governments.[23]

23. It is the local share of national revenues that has been shown in previous research by political scientists and economists to have a significant impact on economic growth and other valued outcomes; see Hatfield (2015) and Boix (2003, chap. 4). The state and local share of

The direct representation of local and state governments in the national legislature ensures the voice of local interests in setting national policy. The two
paths from the share of national revenues under local control to rights illustrate
the importance of politically independent local governments for these protections. The links are statistically significant and lend empirical support to the
legal arguments for a strong role for state and local governments in democracies.[24] Sixth, the paths from property, civil, and political rights to output per
worker show the importance of rights for national economic performance, a
result found consistently in previous economics research explaining cross-
country growth rates and national incomes.[25] Stronger property rights protect
and encourage investment in physical capital, while stronger civil and political
rights protect and encourage investments in human capital. Both investments
increase output per worker. The estimated impacts of rights on incomes are
sizeable.[26] It is most likely through this path that democracy and Democratic
Federalism improve a country's economic fortunes, as we have estimated in
Table 1.1. Finally, Figure 1.1 shows that higher national incomes lead to improved health, measured here by the life expectancy of citizens in 2000, and

---

revenues used here measures locally raised revenues only and thus excludes intergovernmental
transfers. Such transfers may come with substantial national government restrictions. For the
democracies in the sample, both unitary and federal, the means of the percentage of local revenue are .16 and .29, respectively. As a measure of the importance of each institution, the estimated elasticity of percentage of local revenue with respect to N is .14 and the effect size for
$R = 1$ (representation) is .33.

24. The elasticity of both the index of property rights and that of civil and political rights
with respect to the percentage of local revenues is .15. That is, increasing the percentage of local
revenues by one standard deviation from its mean of .29 to .45 (an 55 percent increase) will increase the value of both rights indices by 8 percent, or from their mean index value of .45 to .50,
both within the range of most of southern Europe countries during the sample period. Thus,
plausible increases in the percentage of local revenue will not turn a poorly performing democracy into Switzerland, but it will stabilize rights protections, as is the hope of most legal scholars
supporting federalism; see, for example, Rapaczynski (1985).

25. See, for example, Hall and Jones (1999).

26. The results reported in Figure 1.1 provide a measure of the importance of rights performance for national incomes. The elasticity of output per worker with respect to property rights
is .43 and with respect to political and civil rights is .57. All estimates are for democracies only.
A one-standard-deviation increase in the property rights index, or 40 percent, will increase
output per worker by 16 percent, while a one-standard-deviation increase in the political and
civil rights index, or 50 percent, will increase output per worker by 25 percent.

to increased investments in education for both men and women.[27] Both of these favorable outcomes will "feed back" to increase income at a later date (thus the double arrows).

Table 1.2 and Figure 1.1 are, as advertised, meant to be a "first look" at the possible role for the institutions of Democratic Federalism as they might affect the economic, political, and personal lives of a nation's citizens. On each of our measures of country performance, democratic countries and particularly federal democracies do better. Government and markets are more efficient. Democracy seems more stable. The property, civil, and political rights of individuals seem better protected. Whether these connections are *causal* or *coincidental*, we cannot be certain. But for us, the results strongly encourage a deeper look at the best theoretical and empirical analyses of federal governance and valued outcomes. That is what we propose for the chapters that follow. To anticipate our conclusion, we have emerged even more confident in the virtues of Democratic Federalism.

4. A Quick Tour

By necessity, any successful evaluation of political institutions must be interdisciplinary. Our efforts will be no exception. We draw on work by economists, political scientists, and legal scholars. Each discipline has its own primary concerns: economics with efficiency and growth, political science with citizen participation and democratic stability, and the law with the protection of rights and liberties. Scholars in each discipline focus on their own "means" to their own "ends." The economist uses prices and incentives, the political scientist voting and collective actions, and the legal scholar rules and their enforcement. As social scientists, we should not work in isolation. Much of today's best scholarship borrows freely from, and often contributes to, the understandings of its sister disciplines. A careful evaluation of the strengths and weaknesses of federal governance will require this integrated perspective. Each of our chapters seeks to apply the insights of all three disciplines to our

---

27. The two additional outcomes included in Figure 1.1—life expectancy and average years of education—are measured as follows. Average years of education: years of education for male and female residents over the age of twenty-five, averaged over the period 1965–1989 for democracies, mean = 6.4; SD = 2.63 (Barro and Lee, 2001). Life expectancy: in the year 2000 for democracies, mean = 73.47; SD = 5.84 (World Bank, 2005). The elasticity of the years of education with respect to output per worker is .67 and that of life expectancy is .12. The low elasticity of health with respect to income reflects the impact of income on health after controlling for geography.

central question: *how best to design the institutions of federal governance to achieve the objectives of economic efficiency, democratic participation, and the protection of individual rights and liberties.* Part I, "The Institutions of Democratic Federalism," begins the analysis.

Chapter 2, "Economic Federalism," presents the first of our three models of federal governance. The chapter examines, both theoretically and empirically, the causal connections from multiple local and provincial governments and their local assignment of revenues and services to our three goals of economic efficiency, political participation, and the protection of rights and liberties. Economic Federalism does not require the direct representation of provincial or local governments within the central government. Rather, the central government is managed by a single leader, a president, elected nationally. The president makes and implements all national policies.[28] We review the theory and evidence as to the performance of competitive lower-tier governments and find that allowing citizens variety and choice provides significant economic benefits in efficiency and growth. Technology matters, however. Benefits are greatest for those services that can be efficiently provided to relatively small populations and where service benefits and costs are geographically concentrated within the community. If there are economies of scale in production or spillovers across jurisdictional boundaries, then national government provision will be needed. That is the task of the nationally elected president. We conclude that from the perspective of economic efficiency, there is much to recommend Economic Federalism.

Matters are less clear for how Economic Federalism might perform against the goals of democratic participation and the protection of rights and liberties. While the evidence is supportive of increased citizen involvement with government decision-making at the local level, it is at the national level, for reasons of economies of scale and spillovers, that much of an economy's public dollars will be allocated. Here direct citizen participation, beyond the vote for president, is likely to be minimal. As for the protection of rights and liberties, having many local and provincial governments will allow citizens to choose that community most hospitable to their preferences and way of life. The extension of rights for the LGBTQ community in the United States is one recent and

---

28. In this regard, Economic Federalism would be considered "de facto federalism" as reported in Tables 1.1 and 1.2. Thomas Aquinas's theory of church governance is a theory of Economic Federalism. The pope serves as the "president" and the local parishes as "local governments" to provide education, charity, health care, and religious services to local parishioners; see Beer (1993, p. 50). This governance structure remains in place today; see Kelley (2000).

prominent example. But this advantage is not ensured. Citizens must be able to move if their current local government denies a valued right or liberty. And if local communities separate by incomes, as is likely when efficiency is achieved, the poor local communities may not be able to provide services essential for personal safety and a fair chance at economic opportunity. A strong president has the legal capacity and economic resources to correct these local abuses and deficiencies, but perhaps not the will. With the need to be elected by a national median voter, there is no guarantee that presidential platforms will expand the civil rights and economic opportunities of an oppressed or insular local minority. Facing this limitation, supplementing the presidency with direct local representation in the national government may strengthen federalism's performance along the dimensions of democracy and rights.

Chapter 3, "Cooperative Federalism," describes our second model of federal governance, which replaces Economic Federalism's nationally elected president with a "council" of locally elected representatives. Again there are multiple provincial and local governments with important, possibly concurrent, policy responsibilities and revenues, but now national goods, services, and regulations are the responsibility of a locally elected national council. Representatives may be from larger cities, as was the case with the early Achaean League for the defense of Greek city-states; or from states, as was the case with the U.S. Continental Congress; or from nations, as for the governance of the European Union. To ensure that each city's, state's, or nation's preferences are accommodated, Cooperative Federalism imposes a supermajority, often unanimity, voting rule. The resulting governments are known as *confederal* when representation is by geography, as for Montesquieu (Beer, 1993, chap. 7), or *consociational* when representation is allowed more generally—say, from ethnic, religious, or economic groups, as for Arend Lijphart (1977). The original thirteen colonies governed by the Articles of Confederation from 1777 to 1789 are the most often cited example of Cooperative Federalism, but we argue in Chapter 9 that so too is the European Union.[29]

Since the council decides by a supermajority or unanimous vote, national policies require a consensus bargain. The primary virtue of Cooperative Federalism is its potential to protect the interests of minorities from Economic

29. Wheare (1964, p. 32) and Riker (1964, pp. 8–10) also mention the Dutch Union of Utrecht, the early constitutions of Switzerland, Germany from 1815 to 1867, the North German Confederation of 1867 to 1871, and the German Empire from 1871 to 1918 as other examples of Cooperative Federalism.

Federalism's tyranny of a majority under presidential governance. But minorities must first elect a representative to the national council. This requires being a majority in at least one state or province. In confederations, citizen mobility across states can help to build those majorities. In consociations, the use of proportional representation to elect the national council can achieve the same end.[30] Since the stakes for minority citizens are potentially so high and the influence of each elected representative to the national council so decisive, democratic participation may be encouraged as well.

It is on the dimension of economic efficiency in the provision of national goods and regulations that Cooperative Federalism is likely to fall short. Unanimous, or nearly unanimous, agreements by the national council protect minority interests, but they make the provision of national (or in the case of the EU, transnational) public goods and regulations very difficult. The biggest roadblock to building a full consensus is the need to allocate any policy's economic surplus. Who gets the benefits? Who pays the costs? It was the inability to resolve the financing of the Revolutionary War's debts that led to the calling of the U.S. Constitutional Convention in 1787 and to the drafting of an alternative federal constitution to replace the Articles of Confederation.[31] That new constitution retained state representation to the national government but dropped supermajority in favor of simple majority rule. We call this third alternative *Democratic Federalism*, which we specify first in its "pure" form of legislative governance only, and then with the "safeguards" of a senate, a strong president, an independent judiciary, and finally, organized political parties.

Chapter 4, "Democratic Federalism: The National Legislature," details the likely economic, democratic, and rights performance of a decentralized national legislature with representatives elected from geographically specified local districts. The national legislature is assigned responsibility for national public goods and services and national regulations. Decisions in the legislature are made by simple majority rule. Independent local governments continue to be responsible for important local services, perhaps provided concurrently with the national government.

---

30. A proposal offered by Guinier (1994) for election to one chamber of the U.S. Congress.

31. For the details of failed governance under the Articles of Confederation, see Rakove (1979, chap. 14) and Dougherty (2001). For the profound effect this frustrating history had on the drafters of the U.S. Constitution, see Rakove (1996, chap. 7).

On the dimensions of democratic participation and the protection of rights and liberties, Democratic Federalism is likely to do well, *provided* all citizens are represented in the legislature. Since locally elected representatives can, in principle, each be pivotal to any national majority, citizens have an incentive to vote and engage their representatives with their concerns. Proximity and the relatively small scale of the local districts will encourage not just voting but also "face-to-face" engagement of representatives with their constituents, called the "personal vote." Democratic participation is likely to be encouraged as a result. Further, and as James Madison argued in *Federalist* Nos. 10 and 51, local representation in the national legislature also provides added protections for individual rights and liberties. Represented minorities from local districts can band together to mutually protect each other's rights in legislative voting. Oppressive majorities may not be stable if a new majority of minorities can form to defeat the originally proposed restriction on rights. But as noted, all citizens must be represented. There is no guarantee that an existing federal legislature will willingly open its doors to the disenfranchised. What can be done?

It is on the dimension of economic efficiency that legislature-only Democratic Federalism is most likely to fall short. In contrast to Cooperative Federalism, where the national government might do too little, the national legislature in Democratic Federalism might do too much. The problem arises from the use of simple majority rule for making legislative decisions. As first pointed out by the Marquis de Condorcet in 1785 and shown quite generally by Kenneth Arrow (1951), if there are more than two policies to be decided and local interests over those policies are in conflict, a stable majority-rule outcome cannot be guaranteed. Any one majority coalition can be undone with a small change in policy allocations or payments to create a new majority coalition. Cycling between policies is the result. A tempting and all too common solution is to bundle all policies into a single package, called the *omnibus* or *pork-barrel* policy, from which all local districts get some benefits and for which all share in costs. If policies' benefits are primarily local but costs are shared nationally, there will be a strong incentive for each local representative to demand too much of his or her local good. There is a "common pool problem," where the national tax base is the shared common resource. Further, no one district has an incentive to vote no, as a single vote won't defeat the omnibus policy, nor is there an incentive to remove one district's benefits from the legislation while still paying a share of all others' costs. As a result, the final national budget and the reach of national regulations will be economically too large, perhaps significantly so. There is a risk not only of too much national spending and regulation but also of replacing the local or state governments' provision of those same services. In such instances, all policy becomes "national" policy, what William Riker (1964) has called the "overawing" propensity of locally elected, national legislatures. What can be done?

Chapter 5, "Democratic Federalism: Safeguards," addresses these two weaknesses of Democratic Federalism. First, how can we guarantee all minorities are represented in the legislature? Second, how can we control the national legislature's inclination to usurp all important dimensions of public policy? Chapter 5 evaluates the contributions of three new national institutions: first, an upper chamber called the Senate, elected not from local districts but from geographically larger provinces or states; second, a nationally elected president with agenda and veto powers over legislative decisions; and third, an independent national court to interpret the ground rules for federal governance and, in particular, what constitutes meaningful local assignment and full representation of all citizens. In addition to these three constitutionally created institutions, we also consider the ability of national political parties, if they were to arise, to foster minority representation and to control an overreaching national legislature. We argue that each of these four safeguards contributes positively to the performance of Democratic Federalism, but *only if* a majority of all citizens understands and support the ongoing contribution of these institutions to the goals of efficiency, participation, and protections of rights.

Needed citizen support will arise only as a result of a national conversation as to the implications of each policy choice for the institutions of federal governance. A national tax and transfer policy, for example, may be an attractive redistribution policy, but perhaps not if it removes the future ability or incentive of local governments to set their own levels of local spending in response to the preferences of local citizens. To understand the consequences of policies for institutions, and of institutions for policies, will require a national conversation about the process of federal governance and not just its outcomes. Providing a framework to facilitate this conversation is the objective of Part II, "Encouraging the Federal Conversation."

Chapter 6, "FIST: Having the Federal Dialogue," provides the guidelines for the needed federalism debate by outlining a sequence of evaluative questions that national policy-makers should consider before the passage of any national law that affects one or more of the three institutions of federalism: assignment as to who does what, the number of lower-tier governments, and representation of those governments to the national legislature. The proposed evaluation provides citizens with a Federalism Impact Statement, or FIST, for the proposed policy. As implemented, FIST begins with an analysis of the economic implications of each proposed central government policy by asking whether the national benefits of the policy outweigh its national costs, and whether there might be an alternative policy that is plausibly more efficient. If the proposed policy is viewed as inefficient, by itself or relative to alternative policies, then FIST asks whether there is evidence of, or plausible argument for, compensating benefits from improved local political participation, improved economic fairness, or increased protection of individual rights or liberties. If so, then FIST asks whether these noneconomic benefits can be achieved more efficiently. FIST will not require definitive answers to its questions nor an explicit analysis of the possible trade-offs between efficiency and participation or between efficiency and fairness and rights. FIST only requires that the trade-offs be acknowledged and considered. Not all centrally provided policies would trigger a FIST review; for example, defense spending, foreign affairs, and monetary policy would be exempt, as they are clearly national public goods and must be provided centrally. The execution of FIST would be by an independent agency, such as the Congressional Budget Office or the European Commission, while a national court could ensure that all relevant central government legislation acknowledge, though not necessarily accept, the content and conclusions of the FIST analysis.

Chapters 7 and 8 outline the central principles for efficient policies in a federal economy as a starting point for implementing a FIST analysis. Chapter 7, "Fiscal Policy in the Federal Union," offers the guidelines for efficient taxation and debt financing as well as principles for efficient federal government spending within a federal public economy. Efficient tax policy should seek to minimize horizontal spillovers between local and provincial economies and vertical spillovers between the central and provincial and local governments. Efficient debt policy should seek to align debt payment to future benefits and control possible abuses of local borrowing via balanced-budget rules. Efficient spending focuses on the essential federal task of designing intergovernmental transfers, stressing when matching and lump-sum grants-in-aid are most appropriate to manage public goods, spillovers between states, and the provision of social insurance for differential income shocks across regions, states, or localities.

Chapter 8, "Regulation in the Federal Union," outlines the principles for the efficient regulation of market activities in a federal economy. As with the provision of public services and the assignment of taxing powers, the aim is to allocate regulatory responsibilities between local, state, and national governments so as to ensure efficient allocations. There may be too little regulation as a result of competition by local and state governments for private business and the compensating benefits for residents that those firms might provide, a competition known as "the race to the bottom." The result will be lax environmental, competitive, or financial regulations imposing damages on residents of other localities or states. If those damages are significant and widespread, then national regulation of such activities will be appropriate. On the other hand, national regulations that preempt local regulations may restrict the ability of state and local governments to tailor their own environment or competitive marketplace to meet the specific needs of their residents. Some states may wish to allow more local pollution if it means more jobs, or permit local market collusion if it reallocates local incomes in a way valued by local residents. Allowing local regulatory choice that benefits only local residents and imposes only local costs, and may be copied by other states, may lead to a "race to the top." Chapter 8 provides a template for separating the two "races" and facilitating an informed national debate on federal regulatory policies.

Part III, "On Becoming Federal," concludes our analysis. If Democratic Federalism is an attractive institution for the design and implementation of government policy, how might it then be put in place? Efforts by the countries of Europe to form a working economic union and those of the citizens of South Africa to form a working political union lead to the same conclusion. To be successful, Democratic Federalism begins and ends with a union polity committed to the benefits of shared governance and the spirit of compromise needed to make it work.

Chapter 9, "The European Union: Federal Governance at the Crossroads," details the evolution of EU institutions from a simple six-nation pact to jointly manage the collective production of coal and steel to a 2020 union of twenty-eight members setting common agricultural policies, economic development investments, competition and trade policies, and for nineteen member states, monetary policies and financial regulations. As an economic ("customs") union regulating market policies, there is little doubt that the union has been a success, particularly for the residents of the originally less economically developed member states. As a monetary ("currency") union and as a political ("democratic") union, perhaps less so. The monetary union has reduced the ability of member states to manage their economies in periods of economic downturns, most evident in Europe's lethargic recovery from the Great Recession, and has created adverse incentives for "beggar-thy-neighbor" fiscal policies, most evident in Greek's excessive borrowing and resulting bailout.

Politically the union suffers from a "democratic deficit," with citizens lacking a direct means to debate and collectively decide the direction of EU policies, and a "rights deficit," with the union lacking a means to discipline member states (Hungary and Poland) that threaten the union's foundational commitment to individual rights and the rule of law. The EU is at a crossroads. One path involves modest reforms—which we offer—within the structure of current institutions. The other would entail a full commitment to Democratic Federalism. To be successful, such a commitment must *begin* with a union polity willing to view EU policies as *European* policies, not member state policies for the benefit of each member state alone. The path of modest reforms may be all we can hope for at the moment.

Chapter 10, "Mandela's Federal Democracy: A Fragile Compact," details the central role that the institutions of Democratic Federalism played in South Africa's transition from apartheid to a multiracial democracy, one of the most important political events of the last century. While both apartheid's governing National Party (NP) and the resistance's African National Congress (ANC) agreed that the century of suppression and armed resistance must end, negotiations over exactly how the new democratic government should be designed were far from harmonious. The NP wished to protect the economic interests of the once-ruling elite and rural landowners, while the ANC was committed to a significant expansion of essential public services for the poor: health care, education, and housing. In the background was a desire to avoid the damaging consequences of Zimbabwe's monolithic unitary government, a concern for both the ANC and the NP. They compromised on a middle ground of shared governance with (1) politically independent provincial and metropolitan governments constitutionally assigned to provide all important local services and (2), a separately elected national parliament and president responsible for setting the overall rate of taxation and funding for local services. By its clear national majority, the ANC would determine the overall level of taxation and redistributive funding, but the locally elected provincial and metropolitan governments, some perhaps controlled by the NP or its successors, would decide how national revenues would be spent and local services provided. The institutions chosen to implement this compromise were those of Democratic Federalism. They created the institutional structure for a "hostage game" in fiscal policies to be played between the competing economic interests of the ANC majority and the economic elite and middle class. If the national government taxed "too much," then the middle-class coalitions controlling local spending could allocate funds to middle-class, not lower-income, services. If local governments spent their budgets on middle-class services, then the national government could raise taxes and assume direct responsibility for providing redistributive services. Today the Democratic Alliance and its allies, a broad-based middle-class coalition, control the important provincial government of the Western Cape and the local government of Cape Town. The federal compromise has worked, so far, to the economic benefit of most South Africans. But either side can undo the compromise at any time. The likely outcome would then be an ANC-dominated unitary government, and the risk of a Zimbabwe outcome. The recent tenure of Jacob Zuma as president posed such a threat. The ANC recently removed Zuma and appointed Cyril Ramaphosa, one of the central negotiators of the original federal agreement, as his successor. The future is uncertain. As is the case for the EU going forward, the continued success of South Africa's federal institutions will turn on a commitment of its citizens to the principles of federal governance and a renewed willingness to compromise.

Chapter 11, "Epilogue," summarizes our main conclusions and seeks to place our work in the wider context of democratic constitutional design by addressing the question, Who *should* be federal? While there is much to recommend it, Democratic Federalism may not be for everyone. Any new nation-state seeks to do what smaller and spatially diffuse communities cannot: provide for mutually beneficial public goods, most notably collective security; control intercommunity spillovers; and enforce the rules needed for wider market exchange. Each new state must choose how best to run its affairs. Whether designed as Economic or Cooperative or Democratic Federalism, federal governance is one alternative. But so is a single, unitary government, or perhaps even to remain as separately governed jurisdictions and then manage shared interests by bilateral agreements. There are strengths and weaknesses to each form of governance. While numerous "fundamentals" will be important to the choice of governance—technology, geography, language, ethnicity—we suggest two attributes that may be the most important: heterogeneity of tastes for government services and a willingness to compromise when there is disagreement. When tastes are similar and trust between citizens is widespread, unitary governance may be most appropriate. When tastes are different and trust is absent, remaining as separate states is likely to be the preferred outcome. Democratic Federalism, we conjecture, will be most appropriate for that middle ground where tastes are different but compromise still possible. Hopefully our work here will prove helpful to those considering governance for this middle path.

5. Hardly the Only, and Certainly Not the Last, Word

Our debt to the classics in the analysis of the federal state is perhaps already apparent and will certainly be so by the end of this book. For those who wish to go to the sources themselves, we recommend a close reading of Wallace Oates's *Fiscal Federalism* (1972) for the foundational analysis of the economics of federalism; of William Riker's *Federalism: Origin, Operation, Significance* (1964) for the best analysis of the political economy of federalism; and then, of course, of the essays by James Madison and Alexander Hamilton in *The Federalist Papers* for still the most complete presentation of the constitutional arguments for the federal state.

As will be apparent in the chapters that follow, we have also benefited greatly from reading the new economic, political, and legal literatures on federalism that have emerged over the years since we began this project. It pays to wait. For the economics of federalism, we recommend, first, Dietmar Wellisch, *Theory of Public Finance in a Federal State* (2000). Wellisch is a leading public finance theorist who has provided an excellent overview of the core economic theory of fiscal federalism. The focus of the book is on the efficient provision of public goods and services using local (decentralized) and national (centralized) governments. The economy under study is an open economy with the free movement of labor and capital across all governments. The considerable contribution of Wellisch's book is to provide a general and fully consistent framework for the evaluation of local and central government's fiscal policies in a federal public economy.

Second, we recommend Robin Boadway and Anwar Shah, *Fiscal Federalism: Principles and Practice of Multiorder Governance* (2009). The authors are a leading scholar (Boadway) and practitioner (Shah) of the design and implementation of fiscal policy in a federal public economy. The economic theory of fiscal policy is presented clearly and in a nontechnical way. Topics include tax policy, spending policy, the design of intergovernmental transfers, and the management of macroeconomic policy in federal economies. The strength of the book is its wide use of examples of each fiscal policy from both developed and developing federal economies. It is a valuable reference for those charged with implementing fiscal policy in federal economies.

The new political science of federalism focuses on federal institutions for representation and their likely impact on the design and implementation of policies. Three recent books have made important contributions. First, we recommend Jenna Bednar, *The Robust Federation: Principles of Design* (2009).

While economic theory provides guidance for the appropriate assignment of policy responsibilities in a federal state, *in*appropriate institutions of representation can undo economic theory's best advice. The problem is a locally representative national legislature. Local representatives have an incentive to abuse the national tax base—what Bednar calls "encroachment"—to benefit their narrow local interests. Effective federal governance needs to check such behaviors. Bednar calls these checks the *safeguards of federalism*. Through instructive country-specific examples, she highlights the strengths and weaknesses of each, called structural (presidential and upper-chamber vetoes), political (political parties), judicial (independent supreme court), and popular (citizenry commitment to federal values) safeguards. No one safeguard is decisive by itself. To ensure a *robust federation*, Bednar argues, all must be in place.

While structural protections of federal institutions can be put in place through the adopted constitution, how can we hope to construct viable political parties as a safeguard for federal governance? Mikhail Filippov, Peter Ordeshook, and Olga Shvetsova's *Designing Federalism: A Theory of Self-Sustainable Federal Institutions* (2004) provides one answer. Locally elected national legislatures can be both parochial and shortsighted. Successful political parties must be national in their focus and, as ongoing organizations, farsighted in their vision. Importantly, strong national parties are a complement to, not a substitute for, local representation in the national legislature. National parties find their strength from the financial and election support of local constituencies. In this way, both local and national interests in federal governance are protected.

Finally, in *Hamilton's Paradox: The Promise and Peril of Fiscal Federalism* (2006). Jonathan Rodden applies the insights of Bednar and of Filippov and his colleagues to address the important matter of how the national government can control excessive local government borrowing that might spill over to limit, and even bankrupt, the national fisc. The problem of excessive local borrowing arises because local representatives to the national government favor local bailouts over national solvency. With local political incentives favoring national bailouts, there is no reason for the private market to discipline local borrowing with higher interest rates. If there is a solution to this problem, it is in strengthening the ability of the central government to say *no* to local excesses. Rodden turns to country-specific case studies to find his answers: a strong president in Brazil and strong political parties in Germany. Rodden's book is particularly valuable for illustrating why all institutions of Democratic Federalism are needed.

While the federal constitution sets the ground rules for federal governance, it will be the task of the judiciary, in particular the national courts, to interpret and enforce those rules. How successful can the courts be in this role? Malcolm Feeley and Edward Rubin are skeptical, arguing in *Federalism: Political Identity and Tragic Compromise* (2008) that finding a compelling and judicable standard for enforcing federalism's "rules" is impossible. Without clear, constitutionally defined "bright" lines of what is national and what is local, the court's decisions as to governments' responsibilities can only be responsive to the personal preferences of the justices or to the political pressures of the times. Robert Schapiro in *Polyphonic Federalism: Toward the Protection of Fundamental Rights* (2009) argues that Feeley and Rubin may be asking too much of the courts. Constitutions are compromise documents, and as such it is beneficial to keep the boundaries between national and state responsibilities vaguely defined. If so, what can be the role for the courts as a safeguard of federal governance? Schapiro suggests it will be found, first, in the protection of the institutions of state government as effective channels for local policies—what he calls polyphonic federalism—and then, second, in the courts' oversight of the process of state and federal policy-making to ensure that these protected voices are being heard. Our FIST proposal and its implementation in Chapters 6–8 are one application of Schapiro's insight.

Finally, while we provide examples of federal government performance throughout our book, much of the evidence we offer comes from the U.S. federal public economy. To expand the conversation of what works and when, we offer the following three books of comparative studies as valuable references beyond our analysis here: Richard M. Bird, Robert Ebel, and Christine Wallich, editors, *Decentralization of the Socialist State: Intergovernmental Finance in Transition Economies* (1995); Jonathan Rodden, Gunnar Eskeland, and Jennie Litvack, editors, *Fiscal Decentralization and the Challenge of Hard Budget Constraints* (2003); and Pranab Bardhan and Dilip Mookherjee, editors, *Decentralization and Local Governance in Developing Economies: A Comparative Perspective* (2006).

PART I

The Institutions of Democratic Federalism

DEMOCRATIC FEDERALISM seeks to provide three valued outcomes for its citizens. First, it aims to provide valued public services, including national defense, public infrastructure essential for the efficient functioning of the private economy, and essential services consumed each day for the personal well-being of all citizens, including education, health care, and a clean and safe environment. Second, it strives to ensure fair and open public debate and elections so that all citizens can participate equally in the affairs of governance. Third, it seeks to protect the rights and expand the liberties of each citizen. To promote these ends, and in contrast to a unitary democracy, Democratic Federalism empowers two, and in larger republics, three, levels of governance. At the bottom of the federal hierarchy are local governments providing public services with limited spillovers and no significant economies of scale—for example, K–12 education, local police and fire services, and local environmental protection such as trash collection. Next are state or provincial governments meant to internalize spillovers of modest geographical reach and to provide services with modest economies of scale—roadways, air and water quality, university education, and prisons. Finally, at the top of the hierarchy is the national government, which is designed to provide pure public goods and to manage wide-reaching economic spillovers—most importantly national defense and the public infrastructure and market rules needed for an efficient national economy. Each level of government has its own democratically elected legislature or executive and its own taxing authority. Local and state or provincial governments will each have elected representation to the national government. Each level of government has a separate role to play within Democratic Federalism.

Chapter 2, "Economic Federalism," details the potential contribution of local governments to the three goals of democratic governance. Under appropriate conditions, which we detail, local governments can be efficient providers of local public goods, can serve as active venues for democratic deliberation, and can offer safe havens and protection for individual rights and liberties. For all these virtues, local governments will not be efficient providers of public goods with widespread spillovers or significant economies of scale, nor allow the full voice of citizens in regional or national decisions, nor necessarily protect the rights of immobile or isolated minorities. For these benefits, a national government will be needed. Economic Federalism does so with the national election of a president. With open and competitive elections and informed voters, the elected president will have an incentive to provide national public goods and to regulate national spillovers so as to meet the preferences of the median voter decisive for his or her election, most likely the voter with the national median income. Citizen participation in these decisions will be limited to the single vote, however. Protection of individual rights can only be ensured when it is in the election interest of the president. Rights of isolated minorities will not be protected.

Chapter 3, "Cooperative Federalism," outlines how cooperative agreements between local, or state, governments might address each of these concerns. Voluntary clubs and alliances offer citizens the opportunity to address intercommunity spillovers without sacrificing the autonomy of local control. Rights and political deliberation may be enhanced as a result. What voluntary alliances cannot guarantee, however, is the efficient provision of public goods or a minimal standard of rights and opportunities for all citizens. The hurdle to overcome is the need for unanimous agreement in Cooperative Federalism.

Chapters 4, "Democratic Federalism: The National Legislature," and 5, "Democratic Federalism: The Safeguards," drop unanimity in favor of majority rule by a locally elected national legislature. A national legislature offers the possibility for a more efficient provision of national public goods and regulatory control of national spillovers. A national legislature offers citizens additional channels for democratic participation. Finally, a national legislature provides a further venue for the protection of individual rights and liberties. For all these benefits, a national legislature has risks too. The incentives of locally elected representatives to the legislature are to use the national tax base to overprovide locally beneficially public goods and to overregulate the market economy for the benefit of local producers. Though there is local representation to the national legislature, individual influence over outcomes may be diluted by the sheer size of government. While a national coalition of minorities can band together to mutually protect minority rights, minorities must first be represented in the national legislature. Chapter 5 offers four institutional safeguards to minimize these risks: a separately elected and smaller senate, a separately elected national president, an independent national court, and competitive political parties. Each helps, but only if all citizens have the right to vote, participate in political deliberations, and are informed of the benefits and costs of their national decisions.

2

Economic Federalism

1. Introduction

The economic theory of federalism, first summarized in Wallace Oates's 1972 book *Fiscal Federalism*, has become the starting point for most scholarly and policy discussions of how best to organize the federal state. The objective of Economic Federalism is to correct market failures through government action. Market failures arise whenever cooperative action, rather than private choices alone, is needed to ensure that we get the goods or services we want at the lowest cost. There are three prominent examples: (1) fixed resources that it is efficient to share, called public goods; (2) goods or services for which one person's actions offer benefits or impose costs on others, known as spillovers or externalities; and (3) goods and services favored by society that contribute to the well-being and economic opportunity of others, often the disadvantaged, called merit goods. What is needed in each case is some means for discovering citizens' willingness to pay for the valued good or service and to then collect sufficient payment to cover production costs.

Economic Federalism uses two very specific forms of government to provide for revelation and payment. First, for goods or services whose congestion becomes evident within fairly small (say, ten thousand to one hundred thousand people) populations, and for which the spatial reach of the externality is modest, Economic Federalism recommends using small, local governments. Likely services are K–12 education, police and fire protection, trash pickup and street sanitation, libraries, parks and recreation, and local roadways. Second, for those goods shared by large populations and for externalities and merit goods that jointly benefit large populations, Economic Federalism will use a state, regional, or national government. Here the possible services might be higher education and research, national defense, courts and jails, the protection of property rights and market competition, the protection of air and water quality, a system of exchange and monetary policy, regional and national highways, airports and airways, and equal access to goods and services considered essential for a full and productive life. Economic Federalism's guiding principle is to assign policy responsibility for each government service to the smallest level of government that can do the job. The principle has been formalized by Oates as his *decentralization theorem* and more recently as the principle of *subsidiarity* in the current debates over the governmental structure of the European Community.

We first present the efficiency arguments and evidence for Economic Federalism (Sections 2–4) and then evaluate Economic Federalism from the perspective of the other objectives of governance: political representation (Section 5) and the protection of individual rights, liberties, and opportunities (Section 6). While on balance we conclude (Section 7) that there is much to recommend Economic Federalism, in particular its ability to provide public goods and services efficiently, it is likely to fall short against the objectives of democratic participation and representation and the protection and promotion of rights and liberties.

2. The Efficiency Case for Local Governance: The Tiebout Economy

The economic case for the decentralized provision of government services begins with Charles Tiebout's (1956) powerful insight that when public services are congestible and a "not too large" population allows efficient provision, many small governments competing for informed residents can provide these services efficiently, both in the sense of low production and organization costs and in giving residents services they desire.

The Tiebout public goods economy works like a marketplace. Local governments act as competitive "supermarkets," each offering a service bundle at the cost of the bundle. A family pays for the bundle in two ways. First, they pay an entry fee, much like joining a club or a consumption cooperative, and then they pay the average cost of the bundle of services they consume once in the club. The community that offers the family its preferred bundle at the lowest entry fee and average cost wins the citizen-consumers' business. The entry fee is typically "capitalized" within the price of the home when the family moves into its preferred community, while average costs may be paid for by user fees or annual taxes. Well-run communities with quality services and low average costs can charge a high entry fee that is realized in higher home values. This entry fee provides an incentive for current residents to be efficient, matching future resident demands with preferred services at low cost. The resulting efficiency "rents" also provide incentives for other communities to offer the same preferred bundle of public services. As a consequence, the excess rents, or entrepreneurial profits, earned by the originally efficient communities will be bid to zero. Builders of communities and providers of public services will now earn a competitive rate of return. Citizens in each local community will get the housing and public services they want at the lowest cost. For this Tiebout economy to be successful, six conditions must hold.

T1: Publicly provided goods and services are produced with a congestible technology and can be efficiently provided by small communities.

Congestible public goods will have an efficient population size, one that minimizes the cost per person of providing the public good or service. To be efficient, the Tiebout economy needs sufficient congestion so that there can be enough providers for each bundle and a quality level of public services to prevent collusion in the pricing of the public good. For many public services, small communities are the efficient providers of the service. Communities of ten thousand residents, for example, can maintain a school system of 2,500 students in grades K–12, and such systems can provide all the classes needed to offer a quality education for every student, from the least to the most able. Similarly, communities of ten thousand to twenty-five thousand are sufficient to maintain the levels of police and fire surveillance demanded by most citizens. Larger communities—or sets of communities—may be needed for the efficient adjudication of violations and imprisonment, however. Furthermore, trash can be efficiently collected within small communities, but larger populations will be needed for efficient disposal. The size of the efficient community will depend on the quality of services desired; typically, when the efficient community size is smaller, the desired level of service quality is higher.[1]

T2: There is a perfectly elastic supply of communities, each capable of replicating all attractive economic features of current communities.

1. For an analysis of education, see Andrews, Duncombe, and Yinger (2002); for fire protection, see Hitzhusen (1973); for police, see Douglas and Tweeten (1971); for trash collection, see Stevens (1978); for solid waste disposal, see Collins and Downes (1977); for water and sewerage treatment, see Cosgrove and Hushak (1972); for libraries, see DeBoer (1992); and for efficiency in city bureaucracy, see Southwick (2012).

Two conditions are necessary for T2 to hold. First, there must be a sufficient supply of entrepreneurs with capital so that profitable communities earning high entry fees or capitalized fiscal rents or profits can be replicated. Second, there must be sufficient land area to accommodate all the communities needed for effective fiscal competition. Given that residents typically need to be close to their public facilities and they may also need to commute to work, the Tiebout economy can thrive only in relatively large metropolitan areas.

How large? Perhaps one million residents or more with sufficient land area to accommodate housing preferences for those residents. If five or so communities are needed for effective market competition, then fifty to one hundred communities will allow sufficient competition for efficiency in the provision of ten to twenty different public service "bundles" to accommodate ten to twenty different types of consumers. Given the likely correlations of service demands with resident income, this seems to be more than enough residents for efficient public service competition.[2] The key to condition T2 is whether there will be a sufficient number of community entrepreneurs to ensure adequate competition in supply. When this is not the case, there will be too few communities and perfect sorting by tastes for local public goods will not be possible. In this case, local politics become important to providing the efficient level of local services; mobility is not enough.[3] See Box 2.1.

T3: Households are mobile between communities and value better
     public services when they move.

It is essential for the Tiebout economy that fiscally inefficient communities be punished by the loss of residents and efficient communities be rewarded by attracting dissatisfied residents from their less efficient competitors. Mobile residents willing to leave inefficient for efficient communities provide this discipline. Communities losing residents see their home values' capitalized fiscal surplus decline, while those residents whose communities gain members will see their home values increase. Not all residents need be moving for market discipline to be effective. As in most markets, it is the last buyer and seller who

2. There are fifty-two metropolitan areas in the United States, accounting for about one-third of the nation's population, that meet this threshold. U.S. Census Bureau, *Statistical Abstract of the United States, 2011*, table 23.

3. That local politics can be an important force for local public goods efficiency; see H. L. Wong et al. (2017) for the provision of local roads in Chinese villages and Pradhan et al. (2014) for school services in Indonesian villages.

Box 2.1. Are Local Politics Economically Efficient?

When we lose Assumption T2, we no longer have a sufficient number of local communities to accommodate all types of families with different demands for local public services. As Epple and Zelenitz (1981) show, compromises among residents will be required, and this requires local politics. The important question is, *How well does local government voting do in providing the efficient level of local services (that is, will residents get what they want)?* The answer is, *Pretty well.* The argument moves in three steps.

First, we define economic efficiency using the Samuelson Condition: for efficiency, the sum of all the additional (marginal) benefits citizens enjoy from one more unit of the local public good must equal the additional (marginal) costs they need to pay to provide that extra unit of services. We can write this as $\sum MB(g) = MC(g)$, where g is the level of government services.

Second, we specify a voting process in which the majority-preferred budget is that budget that defeats all alternatives in pairwise comparisons. If there is enough local competition either from other candidates or from other communities, then that budget will be the one that stands in the median (50th percentile) position of all individually preferred budgets; see Inman (1978) and Romer, Rosenthal, and Munley (1992).

Third, compare the median voter's preferred budget to that satisfying the Samuelson Condition for efficiency. Bergstrom and colleagues (1988) examine the ability of local governments to provide school services efficiently. Using household survey data, they first estimate families' marginal benefits from the provision of public education. Knowing the marginal benefits for each family in a community and the level of educational services (g), they compute the sum of marginal benefits for the whole community. As a last step, they compare the sum of marginal benefits with the marginal costs of providing education and ask, Does $\sum MB(g) = MC(g)$? For more than 80 percent of the 497 Michigan school districts in their study, the marginal costs are greater than the sum of marginal benefits. It appears that local governments provide *too much* local public education. Why? The answer is that local school costs are being subsidized by the state and by the federal government at the rate of m, thus lowering $MC(g)$ to an "effective" $(1-m) \cdot MC(g)$. Once this subsidy is considered, the authors find that citizens are provided an efficient level of school services. But why would the state and the federal government subsidize local school services? It may be that there are positive spillovers—these local services are valued by citizens outside the community.

determine the market price for homes, and thus the entrepreneurial profit, from local government performance. In the United States, each year approximately 6 percent of the metropolitan-area population moves for reasons of finding a "better community," one that presumably offers better public services.[4] For a community of ten thousand residents or approximately 3,300 homes, that will be about two hundred home sales a year to new residents who have explicitly considered the benefits and costs of government services.

4. U.S. Census Bureau, *Statistical Abstract of the United States, 2011*, table 31.

T4: Mobile households are well informed about the fiscal performance
of each jurisdiction.

For local communities to earn the rewards of a better fiscal performance,
citizens must know those communities that are doing a good job in providing
public services and those that are not. This requires knowledge of local service
quality and current and future taxes. When such information is costly to obtain, market efficiency cannot be guaranteed. For example, if one resident pays
to discover a high-quality, low-cost community and her bid for a home in that
community reflects that extra quality, others may simply copy the informed
bid when they buy their home. In such instances, market information is a
public good—once discovered, it is revealed to all through market prices. All
buyers will prefer to wait and copy others' informed bids. But then no one
provides the information. One possible result is that expensive and poorly
managed communities will survive.

There are two solutions to this problem. First, not all information about government performance qualifies as public information. Knowing that one family
bid $200,000 for a home does not tell others what they should bid if the public
service attributes of the community—for example, school quality—have family-
specific values. In this case, information is a private good, and it will be necessary
for each family to discover the facts of government performance for themselves.
When information has private value, markets can work. But then, who provides
the information? The market needs a trusted outside party. Real estate agents
seeking to build reputations as honest brokers can play this role. Buyers receive
detailed information from their agent about school quality, school tax rates,
crime rates, fire insurance rates, local parks, trash pickup, trash fees, and bonded
indebtedness for each community they are considering.

Yet, second, some fiscal information remains as public information with a
common value for all new residents. For example, knowing that a community
has a large unfunded public employee pension and that future taxes must rise
to cover this liability imposes a common monetary burden on all residents. If
one family or their real estate agent discovers that burden but others do not,
the informed family who makes an appropriately adjusted lower bid will never
be able to buy a home in the high-liability community. They will always be
outbid by the uninformed households, and the inefficient community will
survive. In this case, the Tiebout market needs outside help. As with any pure
public good, common-value information is best supplied by a higher-level
government. In the United States, states typically monitor and publicize the

fiscal performance of their local governments. With such monitoring in place, condition T4 seems acceptable.

T5: Residents can be excluded from a community if they do not pay the marginal cost of the services they consume.

There can be no free riders in the Tiebout economy. Each community needs a way to exclude those who do not pay their marginal costs. How might exclusion from a community public good be implemented? The simplest means is to just charge residents a "user fee" equal to the marginal cost of the services they consume, and if the fee is not paid, then the service is denied. This will work for services whose "use" can be measured and neighborhood spillovers are slight—say, parks, schools, libraries, and trash. But when use is difficult to measure—say, for local roads or police and fire protection—then a fixed annual charge per family equal to the average cost per resident of supplying the public service is appropriate. Such a charge will be equivalent to a head tax, though such a tax may be difficult to implement politically.[5]

U.S. communities can approximate efficient head taxation through the joint use of property taxation and residential zoning for housing. The argument is due to Bruce Hamilton (1975), and its importance to efficiency in the Tiebout economy is now so central that we shall refer to this requirement as defining the *Tiebout-Hamilton* public goods economy. Here's how it works. First, each resident pays a property tax equal to the town's tax rate (r) times the value of his or her residence (h): $\text{TAX} = rh$. The local tax rate must be sufficient to pay for the costs of local services equal to the cost per person (k) times the number of town residents (N). The local tax rate that will cover these costs is that rate, which, when multiplied by the aggregate value of all properties in the town (H), pays for total costs: $rH = kN$, or alternatively, $r = k/\hat{h}$, where $\hat{h} = H/N$ and is the average value of property per resident. If condition T1 holds and communities have the efficient population size, the marginal cost of providing services to one more family will equal the average cost per family of providing that service: $k = mc$. Each resident's tax payment will be $\text{TAX} = (h/\hat{h})mc$.

Now for the last step. If $h = \hat{h}$, then $\text{TAX} = mc$. Residential zoning plus Tiebout's condition T4, ensuring mobile and informed residents, achieves this result. Zoning prevents anyone from buying a home of value less than $\hat{h}$, and no informed resident will buy a home greater than $\hat{h}$; if they did they would pay

---

5. See Besley, Preston, and Ridge's (1997) evaluation of Prime Minister Margaret Thatcher's failed efforts to introduce a head tax for the financing of local services.

more than the marginal cost of public service—that is, $h/\hat{h} > 1$. Informed citizen-consumers who want larger homes than one community's average value will move to an otherwise identical community where all the homes are the size and value of their preferred larger home. If there are a sufficient number of communities providing the preferred levels of public goods and (now) housing, efficiency can be achieved without user fees or explicit head taxes.[6] Condition T5 will be appropriate. And we do observe sorting of residents by income and their tastes for local public goods.[7] Income and family demographics that determine the demand for public goods also determine the demand for housing.

T6: There are no interjurisdictional spillovers.

When spillovers are present, competitive local governments may under-provide goods and services with valuable, positive spillovers and overprovide goods and services with harmful, negative spillovers. Economic inefficiency results. Unfortunately, community competition may make matters worse when there are spillovers. In an effort to attract firms, jobs, and ultimately new residents to the community, local governments may find it attractive to not regulate firm pollution if pollution's adverse effects are borne by downwind or downstream communities. Or if local firms benefit from local cost-saving ag-glomeration economies, local governments might encourage firm location with firm subsidies for new entrants and with favorable business regulations. In these cases, local government competition may lead to a proliferation of *inefficient* regulations and tax subsidies. Rather than Tiebout's "race to the top," fiscal and policy competition may become an inefficient "race to the bottom."[8]

3. Evaluating Economic Federalism: Efficiency in the Local Economy

If conditions T1–T6 hold, then a competitive local government economy will be economically efficient. The intuition is straightforward. Condition T1 guarantees that the production costs of supplying any public service can be

6. What is needed are local communities sufficiently segregated by income. In the United States this describes most metropolitan areas; see Epple and Sieg (1999).

7. See Epple and Platt (1998) for the analytics and Epple and Seig (1999) and Bayer and McMillan (2012) for the supporting empirical evidence.

8. For how to identify a "race to the top" from a "race to the bottom" for the design of policies to correct any resulting market inefficiencies, see Chapter 8.

minimized with a relatively small population. This allows for many competitors for each quality level of each public service. Condition T2 ensures that there is an elastic supply of potential competitors so no one community can earn monopoly profits or be economically inefficient in the provision of any local public service. Conditions T3 and T4 provide mobile and informed residents; they ensure that communities have an incentive to be efficient and households will receive that bundle of local services that maximizes the residents' economic welfare. Households search until they find that community that gives them their preferred service bundle at the lowest cost. Condition T5 gives each community the ability to exclude any household that does not pay the full marginal cost of consuming the community's service bundle. There will be no "free riding" in the Tiebout public goods economy. Finally, Condition T6 ensures that all social costs and benefits of local services are fully reflected in each community's production cost and in its citizens' willingness to pay those costs. If so, then each community's provision of local services will be efficient. In Tiebout's own words, "*The (conditions)needed in the model of local government expenditures yield the same optimal allocation that a private market would,*" (Tiebout, 1956, p. 421). It is a grand and eloquent theory, but does it work in practice?

Is There Tiebout Shopping and Sorting?

As previously mentioned, in U.S. metropolitan areas, approximately 6 percent of households move each year in search of a better community.[9] In a typical large metropolitan area of five hundred thousand families and one hundred or so communities, thirty thousand families are relocating each year to improve the amenities of their location. If typical homeowners remain in their community for twelve years, long enough for all their children to graduate from high school, then after that period slightly more than half of all metropolitan families will have moved. That is a lot of shopping. But how do they sort? Are they creating Tiebout communities of families with similar demands for local public services?

One answer to this question can be found by comparing family characteristics that are most likely to determine demand for important local public goods within and across communities. Do families sort into communities by income, by occupation, by age, by family size, or by marital status? Pack and Pack (1978) concluded that the answer was yes; communities were more homogeneous on

9. U.S. Census Bureau, *Statistical Abstract of the United States, 2011*, table 31.

these measured attributes than the metropolitan area as a whole. Subsequent work with more recent U.S. Censuses has reached a similar conclusion.[10]

Unfortunately, knowing that there is more homogeneity of measured demand attributes within local communities than in the region as whole is not a test that actual demands are more homogeneous. There may be significant unmeasured determinants of demand for local public goods, what economists call "tastes," that matter too. The only compelling test for Tiebout sorting is to compare community compositions and service levels predicted by a Tiebout economy with the compositions and service levels of actual communities. If the location of families and the communities' provision of local public services predicted by the Tiebout economy do not match the actual locations of families and demands, then this is good evidence for rejecting Tiebout sorting. This is exactly the test proposed by Epple and Sieg (1999).[11] They estimate a model of Tiebout sorting using data from the Boston area for 1980. They predict, with some accuracy, the distribution of incomes within and across communities and the level of public services and housing prices in each locality.

But does such a competitive marketplace of local governments lead to a more efficient provision of local services? We measure efficiency along two dimensions. First, are we producing goods and services at the lowest cost— that is, is there "technical" efficiency?[12] Second, are people able to consume the level of services they desire—that is, is there "allocative" efficiency?

Technical Efficiency in the Tiebout Economy

The best direct evidence examining the impact of Tiebout fiscal competition on local government technical efficiency is provided by Caroline Hoxby in her studies (2000, 2007) of the costs of producing K–12 public education when

10. See Heikkila (1996) and the excellent survey of local public finance by Ross and Yinger (1999, p. 2035); see also Rhode and Strumpf (2003).

11. And Gramlich and Rubinfeld (1982) before them. If the Tiebout model is appropriate, one would expect greater homogeneity of demands in suburban jurisdictions where there is substantial locational and public-sector choice. Within the suburbs of Detroit and several other large metropolitan areas, public service demands were found to be relatively homogeneous, while the demands were less homogeneous in cities with smaller numbers of suburbs or in rural areas.

12. Spending may be too high, either because local governments are inefficient in the production of those services or because there is "capture" of the local provision of those services to favor excessive provision. Those favored are typically thought to be local bureaucrats, as in Romer and Rosenthal (1979) and Brennan and Buchanan (1980).

there are multiple independent local school districts in a given metropolitan area. Hoxby conjectures that having more school districts and thus greater fiscal competition will lower the costs of providing student learning to randomly selected public school students in the region. Hoxby wants to know: Do students in metropolitan areas with higher values of her School Competition Index have higher test scores, controlling for family attributes? If so, are school expenditures then at least constant, but better still, perhaps even lower in those regions? If both conjectures are true, then families in the more fiscally competitive metropolitan areas receive more student learning at a lower cost. Those local schools show greater technical efficiency.[13]

Hoxby's evidence favors both conjectures: students in more competitive metropolitan areas learn more at lower costs.[14] For example, children in a metropolitan area whose School Competition Index is one standard deviation above the mean (fifty districts of equal size) have 4 to 9 percent higher math and reading achievement scores in high school than do children in a region whose School Competition Index is one standard deviation below the mean (say, one large district and three suburban districts). To place these gains in context, the same increase in math and reading performance would occur if the income of a child's parents were to double or if the child's parents were to have a college, rather than a high school, education.[15] Further, this gain in

13. Similar conclusions in favor of decentralization's benefits for technical efficiency follow from the study by Barankay and Lockwood (2007) of the effect of fiscal decentralization in Swiss cantons on the cost of education.

14. Hoxby's analysis is not without controversy. Rothstein (2007) asks whether Hoxby has found adequate "instruments" for the number of local governments in each metropolitan area. It could be that where local governments are more efficient for reasons unrelated to Tiebout competition, citizens favor the use of local governments for providing their services. Hoxby suggests that the number of streams within the metropolitan area would be a good instrument since in many areas the historical boundaries for local governments and school districts were drawn to match the borders of streams and rivers. It is also plausible that streams and rivers are unrelated to current government efficiency. The point of difference between Hoxby and Rothstein is whether large rivers should also be counted when defining the instrument, and if so, how large rivers should be measured. It would be nice if both Hoxby's and Rothstein's approaches gave the same results. They do not. So who is right? We give the nod to Hoxby (2007). To our mind, the small-stream instrument is the better instrument for predicting the number of competitive governments *within* a county. Importantly, our conclusions given later as to overall efficiency of local government fiscal competition do not turn on technical efficiency. The gains in allocating school services to family preferences are sufficient to make the empirical case for local fiscal competition.

15. Hoxby (2000, tables 3, 4); Hoxby (2007, table 3).

student performance is achieved with lower spending per pupil, from 4 to 5 percent lower. Together, these two results imply a percentage decline in the average costs of student learning from 8 to 13 percent. The sources of these cost savings from fiscal competition are most likely found in the labor budgets of local governments. Labor costs are the most important expense for local governments, and local public employees—teachers, firefighters, police officers, and sanitation and maintenance workers—are most often covered by negotiated labor contracts over wages, pensions, and work rules. Competition for residents can act as an important constraint on the levels of negotiated compensation and public employment. Both Inman (1982) and Richard Freeman (1988) find that increased fiscal competition leads to lower wages and, consequently, higher employment in central cities surrounded by suburbs attractive to city residents. On balance, fiscal competition leads to smaller local government budgets, consistent with greater public services at lower cost; see Jeffrey Zax (1989). Consistent with the incentives in the Tiebout economy for families to favor low-cost communities, Joseph Gyourko and Joseph Tracy (1989) find strong evidence that home values are lower in the higher-cost communities.

Finally, as conjectured by Justice Louis Brandeis in his famous 1932 decision evaluating federalism, not only does fiscal competition promote contemporary fiscal efficiencies, it has the potential to encourage the spread of successful policy innovations and thus long-run efficiencies too; see Box 2.2.

Allocative Economic Efficiency in the Tiebout Economy

In contrast to the standard wisdom at the time, Tiebout's central insight in his classic 1950s article was that government did not need politics for economic efficiency; shopping across competitive communities was enough. Fiscal competition could provide people with exactly the services they desire at the lowest cost. The argument was not easily accepted, and it took another fifteen years before economists took the analysis seriously. The question being asked was, How might this Tiebout economy perform in practice?

A compelling answer requires a full specification of the local public goods economy, one where households can move from town to town, where residents vote to set the level of public services, and where the housing market is in equilibrium with the demand for housing in each town equal to its supply. Dennis Epple and his colleagues (Calabrese, Epple, and Romano, 2012) have provided the required general equilibrium analysis for a "typical" U.S. metropolitan economy of one large central city and four surrounding suburbs that

Box 2.2. Evaluating the Brandeis Conjecture: Does Federalism Mean More Innovation?

It is one of the happy incidents of the federal system that a single courageous State may, if its citizens choose, serve as a laboratory, and try novel social and economic experiments without risk to the rest of the country.

—JUSTICE LOUIS BRANDEIS, *NEW STATE ICE*
CO. V. LIEBMANN, 295 U.S. 262 (1932)

Justice Brandeis's argument for federal governance as the mechanism for valuable innovation in government policy has been accepted by the courts, legal scholars, and policy-makers alike. For example, the motivation for relaxing U.S. federal government rules for managing social welfare under the Personal Responsibility and Work Opportunity Reconciliation Act came in part from the Brandeis Conjecture. Congress thought that by relaxing federal rules and allowing state innovation, new strategies for addressing poverty might emerge from state competition and therefore be replicated.

The conjecture finds its theoretical foundation in the economic theory of yardstick competition as developed by Shliefer (1985). Under yardstick competition, comparing the performance of one's local government with that of another's provides citizens with the information they need to encourage their own local officials to adopt more effective policies. The spread of policy innovations has been documented for children's health-care programs (Volden, 2006), state welfare reforms leading up to the Personal Responsibility and Work Opportunity Reconciliation Act (Weaver, 2000), tax reforms and tax rates (Besley and Case, 1995).

While yardstick competition does encourage the spread of efficient policies, the conjecture first needs an innovator. Innovation requires costly experimentation. The potential benefits will be available to all other states without the cost of experimentation or, perhaps most importantly, the political risks of failure. The incentives of local officials will then be to "free ride" on the innovative activities of other local governments. If so, too little innovation will occur (Strumpf, 2002), or if innovation does occur, it will be "state specific" so that it cannot be easily copied (Callander and Harstad, 2015). That state innovations occur at all appears to be largely decided not by economic efficiency but by state political events; see Gray (1973).

The solution for too little policy innovation is to rely on the central government, ideally through subsidies to local governments to pursue innovative strategies. This is exactly what was done when the federal government introduced a matching grant program for the adoption and spread of children's health programs. In contrast, recent federal efforts at welfare reform removed matching rate subsidies for program adoption, and there has been no significant evidence of program innovations as a result; see Rodgers, Beamer, and Payne (2008).

can be poor, middle class, or rich.[16] The distribution of income is chosen to match a national income distribution with a median family income of $37,000, an average income of $55,000 (both in 1999 dollars), and an upper 5 percent

16. Adding more communities did not significantly change any of the conclusions from their analysis.

TABLE 2.1. Does Local Choice Improve Household Welfare?

	Uniform provision (Head tax) (1)	Uniform provision (Property taxation) (2)	Local choice (Head tax/full housing choice) (3)	Local choice (Property taxation/full housing choice) (4)	Local choice (Property taxation/restricted housing choice) (5)
Average property tax rate on housing consumption	NA	.35	NA	.35	.35
Average spending per child	$2,420	$3,830	$3,358	$3,835	$3,878
Housing consumption	2,027 SF	1,313 SF	2,054 SF	1,686 SF	1,794 SF
Efficiency gain per household	0	$1,076	$2,511	$1,031	$2,230
Service equity (g_{LOW}/g_{HIGH})	1.0	1.0	.10	.11	.09

Notes: Housing consumption reported here is measured in square feet and is the population weighted average of housing consumption by the median income household in each community. All efficiency comparisons are relative to the economy with uniform provision of the local public good financed by a head tax. Service equity is measured by the ratio of service spending in the lowest- (g_{LOW}) relative to the highest- (g_{HIGH}) income communities.

Source: Based on data available from Calabrese, Epple, and Romano (2012, table 3).

of families with incomes over \$200,000. The distribution of tastes for the local public good is chosen so as to mimic the observed sorting of families across communities in the Boston metropolitan area. When local choice is allowed, families are free to locate in their preferred community. Communities provide government services and housing. The level of government services, here education, is decided by majority rule. The family with the median demand for the public good is the decisive voter. The family's location decision depends on the family's income and each community's price of housing, available housing at that price, the level of public services, and the local tax rate.

Table 2.1 summarizes the efficiency gains of having competitive local communities rather than one single government provide local services. It provides the answer we need as to whether Tiebout sorting and local choice can provide significant efficiency benefits. Column 1 shows the performance of the local economy when there is just one government and the chosen level of public services are financed by a uniform head (per family) tax. The level of services is that level chosen by the median-income family for the whole metropolitan economy. In this benchmark economy, the average level of public education spending per child is \$2,420, the average level of housing consumption is 2,027 square feet, and because we have just one government, there is perfect tax and spending equity.

Column 2 examines this same economy with uniform provision, but now the good is financed by a common, metropolitan-wide property tax. Again the median voter determines the metropolitan-wide level of school spending. Now all voters pay a tax equal to a common tax rate times the value of the home. That common tax rate (r) balances the government's budget, so $rH = kN$, where H is the value of all housing in the metropolitan area, k is the level of spending per child, and N is the number of children. Assuming one child per house, then $r = k/\hat{h}$, where $\hat{h} = H/N$ is the average value of property. The taxes paid by any one family will be $TAX = rh$, where h is the value of their home. For the median-income family, their tax payments will then be $TAX_m = rh_m$ or $TAX_m = (h_m/\hat{h})k$. Importantly, if the median-income family has a smaller house than the average-income family, then $(h_m/\hat{h}) < 1$. If so, then the median-income family is able to buy school services at less than their full cost (k), and the resulting subsidy for the median-income family leads to voting for more local public goods than under head taxation. The average spending per child rises by almost 60 percent, from \$2,420 to \$3,830.

There is a second important consequence of moving to property taxation. A property tax is a tax on housing, and as such it raises price for housing inclusive of the tax. The effects are highly significant because the implied tax rate on housing *consumption* (that is, rents) is very large. Here that rate is 35 percent.[17] It is the tax on consumption that matters for family decisions. As a consequence of the high tax rate, the median-income family lowers their housing consumption from 2,027 square feet when there is a head tax—and thus no added burden on housing consumption—to 1,313 square feet with the property tax.

These effects of property taxation for the provision of public services and for housing consumption have significant implications for allocative efficiency. First, the good news. Because of the subsidy with property taxation, the median-income family now prefers more local public goods. This means economic benefits for upper-middle and upper-income families who had, in the world of uniform provision and head taxes only, been forced to consume relatively low levels of services; compare average government spending in Columns 1 and 2. It is true that lower-income families now get more services than they might choose on their own, but they also receive a large cross-subsidy from families owning expensive homes with the adoption of the property tax. The efficiency gains from being more "responsive" to the public goods demands of middle- and upper-income families offset the small net losses to lower-income families.

Now, the bad news. The high rate of property taxation on housing consumption of 35 percent leads to a 35 percent fall in housing services for all income levels. This leads to a large efficiency loss. The net efficiency effect of the two changes is still positive, however. In this economy, the gains from a greater provision of education dominate the losses from less housing consumption. The average annual efficiency gain per household from replacing a head tax by a property tax is $1,076, equivalent to about 2 percent of average family income. Finally, since all families get the same level of services and pay the same tax rate, full tax rate and spending equity again hold.

It is the Tiebout economy with family choice and efficient financing of public services using a head tax that offers the largest gains in overall economic benefits; see Column 3. As a Tiebout market, this economy offers local choice to the residents of each of the five communities. Families stratify by income. The poorest families choose to live in one large (central city) community.

---

17. Annual housing consumption is equal to market rents $\rho \cdot h$, and tax payments are equal to the tax rate (r) on home value (h). Thus, the tax rate on housing consumption will equal $(r \cdot h)/(\rho \cdot h) = r/\rho$, where ρ is the competitive market rate of return on rental property. If the property tax rate on home value is .028 and the rental rate of return on home value is .08, the tax rate on housing *consumption* will be $r/\rho = .028/.08 = 0.35$.

There are then two middle-income communities, one upper-middle-income community, and finally, one very rich, exclusive suburb. The family with the median demand for public services in each community determines the level of school services. Because of sorting, there will be better matching of public services to each family's demand. As a consequence, the average level of school spending rises from uniform provision, because middle- and upper-income families can now buy what they want. Since Tiebout recommends the use of a head tax for the financing of local services, there are no adverse effects on housing consumption from a property tax. With the efficiency gains from better matching but none of the efficiency losses from property taxation, this "pure" Tiebout economy provides an average efficiency gain of $2,511 per year, or 4.5 percent of average household income. In contrast to the service provision in a metropolitan-wide economy, now there are significant spending inequities. The poorest families receive only 10 percent of what the richest families receive in educational services.

Of course, U.S. local communities typically use property taxes and not head taxes. The study then examines the effects of combining local communities with property taxation in two possible institutional environments. The first does not allow local zoning, so all families are free to choose their preferred level of housing in whatever community they choose to live in; see Column 4. *Importantly, this local economy violates Tiebout's condition T5.* Spending for the public good increases, but now primarily through sorting by demands and local choice rather than from a subsidy from property taxation. Since there are local communities in this case, the rich can escape subsidizing the poor by relocating. There is income sorting and richer families get better public services. There is no zoning, but the poor are still excluded from the richer communities because of high housing prices. The property tax again leads to inefficient housing choices, however, and this housing inefficiency significantly offsets the benefits of allowing each family to choose its level of local school services. Net gains are now only $1,031 per family. Again because of local choice, the poorest families receive significantly less in school services than the richest families.

What is needed for efficiency is the full Tiebout economy with condition T5 restored. If there is property taxation, then we need zoning, or equivalently fixed residential borders and local housing stocks so new housing construction is constrained; see Column 5. Property taxation is still inefficient because housing consumption is affected by the tax. But if housing consumption is constrained by fixed community borders and preassigned housing stocks, then families can only adjust their housing choice simultaneously with their decision to consume local public services. Effectively, this local economy is close to one with property taxation and exclusionary zoning—the Tiebout-Hamilton economy. Now families sort by their joint choice of housing and public services. With only five communities, not all combinations of family demands for housing and services can be satisfied, so this economy will not be fully efficient. But it might be close. Now the annual efficiency gain is $2,230 per family, achieving nearly 90 percent of the efficiency gain of the pure Tiebout economy.[18] The gain is equal to about 4 percent of the region's annual average income. And once again, allowing local choice leads to large inequities in the provision of public education.

Overall Efficiency Less the Implementation Costs of Local Choice

Introducing local fiscal choice when conditions T_1–T_6 hold offers the promise of efficient government provision of public services, both from lower costs of production from improved technical efficiency and from greater citizen benefits from improved allocative efficiency by the matching of citizen demands to the provision of local services. These two efficiency gains can be combined. Hoxby's analysis suggests that government competition lowers the costs of providing any bundle of local services by as much as 8 to 14 percent. For the average budget of $3,800 per family (local choice with property taxation or fixed boundaries), this amounts to a cost savings of from $300 (= .08 · $3,800) to $530 per family (= .14 · $3,800). As a first-order approximation, these efficiencies can be added to allocative benefits estimated for the Tiebout ($2,511) and Tiebout-Hamilton ($2,230) public economies in Table 2.1. The overall efficiency gains compared with the benchmark economy from introducing Tiebout choice will therefore range from $2,500 to $3,041 per family per year, or approximately 4.5 to 5.5 percent of annual average income.

The last step in tallying the overall efficiency advantages of a Tiebout economy is to estimate its implementation costs. Families need to know the better-performing governments (condition T_4) and then at least some must move (condition T_3). The implementation costs of running the Tiebout market

18. Barseghyan and Coate (2016) extend the model to allow communities to endogenously adopt zoning and set zoning levels to maximize the benefits of current residents. Since current residents always benefit by only allowing houses larger than their own, there is "overzoning" and an inefficiently restrictive supply of low-income housing. Public goods are still efficiently provided, however, and the shortage of low-income housing disappears if there is truly an elastic supply of entrepreneurs capable of filling all market demand—that is, if condition T_2 still holds.

must be subtracted from the technical and allocative efficiency gains. For a moving family, information regarding local services and taxes is typically provided by a real estate broker, for which the moving family pays a one-time fee of (usually) 3 percent of the purchase price of their new home. Once the property is purchased, they need to move to execute the trade. Finally, if families relocate to a community with better public goods but as a consequence must commute additional miles to their jobs, then there may be "wasteful commuting." One should consider these longer, inefficient commutes as an additional cost of Tiebout shopping and sorting. When amortized to an annual cost, we estimate these three decision costs to total perhaps as much as $3,100 per *moving* family.[19]

But not all families need move to achieve the benefits of Tiebout fiscal competition. The 6 percent of residents that move each year to find a "better community" set the price of homes in each community, and it is that price that rewards efficient and punishes inefficient communities.[20] Only movers bear decision costs, but we all benefit from the discipline they impose. (Be sure to thank your new neighbor.) Using the 6 percent assumption, we can average the movers' decision costs over all residents of a metropolitan area. This equals about $190 per family.

In the end, is a Tiebout economy worth it? Would families rather live in a metropolitan area with many local governments and choice or in one with one large government? From the perspective of overall economic efficiency, we think a Tiebout economy is indeed worth it. The average efficiency gain per family from greater choice in the Tiebout economy, when compared with a metropolitan economy with property taxation, is estimated in Table 2.1 as worth from $1,200 to $1,400 per year.[21] Hoxby has estimated the cost savings from fiscal

19. First the cost of relocation. A broker's fee to provide search information to a new resident will be approximately $10,500, and moving expenses are likely to total $4,000. Amortized over the tenure of a typical residence of twelve years at a 5 percent interest rate, the total cost will be an annual expense of $1,600. Further, there is likely to be additional "wasteful" commuting to work; see Hamilton and Roell (1982) and M. White (1988). Assuming that half of the average annual cost of commuting is wasteful (see Small and Song, 1992), the added commuting costs will be about $1,500 per year. Together the amortized moving costs plus the annual inefficiencies in commuting total $3,100 per moving family.

20. For the annual rate of household mobility, see U.S. Census, *The Statistical Abstract of the United States, 2011*, table 31. These families may pay significant premiums in higher home prices for the privilege of consuming those greater service levels at lower cost; see Black (1999) and Fischel (2001).

21. From the efficiency gains in Table 2.1, $1,154 = $2,230 (Col. 5) − $1,076 (Col. 2) and $1,435 = $2,511 (Col. 3) − $1,076 (Col. 2).

Box 2.3. Overdoing Tiebout: The Adoption of Proposition 13

In June 1978 the voters of California approved a sweeping reform for the financing of local public services in their state, Proposition 13. Proposition 13 set a maximum for the local property tax rate at 1 percent of the property's market value. As a result of the lower tax rate, local governments faced a shortfall of $7 billion, which was filled by the state. Indeed, since the approval of Proposition 13, state government has assumed primary responsibility for financing local public services. The fiscal and policy consequences of Proposition 13 have been significant. In 1972, California ranked in the upper quintile among U.S. states in its support for public education, and California students were performing at the same level as their national peers. By 2015, California's spending placed the state in the lowest quintile and students' performance on national tests placed them in the lowest decile. The loss of local control over local public finance seems to have had a significant negative impact on the residents of California. Why then did California give up on local financing of local services?

The primary motivation for the adoption of Proposition 13 was the growing sense that the system of local property taxation was out of control; see Stark and Zasloff (2003) and Martin (2006). The source of rising tax bills was the rapidly increasing home values, coupled with a state requirement to reassess local properties at market values every three years. As a result, residents' tax bills rose with the appreciation of housing prices, which during the 1970s was as high as 10 percent per year. Why were tax rates not reduced?

Overdoing Tiebout was an important source of the problem, particularly in Southern California. For economic efficiency, the population served by government should match the efficient population for each local service, a principle known as "fiscal equivalence" (Olson, 1969). As a result, each family would receive their services from a different district, and each district would set its own tax rate. Economists loved the idea, and so did Los Angeles County. By 1970, Los Angeles had the largest number of independent local governments and special districts of any county in America.

But here's the problem. With so many separate local governments setting the overall tax rate, if a family wanted to complain about its high tax payments, it had to do so to five or more separate governments. Lacking control over rising local taxes, it is perhaps not surprising that Californians, particularly Southern Californians for whom property values were rising the fastest, preferred Proposition 13 and overall state financing. At the time, the state had a $2 billion surplus, making state funding all the more attractive. A better option would have been to sacrifice some economic efficiency for improved local political control by combining local services under a single local government, but in return create a more manageable and responsive structure of local governance.

---

competition as worth perhaps an additional $300 to $500 per family per year. Against these benefits stand the annual organizational cost to run the Tiebout economy of about $190 per family. Add it all up, and you have a net economic surplus for each family of from $1,250 to $1,700 a year, worth from 2 to 3 percent of average annual income. From a lifetime perspective, families would pay from

7 to 10 percent of their home value wealth for the right to have fiscal choice and competitive local governments providing their local public goods.[22] Of course, there is always the risk that a good idea can be overdone. See Box 2.3.

For all of its efficiency advantages, however, the pure Tiebout economy does not solve all market failures. First, by condition T1, Tiebout's communities are limited to allocating only those public goods that become congested at relatively small populations. Public services that are most efficiently provided to large populations, such as national defense, telecommunication and transit networks, and social insurance and income protection, will require financing and production by large governments. Second, by condition T6, the Tiebout economy will not adequately address problems of intercommunity spillovers. Third, like all market economies, the Tiebout economy will not guarantee equal access to local public services. If those services are important to a citizen's future capabilities and economic opportunities, then societal economic fairness will be adversely affected. If Economic Federalism is to be an attractive means for organizing government, then it must provide more than the Tiebout or Tiebout-Hamilton economy. It cannot assume away large-scale public goods, spillovers and externalities, or a societal preference for equal economic opportunity. For an answer to these market failures, Economic Federalism turns to the central government.

4. Evaluating Economic Federalism: Beyond the Local Economy

In Economic Federalism, the task of the central government is to manage those goods and services that cannot be efficiently or equitably provided by private markets or the Tiebout economy. The difficulty is the fact that economic choices by individuals or communities have consequences beyond those making the decision. Individuals free ride on others' provision of large-scale public goods. Local communities are likely to ignore the benefits and costs their decisions impose on their neighbors.[23] And markets may limit an individual's consumption of a socially valued "merit good" such as education, housing, public safety, or clean environment because of an individual's limited ability to pay. In each

---

22. Discounting the annual efficiency gains of $1,250 to $1,710 into perpetuity at an interest rate of .05 implies a lifetime wealth gain of from $25,000 to $34,000. As a share of average household wealth of $350,000, this is a percentage gain of from 7.1 to 9.8 percent.

23. This was first shown formally by Pauly (1970). For an excellent contemporary treatment of the same issues, see Wellisch (2000, chaps. 6, 7).

case the solution requires an institution with the ability and incentive to transcend individual or local interests. This will typically be a central government.

But managed how? Economic Federalism has been silent on this important question. Oates (1972), in his classic treatise on economic federalism, simply says, "As part of the general guidelines [for Economic Federalism], I argued that *the central government* should assume primary responsibility for resolving stabilization and distribution problems and for providing efficient outputs of those public goods that significantly affect welfare of individuals in all jurisdictions" (pp. 31–32). Beyond conjecturing an important role for the central government in Economic Federalism, nothing more is said. We want that government, like our local governments, to be democratic. At a minimum, we could allow for direct democracy and have all these important national issues decided by citizen referenda. There is much to recommend such a procedure when the cost of running a referendum is low and issues are separable in their economic impacts and thus can be decided one by one; see John Matsusaka (2005) and Timothy Besley and Stephen Coate (2008). But individual referenda are often expensive and only affordable for well-organized special interests, and national issues are rarely separable. Setting the level of a national public good, such as national defense or interstate highways, will certainly affect private individuals who will also benefit from other national public goods, such as telecommunication, clean water, higher education, or national health insurance. To even approximate efficient policies, referenda will then need to be over "bundles" of national policies. But who is to decide how to structure the bundle?

One administratively simply solution is to hold a referendum on competitive bundles of national policies all managed by a single democratically elected individual chosen in a simple majority-rule election. Let's call that person a "president" whose campaign platform is the bundle of national policies, perhaps itself decided by a sequences of prior votes or citizen negotiations within "political parties." The candidate with the bundle most attractive to a majority of citizens will be chosen to be the president. The president will be given tax and spending powers and a bureaucracy sufficient to implement the promised bundle. The president will serve a fixed term in office with the option to seek reelection. The competitive election of a president is perhaps the simplest democratic structure for managing national policies. The hope is it will lead to the implementation of efficient national policies. Doing for the presidency and national policies what Tiebout and Hamilton had done for local governments, Besley and Coate (1997) outline the five conditions required for an economically efficient, presidentially managed, central government.

P1: There are open elections and voting.

All citizens who choose to run for the presidency may do so. The entry costs to being a candidate are modest; in particular, a candidate's freedom is not at risk if he or she chooses to run. All citizens can vote (strategically), maximizing their expected utility over candidates who are running, given how others are likely to vote.

P2: All candidates have equal abilities, and information, to deliver on their promised policies.

All candidates who do run are capable of delivering on their preferred policies. Information regarding the likely success of a proposed policy is common knowledge both for citizens and for candidates, and all candidates have access to the same technologies for producing public goods and services. In providing government policies, the president respects the preferences of the citizens. The efficient president understands possible behavioral responses to his or her policies and adopts the best available incentive mechanism for their execution.[24]

P3: Voters are informed of candidate preferences for, and abilities to provide, policies.

Voters cannot be fooled by a candidate who promises policy x but then implements policy y when in office, either because the candidate prefers y over x or because the candidate is not able to provide x. The best indicator of a candidate's policy preferences and abilities is what that candidate has done in prior office. Economic Federalism has an advantage in this regard, since holding office at a lower tier of government provides an important testing ground for honesty of candidates; see Roger Myerson (2006). Newspaper, radio, and television coverage of candidates and campaign advertising and debates are also important sources of information about candidates' preferences. A free and competitive press and policy debates each contribute to economic efficiency.[25] The consequence of this condition is that all candidate campaign promises (policy positions) are credible promises. Only truthful candidates will be successful, and candidates' promises will be based on candidates'

---

24. For the public finance literature on the design of policies recognizing the incentives of policy recipients, see Myles (1995, pts. 2, 3). For the literature on the design of incentives for public bureaucrats who provide policies, see Dixit (1996, esp. pp. 94–107).

25. For a review of the role of media in promoting truthful information about candidates, see Gentzkow and Shapiro (2008).

preferences. Finally, there is no presumption as to what motivates candidates to hold public office, whether it is the maximization of citizen welfare, corporate welfare, or personal income, as long as informed citizens know the difference and the consequences for policy outcomes.

P4: There is policy commitment.

To ensure that dynamically efficient policies will be adopted, the president must be able to commit to the continuation of an efficient policy, even after he or she has left office. If good investment policies can be undone by a subsequent president, then those policies will not be proposed in the first place. There are mechanisms to protect policy continuity. Political parties, viewed as informal agreements between a sequence of like-minded presidential candidates, are one possibility. Internal party politics can reveal future presidents' abilities and preferences, and the party's "brand" serves as a reputation to be protected.[26] Institutional checks and balances provide additional commitment devices for current presidents. Examples include independent courts, independent monetary authorities, and independent agencies. The current president appoints the judges, bankers, and bureaucrats whose long-run preferences agree with his or her own. Future presidents might abolish such agencies (or just ignore their decisions), but then their own ability to use these institutions to ensure their favored long-run policies will be compromised.[27] Finally, the president can devise means within the policy itself that tie future program benefits to assets held by a majority of current residents. As future residents buy those assets, they develop a vested interest in the continuation of the program. For example, owners of land next to interstate highway exits or environmentally protected areas become advocates for the future of those programs.

P5: Majority rule selects the president in two-candidate elections.

Presidents will be elected in a "first-past-the-post," majority-rule election. The election is assumed to involve just two candidates, a result known as

26. On brand name as a valuable, accumulated reputation that allows for the credible introduction of new products—here policies—see Choi (1998). On how party organizations can enforce behavior on senior leaders, see Cremer (1986).

27. Dixit (1996) provides an overview (pp. 62–85). Examples of commitment institutions include Kydland and Prescott (1977) and Lohmann (1994) on the use of independent monetary authorities, Landes and Posner (1976) on the use of independent courts, and McCubbins, Noll, and Weingast (1987) on the use of independent agencies to ensure commitment to long-lived economic policies.

Duverger's Law.[28] In this case, the two candidates will split the voters evenly. No third candidate will enter since no voter will risk switching his or her vote unilaterally to a third candidate, thus making the voter's original second choice a sure winner.

Together conditions P1–P5 describe a world of "citizen-candidates" where anyone can run for president, seek campaign financing, present his or her case to voters, and if the individual achieves a majority of votes, serve as president. Once elected, presidents can implement their policies, subject to the constraints of technology and the incentives of policy recipients, bureaucrats, and public employees. Besley and Coate (1997, 1998) prove that such open two-candidate elections with informed voters will elect a citizen-candidate as president whose policies are efficient in the sense that no other feasible candidate is preferred by another majority of citizens.[29] Much as Tiebout's market competition with many equally efficient communities providing local public goods and informed citizens free to choose their favorite community leads to the efficient provision of local public goods, here Besley-Coate's political competition with efficient candidates and informed citizens can lead to the efficient provision of national public goods, though with one important qualifier— because the technology of national goods often requires a common policy for all citizens, efficiency will be *constrained* efficiency. In contrast to Tiebout's markets, democratic majority rule may leave some citizens worse off with the adoption of the president's policies.[30] Constrained efficiency is a result of Economic Federalism's commitment to our other valued objectives: democratic governance and the protection of individual rights and liberties.

What is the evidence for the efficiency of strong presidential governance? Comparing majority rule, presidential democracies and proportional-representation, parliamentary democracies with multiple political parties, Persson and Tabellini (2003, 2004) find that presidential democracies adopt more efficient public budgets and as a result enjoy higher rates of economic growth. Other studies point in the same direction. When comparing electoral systems with broad rather than narrow geographic representation, broader

28. See Fujiwara (2011).

29. For proof of efficiency in the case of policies that last only for one election cycle, see Besley and Coate (1997, proposition 10). For efficiency in the dynamic setting where policies can extend beyond one election cycle, see Besley and Coate (1998, propositions 2, 3).

30. Only under very special circumstances will this outcome satisfy the (Samuelson) conditions for *potential* Pareto efficiency; see Bergstrom (1979).

elections (such as for a single national president) favor the provision of geo-graphically wide-reaching public goods and more uniform distribution of public pensions and other welfare programs. Finally, majority-rule presidential democracies are less likely to run large fiscal deficits over many years, generally consistent with more efficient intertemporal fiscal policies. More direct evidence comes from studies of U.S. fiscal policies showing how "strong" presidents outperform "weak" presidents in the development of economic policies. Presidential strength is measured in two ways: first, by formal executive powers such as control over the agenda and access to executive vetoes, and second, by the popular support ("political capital") for the president in national elections or surveys. Michael Fitts and Inman (1992) show how a president might use these resources to win legislative approval of economically efficient policies, policies with lower national spending on "local" public goods with all savings returned to citizens as tax cuts.

Finally, case studies of important economic policy reforms favoring efficiency all point to the importance of strong presidential governance for their passage. Prominent examples include Theodore Roosevelt and the passage of the first environmental legislation, Woodrow Wilson and the approval of the Federal Reserve regulation of money and banking, Franklin Roosevelt's promotion of fiscal policy for escaping the Great Depression, Dwight Eisenhower and the adoption of the interstate highway system, Lyndon Johnson and the passage of Medicare and Medicaid, and Ronald Reagan's leadership behind the tax reforms of 1986. In all cases, presidential leadership was necessary for approval of the legislation, and in each case the empirical evidence suggests the reforms contributed significantly to economic growth and market efficiency.[31]

31. See Brinkley (2009, chaps. 15–25) on Theodore Roosevelt setting the national agenda for environmental policy; Meltzer (2003, chaps. 1, 2) on Woodrow Wilson's role in the passage of the Federal Reserve Act of 1913 and M. Friedman and Schwartz (1963) for an economic analysis of the efficiency advantages of centralized monetary policies; A. Schlesinger (1958, chaps. 16–22) and Patterson (1981, chap. 4) on Franklin D. Roosevelt's leadership for the passage of New Deal fiscal policies and the passage of the Social Security Act of 1935 establishing income insurance for dependent children, the elderly, and the blind and A. Schlesinger (1958) and Cole and Ohanian (2004) for an economic analysis; Rose (1990, chaps. 6, 7) on Dwight D. Eisenhower's passage of the Federal-Aid Highway Act of 1956 and Friedlaender (1965) and Small, Whinston, and Evans (1989) for the economic analysis; Patterson (1981, chaps. 8, 9) and Marmor (2000, chap. 4) on Lyndon Johnson's role in the approval of War on Poverty legislation and Blank (2002) and Gruber (2008) for an economic analysis of the War of Poverty; and Birnbaum and

Both the aggregate empirical evidence and the individual policy achievements of Presidents Theodore Roosevelt, Wilson, Franklin Roosevelt, Eisenhower, Johnson, and Reagan suggest the potential efficiency advantages of strong presidential governance for the provision of national public goods, spillovers, and merit wants.

5. Evaluating Economic Federalism: Representation

The aim of democratic representation is to ensure every citizen a fair opportunity to influence the policies of his or her government; political participation is the means to that end. The act of participation can include voting, debating, marching, picketing, contributing time and money, and in the limit when peaceful means fail, perhaps armed resistance. The formal and informal institutions of public decision-making are the most important determinants of the decision to participate, of which federal governance is one, and, for Economic Federalism, local governance in particular. In describing early New England governance in *Democracy in America*, Alexis de Tocqueville was very clear as to the participatory advantages of local governments:

> The native of New England is attached to his township because it is independent and free: his cooperation in its affairs insures his attachment to his interest; the well-being it affords him secure his affection; and its welfare is the aim of his ambition and of his future exertions. He takes part in every occurrence in the place; he practices the art of government in the small sphere within his reach; he accustoms himself to those forms without which liberty can only advance by revolutions; he imbibes their spirit; he acquires a taste for order, comprehends the balance of powers, and collects clear practical notions of the nature of his duties and the extent of his rights. (1969, p. 70).

For contemporary scholars of federalism such as Heather Gerken (2014b), local governance and local participation provide an important additional benefit, protection for the rights of national minorities through their political control of local governments. First, such control gives elected leaders access to a local tax base, though constrained by asset mobility, to finance services benefiting the controlling minorities. Second, through success in local elections,

---

Murray (1987, chap. 7) for Ronald Reagan's role in the approval of the Tax Reform Act of 1986 and Auerbach and Slemrod (1997) for an analysis of the efficiency gains with the new law.

minorities learn the benefits of participating in politics and the skills required to influence the choice of public policies. Third, as Gerken's "loyal opposition" in national politics, minorities can use their positions as elected local leaders both to speak nationally on minority concerns and, more importantly, to organize a national coalition of initially diffused minority communities to influence national elections.

For all these potential participatory benefits of local governments, is there any reason to think that local governance will foster local political participation? On the one hand, small local governments may ensure each citizen more influence over outcomes, whether by voting, debating, or contributing to candidates. Greater influence over outcomes compensates for the personal costs of participating, and this should encourage participation.[32] On the other hand, in very small communities of (nearly) identical citizens, someone will probably participate, and he or she will be just like you. So why bother? Further, larger communities can provide protection through anonymity if one wishes to speak out or protest an abusive political regime. Both the international and the U.S. evidence is supportive of the conjecture that smaller governments contribute to the goal of citizen participation, with one exception. The appropriate testing ground is within country evidence. Robert Dahl and Edward Tufte (1973, chap. 4) survey the early international evidence, and a special issue of *Environment and Planning C: Politics and Space* (2002) has provided an update of their analysis for five European countries. The results have remained consistent over time. The analysis reaches four conclusions. First, for four mature democracies (Britain, West Germany, Italy, and Mexico), citizens report making a greater effort to understand, and having more success in understanding, local rather than national political issues. In the same four democracies, citizens were then more likely to make an effort to influence local rather than national government policies, typically two to three times more likely. Further, a detailed survey of political participation across Swedish cities found that citizens in small communities were more aware of local politics than citizens in middle-size cities and both knew more local political facts than

---

32. Mulligan and Hunter (2003) are skeptical of the view that small governments mean greater individual influence and thus greater participation; even in small towns, the influence of any individual's vote on the outcome is slight. Feddersen (2004) suggests an alternative model of voting behavior, in which individuals view their vote as representative of a "bloc" of like-minded voters, and the bloc—if all vote—can be influential, as described in Palfrey and Rosenthal (1984). Coate and Conlin (2004) find empirical support for this view of local voting in Texas city referenda.

their counterparts in large cities. Second, Swedish citizens felt much more influential at the local than at the national level; typically, half of the citizens in the surveyed countries felt they had no influence over national policies, while only 25 to 30 percent felt powerless at the local level. Third, survey data from Denmark, the Netherlands, Norway, Switzerland, and the United Kingdom found that citizens trusted their local politicians far more than their national representatives and were more active politically (voting, attendance at legislative sessions) the smaller the jurisdiction. Fourth, evidence from the United States, the Netherlands, and Switzerland each showed that politics in larger communities, states, and cantons are increasingly dominated by organized interest groups or political parties. While such groups make participation easier for some citizens, they may also make it more difficult for others. Participation becomes more unequal as governments get larger.

In a series of studies of political participation in small to medium-size U.S. cities, Eric Oliver (2000) reaches similar conclusions. He finds that local participation rates, measured by the percentage of the community's citizens who contact local officials about policy, attend organizational meetings for political activity, and attend community board meetings, are all near 40 percent in communities of 10,000 residents or smaller, while rates of participation in cities larger than 250,000 residents are typically closer to 20 percent. Citizens in smaller communities are "almost always" likely to vote in local elections, while those in the largest cities "rarely" do so. Oliver and Shang Ha (2007) find that citizens in communities of 15,000 residents are from 10 to 20 percent more interested in, and more knowledgeable about, local issues and candidates than even residents in communities of 30,000 residents. Among all communities, those with the greatest degree of citizen political engagement are relatively small and also economically and demographically diverse communities with populations ranging from 25,000 to 50,000 residents.

That diversity improves political engagement supports the hope of Gerken that smaller communities can be the basis for a stronger minority voice in democratic governance. Oliver finds that African American citizens are just as likely as their white counterparts to participate in community politics and significantly more likely to show an interest in local issues and to engage in local political organization. In cities where the minority population is sufficiently large, about 40 percent of registered voters, minority control of local politics is possible.[33] U.S. cities with significant minority populations have elected African American mayors, and their successful tenures there have

---

33. See also C. Cameron, Epstein, and O'Halloran (1996).

lowered racial barriers to the election of African American mayors even in cities with relatively small black populations. Further, these elected mayors have used their mayoral platforms to speak in favor of national policies important to their minority and city constituents generally: gun control, school funding, public housing, public transit, and the reform of policing practices.

The one important exception to the participatory benefits of smaller communities is when the residents of those communities are economically and socially homogeneous and affluent; see Oliver (2000). In such communities, government plays a relatively unimportant role in citizens' lives, other than for education. There is little to contest and little controversy, and thus little reason to be politically active. Citizens in smaller communities are likely to have a lower cost of participation, but there needs to be a reason to participate. There is, when local leaders fail to manage local public finances to the benefit of residents. Just as Economic Federalism requires, Oliver and Ha (2007) finds that residents in smaller communities are significantly more likely than their counterparts in large cities to vote against an incumbent politician when they are unhappy with the policy performance of the local government. The focus of participation in these communities is on electing and supervising civic-minded leaders to ensure the fiscal and administrative efficiency of the local government, in what Oliver (2012) calls "managerial democracies."

For all the virtues of local governance for democratic participation and representation, the fact remains that Economic Federalism offers only one national presidential election, once every four or five years, as the means for setting national policies. The ability of any one citizen, or bloc of citizens, to have influence over national policy outcomes may be slight. It will be the median, most likely median-income, voter who typically proves decisive in such elections. It is perhaps no surprise then that the international evidence reviewed by Dahl and Tufte (1973, chap. 4) showed that a majority of European voters felt disconnected from national policy deliberations and as a consequence made less effort to understand such issues. Citizens' political engagement is likely to be lower the less they have the opportunity to directly influence the president and his or her advisers in the formation and passage of policy. U.S. citizens who felt less "efficacious" as to the impact from voting and campaign activities in national elections participated less, and less participation increased the voters' sense of powerlessness in subsequent elections.[34] In countries with strong presidents, as measured by their ability to operate independent of

34. See Finkel (1985).

legislative or judicial oversight, voter participation is 10 percent less than in countries with such oversight.[35] As a result, there is a potentially significant "democratic deficit" with Economic Federalism's strong president, even when the strong president is democratically elected.

6. Evaluating Economic Federalism: Rights and Equity

From early political theorists such as James Harrington, Baron de Montesquieu, and James Madison to contemporary republican theorists such as Richard Pettit and Bruce Ackerman to libertarian philosophers such as Robert Nozick to leading legal scholars such as Gerald Frug, Andrzej Rapaczynski, and Akhil Reed Amar, the primary virtue of federal governance is in its ability to protect individual rights and liberties: the economic rights to own and allocate property, the political rights to vote and speak one's mind, and the civil rights of religious expression, privacy, and freedom to travel.[36] Alexander Hamilton, in *Federalist* No. 28, outlined the argument for how Economic Federalism's dual institutions of local governance and a strong central government, here a democratically elected president, might provide such protections: "Power being almost always the rival of power; the General Government will at times stand ready to check the usurpations of the state governments, and these will have the same disposition towards the General Government. The people, by throwing themselves into either scale, will infallibly make it preponderate. *If their rights are invaded by either, they can make use of the other as the instrument of redress*" (Hamilton, Madison, and Jay, 1982, p. 136; italics added).

Local governments defend individual rights and liberties in three ways. First, with a guaranteed right of free mobility, they can check rights abuses by other local governments. If any one jurisdiction restricts the rights of its citizens on any dimension, residents are free to relocate to a more hospitable community. Not only are rights protected for those who move, but the loss of potentially productive labor from the oppressive community imposes a

35. See Dettrey and Schwindt-Bayer (2009).

36. For the best summary of the arguments of the early scholars on how federalism might protect individual rights, see Beer (1993, chaps 3, 7, 8), and for the arguments of Publius in *The Federalist Papers*, see Amar (1987). For the arguments of contemporary scholars as to how the institutions of federalism might protect rights and liberties, see Ackerman (1991, chap. 7), Pettit (1997, chap. 6), Nozick (1974, chap. 10), Frug (1999), and Rapaczynski (1985).

penalty on those residents (the oppressing majority) who remain. The exit of African American workers from the South to the North, finally possible after World War I, is a case in point (Leah Boustan, 2016). Today, cities that have been hospitable to the gay and lesbian community have benefited economically (David Christafore and Susane Leguizamon, 2012). Even without mobility, observing freedoms in neighboring communities can create demands for comparable freedoms at home, leading to political pressure within the more oppressed community for an expansion of rights. This has proved to be the case in the United States with the recent expansion of marriage rights for same-sex couples. Perhaps the most recent examples of how such "yardstick competition" can encourage the expansion of individual rights and liberties are the fall of communist Poland, then East Germany, and finally the breakup of the Soviet Union.

How competition between local governments may act to protect individual rights and liberties from central government overreach is illustrated by what Barry Weingast (1995) has called "market-preserving federalism"; see Box 2.4. If the national government and local governments both value the long-run rewards that follow from stable rights more that a large one-time reward from a rights abuse, then market-preserving federalism can endure. Weingast argues that this was the case for England establishing its Glorious Revolution, for the United States following its War of Independence, and finally, for China today with its decision to decentralize business taxation and regulation to its major cities and provinces (Jin, Qian, and Weingast, 2005).

Second, as argued by Rapaczynski (1985) and Amar (1987), local governments can provide a direct line of defense against an abusive central government. Local governments stand "at the ready" for any historical moment when a central government threatens individual rights and liberties. Local governments have local police forces, perhaps a local militia (in the United States, the National Guard), and most importantly, a functioning institutional apparatus already in place to organize local resistance to central government overreach. Such protections may not always work, however; the failure to protect market rights in modern Nigeria is an example. Central government politicians have routinely placed a high value on exploiting local oil revenues for their private gain at the expense of long-run political and economic stability. The results have been periodic wars between the states and the central government and zero real growth in per capita incomes since independence in 1960.[37] For both Rapaczynski and Amar, what

---

37. See Suberu (2001) and Adamolekun (2005).

Box 2.4. Market-Preserving Federalism

How should a market economy protect individual property rights from an overarching central government—what Thomas Hobbes has called Leviathan? While in theory the central government can protect individual rights and liberties, in practice there remains the risk that a powerful central government could be captured by those who violate individual rights for their personal gain. How might we design federal institutions to check such abuses?

Brennan and Buchanan (1980) and more recently Weingast (1995) have suggested local governments with clearly delineated local powers. For Brennan and Buchanan, the list of assigned local powers must include taxation of mobile factors of production—labor and capital—and for Weingast, assigned local powers must include regulation of business activities. For both, however, the central government assumes responsibility for national public goods and for ensuring free trade and free mobility of resources across the borders of the subnational governments. Weingast argues that citizens, through their local governments, have a collective long-run interest in resisting central government violations of policy assignments and individual rights. Given this resistance, the central government has a long-run interest in respecting rights and maintaining open borders for goods, capital, and people. Such a federal organization for government protects individual property rights and encourages the efficient taxation of mobile human and physical capital. Weingast calls such an arrangement "market-preserving federalism."

Here is the intuition for how it works. Citizens, through their local governments, can refuse to pay revenues to the central government, but then they risk losing all the economic benefits and rights protections—in particular preventing wars between the local units—that the central government provides. Perhaps it takes one year before those losses appear. In the meantime they enjoy one year of no central government taxation. These short-run gains may make withholding local taxes a tempting option. The central government is tempted too. It might choose to centralize all regulation and taxation and then capture those resources for its own use. But if it does so, the local governments withhold local tax revenues from the central government. Then everyone loses. All this adds up to a prisoner's dilemma. If both local governments and the central government adopt their "temptation" strategies, we have a standoff: local taxes are not paid, but no central services are provided.

The hope is that both the central government and the local governments take the long view. If the central government and local citizens both value a smaller but steady long-run reward from stable rights and efficient markets to the larger temporary gains of the "temptation" strategy, the preferred outcome of protected rights and competitive local outcomes can be sustained. The long view will be possible with stable national and local governments where residents capture the rewards of competitive efficiencies, as, for example, under Economic Federalism and Tiebout competitive local governments.

must be protected are the institutions of local governance: the election of local representatives, local democratic deliberations, and the independence of local police and fiscal powers. The last has been missing in Nigeria.

Third, local governments provide a valuable testing ground for the inclinations and abilities of future national leaders as protectors of individual rights and liberties. The rights performance of an elected local leader provides a clear signal of how he or she might perform if elected president of the central government. The racist track record of Governor George Wallace of Alabama that made him a popular candidate in portions of the South also prevented his election nationally as president of the United States in 1968. Conversely, the civil rights records of Governors Jimmy Carter of Georgia and Bill Clinton of Arkansas motivated a significant increase in minority turnout and thus aided Carter's and Clinton's elections as president.

Together the three arguments make the case for local governments and policy decentralization as providing important protections for individual property and civil rights. Our cross-country empirical results presented in Chapter 1 provide strong empirical support for this conclusion. While arguably a necessary institution for a fully free and democratic society, local governments alone may not be sufficient. As anticipated by Hamilton in *Federalist No. 28*, citizens may also need a strong central government if, and when, local governments abuse individual rights and liberties and the protection provided by citizen mobility is not available. The United States' struggle to remove slavery and to ensure full rights for African Americans is a case in point. Without strong presidential action, first by Lincoln in pressing for a Northern victory in the U.S. Civil War, then by Eisenhower in enforcing school integration, and finally by Johnson in securing the passage of the Civil Rights Act of 1964 and the Voting Rights Act of 1965, it is very possible that U.S. southern states would still be, at least de facto, segregated and restricted societies for African Americans.[38]

National leadership will also be required to ensure equitable access to goods and services required by individuals to achieve their full potential, what economists Richard Musgrave (1959) and Amartya Sen (1999) described as "merit goods" and "capabilities," political philosophers Isiah Berlin (1969) and

---

38. Lincoln embraced the cause of emancipation as a central additional justification for the Civil War; see Gienapp (2002, chap. 5). Eisenhower, though initially reluctant, acted decisively to protect the schoolchildren of Little Rock, Arkansas, when local resistance to the court-ordered integration of Little Rock schools became violent; see Anderson (2010, chaps. 2, 3). Two years later, Eisenhower introduced the first civil rights bill, which led eventually to the Civil Rights Act of 1964 and the Voting Rights Act of 1965 under the presidential leadership of Lyndon Johnson. Eisenhower's support giving political cover to conservative Republicans and Johnson's relationships with southern Democrats both helped to neutralize opposition in Congress to the legislation; see Loevy (1997, chaps. 1, 2). These protections of minority rights would not have been possible without strong presidential leadership.

John Rawls (1971) as "positive liberties" and "primary goods," and legal theorists Frank Michelman (1977) and Ronald Dworkin (1986) as "just wants" and "essential resources." The ability of local governments to provide such goods on their own is limited by local fiscal resources, however. Poor communities cannot provide the same levels of education, safety, and environmental quality as richer communities. And because of local fiscal competition and the sorting of households and businesses across communities, these resources will be unequally distributed.[39] The U.S. evidence comparing local service provision across communities and states is quite clear on the point.[40] Achieving significant equity reforms without strong central government leadership appears very difficult. See Box 2.5.

The institution of Economic Federalism needed for the equitable distribution of merit goods and services is the elected president. Since resources must be redistributed from rich to poor localities, strong national leadership will be required. What the president can accomplish, however, will inevitably be constrained by the wishes of his or her majority coalition, most likely median-income voters.[41] Only when the middle class itself feels threatened by the causes of income and merit goods inequality is significant income redistribution and protection of positive rights likely under Economic Federalism. There have been such moments within U.S. federalism, but in each case the successful reform was led by a president with significant middle-class support for the expansion of economic rights. The New Deal of Franklin D. Roosevelt introduced progressive income taxation, unemployment insurance, Social Security, and income insurance via welfare payments as a response to a Depression whose adverse economic consequences reached far into the middle class.[42] The War on Poverty passed under the leadership of Lyndon Johnson included health insurance for the poor but also, most important politically, health insurance for *all* elderly.[43] And most recently, Barack Obama's signature policy, the Affordable Care Act, provided for the significant expansion of health insurance to lower-income households and, again important politically, to self-employed, middle-income households.[44]

---

39. And the evidence from Feldstein and Wrobel (1998).
40. See Inman and Rubinfeld (1979) and Murray, Evans, and Schwab (1998).
41. See, for example, Meltzer and Richard (1981) and Boadway and Wildasin (1989).
42. See A. Schlesinger (1958, chaps. 16–22).
43. See Patterson (1981, chaps. 10, 11).
44. See Carman, Eibner, and Paddock (2015).

For the goal of economic efficiency, Economic Federalism assigns responsibility for the provision of ("congestible") public services, those that can be provided efficiently with relatively small populations, to local governments. Examples include public education, public housing, health services, and police and fire services. When provided locally, the level of provision in each community will depend on the preferences and economic resources of residents and local politics. Rich communities and those whose elected officials value the local service will receive relatively more local services. This is as it should be for the goal of economic efficiency, but not if the goal is service equity. Wide disparities in the provision of local services are often the result. If the local service is viewed as a "merit good," then central government policies to narrow local disparities will be required. Chapter 7 suggests such policies. The first step, however, is to persuade Economic Federalism's nationally elected leadership that local service equity is a national priority.

The experience of U.S. states to achieve equity in the financing of local public education provides an important lesson. The economic evidence is overwhelming that a quality K–12 education is essential for a child's long-run economic future. Equity in the provision of K–12 education is essential for future fairness in the distribution of personal economic opportunities and national incomes; see Fernandez and Rogerson (1996). By 1970, inequities in the provision of K–12 education were clearly evident to U.S. policy scholars, and the cause was identified as disparities in the resources available to local governments assigned the responsibility for local schools; see Coons, Clune, and Sugarman (1970). The solution was to channel more fiscal resources to fiscally poor communities. This could only be achieved if the state or, ideally for those advocating greater equity, the national government were willing to tax richer communities and transfer education aid to poorer communities. To motivate state or national government action, advocates for greater local service equity appealed to the state and national courts for relief under the argument that Economic Federalism's local financing of public education violated a constitutional provision for equal educational opportunity for all children in the state (for example, *Serrano v. Priest*, 487 P.2d 1241 [Cal. 1971]) or even the entire nation (*San Antonio Independent School District v. Rodriquez*, 411 U.S. 1 [1973]). Eight state supreme courts have since overturned full local financing for K–12 education as a violation of their state's constitutional requirement for equal educational opportunity and thus required state reforms to increase local fiscal equity; the U.S. Supreme Court did not find such a requirement in the U.S. Constitution and thus did not impose a national remedy for national funding inequities.

The ensuing thirty years of reforms have shown only modest gains in overall equity in the eight affected states when compared with the forty-two states not required by their courts to reform local finance; see Murray, Evans, and Schwab (1998) and Hill and Kiewiet (2015, table 2). This is for four reasons. First, state policies typically did only the minimal level of fiscal redistribution needed to meet state court requirements for "equal opportunity." Second, state policies were constrained by the preferences of middle-class families *not* to have their level of school funding reduced. While poor districts got more state assistance, all local governments got additional state funding. Third, local preferences matter, and where unaffected by court decisions, higher-income communities chose to allocate a greater share of their tax dollars to education. Fourth, and perhaps most importantly, while local fiscal resources can improve educational opportunity, the local nonfiscal environment—in this case, classmates—is just as important. The central lesson from the U.S. experience with school fiscal reform seems clear: to achieve meaningful service equity in Economic Federalism, direct central government provision will be required.

From the arguments and evidence presented here, we conclude that the institutions of Economic Federalism can function as a positive force for human rights and economic equity. Economically and politically competitive local governments can provide an important check against rights abuses by each other and by the central government. But as the U.S. history of civil rights makes clear, local government protections alone are not sufficient. For the protection of individual rights against possible local abuses and for equal access to merit goods, a strong central government will be needed. In Economic Federalism, that will be a competitively elected president. From the U.S. experience, presidents have, though not often, provided the needed protections and redistributions. But in all instances, they have been constrained by the realities of majority-rule politics and thus the goodwill of their, most likely middle-class, coalition.

7. Summing Up

Economic Federalism offers a good start in the search for a well-functioning federal system. Local governments can be efficient providers of appropriately assigned "local" goods, provide active venues for democratic dialogue and deliberation, and offer safe havens and protective shields for individual rights and liberties. For all those virtues, local governments will not be efficient providers of national public goods or local goods with significant positive or negative spillovers, nor will they equitably provide merit goods seen as necessary for a full and productive life. For these services, a central government will be required. Economic Federalism proposes a simple institutional structure: a democratically elected president serving a four-year term of office. The elected president's efficiency can be *constrained efficient* in the sense that no other candidate is preferred to the elected president, but many citizens may inevitably remain dissatisfied with the final allocations. Presidential elections help, but other than every four years, dissatisfied citizens may have no other means to have their voices heard; representation and democratic participation are likely to suffer as a consequence. Further, presidential policies are constrained by the preferences of the decisive election coalition, with the risk that minority preferences will be ignored at best and minority rights may be abused at worst. It is useful, therefore, to examine the performance of possible alternative forms of federal governance.

In Chapter 3, we replace Economic Federalism's single national government with a network of voluntary agreements among local governments, to form

Cooperative Federalism. Cooperative Federalism ensures that each local government, or a voluntary coalition of such governments, can veto any central government constraint on its own domain of policy. In Chapters 4 and 5 we consider a hybrid form of governance, Democratic Federalism, that seeks to capitalize on the relative strengths of Economic and Cooperative Federalism. Democratic Federalism will stand as our preferred institutional middle ground, offering wider democratic engagement and more assured protection of rights and liberties than Economic Federalism, but greater economic efficiency and equity than Cooperative Federalism.

3

Cooperative Federalism

1. Introduction

Economic Federalism has much to recommend it. As a structure of governance, it creates a competitive network of small governments that efficiently provides government services with modest (that is, local) economies of scale and that entails no significant economic spillovers onto neighboring communities. Further, because communities are relatively small and citizens are able to choose where to live and consume services, Economic Federalism is responsive to citizen preferences for these local public goods. Finally, if citizens are free to move to new communities, no one community can exploit its citizens without their leaving. As a result, rights are secure. For the provision of public services with significant (that is, national) economies of scale, for the control of ignored economic spillovers, or to ensure greater economic opportunities, Economic Federalism proposes a nationally elected president to set policies. It is here that Economic Federalism loses some of its luster. The president will set policies in response to the preferences of the median voter, most likely the voter with the median income. Citizens with preferences away from the median will find that the president provides either too little or too much of a national public good, fails to manage spillovers, and is not likely to expand economic opportunities for all citizens. Further, if a small group of citizens are exploited by their local communities but cannot move, it is unlikely that a nationally elected president will provide the needed relief.

Cooperative Federalism offers an extension of Economic Federalism to address these concerns. In Cooperative Federalism there is no nationally elected president. In his or her place will be a network of local communities banded together by voluntary agreements to provide more or less of a national public good, to resolve the inefficiencies of their intercommunity spillovers or not, and to offer more or fewer economic opportunities, as the residents of cooperating local governments might prefer. Citizens will be free to choose among and between cooperating local governments. Political theorists will recognize Cooperative Federalism as Montesquieu's "Confederate Republic," where the "political process of central government is a matter of balancing and bargaining among respective interests of the member republics."[1] Economic theorists will recognize Cooperative Federalism as an application of Ronald Coase's "Theorem," where, with "a precise allocation of property rights and absent any cost of information or negotiation, two parties will arrive at a bargain that would internalize any externalities between them."[2]

We begin our evaluation of Cooperative Federalism with an overview of the theory underlying its potential benefits. Seven conditions must hold for Cooperative Federalism to economically benefit residents of all bargaining communities. Two of the requirements prove particularly problematic. Community preferences must be revealed to all those participating in the bargain, and the bargain, once in place, must be enforceable. Lacking revelation and enforceability, Cooperative Federalism cannot guarantee economically fully efficient allocations, although in certain settings it can come close. We will clarify when efficiency might be possible. Even if inefficient in each agreement, however, Cooperative Federalism may still provide an attractive alternative to the failings of Economic Federalism. Those with low and high demands for national public goods may do better with a cooperative agreement among those with similar demands than with the single allocation provided by Economic Federalism's national president. Further, the fact that all cooperative agreements are voluntary provides an added layer of protection for property rights and personal liberties over that available with Economic Federalism.[3] As a possible cost, however, increased economic opportunities funded by involuntary redistributive transfers are not available.

---

1. Beer (1993, pp. 230–231). A contemporary variation of the "confederate republic" is Lijphart's governance by "consociation," which combines proportional representation of groups—which may, or may not, already be organized as separate political states—with decision-making by unanimous agreement; see Lijphart (1997).

2. See Dixit and Olson (2000, p. 310) in their summary and analysis of Coase's argument.

3. See Nozick (1974, chaps. 7, 10).

2. The Efficiency Case for Cooperative Federalism: The Coasian Economy

In his pathbreaking article "The Problem of Social Cost," Ronald Coase (1960) challenged the then-accepted wisdom that only government with the powers of taxation and spending could efficiently manage the provision of national public goods or regulate positive and negative spillovers between citizens and their communities. From Coase's argument, if there were benefits to cooperation, benefits were known, and there were no significant barriers to cooperation, then private motives alone would be sufficient for the joint provision of the public good or control of the spillovers. No formal government would be needed. Voluntary agreements between cooperating parties would be sufficient for economic efficiency. Now known as the Coase Theorem, the insight was simple but profound. Cooperative Federalism seeks to apply Coase's insight to provide an institutional alternative to the strong president of Economic Federalism for the provision of intercommunity public goods and spillovers. Rather than elect a president, can the communities of Economic Federalism bargain their way to economic efficiency?

Coase's Theorem

Implicit in Coase's original argument are seven conditions now understood as necessary for bargaining between economic agents—here, communities—to be efficient. They are the following:

C1: *Participation is voluntary.*

All participants to the Coasian bargain retain the option to participate in the agreement and to exit the agreement at any time that they feel the terms of the agreement have been violated.[4]

---

4. The importance of voluntary participation for the Coase Theorem was implicit in Coase's (1960) original analysis, but he did not consider the implications of allowing voluntary participation for the process of bargaining itself. Dixit and Olson (2000) extend Coase to allow such a "first-stage" decision. Crucial to their argument is an assumption that nonparticipants can still enjoy some of the benefits of the Coasian agreement as free riders—say, its clean(er) air or its deterrence of a common aggressor. The decision to join the bargaining process will require coordination among many possible communities, where a minimal number will be required to cover the fixed costs of the public good. If too few communities agree to participate, then no bargain will take place.

C2: *Bargaining agents represent citizen preferences.*

Bargaining agents for the community must represent citizen preferences accurately when negotiating with other communities.[5]

C3: *Community property rights are clearly specified.*

All parties entering into the agreement have clearly known and respected property rights, either from precedence or from armed security.[6]

C4: *Preferences are known.*

Participants' preferences for the outcomes of the bargain are known to all participants.[7]

C5: *Bargaining is costless.*

There are no costly barriers to reaching an agreement once the participants agree to meet and bargain.[8]

---

5. Jéhiel (1997) provides an example in which the community's representative does not bargain in the best interests of its residents. With free mobility—which we assume—this will be to provide a common level of welfare, u. As citizens are mobile between communities, the final bargain may affect the population within each community. Communities relatively favored by the bargain will gain residents, and those favored less will lose residents. Rather than seeking to maximize individual welfare, the community's representative might "mistakenly" seek to maximize the aggregate utility of community residents, $N \cdot u$. Since populations are mobile, decisions that maximize $N \cdot u$ will not be decisions that maximize u alone. This might occur when campaign donations from developers or local businesses depend on increasing N.

6. Well-specified property rights are required to define the starting point for intercommunity bargains; see Mueller (2003, pp. 34–35). Coase (1960) assumed such protections were in place before bargaining. He then conjectured that the final allocation would be unaffected by this initial distribution of rights, a result requiring benefits from the agreement to be independent of community wealth.

7. Myerson and Satterthwaite (1983) show that when participants know their own benefits from the bargain but not those of other bargainers, there is no guarantee that the Coasian bargain will be efficient.

8. Dixit and Olson (2000) consider a bargaining game where participants announce they are "in" the bargain if enough other players announce they are also in but announce they are "out" if most others are also out. If the number who are out is high enough, then the benefits from the bargain for those who are in will not be sufficient for a bargain to occur. For example, those who are in may not be sufficient to profitably share the fixed costs of the public good's facility. Bargaining costs raise the fixed cost of providing the facility and may therefore turn an initially successful bargain into one that is no longer feasible.

C6: *Participants can agree to a division of the benefits.*

All voluntary agreements create both benefits for the participants and a mutually accepted division of those benefits among participating communities.[9]

C7: *Agreements are costlessly enforceable.*

Once an agreement is reached, the utilization and contribution of each participant can be monitored, and if a violation to the agreement is discovered, the participant can be penalized or excluded from the agreement.[10]

The process by which economically efficient Coasian bargains among local communities can be reached is as follows. First, representatives from local jurisdictions are the bargaining agents for their citizens and perfectly represent the preferences of the citizens in each community (C2). The bargaining agent, perhaps the community's mayor or governor, does not have his or her own agenda. The representatives not only find it beneficial to reach an agreement but also have no interests outside of the current bargain that might induce them to forgo an agreement that is most preferred by community residents. Second, when the bargaining begins, there are no secrets. Community representatives know the wealth and resources of all other participants (C3), as well as the preferences (C4) of all other citizens. No community can plead "poverty" or claim "too few benefits" when asked for a contribution. Third, the process of bargaining itself does not entail any significant costs, either in bringing participants together or in negotiating delays once the bargaining begins (C5). Participants meet and agree. Fourth, in completing the terms of the agreement, the parties agree how to use the new public facility or common property (for example, land, water, or air) and how to share the costs of building and maintaining the facility or common property (C6). Agreeing to share use and costs is an agreement to share the aggregate net benefits of providing

9. Cooter (1982) stresses that participants must agree to a division of the total benefits of the bargain before the bargain can be implemented. Benefits are shared by adjustments to the rate of utilization of the facility or commons and costs are shared by adjustments to the rate contribution to maintain the facility or commons. Efficient bargains may not be accepted, however, if the distribution of benefits and costs violates one party's sense of fairness—see Roth (1985)—or if the political incentives of a community's elected representatives demand a quicker return than what the efficient bargain might allow—see Bagwell and Staiger (2005).

10. See Ostrom (1990, chap. 5) for examples of Coasian bargains that are successfully enforced. What is needed is a low-cost technology to credibly monitor the behavior of all participants and an easy-to-administer penalty when a violation is discovered.

the facility or protecting the commons. There is always the risk of a "holdout" to an agreement, but if wealth and preferences are known (and parties are rational), there will be a division of net benefits that is mutually advantageous to all parties. Fifth, once an agreement is in place, it is easy to monitor the use and contribution of all participants (C_7). Those who violate the agreement can be disciplined at relatively low cost, most typically by denying the violator access to the public good or the shared common.

Finally, and most importantly for why Cooperative Federalism is potentially attractive, all agreements between communities are voluntary (C_1). Communities are free to join or leave the coalition in accordance with its entry and exit rules. Joining may require payment of an entry fee to contribute to the coalition's fixed costs, and leaving may require an exit fee to discourage ex post free riding. In contrast to Economic Federalism with its elected president, no community is required to contribute to the coalition's economic mission unless that contribution returns a compensating benefit sufficient to make all in the community better off against its next best alternative.

Final agreements might involve all communities in one grand coalition or be a scattering of regional agreements with some involving a few communities and others, many. Agreements may not be possible when property rights are unspecified, preferences unknown, participants intransigent, or terms unenforceable. That is, without conditions C_2–C_7, efficient, voluntary agreements are not possible.[11] It is instructive to consider two alternative settings where efficient agreements may, or may not, be possible.

Coasian Clubs

As for local public goods allocated within the Tiebout economy of Economic Federalism, congestion can be a prominent feature of national public goods as well. The difference is one of scale. While local public goods can be

11. It may be possible to satisfy conditions C_2–C_7 by investing resources to gather information about citizen wealth and preferences, to facilitate communication about offers, and to hire arbitrators to suggest fair divisions, accountants to monitor contributions, and guards to control usage. Together such expenditures are the "transactions costs" of a Coasian agreement. By assuming conditions C_2–C_7, the original Coase Theorem sets all these costs to zero. An expanded version of the Coase Theorem, what Dixit and Olson have called the "Super Coase Theorem," would be the following: *efficient economic agreements net of transaction costs will be achieved by voluntary bargaining among all affected parties.* The corollary is this: if expected transaction costs are too high, then no agreement will be the efficient outcome.

efficiently provided to populations of five thousand to one hundred thousand residents, national public goods often require populations of one hundred thousand to one million residents or more to reach the efficient scale. Some goods of course are only efficiently provided to all residents of a nation, and the common example is national defense.

But public services such as local transportation networks (including airports and rail hubs that provide access to a national transit network), water and waste management, prisons, arts and cultural facilities, and the maintenance and protection of recreation and natural resource areas can all be efficiently provided with fewer than one million residents. Rather than leap all the way to a national government run by an elected president, why not allow ten or fifteen local communities to band together to jointly provide those services with significant but not full national economies of scale? In the United States such coalitions of local governments might be called "counties," and in other federal economies, "metropolitan" or "regional" governments. In Cooperative Federalism, such government coalitions come with a twist, however. Joining is voluntary and the voluntary union becomes a *Coasian club*. Local communities joining the club agree to pay an entrance fee to cover the fixed costs of the public facility and an annual maintenance fee equal to the marginal costs (including depreciation) for each community's use of the facility. In return the residents of each member community have access to the public facility, common area, or services provided by the club. Examples of Coasian clubs have included cooperation among the local communities of ancient Greece called *koinons*, and among the communities in Southern California today called the Lakewood Plan; see Box 3.1.

When might such Coasian clubs be economically efficient? When all of the seven requirements, Conditions C_1–C_7, for efficient Coasian bargains are met. Here's how.[12] Begin with condition C_2. When deciding to join a Coasian club, each community will be represented in its negotiations by an elected representative from the community who will bargain so as to maximize the economic welfare of the community's "typical" resident. For the small communities in Economic Federalism, the typical resident will be the community's average resident. If so, condition C_2 will hold. To satisfy condition C_3, the initial property rights of all joining communities must be respected. Conditions C_4–C_7 will hold when the technology of the club's public goods has this essential feature: *exclusion from use of the public facility is inexpensive*. If so, then

---

12. Buchanan (1965) was the first to outline a theory of Coasian clubs.

Box 3.1. Coasian Clubs, Old and New

The Greek *Koinon*

Over the period from 450 BC to early 300 BC, 183 of the 456 local communities (called *poleis*) of mainland Greece and the Peloponnese organized themselves into regional governments known as the *koinon*. While some koinons were formed by a military takeover by a dominant community, most were voluntary associations between geographically contiguous communities. Local communities were free to join or exit as the residents preferred. A typical koinon involved a merger of from ten to thirty poleis into a regional union. The koinon served three important functions. First, it provided military protection for the members, with each agreeing to provide armed forces if any one member were attacked by those outside the koinon. Second, the koinon served as an economic union, providing a common coinage, removing trade barriers between participating local communities, and providing arbitration services for trade disputes. While there was free trade within the koinon, the koinon imposed duties on imports and exports. Third, koinons often oversaw and promoted a common religion and encouraged intermarriages between families of separate communities. Each polis was expected to pay taxes to fund the military. Failure to pay taxes or to provide trained soldiers led to expulsion from the koinon. Decisions were made by unanimous agreement among elected representatives from each polis. Koinons proved a very successful compromise "between complete poleis autonomy and a fully centralized state. [The koinon] was adopted as a political solution by nearly half of mainland Greece and the Peloponnese by the fourth century, and by even more in the Hellenistic period."[a]

The Lakewood Plan

The Lakewood Plan was created by the small community of Lakewood, California, in 1954 when it arranged with the County of Los Angeles to provide services to its residents for a per-unit fee plus an annual contribution to the fixed costs of county services. Purchased services included police and fire protection, street maintenance, trash collection and disposal, judicial services, prisons, ambulance services, building inspections, and tax collection. Other small communities followed Lakewood's lead. The county soon became a primary provider of services to local communities, particularly the new, small communities in the growing suburban areas. Participating communities had populations ranging from ten thousand to fifty thousand residents. Each community was free to select its preferred bundle of services; fees were negotiated individually with the county. Communities could add services, subtract services, or leave the contract entirely at any time. By 1964, seventy-six communities were using the county as the sole provider of at least one community public service, with the provision of fifteen services in a typical contract. County officials saw the plan as a "partnership of cities and the County to provide joint services at the least cost while [allowing] both to retain the power of self-determination and home rule."[b] Problems arose, however. County services were of uniform quality and could not be targeted easily to a community's specific needs. Fees were presented as "all-or-nothing" offers and were often viewed as excessive relative to service quality. While exit was possible with a sixty-day notice, county officials often put political pressure on local community representatives to continue the contract. Facing a monopoly supplier of intercommunity services, communities had only two choices: use the county or go it alone at a significantly higher cost for provided services. When given a choice by the state to continue to use the county for services, to return to community-provided services, or to reorganize as a new regional government providing uniform services decided by a locally elected board of supervisors, most local communities opted to remain in the Lakewood Plan. As for ancient Greece, Cooperative Federalism proved an effective means for coordinating the economic affairs of similarly situated small communities.

[a] Summarized from Mackil (2008).
[b] Quoted in Cion (1966, p. 274)

---

the preferences of any community will be revealed, as required by condition C_4, through negotiations over access to the facility. Each club requires an "entrepreneur" to do these negotiations; the entrepreneur might be the community with the highest valuation for the provision for the public good.[13] If the economies of scale of the public facility are relatively modest—say, efficient at five hundred thousand residents—then negotiations need only be with twenty or so communities and, as required by condition C_5, bargaining costs for the efficient club will be relatively modest and incurred as a one-time fixed cost. Further, since exclusion is possible, communities will only be allowed access to the facility if they agree to their negotiated rates of usage and contributions. As a result, the distribution of net benefits is decided and condition C_6 is satisfied. Finally, the assumption of low-cost exclusion provides most of what is needed to satisfy condition C_7 of (nearly) costless enforcement. A Coasian club will also need a gatekeeper to monitor usage and an accountant to monitor contributions; the costs of both are likely to be modest.

This leave condition C_1—voluntary participation. For Coase, assuming voluntary participation was axiomatic. For the efficiency of Coasian clubs, however, voluntary participation must be guaranteed by the economic environment within which the clubs arise. To truly meet the requirements of condition C_1, communities need not only a choice to join or exit a Coasian club but also a selection of alternative clubs from which to choose. For efficiency there must be market competition between clubs. To ensure a sufficient supply of competitive clubs, three conditions must hold. First, the efficient scale of services provided by the club, though greater than that of local communities,

---

13. For how these negotiations might be conducted as a sequence of all-or-nothing offers to a prospective club member, see E. Thompson (1968). Negotiations are likely to result in price discrimination across club members, and therefore the exclusion technology must prevent residents from low-price communities from selling their services to members in high-price communities. This is certainly possible for services provided by residence (trash disposal) and through the use of identity cards for services provided on-site (museums).

must be modest enough to allow at least three or four clubs to form for each desired level of club services. Public services that entail significant economies of scale, such as an interregional transportation network, or spillovers with a wide geographic reach, such as air quality, cannot be efficiently provided by a network of competitive Coasian clubs. Likely services suitable for Coasian club competition include waste and water treatment, regional transit networks and hubs, higher education, and centers for recreation and community learning. Yet, second, even for these services, a relatively densely populated metropolitan area will be required to ensure a sufficient number of competitive clubs. Third, the formation of new clubs must be relatively easy. Capital must be available and, perhaps most importantly, so too must there be a sufficient supply of "entrepreneurs" who understand the benefits of creating a Coasian club. If a sufficient number of clubs does arise, efficiency will be the result.[14]

Lacking sufficient competition, efficiency is still possible if the one Coasian club acts as a price-discriminating monopolist. With just one Coasian club, however, the marketplace may not be stable. Now Cooperative Federalism's requirement of voluntary participation (C_1) creates problems for economic efficiency. Communities placing a high value on the intercommunity public service or controlled spillover and thus paying a high price to the monopoly club may exit that club to form a smaller but less efficient alternative for high demanders only. But then why not admit a few low demanders at a low price to get some additional contribution to overhead, and perhaps form a new monopoly club? The outcome might be many inefficiently small Coasian clubs composed only of high-, middle-, and low-demand communities, or alternatively a competitive cycling between monopoly clubs. Lacking sufficient competition for efficiency, the club marketplace based on voluntary participation may unravel with no stable outcomes.[15] If we insist on keeping condition C_1, as we must to stay true to the aims of Cooperative Federalism, the only answer is to accept an unstable marketplace with either of two outcomes: no clubs or a monopoly Coasian club. In either case we are likely to have an underprovision of the intercommunity public good or management of intercommunity

14. See Scotchmer (1997), who concludes for an economy of Coasian clubs that there will be an efficient equilibrium in a sufficiently large economy.

15. A point first made by Pauly (1967), who argued that there is no equilibrium (called the core) in a Coasian club economy if there are communities outside an existing club that can successfully bribe members in the club to accept a membership in a new club with the outsiders.

spillovers, with a monopoly club preferable to no clubs at all.[16] We will call such monopoly clubs *Coasian alliances*, and we will consider next how well they might do in providing intercommunity public goods and controlling spillovers.

Coasian Alliances

A Coasian alliance is a cooperative provider of the intercommunity public good or manager of intercommunity spillovers with explicit rules for members' use of the public good, required contributions, and expected behavior with regard to intercommunity spillovers. Members can be expelled from the alliance for failure to abide by alliance rules regarding the use and funding of public goods or common properties. Consistent with Cooperative Federalism, however, membership in the alliance is voluntary. Alliances are Cooperative Federalism's best response for providing intercommunity public goods when those goods involve significant economies of scale and for managing intercommunity spillovers when those spillovers have a wide geographic reach. Examples include trade agreements to manage the flow of goods and services between communities' markets, such as the World Trade Organization (WTO); environmental agreements to manage air and water pollution across borders, such as the Paris Agreement; health agreements to manage the spread of communicable diseases, such as the World Health Organization; national defense pacts to deter common aggressors, such as the North Atlantic Treaty Organization (NATO); and economic and monetary agreements to facilitate the free movement of households, labor, and capital between member communities, such as the European Union.

To successfully provide its public goods or to manage its spillovers, the alliance must solve two problems. First, members must reveal their valuation of the good or spillover so that each member's use and charges can be efficiently assigned. Second, the alliance must be able to enforce each member's assigned use and charges. Revelation and enforcement are required for an efficient alliance. The original solution for efficiency in Coasian alliances was first proposed by Swedish economists Knut Wicksell (1958) and Erik Lindahl (1958) and later formalized by Norwegian economist Lief Johansen (1963) as the Wicksell-Lindahl process for the provision of public goods; see Figure 3.1.

---

16. With no clubs, each community "free rides" on its neighbors' provision of the public good. As the provision by the neighbors increases, its own provision declines and in the limit reaches zero for a large number of local communities; see Chamberlain (1974).

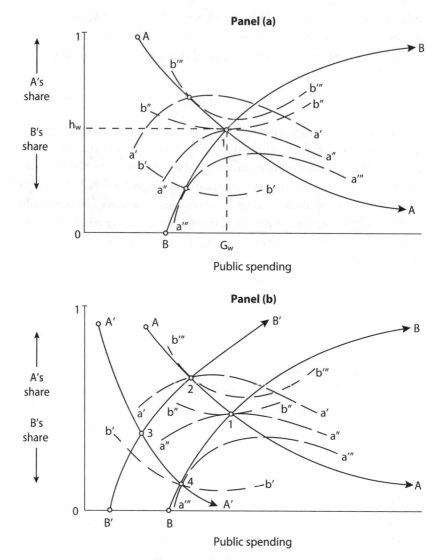

FIGURE 3.1. Wicksell-Lindahl Bargaining in a Coasian Alliance

There are two communities in the alliance, community A and B, and they agree to share the costs of providing a joint public good (G), where h is the share of the costs allocated to community A with $(1-h)$ allocated to community B. Each community's preferred level of G varies with h and is shown by demand curve AA for community A and demand curve BB for community B. As h declines, A pays less of the costs for G and demands more G along AA, but conversely, B pays more and thus demands less along BB. As h approaches zero, B assumes the full cost and therefore demands that level of G that they would buy on their own (Point B, when $h = 0$). Similarly, as h approach one, A pays for the full costs of the public good and demands that level of G that they would buy on their own (Point A, when $h = 1$).

Wicksell and Lindahl argued that there would be one tax share where the two communities would agree on a common level of services. That is Point 1 in Panel (a), where $h = h_w$ and $G = G_w$, and where the two communities' demand curves cross. Point 1 is known as the Wicksell-Lindahl equilibrium. Johansen then showed that at Point 1, the public good is efficiently provided. This is seen in Panel (a) by the fact that at Point 1 the peaks of the two "indifference curves" for A and B just touch. There is no reallocation of the tax share or the level of the public good that can move both communities A and B to a better allocation along a preferred (lower) indifference curve for A and also along a preferred (higher) indifference curve for B. Residents in A are doing as well as they can given how well the residents of B are doing, and conversely so for B. Point 1 is therefore economically efficient.[17]

To reach Point 1, the representatives from the two communities must truthfully reveal each community's demand curve, AA and BB. If they do, then the alliance knows where the demand curves cross, and the efficient allocation is revealed. Unfortunately, representatives may not be truthful. The Wicksell-Lindahl process in effect grants a veto to the low-demand community for each value of h, and thus each community has an incentive to appear as the low-demand community. Suppose, for example, that community B has always cooperated and announced its true demand curve BB. Knowing BB, community A can hold out until a low h is announced before agreeing to an allocation for G, say at Point 4 in Panel (b). Although there is less of the public good provided at Point 4, A's lower tax share has provided more than enough compensation to move community A to a better (lower) indifference curve marked as a''' at Point 4. Community B, of course has the same incentive to understate its true demands for G for any value of h, and its best reply if A tells the truth

17. Point 1 will satisfy the Samuelson Condition for economic efficiency in the provision of a public good requiring the sum of A's and B's benefits from the shared good equal to the marginal cost of providing that good. Point 1 is not the only efficient point. There will be a "contract line" of such efficient points (not shown in the figure) defined by where the indifference curves of community A and community B are tangent to each other. Some of those efficient points will have low values of h, benefiting the residents of community A, and others high values of h, benefiting the residents of community B. The alliance can be both redistributive, by varying h, and efficient, by selecting a value of G along the contract line. Chen and Zeckhauser (2018) apply the Wicksell-Lindahl mechanism to find an efficient International Environmental Agreement.

results in an allocation at Point 2 moving B to a better (higher) indifference curve b‴. Community A would like community B to believe its true demand curve were $A'A'$, with lower demands for any value of h, just as community B would like A to believe its true demand curve were $B'B'$. When both representatives lie as to their true demands, the outcome will be at Point 3, where $A'A'$ intersects with $B'B'$, with too little of the public good provided. Without the truthful revelation of community demands, therefore, the alliance will underprovide its public goods.

The central challenge facing members of the alliance is in solving the prisoner's dilemma implicit in members' strategic announcements of their demand curves for the public good. If both communities in the alliance tell the truth and reveal their true demands for the public good, then the efficient allocation at Point 1 results. However, if community A "cheats" while community B is "honest," then the allocation will be at Point 4, where A gains and B loses. Alternatively, if community B cheats and A is honest, then the allocation will be at Point 2, where B gains and A loses. And if both communities cheat and announce $A'A'$ and $B'B'$, then the allocation is at Point 3, and both will lose. Unfortunately, both have a dominant incentive to cheat and fail to reveal their true demands for the public good. If so, the result is an inefficient underprovision of the public good.

Is there any hope for an efficient allocation when alliance members face the incentives within a prisoner's dilemma game? Even if true preferences for the public good or spillover are revealed, alliance members must be held accountable for any deviations from an agreed-to efficient allocation. The alliance is voluntary; efficient behavior is not guaranteed. If the alliance is temporary, valuable to the communities for only a short period of time, after which benefits disappear, it will be difficult to sustain any behavior by the participants other than to cheat. But if the benefits of cooperation are ongoing, then cheaters can be disciplined in future periods by denying them access to the public good for a time, or by having the other members of the alliance also cheat for a time and force everyone into an inefficient allocation.

One approach to providing discipline is the strategy called tit-for-tat. If one member of the alliance violates the efficient, cooperative agreement, others penalize that member by not cooperating themselves for a time, and then if the cheater returns to the cooperative contribution, all agree to cooperate going forward. Of course, to impose that penalty of noncooperation on the cheater is itself costly to all the honest members of the alliance for as long as they do not cooperate. But if the benefits of cooperation are significant and ongoing

and the members of the alliance value those future benefits, an efficient allocation may be possible. With tit-for-tat, cheaters will capture the one-time gain
from overuse or undercontribution, but then face a penalty of reduced benefits
for a time, or perhaps no benefits at all going forward. If the potential cheater
values these lost future benefits enough, then they will be discouraged from
cheating. The extreme tit-for-tat penalty—known in the theory of alliances as
the "grim-trigger" strategy—is to have a rule that if any member of the alliance
cheats, the alliance is disbanded. There are, fortunately, less demanding tit-for-
tat strategies, but if the grim-trigger enforcement rule cannot guarantee cooperation, then no other, friendlier rule can either. Continued successful cooperation will depend on significant net benefits from the alliance, their longevity,
and members who value the continuation of the alliance.[18]

How well have contemporary Coasian alliances done in providing mutually
beneficial public goods and in controlling mutually damaging spillovers? The
record is mixed and depends on the willingness of alliance members to reveal
their true benefits and the alliance's ability to then enforce the efficient cooperative allocation. International Environmental Agreements have had the
greatest difficulty in achieving an efficient allocation, because true country
preferences for clean air, water, and control of climate change are difficult to
infer and, even if known and an agreement is reached, enforcement has been
lax. Country preferences balance the benefits of a cleaner environment against
the economic costs of moving to cleaner technologies and will be specific
to each country's economy. It is easy to say that benefits are low and costs
are high when environmental standards are being negotiated.[19] Once an

18. The grim-trigger strategy sets the boundary for other feasible tit-for-tat strategies; see Morrow (1994, chap. 9). For example, if the two alliance members cooperate, there will be a benefit to
each of B dollars. If they both cheat, then their joint benefits will be L. If one cheats by not contributing to the public good but the other continues to contribute, then the benefits for the cheater
will be C dollars and the benefits for the (naive) cooperating member will be S dollars. In the
prisoner's dilemma, $C > B > L > S$. With the grim-trigger strategy, if both members of the alliance
cooperate forever, each will receive $W(\text{Cooperate}) = B + \delta B + \delta^2 B + \delta^3 B + \ldots = B/(1-\delta)$, where
$\delta = 1/(1+r)$ is the community's discount factor, and r is the community's rate of time preference.
If a member cheats, then they will receive C for the year they cheated, but then L for all years thereafter by the grim-trigger strategy. $W(\text{Cheat}) = C + \delta L + \delta^2 L + \delta^3 L + \ldots = C + \delta L/(1-\delta)$.
$W(\text{Cooperate}) > W(\text{Cheat})$ if $\delta > (C-B)/(C-L)$. As long as communities value the future
enough (i.e., have a low rate of time preference for dollars "today" so δ is near 1) and gain only
modestly by cheating (B close to C), then the grim-trigger strategy can enforce cooperation.

19. Kolstad (2007) shows that the size of the alliance shrinks, and free riding increases, as
uncertainty over the net benefits of potential participants increases. Barrett (1994) shows that

agreement is in place and pollution standards set, deviation from the agreed-to environmental protocol is also relatively easy. There is no easily enforceable penalty for those who cheat on the agreement, as those who cheat will still benefit from the efforts of those who remain. Without an effective exclusion mechanism, free riding on the International Environmental Agreement is the dominant strategy for signees. Studies of enforcement of the Montreal Protocol, which seeks to regulate chlorofluorocarbons, and of country promises for carbon reduction included in the Paris Agreement both show significant free-riding behaviors. Performance under both agreements shows final allocations closer to the inefficient Point 4 in Figure 3.1 than the efficient Point 1.[20] Countries generally contribute what they would have contributed on their own.

Defense alliances can control free-riding behaviors. If contributions are not paid, then the alliance will not protect your borders. But contributions may still be too little, if members can conceal their true benefits from belonging to the alliance. This has been the case for NATO. Twenty-three mainland European countries, including all those bordering Russia, now belong to NATO, plus Greece, Turkey, the United Kingdom, Canada, and the United States. NATO provides two defense "goods" to its members. First is the pure public good of general deterrence to the threat of aggression by Russia or China; the second is the private good of direct border protection against Russian incursions or threats of terrorism. As first stressed by Mancur Olson (1965) in his path-breaking book on the cooperative provision of public goods, alliances can maintain member contributions if the alliance also provides a valued private good with the public good. Enforcement of contributions is therefore possible within NATO. The issue for NATO is how to reveal each country's true benefits when setting contributions. NATO attempts to do so by hypothesizing a benefit share and setting each member's share of total NATO spending to the product of each country's share in NATO's population, GDP, and exposed borders.[21]

---

voluntary environmental agreements are difficult to enforce when the benefits to cheating are significantly greater than the benefits of cooperating and the time horizon of the participating governments is relatively short.

20. See Murdoch and Sandler (1997) for evidence of Nash cheating behaviors (Point 4 in Figure 3.1) for the Montreal Protocol and Chen and Zeckhauser (2018) for a similar conclusion evaluating the country submissions for the Paris Agreement.

21. With a valid estimate of each country's benefit share, setting each country's contribution equal to its benefit share multiplied by total costs will lead to the Wicksell-Lindahl efficient allocation.

Todd Sandler and James Murdoch (1990) have compared actual contributions with proposed contributions within two models of contribution behavior, one derived from cheating behavior where a member's own contributions decline as the expected contributions of other members increase and a second where contributions are honest and are best explained by the cooperatively proposed benefit share. The evidence is strongly in favor of the cheating strategy; members' own contributions decline as the contributions of others in the alliance (particularly the United States) increase. Though enforcement is possible, expected benefit shares have not been paid, with each delinquent country arguing that the benefit formula is ad hoc and does not represent its true benefits.

Alliances do work, however, when both preference revelation and enforcement are possible. This has been the case for free trade agreements enforced by General Agreement on Tariffs and Trade/WTO supervision of compliance. The WTO treaty, now signed by over 150 nations, and its precursor the General Agreement on Tariffs and Trade, signed in 1947, provide an impartial "court" of adjudication to settle disputes between trading partners. Trade agreements are voluntary, as is membership in the WTO.[22] Trade agreements may involve just two countries or many. Since both parties agree and can leave the trade pact at any time, the presumption is that agreement is beneficial to all parties. Evidence is overwhelmingly in favor of the aggregate benefits of free trade agreements to all participants. Though benefits are "private" to each participating country, the observed terms of the agreement reveal each country's gains, at least on the margin, from the alliance.

The only issue is enforcement. While trade agreements do reveal the point of mutual benefits for the trading partners, each has an incentive to deviate from the agreement (cheat) by unilaterally imposing a domestically beneficial trade barrier while still exporting freely to its trading partner. If both parties cheat, we have the inefficient outcome of high tariffs. Trade agreements are another example of the prisoner's dilemma. It is the job of the WTO as the supervisor of trade agreements to hold all countries to the terms of the original efficient agreement. It does so by adjudicating disputes between the partners by efficiently implementing the tit-for-tat penalty structure required for the long-run enforcement of the cooperative—free trade—allocation of the

22. Only thirty-four countries are not in the WTO, the largest of which is Iran as the twenty-seventh-largest world economy. Algeria (fifty-fifth-largest economy), Sudan (sixty-third), Belarus (eighty-third), and Serbia (ninety-second) are the other four largest economies not in the WTO.

original prisoner's dilemma. The WTO does so in three steps.[23] First, a neutral WTO panel determines whether the actions of one country nullify or impair the benefits for a trading partner for its own gain—say, by imposing a new trade barrier. Second, if an infraction of the agreement has occurred, the panel recommends that the offending country correct the offense. Third, if the trade deviation is not rescinded immediately, the offended country may request compensation for the original offense—the "tit" for the original "tat"— perhaps granted as a most favored nation clause for goods exported by the originally harmed country. The WTO panel evaluates such a proposed change to the trading agreement to ensure that the new agreement is fair to both trading partners.[24] The new agreement is then approved by the WTO. The original offending party need not comply with the new arrangement, but if it does not, the trade agreement can be declared void. In most instances the new agreement is accepted. Most trade disagreements submitted to the WTO resolve themselves quickly at the second step. The reputational costs of going to trade arbitration appear to be a strong enforcement mechanism.[25]

23. Bagwell and Staiger (2010, pp. 237–241) provide a comprehensive overview of how the WTO plays this important role.

24. Implemented by a "principle of reciprocity" whereby the WTO "allows" changes in the value of a country's imports to be offset by an equal dollar change in that country's exports. Thus a country harmed by an increase in tariffs can raise tariffs on the other country's exports so as to neutralize the net trade benefits of the original tariff increase. The "tit" is then economically equal to the "tat." A preferred implementation of "reciprocity" would be to renegotiate the treaty to grant the affected country a most favored nation concession on other of its exports.

25. Playing the same role as the WTO are U.S. federal courts that oversee Coasian alliances between communities and states for the provision of regional public goods and for managing regional spillovers as part of what we will call contract federalism; see Chapter 8. Regional agreements are voluntary. Compliance turns on the acceptance by participants of the supervisor's or court's rulings. Successful examples include (1) an agreement between New Jersey and New York for disposal of New York City waste off the shores and beaches of New Jersey (*New York Times*, November, 27, 1987); (2) the creation by the legislature of California of the Southern California Metropolitan Water District as an alliance of fourteen cities and twelve local water districts to build and manage the Colorado River Aqueduct with supervision provided by a locally elected water district board of supervisors and expenses allocated to each member as its share of assessed property values in the district (Zetland, 2009); and (3) an interstate compact between Washington and Oregon to manage the Columbia River Gorge through an oversight organization called the Friends of the Columbia Gorge with the power to bring lawsuits against parties threatening the environmental quality of the gorge (McKinney, Parr, and Seltzer, 2004). Additional U.S. examples include the Tennessee Valley Authority and the Delaware River Basin

Summary

We conclude that Cooperative Federalism can be an efficient provider of intercommunity public goods and spillovers if (1) the extent of economies of scale and the spatial reach of spillovers are modest and there is a sufficient number of communities to allow the formation of competitive Coasian clubs, *or* (2) economies of scale and the extent of spillovers are significant but the provision of those goods and the management of those spillovers permit Coasian alliances in which community preferences are known and community use and contributions can be enforced. Efficient Coasian clubs and alliances are only possible if the public goods technology or the reach of spillovers allows the club or alliance to exclude communities that do not pay their fair share of costs or that overuse the facility. If not, the voluntary provision of the public good or spillover will be economically inefficient.

That was the hard lesson learned by the thirteen U.S. colonies as they searched for a new form of national governance following the Declaration of Independence and the beginnings of the Revolutionary War. After decades of economic and civil rights abuse under British rule, the colonies were justifiably skeptical of centralized powers to tax and regulate. The first established government bound the new thirteen states together under an agreement called the Articles of Confederation. The Articles empowered a representative Congress to provide for a common defense, enabled free movement of citizens between all states, and allowed Congress to manage international relations. Passage of any national law would require the approval of nine of the thirteen colonies. Funding for any national public project, including defense, would be by voluntary payments from the states based on the state's share of national land. By all measures, the Confederation failed. Its failure was the stimulus for a new form of national governance—Democratic Federalism; see Box 3.2.

3. Representation and Rights

For whatever weaknesses Cooperative Federalism may have in the provision of national public goods or in the control of significant interregional spillovers, it has the virtue of guaranteeing all citizens the right to leave any alliance they find does not fully meet their needs. Taxes need not be paid unless there

---

Commission, both created by an act of Congress, but in response to needs of the states to jointly manage important regional water resources; see Derthick (1974, chaps. 2, 3).

Box 3.2. The Failure of the U.S. Experiment: Articles of Confederation

Entering into the War of Independence against the British in 1776, the colonies required a place to meet and means to provide for the collective goods of the new republic, the most important of which was to finance the war efforts against the British. To this end the states drafted as their governing document the Articles of Confederation on November 15, 1777. The Articles remained in force until the approval of a new constitution on September 13, 1788, and the convening of a new congress on March 4, 1789.

The Articles outlined four governing principles for the new nation.[a] Jointly the four principles define a Coasian alliance. First, the new legislature, the Congress of the Confederation (more popularly, the Continental Congress), would be composed of representatives from each of the thirteen states, with each state granted one vote. Nine of the thirteen states were required to approve any new legislation. Amendments to the Articles would require unanimous approval. Because of distance, achieving a quorum of nine states was often difficult, however. As a result, decisions were most often made by unanimous agreement of those in attendance. Second, there would be no formal executive with executive powers. Congress would administer its laws through appointed congressional committees. Third, there would be no national judiciary. Enforcement of national laws would be left to the discretion of state courts. Fourth, the Confederation was limited to address only those matters *expressly delegated* to it by the Articles. These included the following: to provide for the common defense of the states (Article II), to ensure the free movement of individuals (Article IV), and to manage foreign affairs (Articles VI and IX). Revenues for the new government would be assessed against each of the states according to the value of property within the state, with each individual state responsible for raising its own required payments (Article VIII). All other important activities of government—the provision of public goods, regulation of trade and tariffs, and the protection of individual rights and liberties—would lay with the states.

By most measures, the new confederation was a failure.[b] Since the Articles left economic policies to the state legislatures, beggar-thy-neighbor tariffs and taxes for cross-border transactions were common and efficient trade discouraged. Further, without national coordination, interstate public goods (roads, bridges, canals, and so on) were not funded. Most states failed to contribute to their common defense, the classic pure public good. Contributions that were made were for state armies that protected local lands and residents (a private good). National tariffs and needed revenues were consistently defeated because of intersectional rivalries between the industrial North and agricultural South. As a result, Revolutionary War debts owed to France, Holland, and Spain were left unpaid. The inability of the national government to collect revenues came to head with a taxpayer "strike" known as Shays's Rebellion of 1786. Territorial disputes with England and France along the Great Lakes and with Spain in New Orleans further convinced state leaders that the Articles needed to be amended to strengthen the powers of the national government.

The result was the Federal Convention of 1787, establishing a new federal republic with legislative representation in proportion to population, a strong executive with enforcement powers, and a national judiciary with the powers to adjudicate, and balance, state and national interests. The central objective of the new constitution was to provide a government capable of managing national affairs for the general welfare of citizens nationally. The practical failures of the Articles made clear the fundamental weaknesses of Cooperative Federalism as the basis for governing a modern nation.

---

[a] See Maggs (2017) and Riker (1987).
[b] See Dougherty (2001, chaps. 4, 5) and Rakove (1979, chap. 14).

---

are compensating benefits. As in Economic Federalism, citizen representation in such agreements mirrors their representation in their local community, which selects their representative, but it is diluted by the fact that their representative's preferences for an outcome must align with the preferences of the other communities in the club or alliance. If decisions are made by unanimity, then each of the communities in the Coasian club or alliance has an equal say. If so, then each community representative has an equal chance of being decisive in the club's or the alliance's final choices.[26]

If the number of participating communities is relatively small, citizen influence on collective choices will be nearly that enjoyed under Economic Federalism. But when the number of communities is large, as it will be for the efficient provision of pure public goods or the management of widespread spillovers, the possible loss of citizen influence and participation can be significant. The dilution of citizen influence is likely to be greatest, therefore, when the alliance is most economically beneficial. The same tension between economic efficiency and citizen influence that arose with the use of a nationally elected president in Economic Federalism is evident with the use of large alliances in Cooperative Federalism.[27] When the efficient allocation requires the participation of all citizens, the ability of any one group of citizens to influence outcomes will be modest to nil. There is no avoiding this reality. What Cooperative Federalism does provide that Economic Federalism does not, however, is the opportunity for each citizen to balance this trade-off between economic efficiency and representation. Because participation in any club or alliance is voluntary, Cooperative Federalism allows each community to select that club or alliance which provides the preferred mix of efficient allocations and influence over outcomes. Facing

---

26. If there are N communities in the club or alliance, then $(1/N)$ is the probability that any one of N equal communities will have veto power over a decision of the alliance when all communities have one vote. This probability is also known as the Shapley value or "power index" of a cooperative game; see Riker and Ordeshook (1973, chap. 6).

27. A concern that has become known as the "democratic deficit" in the European Union; see Chapter 9.

the prospect of paying for the level of a national public good most preferred by Economic Federalism's median voter, those in the tails of the distribution of demands may prefer Cooperative Federalism and provide that good less efficiently but closer to their preferences within a smaller club or alliance.

Among individual liberties and rights, that most protected by Cooperative Federalism is the right to own and allocate one's property, including the product of one's labor, as one sees fit.[28] Voluntary participation guarantees that no taxes can be levied against one's assets or earned income unless the individual's community chooses to participate in the taxing Coasian club or alliance. Voluntary participation by one's community also protects individual rights to free speech, the practice of religion, and privacy. Just as Economic Federalism uses the free mobility of citizens between communities to protect individual rights, so too will Cooperative Federalism use a community's right of voluntary participation in the club or alliance. Communities can exit a club or alliance when their citizens' rights are threatened, a concept called "right-sizing" by Brendan O'Leary and his colleagues (2001). The short-term costs of separation (that is, secession) in lives and property may be high, but the long-run gains from a more assured protection of individual rights against ethnicity-based suppression stands as compensation.[29] Examples include the division of Yugoslavia into the separate states of Bosnia-Herzegovina, Croatia, Kosovo, and Serbia; the separation of Sudan into Muslim Sudan and Christian South Sudan; and the division of British India into Muslim Pakistan and Hindu India.

The rights not guaranteed by Cooperative Federalism are those that promise a minimal level of income, an equal educational opportunity, adequate health care, or a clean environment. Such economic rights can be provided in Cooperative Federalism but only if voluntarily paid for by the more fortunate communities in a club or alliance.[30] Viewing the European Union as Cooperative Federalism, as we do in Chapter 9, illustrates this point. The alliance

---

28. For a foundational argument for such a right, see Nozick (1974, chap. 7). For Nozick, the one exception to the protection of the right to property would be if that property had been unjustly acquired by violating another's right to property, say, by slavery or theft.

29. See Downes (2004).

30. See Pauly (1973). Perhaps it is not surprising that when negotiating the new constitution for democratic South Africa, the apartheid National Party adopted as its original negotiating position a governance structure that resembled an alliance of provinces with provinces assigned primary responsibility for the financing and provision of redistributive services and incomes; see Lowenberg (1992). Nor should it be surprising that the African National Congress rejected this proposal. The final compromise was to assign financing by progressive taxation to the national

provides valuable public goods to its members through the coordination of trade and market regulations, monetary policy, and foreign diplomacy, but it does not tax and redistribute income or ensure merit goods across citizens of different member communities. To do so would threaten the union itself.[31] Because of voluntary participation, the institutions of Cooperative Federalism cannot guarantee economic rights.

4. Summing Up

Cooperative Federalism is offered as an alternative to Economic Federalism. Like Economic Federalism, Cooperative Federalism allows residents to voluntarily gather in small communities for the provision of public goods and services and for the protection of residents' liberties and rights. Unlike Economic Federalism, however, Cooperative Federalism responds to the need for national governance not with a nationally elected president with unitary powers to tax and spend but with voluntary agreements between communities to respond to the same agenda. Rather than the "coarse" representation of community preferences that comes with having a single decision-maker, Cooperative Federalism's voluntary agreements offer communities multiple choices for how best to meet their collective needs.

To be successful, however, intercommunity agreements must satisfy seven conditions, a group now known as the Coase Theorem. Three are particularly important, and the most difficult to satisfy: condition C4, community preferences are known to all communities in the agreement; condition C6, participating communities can agree to a division of the economic surplus from the agreement; and condition C7, agreements are enforceable by the communities themselves. If the seven requirements are met, economic efficiency will result. Two important, real-world applications of the Coase Theorem are presented: Coasian clubs and Coasian alliances. Clubs are agreements involving only a few communities providing goods with modest economies of scale and spatially limited spillovers, perhaps to between one hundred thousand and five hundred thousand residents in close proximity. Examples of efficient clubs include the shared provision of trash disposal, water treatment, public transit, cultural and religious activities, and historically, agreements for free trade and a common

---

government (controlled by the African National Congress) but the provision of services to decentralized provinces (one of nine controlled by the National Party). See Chapter 10.

31. Illustrated by the possible voluntary exit of Britain from the European Union; see Box 9.1.

currency. Alliances are agreements to provide public goods with significant economies of scale or to manage widespread spillovers, perhaps to large regions or the nation as a whole. Successful present-day examples of alliances are international trade agreements with agreed-to enforcement by a larger (and still) voluntary alliance, the WTO. Modern alliances that have not proved efficient— primarily for their failure to satisfy conditions C4, C6, and C7—include those seeking to control environmental quality (the Montreal Protocol and the Paris Agreement) and to provide for a common national defense (NATO). For much the same reasons, the European Union has proved only a mixed success.

What Cooperative Federalism offers in return for any loss in efficiency relative to Economic Federalism is greater flexibility in providing for citizen representation in intercommunity decisions and greater protection of individual rights and liberties. That flexibility comes from Cooperative Federalism's commitment to voluntary participation for all communities to any agreement. Communities can select that club or alliance that provides their preferred mix of representation and economic performance. Smaller clubs or alliances may be less efficient than the single president of Economic Federalism, but individual communities will have more influence over final allocations. The flexibility available within alliances also provides another layer of protection for individual rights to free speech, the practice of religion, and privacy. Communities can exit an existing alliance to form a new alliance when citizens' rights are threatened, a concept called "right-sizing" the state. Right-sizing has proved a valuable solution to the threat of "ethnic cleansing" in the once-larger states of Yugoslavia, Sudan, and British India. What the voluntary alliances of Cooperative Federalism cannot guarantee, however, are the economic rights to a minimal standard of living; an equal education; or to safe, clean, and healthy environments. Rich communities can pair with poor communities to offer such protections, but they are not required to do so.

There is middle ground between Economic and Cooperative Federalism. Like Economic and Cooperative Federalism, local governments remain important providers of public services to citizens. Like Economic and Cooperative Federalism, a central government will decide allocations of those goods and services with significant economies of scale or having important intercommunity spillovers. Unlike Economic Federalism but like Cooperative Federalism, central government decisions will be decided by a legislature of local representatives. But unlike Cooperative Federalism, that legislature will make decisions by simple majority rule, not unanimity. This alternative, Democratic Federalism, becomes our agenda for Chapters 4 and 5.

4

Democratic Federalism

THE NATIONAL LEGISLATURE

1. Introduction

While both Economic and Cooperative Federalism have their virtues as ways of organizing the public sector, they have their weaknesses as well. Economic Federalism is likely to be efficient, or nearly so, in the provision of both local and national public goods, but may not be so if there are economic activities with regional spillovers or if local jurisdictions cannot manage local public goods at an efficient scale. For spillovers not covering the nation as a whole, Cooperative Federalism—allowing for regional bargains across affected local communities—might be an answer. But as we have seen in Chapter 3, these bargains will only be efficient if the number of bargaining governments is small and the information about the benefits from each bargain is well known. This seems unlikely. There are concerns as well as to the ability of Economic and Cooperative Federalism to guarantee personal rights and to provide economically fair outcomes. Given these potential failures, perhaps we can do better. We examine here and in Chapter 5 a third alternative—*Democratic Federalism*.

Democratic Federalism begins by organizing local governments most efficiently by geographical proximity into a second subnational tier of governments that we call *districts*. Districts (sometimes called provinces and sometimes called states) will serve both an economic and a political function. Economically, each district government can coordinate policies among its local governments to provide public goods that entail significant economies of scale beyond the local level (for example, public transit and roadways) or to manage spillovers across local jurisdictions (for example, environmental policy). Politically, districts also will be used to provide citizens a direct voice in national policy. The citizens of each district will elect one representative to serve in a national legislature. The elected representative is assumed to vote in the interest of district citizens, typically represented by the citizen with median preferences.[1] Representatives are elected, or reelected, when citizens believe the legislator has the best chance to attract benefits to their district.[2]

The centerpiece of Democratic Federalism will be the locally elected national legislature. The national legislature will decide policy to provide national public goods and perhaps to facilitate regional cooperation among subsets of districts to resolve more narrowly specified, cross-district spillovers. Decisions will be made by simple (50 percent) majority rule. Together, local districts, the states, and the national legislature provide the starting point for the institutional political structure that James Madison has called the "compound republic" and that we call Democratic Federalism.

2. Legislative Voting Cycles

The task of the national legislature is to find a policy on which a majority of members can agree. There is a fundamental problem that must be overcome, however. It is the problem of voting cycles, and it is endemic to any majority-rule legislature. As Kenneth Arrow (1951) first showed, under a set of reasonable conditions the decisions of legislatures cannot be both democratic and economically efficient.[3] In theory, matters may be even worse; there may be endless voting cycles across alternatives, and thus no stable agreement. Figure 4.1 illustrates the difficulty created by legislative voting cycles in which no one policy is guaranteed to be the overall winner. To illustrate, imagine that

---

1. See E. Gerber and Lewis (2004), which relates citizen preferences as revealed in referendum voting over policies to the voting behavior of their elected, national legislators in Congress.

2. See Mayhew (1974).

3. Arrow's five conditions, which one might hope every democracy might satisfy, are (1) *unrestricted domain* (a decision can be reached for all possible orderings of outcomes by citizen preferences); (2) *independence of irrelevant alternatives* (only the outcomes actually in the vote are relevant for the outcome of the vote); (3) *rationality* (if outcome A is preferred to outcome B and outcome B preferred to C, then A will also be preferred to C); (4) *Pareto optimality* (if everyone prefers outcome A to outcome B, then outcome A will be chosen); and finally, (5) *nondictatorship* (there is no one citizen who always gets his or her way even if everyone else opposes that person's choice). Arrow shows that there is no process of collective choice that can satisfy all five conditions.

Proposal rank	Legislator I	Legislator II	Legislator III
First choice	A	C	B
Second choice	B	A	C
Third choice	C	B	A

If Legislator I is agenda-setter, then:
B vs. C ⇨ B wins. B vs. A ⇨ A wins.

If Legislator II is agenda-setter, then:
A vs. B ⇨ A wins. A vs. C ⇨ C wins.

If Legislator III is agenda-setter, then:
A vs. C ⇨ A wins. C vs. B ⇨ B wins.

FIGURE 4.1. Majority-Rule Decision-Making in Legislatures: The General Case

the legislature must decide on how best to invest in pollution control projects. The wind blows from district I toward district II, and then finally toward district III. There are three projects, one located in each district. Project A in district I is the least expensive and provides spillover benefits to its downwind district II. Project C in district II is the most expensive and provides spillover benefits to its downwind district III. Project B in district III is the second most expensive, costing more than A but less than C. There is no district downwind from III and therefore no spillover benefits. Only one project can be funded.[4]

The figure shows how the legislators rank each of the three projects from best to worst. The legislator from district I prefers project A, located in his home district. He gets no direct benefits from the projects in districts II and III but prefers project B, in district III, because it costs less than project C, located in district II. Thus legislator I will vote for A over B, B over C, and finally, A over C. The legislator from district II prefers pollution control project C, located in his district. He then prefers project A, located in his upwind district I. Project B, in district III, is least preferred as it is relatively expensive and provides no spillover benefits. Finally, the legislator from district III prefers project B, in his district, then project C, in district II; even though C is expensive, it provides significant downwind spillover benefits that compensate for much of those costs. The least preferred is project A, in district I, which costs money and provides no significant spillover benefits to district III.

4. There is a budget of C dollars, and project C costs more than B, project B costs more than A, and doing both projects A and B together costs more than C dollars.

What will the legislature decide when voting is by majority rule and comparisons are pairwise? If the comparison first pits project A against project B, then A wins, two votes to one. Then A is paired against project C and project C wins, two votes to one. Clearly the legislator from district II would like this outcome. But if the comparison begins with project B versus project C, then project B wins, two votes to one. Now the vote is between project B and project A and project A wins, two votes to one. The legislator from district I likes this outcome. Finally, begin with a vote between project A and C; C wins as before. Now pair project C and B; project B wins. Legislator III prefers this result. There is no one project that wins all the time. We are caught in a voting cycle, where project A can defeat project B, and project B can defeat project C, but then project C can defeat project A.[5] The order in which the proposals are considered dictates the final outcome. Or to put it another way, whoever controls the agenda controls the legislature's choice for the final project.[6]

There is one circumstance in which the legislature can avoid a voting cycle and actually make a decision that sticks. This is when legislators' preferences for policies can be ordered along a single dimension and each legislator has a most preferred outcome along this one dimension. The further the chosen policy is from the most preferred policy, the less the legislator likes the outcome. For these "single-peaked" preferences, each legislator's "preference peak" occurs at his most preferred outcome. The preference peaks can differ from legislator to legislator. Preferences for a single, national public good that provides the same good or service to all citizens can often be arrayed along such a dimension, usually from less to more. Examples include national defense, research, public health, social insurance against common risks, monetary policies, and trade and competition policies. Figure 4.2 shows the three legislators' preferences in this case, where option A is a small budget or a relaxed regulatory regime, option B is a medium-size budget or flexible regulatory regime, and option C is a large budget or stringent regulatory regime. Legislator I is the policy conservative preferring little spending and relaxed regulation. Legislator II is a policy

5. The example assumes that the three legislators vote sincerely. Voting strategically can alter outcomes here. For example, when legislator I is the agenda-setter and the legislators vote their true preferences, the outcome is A. But A is the worst outcome for legislator III; III would prefer either B or C to A. Legislator III cannot get option B, his first choice, but he can get option C if he votes strategically in the first pairwise comparison offered by legislator I. If III votes strategically for C rather than B, then C wins in the first round. Then when C opposes A, C wins, and C is better than A for legislator III. Unfortunately, voting strategically does not solve the problem of cycling.

6. This result is quite general; see McKelvey (1976).

Proposal rank	Legislator I	Legislator II	Legislator III
First choice	A	B	C
Second choice	B	C	B
Third choice	C	A	A

If Legislator I is agenda-setter, then:
B vs. C ⇨ B wins. B vs. A ⇨ B wins.

If Legislator II is agenda-setter, then:
A vs. B ⇨ B wins. B vs. C ⇨ B wins.

If Legislator III is agenda-setter, then:
A vs. C ⇨ C wins. C vs. B ⇨ B wins.

FIGURE 4.2. Majority-Rule Decision-Making in Legislatures: When Preferences
Are Single Peaked

moderate preferring the middle of the policy spectrum, while legislator III is the liberal preferring high spending and strict regulation. Now, no matter who the agenda-setter is, the middle option, B, wins, a result known as the Median Voter Theorem. When policy options can be arrayed along a single policy dimension and voters' preferences are single peaked, then the median or fiftieth percentile option wins. A small move away from the median in the direction of the more liberal position will be defeated by the median voter plus the 50 percent of voters who are more conservative, and similarly for a small move in the direction of the more conservative position.

The primary difficulty for legislatures as democratic bodies arises not when legislators' preferences are one dimensional and single peaked but when preferences regarding government activities are multidimensional. In this case we cannot rule out voting cycles. With two or more policies, it will be the combination of policies that matters for determining legislators' votes. If policies A, B, and C in Figure 4.2 are not single policies but rather combinations of policies open to manipulation by some agenda-setter, then it would be easy to construct non-single-peaked preferences regarding "packages" by simply manipulating the policies in each package. Again, legislative voting is open to manipulation and voting cycles.[7] To make choices, Democratic Federalism must solve the challenge of voting cycles.

7. In two special circumstances, we can avoid these problems. First, voter preferences regarding multidimensional policies can be projected onto a single dimension, along which voters can be aligned; see Grandmont (1978). Second, if voters' preferred allocations are symmetrically

3. Solving the Voting Cycle in Federal Legislatures

There is no single best solution to the problem of voting cycles, but there are alternatives from which to choose. The strategies we focus on here will constrain the policy choices the legislature can consider through the use of formally approved, or informally agreed-to, rules setting the legislative agenda.[8] The typical means for setting the agenda is to appoint a single legislator (the "Speaker") or a small group of legislators (a "committee") to set the agenda for consideration by the full legislature. How the agenda-setting strategy works, and ultimately the final policy choices, will depend crucially on the type of policy under consideration. Two cases seem the most important, that of *national* public goods whose technology requires a common level of service for all citizens and that of *local* public goods, which can be divided and then provided in varying amounts to separate legislative districts.

Setting Policies for National Public Goods

For national goods, agenda-setters will propose single policies that may be limited to one good, such as defense spending, or a package of national policies, such as defense spending, foreign policy, and trade policy. We will assume that for reasons of efficiency in the evaluation and the provision of policies, the legislature's agenda-setters will group policies to allow for all-important preference interdependencies or production complementarities. Formally, such groupings will form "separable" policy domains such that debates and decisions over one domain can proceed independent of, without loss of efficiency or relevance, the decisions in the other domains.[9] Thus national defense and foreign affairs might be assigned to one agenda-setter, competition and trade policy to a second, monetary policy and financial regulation to a third, environmental policies and national parks to a fourth, and interstate travel by

---

spaced so that for every voter in favor of a given change, there is exactly one voter against that change, then the central point wins; see Plott (1967).

8. Alternative strategies might include the election of a single "super legislator" whose preferences alone set policy, at least for his or her term in office; this would have been our president in Economic Federalism. Or the legislature might allow for voting to express intensity of preferences to determine outcomes.

9. Formally, this will involve grouping national public goods into "composite goods." Each composite good can then be treated as "separable" from the others for the purposes of performance evaluation; see Deaton and Muellbauer (1980, pt. 2, esp. chap. 5).

roads, air, and trains to a fifth. The agenda-setters for each group of services may be a single legislator or committees of the whole composed of representative subsets of legislators. We will assume that committees of the whole set the agendas for each cluster of national goods and develop expertise in evaluating and recommending policies in each domain.[10]

What will each committee decide? *If* voting on the composite policy is by simple majority rule and *if* committee member preferences for the composite policy are single peaked for the policy bundle, then the favored policy by each committee will be the median favored position of committee members. Since each policy committee is representative of the entire legislature, the committee's proposed policy will also be approved by the median voter of the entire legislature. Finally, because each committee's policies are functionally separable from the policies of all other committees, the legislative decisions on each national good policy will stand as votes are taken on all other national good policies. In the end, the full bundle of chosen national policies will be the sum of the median preferred allocations or policies across each of the composite public goods.

Political economists know this solution to legislative voting cycles as a *structured induced equilibrium*, an approach pioneered by Kenneth Shepsle (1979).[11] As here, Shepsle assumes that the agenda-setting committees are committees of the whole. There is a risk, however, that committees may be captured by "high demanders" who use their agenda powers to increase the adopted policy to exceed that preferred by the median voter.[12] Closed rules, where a committee's proposal is the only proposal, will lead to the greatest increase, but even open rules where amendments are allowed will result in an outcome considered excessive by the median legislator. The construction of agenda-setting committees will therefore have important implications for the national public good policies.[13] That said, agenda-setting committees still solve the cycling problem.

---

10. For a theory of how committees of the whole perform, see Gilligan and Krehbiel (1990). For evidence that most national public good committees in the U.S. Congress are representative of the entire legislature most of the time, see Londregan and Snyder (1994, fig. 1).

11. We assume truthful, or sincere, voting by legislators. If committees are designed to meet the assumption of policy separability, single-dimension voting results and sincere voting is the appropriate assumption; see Shepsle and Weingast (1981).

12. See Romer and Rosenthal (1979) for the single-dimension case and MacKay and Weaver (1981) for the more general case.

13. Riker (1980) pointed out that the choice of committees itself becomes susceptible to cycling. While legislative "structure" as argued by Shepsle can lead to stable policy choices, that

Setting Policies for Local Public Goods

The national legislature may also have the option to provide local goods. On its face this may seem unlikely. Since the only beneficiaries of a local good are the residents of the district receiving the good, and residents in all other districts must pay for the good through the national treasury, every vote should be unanimity less one against the national provision of a local good or beneficial regulation.

That answer is too easy. What if a majority of the N locally elected district legislators forms a coalition to provide each of their individual local goods from the national treasury, leaving a minority of districts to pay a share of the collective costs but to receive no local goods for their district or state? That bill will pass. The majority gains, while the minority loses. But this answer is also too easy. Districts in the losing minority have an incentive to offer a bit more of the local good, or a bit less of the collective costs, to encourage one of the majority's districts to leave the first majority coalition and join the minority to form a new majority. But once there is a new majority, the resulting new minority repeats the strategy to form yet another new majority. And so it goes. Just as there may be voting cycles over national public goods, so too can there be voting cycles over local goods.

Two strategies have been suggested for controlling voting cycles in federal legislatures that seek to provide local goods. The first picks one legislator to be the single agenda-setter, perhaps by seniority or by lottery. This agenda-setter builds a majority coalition just large enough to pass a bill that favors his or her district and gives just enough to other districts so that being in the coalition is better than being out. If so, the majority is protected against amended policies by those in the minority. Such a legislature is called a minimum winning coalition (MWC) legislature.

The second strategy shares power among all the legislators by giving each member his or her first choice in the provision of the local public good of that member's district. All preferred levels of each local good are then aggregated into a single omnibus policy, which is approved unanimously. This legislature

---

structure, here committees, must itself be chosen by the legislature in an "unstructured" way. Once a structure has been chosen, by whatever means, it can be a stable structure if deviating from the rules leads to worse outcomes for any coalition of legislators operating on its own; see Calvert and Fenno (1994). Against the alternative of cycling and the possibility of deadlock, representative committees with agenda control may still be an attractive way to organize the legislature.

has been called a universalistic (U) legislature, given that everyone has influence. Every representative gets his or her district's favorite policy but has to pay for the policies of the other legislators. U legislatures only work if the district's benefits for each legislator's own policy exceed his or her district's share of the total costs of all local goods. If so, everyone gains at least a little bit.

Which strategy will be preferred by the members of the legislature? We argue here that if put to a vote at the beginning of each legislative session, the U legislature is likely to be preferred to the MWC legislature by a majority of legislators. Here is the argument, which builds on a deeper understanding of the MWC legislature.

THE MWC LEGISLATURE

To resolve the cycling problem over the provision of local goods, an MWC legislature selects one district representative to be the agenda-setter. But who? One approach first suggested by David Baron and John Ferejohn (1989) and Joseph Harrington (1990) is for legislators to take turns, with each legislator's name drawn at random to be the agenda-setter and to propose an allocation that might win a majority of votes. If everyone is equally qualified, then every legislator has an equal $(1/N)$ chance of being recognized as an agenda-setter. If the agenda-setter's proposal wins a majority, everyone agrees that will be the final allocation. In this case the legislature is said to operate under a "closed rule." If the proposal is defeated, there is a new drawing for the next agenda-setter who submits a proposal for approval, and the process continues. Clearly the first legislator chosen to set the agenda has a strong incentive to offer a winning proposal. To understand what that proposal will be, we need to look at the voting incentives of the "non-agenda-setting" legislators needed for a majority.

Legislators not chosen for the role of agenda-setter will only vote for a proposal if that proposal promises them at least what they could expect if they voted no and then reentered the lottery to be chosen as the next agenda-setter. The value of voting no and waiting is called the legislator's "continuation value" and will equal the expected value of participating in the agenda-setter lottery one more time.[14] Each legislator is allowed to select his or her own

---

14. Formally, the expected value $v(MWC) = (1/N)[B(x_p) - C(x_p)] + ((M-1)/N) \cdot [B(x_m) - C(x_m)]$, where N is the size of the national legislature and $(1/N)$ is the chance that the legislator will be chosen as the next proposer, $B(x_p)$ is the benefit his or her district will receive

favorite district project specific to the needs of the legislator's constituents—for example, highways for rural districts, housing for urban districts, industrial subsidies for manufacturing districts, crop price supports for agricultural districts, or dams and levees for districts prone to flooding. Since by definition these district projects provide no spillover benefits to the proposer's district, legislators not needed for the MWC will receive no project from the agenda-setter.[15] The final national budget for local goods will consist of the preferred district spending for the proposer's local good (x_p) plus spending for projects offered by the proposer to all other districts (assumed to be a common, x_m).[16] The lucky legislator chosen to be the first agenda-setter will make the selection of x_m for his or her majority coalition so that receiving that project with certainty is more attractive for those in the agenda-setter's majority than voting no and entering another agenda-setter lottery.

The size of the agenda-setter's preferred project for his or her district will be determined by balancing the marginal benefit of a project specific to the legislator's constituents against the marginal cost that those constituents pay for the project when financed by the national government. This is shown in Figure 4.3, where the curve MB is the marginal benefit of a district project for a typical constituent, MC is the marginal cost needed to produce that project, and $(1/N) \cdot MC$ is the share of those marginal costs paid by a typical constituent in the agenda-setter's district when those costs are shared among taxpayers from all N districts.[17] Doing the best possible for his or her constituents, the

---

from the project of size x_p, $C(x_p)$ is the cost of that project, and $(M-1)/N$ is the chance that he or she will be chosen as one of the (assumed identical) members of the supporting majority coalition, where N is the number of districts and legislators, M is the number of legislators required for the winning majority, and $(M-1)$ is the required number of votes needed in addition to that of the proposer. Finally, $B(x_m)$ and $C(x_m)$ are the benefits and costs of the project x_m offered by the agenda-setter to each of the legislators in his or her supporting coalition.

15. We assume for simplicity that all legislators have the same demand for local goods. When chosen to be in the majority, the legislator receives a project of size x_m and shares $(1/N)$th of all project costs. If not chosen, the legislator receives no project but continues to share $(1/N)$th of all project costs.

16. This final allocation is the best economic strategy for each legislator given what all other legislators are likely to do. See Baron and Ferejohn (1989) and Harrington (1990) for the proof of this result and Eraslan (2002) for a generalization for a legislature where legislators have different probabilities of being selected as the agenda-setter (higher probabilities never hurt) and varying rates for discounting the costs of waiting for a final solution (patience never hurts).

17. This assumes constant returns to scale. For a generalization that allows for increasing returns to scale in the provision of services, see Primo and Snyder (2008).

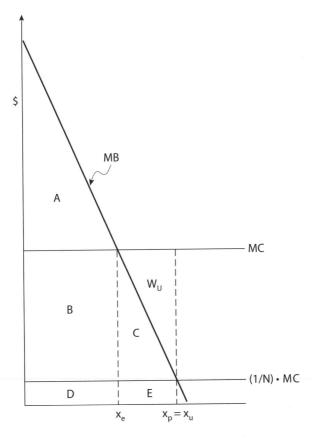

FIGURE 4.3. District Goods and the U Legislature

agenda-setter will select x_p units of the local good, where the typical constituent's marginal benefit (MB) is equal to the constituent's share of marginal costs $((1/N) \cdot MC)$.

Setting a level of nationally funded district services (x_m) for the other members of the agenda-setter's coalition also requires a balancing of marginal benefits and marginal costs, but now for districts that might join the coalition. While project costs are typically known, the agenda-setter may not know the benefit curve for residents in the other districts. How then will x_m be decided? The answer is to run a competitive auction where other legislators offer to join the majority coalition if their district can be promised a project of size x_m.[18]

18. See E. Thompson (1968) and more recently Snyder (1991) for specifications of this auction process.

The agenda-setter will accept the smallest 50 percent of all offers, since this will minimize the taxes borne by his or her constituents. Given that everyone wants to be in the coalition and have a project rather than being outside the coalition and receiving nothing, the 50 percent of the smallest projects may be very small indeed.[19] Those most likely to "win the auction" and be in the agenda-setter's coalition will be those legislators who get the highest constituent benefit for each federal dollar spent in their district. They need the fewest federal dollars to get reelected. These high-marginal-benefit districts are likely to be the richest districts.[20]

The need to win the support of additional legislators offers some check on the agenda-setter's powers, but for all practical purposes he or she will be a dictator when determining how the national government treats the districts when allocating local public goods. The final allocation is likely to show wide disparities in national government spending for local goods. Facing such outcomes, elected district representatives might look for an alternative to closed-rule MWC politics as a way to run their legislative affairs.

One alternative is to allow amendments to the agenda-setter's original proposal, using an "open rule" for legislative voting. Here, the legislators excluded from the initial winning majority coalition are free to offer an alternative proposal as a competitor to the agenda-setter's initial proposal, and if the alternative wins in a majority vote, it will then be adopted as the preferred budget. If the alternative loses, however, then the agenda-setter's original proposal becomes the adopted policy. With an open rule, agenda-setters cannot be quite so greedy in selecting their most favored projects and by offering only very small allocations to their coalition members. If they do, another legislator can propose an alternative that is just "sweet enough" to those in the original coalition, or more likely to the excluded legislators now getting no project at all, and defeat the original proposal.

While open rule reduces the power of the agenda-setter, he or she still has power. With open rule, the risk of endless cycling returns as competitors

19. But not one cent, since there is always the option of not joining the coalition and taking a chance that you will be agenda-setter in the next round. The current agenda-setter still has to beat each legislator's continuation value.

20. If income has a positive effect on constituents' demands for local goods, constituent willingness to pay for each unit of the good will be greater in richer districts than in poorer districts. For the same political support, the legislator from the richer district need bring home less of the local good than the legislator from the poor district. It follows that the legislator from the richer district will be more attractive to the agenda-setter in building his or her majority coalition than the legislator from the poorer district.

scramble to put together a competitive proposal. For every proposed alternative, there is another that may also beat the agenda-setter's budget. If so, no winning alternative may arise, or if one does, it may take time for all the other legislators to reach agreement. Against this risk of gridlock, the original agenda-setter can choose a budget that discourages competitive open-rule alternatives. To do so, however, the agenda-setter must cut spending on his or her own favored project, increase the spending for those in the majority coalition, and perhaps expand the size of the coalition of project recipients to include some of those legislators initially denied projects. Baron and Ferejohn (1989) and Baron (1990) show that in most reasonably sized legislatures (more than ten legislators), the agenda-setter will still succeed in passing his or her proposal with a bare 51 percent majority, but the allocation of final projects will now be more equitable—less for the agenda-setter and more for the legislators in the MWC.

Open rules help. But in most cases, 49 percent of the legislators and the citizens of their districts are still likely to lose out. With simple majority rule and a randomly chosen agenda-setter, one can never be sure he or she will not be in the losing minority. Against this reality, legislators might look for another way to run their affairs.

THE U LEGISLATURE

Rather than select one legislator to be the agenda-setter, might not the legislators all agree to share agenda powers but limit those powers to the national provision of only their own district's local public good? Barry Weingast (1979) has called this sharing of agenda powers *universalism*. Here, legislators propose their preferred level of their own district's public good, then all district proposals are "stapled" together into omnibus legislation, and a vote is held on the full package. Since everyone gets what they want, there is no incentive to vote against the legislation, at least for any one legislator. Omnibus bills are approved unanimously. Of course, such a legislative agreement could not by itself be a stable outcome. There is always a majority that might rise up to prevent granting a minority its own district powers, exclude their project from the omnibus bill, and then approve the smaller bill by a bare majority. But such behavior again leads to cycling and the risk of gridlock. To avoid cycling, all legislators must agree not to undo the original universalistic legislation and, importantly, there must be an institutional mechanism for holding these agreements in place.

Whereas the MWC legislature uses a single agenda-setter to set budgets, the U legislature uses multiple agenda-setters. In practice, these agenda-setters will be legislative committees and, by agreement among all legislators, each committee is granted a monopoly right to set allocations over a unique, and perhaps narrow, set of policies. Membership on each committee is allocated by rank-order bidding among representatives.[21] Representatives are assigned to their preferred committee, typically the one most closely aligned with the policy interests of their district, and retain a "property right" to committee membership. Representatives from rural districts will opt for the agriculture committee, those from urban districts for the housing and infrastructure committee, those with military installations for the defense committee, and those from mining and extraction districts for the natural resource committee. Finally, there may be a single overarching "budget committee," composed of trusted members from the legislature at large whose objective will be to fashion a single, omnibus budget bill aggregating the requests of the individual committees and, at times, constraining those requests if they get out of hand.[22] Finally, to ensure that no small majority in the legislature undoes universalism's grand agreement, the legislature's leadership discourages amendments to the omnibus bill by punishing those who deviate, perhaps by removing their district's own projects from the omnibus legislation. Enforcement of the U legislature's grand agreement is done through a "norm of deference"— that is, "I'll scratch your back if you scratch mine."[23]

Figure 4.3 also shows the level of preferred spending in a U legislature for a district public good preferred by a typical district representative. Each legislator selects that level of his or her district's nationally provided local good where the constituents' marginal benefit (MB) equals the constituents' share

21. See Shepsle (1978) and Weingast and Marshall (1988).

22. See Schick (1980). Matters may "get out of hand" when the aggregate tax costs of local goods requests impose a total burden on all citizens that exceeds the sum of the total benefits that those local goods can provide. It will then be the job of the oversight committee to cut back each district's spending.

23. The argument for enforcement of this "norm of deference" is formally developed in Epple and Riordan (1987). Examples of the use of this enforcement mechanism in the U.S. Congress are reported in Weingast (1979, p. 253) of Senator Buckley's failed efforts to remove projects for public works in all districts (only Buckley's New York projects were removed) and in Ferejohn (1974, pp. 114–115) of Senator Proxmire's attempts to remove wasteful projects, which resulted in a cutback in only his district's favorite project. Both were punished for their efforts to undo the norm of deference.

($1/N$) of the good's marginal cost (MC). The level is x_u and, not surprisingly perhaps, is the same level of spending x_p as chosen by the agenda-setter in an MWC legislature. Now, in the U legislature, all representatives are agenda-setters, each for his or her own district's local good. Total spending for each district's good will be the cost of providing x_u. Each district contributes an equal share of the total cost of its own local good as well as an equal share of the cost of spending in all other districts. Together, these contributions cover the costs of each district's spending and the aggregate budget is in balance. That's the good news.[24]

The bad news is that the national budget for local goods may be very inefficient. Economic efficiency requires the full marginal cost of providing the local good to be equal to the marginal benefit. This is shown as spending x_e in Figure 4.3. But each district representative asks for x_u. This is inefficiently too large relative to x_e, given that the marginal cost of providing all levels of spending beyond x_e exceeds the marginal benefit. The inefficiency is measured by the area $[W_u]$ (for social waste) and equals the difference between marginal costs and marginal benefits summed over all units of the local good from x_e to x_u. Happily, spending on the units of the local good up to the efficient level, x_e, provides services whose marginal benefits are above its marginal costs by area $[A]$. The overall economic performance of the U legislature is measured as the difference between these net gains and net losses, or by the average over all districts of {area $[A]$ − area $[W_u]$}.[25]

Why does each district's representative not ask for the efficient level of the local good? Since national taxes will fall as x_u is decreased to x_e, all other

24. Well, sort of. The bills are paid, but maybe with excessive borrowing. Velasco (2000) extends the argument here from a single period to multiple budget periods and shows that even with infinitely lived legislators, one plausible equilibrium is for each legislator to vote for excessive borrowing if all legislators behave the same—that is, adopt universalistic behaviors with regard to the country's future tax base. The result is to exhaust the country's future taxing capacity sooner than would be optimal if all districts cooperated.

25. When legislators make the efficient choice, there is a net benefit of area $[A]$. Area $[W_u]$ is then the economic inefficiency or social waste in the provision of each local good by a U legislature. Bednar (2009) calls area $[W_u]$ legislative "shirking," and rightly so. Legislators are not doing their job to provide an efficient national government. The one potentially important exception to using $[W_u]$ as the measure of economic inefficiency from the U legislature is when a district's local public good provides positive spillovers to its neighbors. In this case, the district MB curve underestimates the social MB curve from the provision of the local good. With $x = x_u$ from district choice but with a higher social MB curve, the area $[W]$ of social waste will be reduced, an important point stressed by Besley and Coate (2003b).

representatives will appreciate the gesture. But constituents will not. They still must pay for all the other districts' inefficient projects, while they lose all *their* marginal benefits from the local good greater than *their* marginal costs as the good is cut from x_u to x_e. This is the area $[C]$. Since the representative in this legislature is elected for acting in the best interests of his or her constituents, not those of the nation as whole, the representative will lose the election.[26] Reasoning alike, all legislators submit a request for the x_u level of spending, and the final budget is simply the collection of all these inefficient district projects.[27] Aggregate inefficiency will equal the number of districts (N) proposing inefficient projects times the area of inefficiency $[W_u]$. Aggregate inefficiency increases as the number of legislative districts increases for two reasons. First, more districts means more legislators needing to satisfy their local constituents and thus more local goods creating waste. Second, more districts means a lower price for each district's good, thus increasing the demand by each district.

Finally, might legislative committees discipline the individual legislators that ask for too much? The problem is knowing x_e. While each legislator knows his or her district's most preferred level of local goods spending from communication with the constituents, other legislators will not. If asked, each legislator simply says, "x_u is efficient." Committees might hold hearings to reveal each district's true *MB* and *MC* curves, and while knowledge of true project costs is likely available, knowledge of true project benefits typically is not. This requires information about citizen preferences.[28] In the end, the legislature's inability to measure each local good's true benefits and the incentive for each legislator to overspend creates an excessively large and inefficient budget

---

26. In his survey of congressional elections, Mayhew (1974, p. 57) notes that congressional representatives may not know the exact impact of local goods spending on election outcomes, "but it would be hard to find a Congressman who thinks he can afford to wait around until precise information is available. It is the lore that they [local goods] count." For direct evidence that they do matter for election outcomes, see Levitt and Snyder (1997).

27. In discussing the best size of the national legislature, Madison seemed to have sensed this weakness of large legislatures when he wrote in *Federalist* No. 55 that the "number ought at most to be kept within a certain limit, in order to avoid the confusion and intemperance of the multitude. In all very numerous assemblies, of whatever characters composed, passion never fails to wrest the scepter from reason" (Hamilton, Madison, and Jay, 1982, p. 281).

28. If you ask each legislator, or his or her constituents, to report project benefits, each has an incentive to overstate true benefits. These arguments are developed formally in Kessler (2014) and are shown to lead to universalism and overspending on local goods.

for local goods. Legislators seem to have always understood the problem. In commenting on the River and Harbors Omnibus legislation of the 1880s and 1890s, Representative Emory R. Johnson noted, "Representatives of the people have, of a truth, secured appropriations for works in their districts more to further their personal ambition than to promote the general welfare. Logrolling has been and is now employed to secure such legislation" (quoted in R. Wilson, 1986, p. 736).

WHICH LEGISLATURE IS PREFERRED?

From the perspective of any individual legislator hoping to do the best he or she can for the constituents, the choice for how to run the national legislature for the provision of local goods is not obvious. An absence of legislative leadership will typically mean endless cycling between policies and no decisions at all—gridlock. Voting to appoint an agenda-setter will mean a voting cycle over that appointment. That won't help. The two strategies that remain are to randomly select an agenda-setter, as in an MWC legislature, or to allow everyone to be an agenda-setter, as in a U legislature. Assuming gridlock is never the preferred choice by individual legislators, then between an MWC and U legislature, which is preferred?

The choice of legislative rules will need to balance each district representative's expected benefits less costs within the two legislative regimes. The MWC legislature is likely to be more efficient as only one district, that of the agenda-setter's, is allowed to significantly overspend on local goods. But of course not being chosen as the agenda-setter means facing a significant risk of only a modest level of the local good, or worse yet, receiving no local goods at all. Doing business with an open rule that allows amendments to the agenda-setter's budget helps somewhat, but the risk of being out of the winning majority is still sizeable. In contrast, life in a U legislature is less risky for each legislator, but because of incentives created by the norm of universalism, the final budget, and thus taxes paid by all constituents, will be inefficiently too large.

At the start of each legislative session, we adopt the perspective of a typical legislator who asks, Are my reelection prospects higher with an MWC legislature or a U legislature? The answer turns on a comparison of what the legislator can expect in constituent net benefits from each legislative structure. Within an MWC legislature, the legislator has a $(1/N)$th chance of being the agenda-setter and receiving x_p and a bit less than a fifty-fifty chance of being chosen as part of the agenda-setter's winning majority and receiving x_m. But there is also a nearly fifty-fifty chance that the legislator will be part of the losing minority and that his or her district will receive nothing from the national legislature. Will the constituents be better off under a U legislature? Under this legislature structure, each district's constituents receive the benefits from their project minus their share of total costs. If all districts are alike, this will be equal to {area $[A]$ − area $[W_u]$} in Figure 4.3.[29]

Which, then, is larger? The answer turns on how inefficient the U legislature is versus how averse the typical legislator (or the legislator's constituents) is to the risk of receiving very little or no federal spending for his or her district in the MWC legislature. The U legislature will be preferred if each legislator's *certain* net benefits with universalism after paying for everyone's preferred project are greater than each legislator's *expected* net benefits from being in the majority using MWC politics. If the certain, but inefficient, net benefits under universalism are greater than the riskier, but perhaps more efficient, net benefits with a MWC lesislature, then the U legislature will preferred. If not, and the inefficiencies in the U legislature are very large, then the MWC legislature will be favored.

The limiting case most favorable to the MWC coalition option is when legislators are risk neutral and their local districts are able to supplement any national provision of the district's local public good through local taxation. In this case, the legislator lucky enough to be chosen as the agenda-setter will get x_p, those in the MWC will get what the agenda-setter allocates for their district from the national treasury, and then all other legislators get nothing in nationally funded local public goods. But with supplementation, legislators in the MWC and those receiving no local public goods can encourage their local governments to provide local goods efficiently.[30] With no national assistance,

29. Total benefits for a typical district will equal areas $[A] + [B] + [C] + [D] + [E]$, while total costs will equal areas $[B] + [C] + [W_u] + [D] + [E]$. The average district's net benefits will then be area $[A]$ − area $[W_u]$. More precisely, the expected value for each representative in the U legislature will be $v(U) = B(x_u) - (1/N)C(x_u) - [(N-1)/N]C(x_u)$, where constituents get the benefits of x_u in their own district, pay $(1/N)$th of the costs of their own project, and pay $(1/N)$th of the costs of everyone else's projects, each of which has a cost of $C(x_u)$ for the average-size project (x_u) from all other states (assuming constant marginal costs). If most states' preferred projects are about the same size, then $v(U) = B(x_u) - C(x_u)$, which is area $[A]$ − area $[W_u]$ in Figure 4.3.

30. Keeping the argument as favorable as possible for the MWC legislature, we will assume that locally elected national legislators will not suffer any political consequences from *not* providing the local public good from the national treasury. This is very questionable for locally elected legislators to the U.S. House or Senate; see Mayhew (1974) and Atkeson and Partin (1995).

local governments will pay the full marginal cost (MC) for their local goods and thus will provide x_e in Figure 4.3. In this special and most favorable case, the MWC legislature provides the average legislator an expected net benefit equal to his or her fifty-fifty chance of being in the majority times his or her net benefits with supplementation—that is, area $.5 \cdot$ area $[A]$ in Figure 4.3. This expected net benefit from the MWC legislature must then be compared with the certain net benefits from the U legislature equal to $\{$area $[A] -$ area $[W_u]\}$. The MWC legislature will be preferred when it provides larger expected benefits than those available from the U legislature, or when $.5 \cdot$ area $[A] >$ area $[A] -$ area $[W_u]$, or equivalently, when area $[W_u] > .5 \cdot$ area $[A]$. In other words, the MWC legislature is preferred when the inefficiencies of the U legislature are very large compared with the net benefits available from direct local provision of the local public good.[31] And conversely.

We now have an upper bound for how inefficient the U legislature can be and still be preferred to the MWC legislature by legislators when setting their rules for national governance of local public goods. If inefficiencies from a U legislature are relatively small compared with the benefits of local public goods, or $.5 \cdot$ area $[A] >$ area $[W_u]$, then the U legislature will be preferred. If local public goods are nationally provided, economically important, and relatively inelastically demanded by local constituents, then area $[A]$ is likely to be relatively large when compared with area $[W_u]$, and universalism will be the preferred legislative structure. However, if demand for local goods is very elastic, then the inefficiencies from universalism will be relatively large. If controlling inefficiencies is important, then the MWC legislature will be preferred. If not, then the U legislature will be preferred. If the economic evidence favors relatively inelastic demands for local public goods, then preference by legislators will be for the U legislative structure.[32] That's the theory.

What's the evidence from actual legislatures? When left on their own, and without the discipline of either presidential leadership or strong political parties (see Chapter 5), U.S. legislatures have revealed voting behaviors more

---

31. This can be shown more precisely by comparing $\upsilon(MWC)$ as specified in fn. 14 to $\upsilon(U)$ as specified in fn. 29 with the assumption that $x_m = x_e$ when local supplementation is allowed. See also Weingast (1979) and Niou and Ordeshook (1985).

32. For a linear demand curve, one can show that $.5 \cdot$ area $[A] >$ area $[W_u]$ is the likely case when the price elasticity of demand for nationally provided local public goods is 1.0 or lower (in absolute value); see Inman (1979) and DelRossi and Inman (1999). Price elasticities above 1.0 occur when local public goods have close private good substitutes. This is unlikely for most local public goods.

consistent with a U, rather than an MWC, legislature. First, legislation passed by the U.S. Congress for district project spending is rarely if ever approved by bare majorities. More common are large, often 90 percent, majorities; this was particularly the case during the period 1965 to 1981 when U.S. political parties were weak and individual members of Congress operated largely as independent political agents.[33] Second, the management of the U.S. Congress, even from its inception, is more consistent with the U than an MWC legislature.[34] Membership on legislative committees responsible for the allocation of local public goods is typically decided by constituent interests as required by a U legislature.[35] Formal tests comparing the composition of committees responsible for local public goods with the full legislature find that those committees are controlled by those with a direct constituent interest in the local good—for example, those setting policies for defense contracting and army bases, agriculture assistance, urban affairs, public works, and services to the District of Columbia.[36] Finally, budgetary oversight committees, which we do observe, will be important in U legislatures to constrain excessive spending requests for local goods by district legislators.[37] There is no need for such committees in MWC legislatures, since by definition the agenda-setter manages the local goods budget.

While contrasting vote totals and legislative organization is instructive, a sharper test is to compare actual policy outcomes with predicted outcomes under the two legislative structures. In particular, what happens to the total size of the local goods budget, and to the choices of individual legislators, as the number of representatives increases? The U legislative structure predicts that aggregate spending on local goods should increase with the number of

33. See Collie (1988) and Panning (1985). See also Ferejohn's (1974) study of infrastructure voting and Baron's (1990) study of voting on preservation of local Amtrak train lines, as well as Stockman (1975) and Schick (1980). R. Wilson's (1986) study of infrastructure spending in the late nineteenth century finds a similar increase in omnibus voting as the discipline of political party leadership disappears.

34. See Gamm and Shepsle (1989).

35. The paradigmatic example involved the assignment in 1969 of Shirley Chisholm, a newly elected member to the U.S. House of Representatives from New York City. Representative Chisholm held a news conference on the steps of the capitol protesting her assignment to the Agriculture Committee by the House leadership. She had been elected by an urban district and could not represent her constituents if assigned to agriculture. The leadership quickly moved her to the House Banking and Urban Affairs Committee.

36. See Londregan and Snyder (1994) and Adler and Lapinski (1997).

37. For the historical evidence as to the importance of such oversight committees for budgeting on local goods in U.S. congresses, see Inman and Fitts (1990).

legislative districts, as should spending per capita within each individual district. Aggregate spending rises because there are more districts each receiving its local good.[38] Spending per capita within each district rises because more districts share the cost of any one district's local goods. There will be an increase in spending in larger MWC legislatures too as the agenda-setter must increase his or her winning coalition, but spending per new member is typically small and needs to be paid to only half of the new legislators. Both the U.S. and international evidence are consistent with the predictions for the U legislature of significant spending increases, both in the aggregate and within each district, with increases in the size of the legislature.[39]

On balance, we conclude that the most likely structure for legislative decision-making in Democratic Federalism when members are unconstrained in their choices will be the U legislature. It avoids gridlock and allows elected representatives to make decisions to benefit their constituents and thus to ensure their reelection.

4. The Efficiency Performance of the Federal Legislature

How efficient, then, will Democratic Federalism's national legislature be in its provision of national and local public goods? In the case of national public goods and spillovers, performance is likely to be comparable to the performance of Economic Federalism and preferred to that of Cooperative Federalism. In the case of nationally provided local public goods, performance is likely to be less efficient than with either Economic or Cooperative Federalism.

National Public Goods

When the goods to be decided are national public goods whose benefits are shared uniformly by all citizens, Democratic Federalism's choices will reflect the median preference among all legislators. To avoid voting cycles, congressional committees will be selected to act as agenda-setters for each national

---

38. See Stein and Bickers (1995, chap. 3).

39. At the U.S. federal government level, see Inman and Fitts (1990). At the U.S. district level, see Gilligan and Matsusaka (1995), Gilligan and Matsusaka (2001), and Primo (2006). At U.S. local level, see Southwick (2005), Bradbury and Crain (2001), Baqir (2002), and Bradbury and Stephenson (2003). Internationally, see Jones, Meloni, and Tommasi (2012) on Argentina; Rodden (2003) on Brazil; and Golden and Min (2013) for a general review of the international evidence.

public good. Committees will then propose a policy for their assigned national public good that will be voted on by the full legislature.

The provision of national public goods by the national legislature will be efficient, that is, the final allocation will equate the average citizen's marginal benefits to the average share of marginal costs, if the following conditions hold:[40]

> L1: Each committee's assigned policy responsibility is for national public goods whose economic benefits are "separable" from those of other committees and thus independent of decisions made by other committees;
>
> L2: Representation to each committee reflects the distribution of legislators' preferences in the entire legislature—that is, is a "committee of the whole";
>
> L3: Decisions within each committee are made by simple majority rule with the median legislator's preferences decisive for the committee's recommendation; and,
>
> L4: Legislator preferences for providing national public goods reflect citizen preferences, those preferences are symmetrically distributed, and citizen taxation is proportional.

When is this benchmark case likely to hold? Condition L1 seems to be a common feature of most legislatures allocating national public goods. Committees are typically organized by related policies—for example, defense and foreign affairs, monetary policy and financial market regulation, national public goods infrastructure spending, health policies and social insurance—and committee members develop expertise in their committee' policy domain.[41] As required by condition L2, membership on these national public goods committees reflects the distribution of interests in the legislature as a whole.[42] As required by L3, simple majority rule determines committee decisions.

It is condition L4 that is the most likely to be violated. For national public goods whose citizen demands are positively related to income, a nonsymmetric

---

40. Conditions L1 to L3 ensure that legislative decisions match citizen preferences, and condition L4 ensures that the final decision based on those preferences equates aggregate marginal benefits for the national public good to its marginal costs.

41. See Gilligan and Krehbiel (1990). For the argument that the overall allocation for national public goods is an aggregation of these committees' median recommendations; see Krehbiel (2006).

42. See Londregan and Snyder (1994).

distribution of income will lead to a divergence between median and average demands. Most distributions of income are skewed to the right, with the average level of income greater than the median level of income. If so, then the median citizen, and thus his or her representative, will demand less of the national good than will the average citizen. As a result, there will be a legislative bias toward too little provision of the national good. *But* if the national tax is a proportional (or even progressive) tax on citizen incomes, then the median citizen will pay a smaller share of the cost of the national good than the average citizen. If so, then the median citizen, and thus his or her representative, will demand too much of the national public good. How do the two effects balance? There is no compelling empirical evidence suggesting that there will be too much, or too little, provision of national public goods. But we can say this: the resulting bias in efficiency performance of Democratic Federalism will be no worse, but no better, than that for Economic Federalism with a president elected by his or her national median voter.

If there is a difference between the efficiency performance of Economic and Democratic Federalism in the provision of national public goods, it will come from a possible difference between the preferences of the median national legislator, who decides policies in Democratic Federalism, and the preferences of the median citizen, who elects the national president in Economic Federalism. We expect this difference to be small if there are a large number of legislative districts. When a distribution of preferences, even a skewed distribution, is divided into many small segments, the median of segments will be close to the median of the whole distribution.[43] Thus, for large legislatures, the median allocations for national public goods under Democratic Federalism should closely approximate those under Economic Federalism with a single, national president. No better, but no worse. However, we can say, from the analysis in Chapter 3, that both Economic and Democratic Federalism will be more efficient in the allocation of national public goods than Cooperative Federalism.

---

43. If we partition a skewed distribution of national preferences into N districts (where, for simplicity, N is odd), the median of the medians (the median legislator) will be the median lying between the $\{[(100/N)(N-1)]/2\}^{\text{th}}$ percentile and the $\{(100/N)(N+1)]/2\}^{\text{th}}$ percentile. For $N > 50$ the median of the medians would lie somewhere within the forty-ninth and fifty-first percentiles for the full distribution.

Local Public Goods

If there is an efficiency weakness to Democratic Federalism, it will be in the provision of local public goods. The problem arises when legislators opt to run their affairs as a U legislature with allocations at x_u, as in Figure 4.3, with an economic inefficiency of area $[W_u]$. These local inefficiencies can be avoided under Democratic Federalism if:

> **L5:** The national legislature is a MWC legislature and local supplementation of nationally provided district goods is allowed.

But as noted in our analysis of legislators' preferences for running their legislative affairs, condition L5 is unlikely to hold. The U legislative structure will typically be preferred. If so, each legislator will select x_u as his or her preferred allocation and an economic inefficiency of area $[W_u]$ will result for every legislative district. The resulting inefficiency comes from each legislator's overspending on local public goods, with each legislator yielding to the temptation to use the national tax base as a "common pool" for his or her constituents' local benefits.[44]

Recent estimates of area $[W_u]$ for the U.S. Congress have all reached much the same conclusion: area $[W_u]$ is from 16 to 37 percent of the average dollar spent by the national government for local public goods and for local tax subsidies.[45] Applying those percentages to the current federal spending on local goods and district-specific tax favors of $612 billion (about 16 percent of the U.S. national budget) implies a per capita level of economic inefficiency for the U.S. economy ranging from $326/person to perhaps as much as $750/person. Not enough to undo aggregate economic performance, but wasteful nonetheless and equal to about 3 to 6 percent of the median income family's annual income.

In one instance, however, locally motivated fiscal inefficiencies nearly bankrupted a national economy: Brazil in 1993. The crisis revolved around excessive government borrowing to finance local goods.[46] State governments had been given the right to borrow in the national and international capital markets to finance local goods. But when the state debt fell due, state taxation was not

---

44. See, for example, Bednar (2009).

45. See Inman (1988) for federal grants for the financing of district government services, DelRossi and Inman (1999) for federally funded local water projects, Knight (2004) for federally funded district transportation projects, and Inman and Fitts (1990) for the aggregate level of local goods spending including tax subsidies that favor district industries.

46. The story is well told in Rodden (2003).

sufficient to both repay that debt and maintain core state services. Brazilian states then turned to the national legislature for help. Because each state's legislator saw the cost of his or her own state's bailout as only $(1/N)$th of the full cost, each legislator proposed a full local bailout. But so did representatives from all other states, each for his or her own state. Bailouts were paid not by direct national taxes but rather by an "inflation tax" imposed by expanding the money supply. Anticipating bailouts, states continued to borrow, and aggregate annual government deficit rose to more than 6 percent of national GDP and inflation rates reached over 2,000 percent per year. Capital left the country, unemployment rates doubled, and national real incomes fell by 5 percent. Only when a strong president, Fernando Henrique Cardoso, introduced a reform in 1994 creating a new currency (the real) pegged to the value of the dollar, established balanced budget requirements for all state governments, and raised national income tax rates to repay past debts, was inflation finally broken and the country returned to a path of positive and sustained economic growth.

In summary, Democratic Federalism should be seen as no better, but no worse, than Economic Federalism for the efficient provision of national public goods—and both are better than Cooperative Federalism—but significantly less efficient than either Economic or Cooperative Federalism in the provision of local public goods. If there is a uniquely positive case for Democratic Federalism, it will need to be made along the other dimensions of constitutional performance.

5. Representation, Rights, and Fairness

As we have done for Economic and Cooperative Federalism, here we evaluate the potential impact of Democratic Federalism on the valued outcomes of political participation, the protection of rights and liberties, and the promotion of economic fairness. It was the hope of James Madison that a locally elected national legislature would make a significant contribution to all three, providing the democratic voice of the citizenry (*Federalist* No. 10), safeguarding individual civil and religious rights through the competing interests of representative factions (*Federalist* Nos. 10 and 46), and protecting the economic interests of the less fortunate because of all citizens' shared uncertainties (*Federalist* No. 51). The historical record and contemporary evidence provides support for Madison's vision for Democratic Federalism, but with one important qualification: protection is *only* provided to those citizens represented within the legislature.

TABLE 4.1. Democratic Federalism and Voter Participation

Panel A: International Comparison, Federal Governments

Mean participation = .69; standard deviation = .16

$$PART = .70 + .18 \cdot (\%\ \text{years democratic}) - .042 \cdot ln(N) - .005 \cdot (Pop/N) + [\text{CONTROLS}] \qquad R^2(\text{Adj}) = .40$$
$$\ \ (.07)^{**} \qquad (.06)^{**} \qquad\qquad\qquad\quad (.013)^{**} \qquad\quad (.002)^{**}$$

Panel B: United States Comparison, Aggregate U.S. House Elections, 1822–2012

Mean participation = .54; standard deviation = .12

$$PART = .95 - .064 \cdot ln(N) - .334 \cdot (Pop/N) + [\text{CONTROLS}] \qquad R^2(\text{Adj}) = .55$$
$$\ \ (.36)^{**} \quad (.064) \qquad\quad (.075)^{**}$$

Panel C: United States Comparison, U.S. Senate Elections by States, 1980–2010

Mean participation = .68; standard deviation = .14

$$PART = .44 - .006 \cdot (Pop/N) + .0002 \cdot (Pop/N)^2 + [\text{CONTROLS}] \qquad R^2(\text{Adj}) = .54$$
$$\ \ (.02)^{**} \quad (.002)^{**} \qquad\quad (.0001)^{**}$$

Notes: Standard errors are in parentheses . Estimation of Panel A's cross-country regression is by OLS. Estimation of Panel B is by a Newey-West estimator with one lag to account for possible autocorrelation. Controls are the level of government spending and dummy variables for whether the election was held in year of a presidential election, held in a war year, held after the passage of the Nineteenth Amendment (giving women the right to vote), and after the passage of the Voting Rights Act of 1965. Estimation of Panel C's cross-state regressions is by OLS, controlling for real campaign expenditures per voting-age population, percentage of population black and Hispanic, percentage college graduates, winning plurality above .50, years of incumbency, and whether the state qualified for federal government supervision under the Voting Rights Act.

** Indicates statistical significance at the 95% level of confidence.

Representation

For Madison and the original Federalists, a locally elected national legislature would be the center of political decision-making in the new federal democracy. Representatives would be elected from equally populated regions within the country. A citizen's decision to participate in the deliberations of governance, whether through voting or more informally through political action, will involve a direct balancing of the individual's benefits and costs of such activities. In Democratic Federalism, both are likely to depend on the number of districts represented in the national legislature, in at least two ways. First, having more districts and representatives gives each citizen a better chance of influencing his or her legislator, either through voting or by personal contact. Second, as an offsetting influence, more districts and thus more representatives will diminish the legislative influence of any single legislator and thus potentially discourage citizen involvement. How these offsetting effects finally influence citizen participation is an empirical question.

Table 4.1 provides evidence on the point, both from international federal unions and from an analysis of voting in U.S. House of Representatives and Senate elections. Panel A shows both effects at work for voting in a sample of thirty world federal governments. The estimated relationship between the thirty-year average rate of voter participation in national elections $(PART)$ depends on (1) legislators' potential influence in the national legislature measured by the number of states or provinces represented in the national legislature $(lnN,$ to allow for exponentially declining effects) and (2) citizens' influence over legislators measured by population per representative (Pop/N), while also controlling for the history of democratic governance measured by the percentage of the thirty-year period that the federal country was considered a democracy (% years democratic). The average rate of thirty-year voter participation in national elections for this sample is .69. We conjectured that voters would be discouraged in voting as the number of states (lnN) in the legislature increased and representative influence declined but would be encouraged to vote as the number of citizens represented by each state legislator (Pop/N) decreased. Both hypotheses are confirmed. In addition, significantly higher average rates of voter participation are also observed in countries with stronger democratic traditions.

The U.S. voting record in legislative elections tells a similar story. Panels B and C report results for voter participation in U.S. House of Representative and Senate elections. The House results are for the national average rate of voter participation in elections for representatives for the period 1822 (the first year the aggregate data were available) to 2012. The Senate results are for voter participation in all state Senate elections from 1980 to 2010. As we found for the international sample, voter participation in U.S. representative elections increases as the population per representative (Pop/N) declines and declines as the number of elected representatives increases (lnN), though this later effect is statistically insignificant; see Panel B. The Senate results in Panel C confirm the negative effect of (Pop/N) on voter participation, where population is the number of registered voters.[47] The Senate regression also includes the variable $(Pop/N)^2$ as an additional control for the possible influence of voting in a very large state. The estimated effect of $(Pop/N)^2$ is positive, implying participation is U shaped in (Pop/N). The estimated state population of registered voters where participation is at a minimum is fifteen million voters. Only California, New York, and Texas are above that population level, and the effect of these very large populations on Senate voter participation is modest, increasing participation by no more than .025 percent for the largest state, California.

The results from all three samples are in agreement. The impact of increased partitioning of the national population into more voting districts has only a very small overall impact on the final rate of voter participation, at least over the sample ranges considered here. From the results for the international sample, for example, the average federal country has a population of 44.3 million residents and seventeen states; thus mean district size is 2.6 million residents. Doubling the number of states from seventeen to thirty-four (a one-standard-deviation increase) will halve the number of residents in each represented state. The overall effect is to reduce the mean rate of voter participation by only .02, from .69 to .67. From the U.S. results for representative elections, a 20 percent increase in the size of the current legislature from 435 members to 520 members (reducing average district size from 710,000 to 570,000 citizens) would increase the rate of voter participation by only .034 percent. Finally, from the results for Senate elections, increasing the number of senators representing each state from two to three (lowering the mean number of registered voters per senator from 2.61 to 1.75 million) would increase the rate of voter participation by only .01. From Table 4.1, we conclude that adding or

---

47. The number "district representatives" in the U.S. Senate over the sample period remained constant at $N = 100$; N is therefore excluded from the regression explaining voter participation in Senate elections.

subtracting to the number of national legislative districts will have only a very small effect on voter participation.

Voting is not the only means for influencing national policy in Democratic Federalism. Citizens can express their views directly. Here Democratic Federalism has a significant advantage over Economic and Cooperative Federalism, where locally elected representatives often serve their constituents as relatively low-cost, but motivated, ombudsmen to the national government. This avenue of citizen influence is not available in either Economic or Cooperative Federalism. There are no locally elected representatives to the national government in Economic Federalism, and while there is local representation in Cooperative Federalism, each representative is only one of many in a bargaining game required by unanimity voting. In Democratic Federalism, however, if there is a local problem with the national government, citizens can complain directly to their locally elected national legislator and, because of the desire for reelection, expect that representative to use the institutionalized channels of policy, most likely created by a U legislature, to respond and solve the problem.[48]

In their study *The Personal Vote* (particularly chapters 4–7), Bruce Cain, John Ferejohn, and Morris Fiorina (1987) document the importance of this channel. To satisfy citizen demands for legislative service, representatives often return weekly to their local districts, and the visits are more than a "meet and greet." Citizens want performance, either in the form of local grants and services from the national legislature or as assistance in navigating national regulations and bureaucracy. Legislators who provide such services are rewarded with reelection. Only in Democratic Federalism can citizens so easily and effectively share their views, ask for favors, and complain when those views or requests are ignored. Giving citizens a clear sense that their voice is heard and that government can meet their individual needs is an important safeguard for continued democratic rule provided by Democratic Federalism.

---

48. Treisman (2007, chap. 7) argues that local field agents from Economic Federalism's national bureaucracy can serve the same ombudsman function as that provided by the locally elected district representative. The question becomes, Who, elected or appointed, will be best motivated to respond to the concerns of local citizens? Having an elected agent whose compensation is directly dependent on performance and who can be "fired" if that performance is found wanting—as is the case for an elected representative—is likely to be preferred to a nationally appointed bureaucrat; see Dixit (1996, chap. 2). For evidence that directly elected officials are more responsive to constituents than are appointed officials, see Besley and Coate (2003b).

Protecting Rights

If there is one virtue of Democratic Federalism heralded by its proponents, from Harrington to Madison to contemporary republican scholars, it is in the ability of a *locally* elected *national* legislature to protect the civil and property rights of all represented citizens. This faith in Democratic Federalism was shown to be well grounded in the international evidence reported in Chapter 1. We found there that a necessary condition for the protection of property and civil rights was democratic governance. But once democratic, the introduction of federal institutions—states with independent powers coupled with district and state representation to the national legislature—significantly improved rights protections over those provided by unitary democracies. How might this happen? Our evaluation of the rights performance of Economic and Cooperative Federalism suggests that free mobility of citizens across states, and state competition to attract citizens, offers a first line of defense. Citizens discriminated against, or whose private property and labor skills are taxed at exploitative rates, may migrate to a more welcoming location. That protection is available for Democratic Federalism as well.

Madison, however, feared that free mobility would not be sufficient. Citizens who cannot move easily, or property in place, are not protected. There is a need for another line of protection, and for Madison it was to be found in a representative national legislature, one that recognized and protected individual rights no matter where the citizen might reside. First, elected representatives from districts would ensure that all citizens eligible to vote would have someone to represent their cause if their rights were challenged. Second, each representative would come to appreciate that any national coalition he or she might be tempted to join to exploit the citizens of another representative could just as easily turn against the first representative's constituents at a later date. For Madison, this legislative uncertainty makes it difficult to form a stable, majority coalition for the oppression of a minority. Such coalitions become more difficult the larger and more diverse is the legislature:

> The majority . . . must be rendered, by their number and local situation, unable to concert and carry into effect schemes of oppression. . . . Extend the sphere [of representation], and you take in a greater variety of parties and interests: you make it less probable that a majority of the whole will have a common motive to invade the rights of other citizens, or if such a common motive exists, it will be more difficult for all who feel it to discover their own strength, and to act in unison with each other. . . . Where there is a consciousness of unjust or dishonorable purposes, communication is

always checked by distrust, in proportion to the number whose concurrence is necessary. (Hamilton, Madison, and Jay, *Federalist* 10, 1982, p. 48)

For modern political economists the reason for Madison's confidence in the legislature of Democratic Federalism is not obvious.[49] An example illustrates the danger. Imagine that there are three districts represented in the national legislature, and each district controls a natural resource important to the production of national output: a harbor district (H), a mineral resource district (M), and an agricultural production district (A). When property and civil rights are respected, each district contributes its efficient output of ten dollars to the national economy, and national income will be thirty dollars. Suppose, however, that District H proposes to expropriate the land from District A and turn production from food production to coffee production for increased exports. The benefit for District H will be greater use of its harbor and increased harbor incomes. With the less efficient use of land, however, District A's income falls. Finally, national food production falls, which raises the cost of living for everyone. In the end, District H's residents have a net income of twelve dollars. District M's residents lose because of higher food prices and their real incomes fall to nine dollars. District A's residents lose control of their land and also face higher food prices, so their real incomes are now only five dollars. National income falls to twenty-six dollars. If this were the entire story, both Districts A and M would oppose H's expropriation proposal and the proposal would be defeated. Madison would be right.

But this need not be the end of the story. H might think strategically and play District A against District M. Rather than introduce an expropriation bill against District A, H might first go to A and propose expropriation of M's mineral rights and a reallocation from coal production to bauxite production to again increase exports. This again increases H's income to twelve dollars, now lowers M's income to five dollars, and raises the costs of heating homes to everyone, thus lowering A's real income to nine dollars. Now both Districts M and A are at risk. If they can coordinate their strategies, they should both vote against expropriation whenever H suggests the policy. Yet every year there is the risk that the other district will agree with H—indeed, H should sweeten the deal by offering to discount the harbor fees for whomever joins its coalition. Fearing the other district will join with H, now M and A may rush to defect and agree to expropriation. Matters can be even more precarious. Since Districts M and A also control an important natural resource, they too

---

49. See Weingast (1997, 2005).

might play the expropriation game against the other districts. Now Madison may have it wrong. There is no guarantee that a national legislature of diffused interests will protect property and civil rights.

When might the expropriation game be held in check and Madison's conjecture prove correct? Four assumptions need to hold. First, protected rights must be collectively recognized as rights and the consequences of violating rights must be clearly understood. Second, violating rights, while perhaps beneficial to some, must be costly in the long run to a majority. Third, all affected legislators and their constituents must be sufficiently farsighted so that the long-run benefits of protecting rights are more valuable than the short-run benefits of joining an expropriation coalition. Fourth, to control the "race to expropriation," all legislators must be committed to the collective protection of those rights, *provided* all others have that commitment too. These four assumptions are what is needed for the legislators to escape the prisoner's dilemma embedded within the expropriation game that might be played in any one legislative session.[50] As Madison himself stressed, multiple factions are needed within the legislature, and the more the better: "In an equal degree does the [i]ncreased variety of parties, compromised within the Union, [i]ncrease this security. Does it, in fine, consist in the greater obstacles opposed to the concert and accomplishments of the secret wishes of an unjust and interested majority? Here again, the extent of the Union gives it the most palpable advantage" (Hamilton, Madison, and Jay, *Federalist* 10, 1982, p. 48).

The first legislatures following the approval of the U.S. Constitution were successful in protecting one right, the free expression of religion, but not so with another, freedom of the press. The first three conditions for the legislative protection of rights were met in both cases. First, both were publicly recognized and codified in the Bill of Rights. Second, there is little doubt that these rights were highly valued by the citizens at the time of the adoption of new constitution. Initial approval of the Constitution by all the states required a promise for inclusion of an explicit bill of rights, and approval of that bill was one of the first important acts of the new legislature.[51] Third, the enduring nature of both rights

---

50. See Weingast (1997).

51. See Rakove (1996, chap. 5) and particularly McConnell (1990). The consequential importance of religious freedom, free speech, and a free press should be contrasted with some of the other candidates for inclusion in the Bill of Rights. Proposed for inclusion, for example, was the right to "fowl and hunt in seasonable times . . . and in a like manner to fish in all navigable waters without being restrained" (Rakove, 1996, p. 330).

was recognized explicitly in the debate over their inclusion in the Bill of Rights.[52] What was true for freedom of religious expression but not for the freedom of the press was meeting Madison's fourth requirement, that of having multiple legislative factions jointly committed to the protection of the right.

That this requirement was met with regard to the protection of religious freedom is clear from the wide variety of religious backgrounds of the legislators. The wide geographical dispersion of religions across the states ensured a diversity of religious representation in the legislature. With the exception of Connecticut, Massachusetts, and New Hampshire (83 percent or more of the churches, Congregational) and Virginia (76 percent or more of the churches, Anglican), all other states had at least two significant religious sects (Delaware, Georgia, Maine, Maryland, North Carolina, and Rhode Island), and often as many as four (New York) or five (New Jersey, Pennsylvania, and South Carolina).[53] Along with the first three of Madison's requirements, having multiple factions represented in the legislature ensured no significant challenges to the free expression of religion from the early congresses.[54]

Not so for the freedom of the press. In the summer of 1798, Congress passed the Alien and Sedition Acts, which challenged directly the constitutionally promised rights of free political expression. Congress at the time was dominated by a single political party, the Federalists, led by Alexander Hamilton and President John Adams. The intent of both pieces of legislation was to limit the political influence of the minority party, the Democratic-Republican Party, led by Madison and Vice President Thomas Jefferson. The Alien Act gave the president the power to deport any foreign-born resident deemed dangerous to the peace of the nation. Immigrants were important supporters of the Democratic-Republicans. The Sedition Act was directed at the press critical of President Adams, the Federalist Congress, and their policies. A particular target was the Democratic-Republican paper, the *Aurora*. In one editorial, Benjamin Franklin Bache (Franklin's grandson) accused the "blind, bald, crippled,

---

52. That the rights of free religious expression and of free speech were seen as "permanent" or "far-sighted" is evident in the widely shared view of the rights as "inalienable" or "fundamental" and ones from which other civil or "alienable" rights might be derived; see Beer (1993, pp. 270–278).

53. See Gaustad and Barlow (2001, appendix B).

54. Nor from the individual states. Beginning with Vermont's entry into the Union in 1786, all new states formally recognized religious freedom as a right, made no commitment to an "established" church, and prohibited religious tests for public office; see Lambert (2003, p. 288).

toothless, querulous Adams" of nepotism and kingly ambitions.[55] Bache was arrested in 1798 but died before his trial. There were twenty-five arrests of journalists for libel and seventeen indictments under the act, mostly of journalists employed by Democratic-Republican newspapers in Federalist-dominated states.[56] Five of the six most prominent Democratic-Republican papers were prosecuted by Federalist-appointed judges under the new laws.[57] The acts clearly targeted the growing influence of the minority political party of Madison and Jefferson. In this instance, the national legislature alone was not sufficient protection for a fundamental right.

Protection for a free press ultimately came from two institutions outside the national legislature. First, Madison and Jefferson mobilized the Democratic-Republican Party to defeat the Federalists and gain control of Congress and to elect Jefferson as president. Second, President Jefferson used his executive powers to not enforce the acts and then allowed both acts to expire.[58] The right of free speech was protected not by a Madisonian consensus in the national legislature but by the use of two nonlegislative institutions, political parties and a nationally elected president.[59] We evaluate the potential contributions of both institutions to the goals of Democratic Federalism in Chapter 5.

Economic Fairness

For Madison in *Federalist* No. 51, "justice is the [aim] of government . . . the [aim] of civil society." And to this end, the *"republican cause . . .* carried to a very great extent by a judicious modification and mixture of the *federal*

---

55. Miller (1951, p. 29).

56. J. M. Smith (1956, pp. 185–187).

57. Chernow (2004, p. 575).

58. Miller (1951, p. 230).

59. Madison also proposed a third line of defense against legislative abuse, but it too can fail without cooperation among the affected districts or states. In *Federalist* No. 46, he stated the hope that the politically independent states would rise in unison to oppose any national legislative threat to citizen rights, a line of defense promoted by Rapaczynski (1985) in his argument for the legal protection of state governments and developed more formally by de Figueiredo and Weingast (2005). In the case of the Alien and Sedition Acts, this did not happen. Madison wrote a resolution of resistance to the acts for the state of Virginia and Jefferson did the same for Kentucky. The Virginia and Kentucky resolutions specifically challenged the acts as a violation of the Constitution and its protections for the freedom of speech and the freedom of the press. The resolutions were a call for all states to act in unison against the national government. All Federalist state legislatures rejected the resolutions. See Miller (1951, pp. 169–181).

principle" can ensure a government where the strong and well endowed "submit to a government which may protect the weak as well as themselves" (Hamilton, Madison, and Jay, 1982, p. 265; italics in the original). It is an argument that Madison's predecessors (Harrington) and followers (Philip Pettit) have equated with greater equality of physical assets (specifically farm land, for Harrington) and human capabilities (specifically education, health, and shelter for Pettit).[60] How well, then, might Democratic Federalism's legislature do in ensuring economic fairness? Its impact turns on three decisions. The first is a decision by the national government to pay transfers for low-income support, national health insurance, and old-age pensions. The second is the decision to use national taxes for the financing of "meritorious" local goods and services. The third is the decision to adopt a proportional or progressive national tax structure.

In setting policy, the legislature must live within its means and spend no more than the national tax base allows. National revenues are determined by the national average tax rate (t) multiplied by the national tax base per citizen (B), where, because of the likely adverse incentive effects of tax rates on work effort, savings, and investment, the tax base will be a declining function of the tax rate. Total revenues per citizen will equal $t \cdot B(t)$. Total revenues rise with the tax rate, but when tax rates are very high, the loss of tax base may more than offset the increase in tax rates and revenues may actually decline. There will be a "revenue hill" where revenues rise as rates rise, reach a maximum at a tax rate, t^{max}, and then decline.[61] Given the legislature's choice of the average tax rate, resulting revenues per citizen will then be allocated to pay for transfers per citizen, τ (low-income assistance, old-age pensions, health insurance);[62] for national public goods spending per citizen, g (national defense, infrastructure, and repayment of national debt); and for the financing or direct provision of local public goods per citizen, x. The legislature's budget constraint is therefore $t \cdot B(t) = \tau + g + x$.

60. For a discussion of Harrington's argument for a more equitable distribution of farmlands, see Beer (1993, chap. 3) and for a republican argument for a more equitable distribution of essential goods, see Pettit (1997, chap. 5).

61. Most national economies are still on the rising portion of their national revenue hill. Estimates for the U.S. economy suggest that t^{max} is in the range of .71 to .89; see Gruber and Saez (2002).

62. For simplicity, we treat all transfer programs as one. For evidence that, at least in the United States, policy-makers do view the transfer budget as "one program," treating increased assistance in one program (e.g., food stamps and health benefits) as compensation for a reduction of benefits in another (income aid), see Moffitt (1990).

The legislature must choose t, τ, g, and x, but because of the discipline of the national budget constraint, any three fiscal choices will dictate the fourth.[63] We will assume that the legislature focuses on spending, by choosing transfers to households and the level of national and district public goods. Given spending, the government's budget constraint specifies the level of needed revenues, and thus the national average tax rate.[64]

How, then, will the national legislature make its spending choices? In Section 3 we argued that the legislature will defer to the national median (usually median-income) voter when setting the levels of national public goods and to the individual legislators from each district when setting the levels of local public goods spending to each district. Having set the level of national and local public goods, the budgetary choice now reduces to deciding the level of transfers and the national average tax rate. There will be one national transfer for all citizens and one resulting national average tax rate.

What should we expect? Constituents with high incomes, good health, and well-funded private pensions will want their district representative to vote for low transfers and thus a low tax rate. Middle-income households facing income, health, and retirement uncertainties will want their representative to vote for a modest transfer as social insurance and a middle-level tax rate. Finally, poorer, sicker, and older constituents will want a guaranteed high transfer financed by a high average tax rate. Under Democratic Federalism the legislature will decide the transfer and, from the budget constraint, the national tax rate. The redistributive preferences of the median legislator will be decisive. If the distribution of constituent preferences in the legislature approximates

63. For simplicity, we ignore the level of national debt. Having the option to borrow to finance transfers, national public goods, and local goods is a temptation that U legislatures may not be able to resist; see Velasco (2000). The use of debt to finance current services raises the possibility of redistribution from future to current generations and the need to consider intergenerational equity as well. See Auerbach and Kotlikoff (1987) for the theory and Gokhale and Smetters (2003) for an application to U.S. fiscal policy.

64. Assuming the legislature first selects spending and then takes the tax rate as given from the budget constraint seems to conform well with how legislatures actually decide their budgets. The 1974 passage of the Congressional Budget and Impoundment Control Act sought to reverse the sequence by first setting the tax rate and revenues using budgetary committees to set aggregate spending and revenue targets. It was thought this might bring discipline to what had been seen as a runaway spending process; see Penner and Abramson (1988). It has not worked. The constraint has rarely proved binding and the Budget Committee recommendations have evolved into guidelines rather than constraints.

the distribution of voter preferences generally, then the legislature will choose a level of national transfers and the degree of tax progressivity around the average tax rate.[65] If so, the final choice for redistributive transfers will be similar in structure, if not the exact level of financing, to that under Economic Federalism.[66]

In one respect, however, Democratic Federalism may be more equitable than either Economic or Cooperative Federalism. This is the financing of local public goods through the national (not local) tax base when the national legislature decides local goods as a U legislature. As argued in Chapters 2 and 3, community sorting by incomes and local financing under Economic and Cooperative Federalism is likely to lead to significant inequities in the financing and provision of local goods. Residents of lower-income communities face higher tax rates and receive less in services than residents in middle- and upper-income communities. If these local services—for example, education, safety, or environment quality—are viewed by society as "merit wants" and essential to the lifetime welfare of residents, then a significant societal inequity results. One solution is to give all communities access to the same tax base when purchasing those services.[67] This in fact occurs under Democratic Federalism with a U legislature. Here each local district finances local public goods spending from the national tax base, paying only its share of all national spending for local goods. The "effective" price for district public goods is approximately the same for all districts (as shown in Figure 4.3) and significantly lower

65. See Snyder and Kramer (1988).

66. The U.S. Congress, for example, uses a single tax or budget "committees of the whole" to represent each segment of the legislative preference distribution when setting transfer policy; see Ferejohn (1986). This committee process then identifies the median legislator as the decisive voter on transfer policies; see Bartels, Clinton, and Greer (2014). Finally, for evidence that this median legislator is likely to represent constituents with the median income or age, see Meltzer and Richard (1981) generally; Krusell and Ríos-Rull (1999), and Bredemeier (2014) with applications to income transfer policies; Gouveia (1997) and Jacob and Lundin (2005) for an application to national health insurance; and Boadway and Wildasin (1989), Congleton and Shughart (1990), and Cooley and Soares (1996) for an application to old-age pension insurance.

67. A policy first proposed by Coons, Clune, and Sugarman (1970) in response to inequities in the financing and allocation of local education. The policy was called "District Power Equalization." School districts retained control (District Power) over the level of local spending, but all financing was done through the taxation of a common (Equalization) state or national tax base. See Box 2.5. For the design of national policies to address these inequities, see Inman (1978).

than local costs, resulting in an increase in local public goods spending in all districts.[68] It is likely that the increase in spending will be relatively greater in the poorer districts, and as a result, the *relative* gap in the provision of local public goods is "tighter" with a U legislature.[69] For socially meritorious local goods—education, safety, environmental quality—this is a significant equity advantage for the U legislature and thus Democratic Federalism.

But All Begins with the Franchise

Increased representation, greater protection of rights, and increased economic fairness each begins with the representation of *all* citizens in the national legislature of Democratic Federalism. This is not guaranteed, certainly not in the first years following the adoption of the U.S. Constitution. Voter eligibility was decided then by individual states and was typically limited to free, male property owners. Excluded from the franchise were most African Americans, all women, and all without sufficient wealth. Property qualifications for the vote were removed gradually over the new democracy's first seventy years, but by state decisions, not the national legislature. The vote was not extended to all male citizens without regard to race or color until 1870 with the passage of the Fifteenth Amendment. Universal suffrage for women was not available until approval of the Nineteenth Amendment in 1920. Indigenous peoples were allowed to vote only after 1924. In 1971, the Twenty-Sixth Amendment lowered the voting age to eighteen, the same age at which a citizen qualifies for military service. In each instance the central impetus for extending the franchise came

---

68. The same reduction in the price of local public goods also occurs when an MWC decides local spending, but here only the agenda-setter benefits from the large fall in the price of local public goods. Thus there are no significant equity gains in the provision of local public goods under MWC politics.

69. The *relative* impact of national financing on local provision is determined by the relative price elasticities of demand in poor and rich communities. Price elasticities are likely to be greater for communities with a lower initial level of services—that is, in poorer communities. If so, the percentage increase in spending for local goods with national financing will be greater in poorer districts than in richer districts, and thus the relative gap measured by the ratio of richer to poorer district spending or the coefficient of variation of spending will narrow. Whether national financing closes the *absolute* difference in spending between richer and poorer districts will most likely require larger price reductions for poorer communities than richer communities. That will require that the U legislature adopt a specific policy to reduce local public goods prices—for example, a matching grant with higher matching rates for poorer communities.

not from the national legislature but rather from outside pressures originating within individual states or from a strong president or national political parties. Perhaps not a surprising outcome, given that each year's representatives to the national legislature are responsible only to the current voters who elected them into office. Extending the franchise and thus the benefits of participation, rights protection, and economic fairness to all citizens will require institutions beyond Democratic Federalism's single, national legislature. What those additional institutions might be is addressed in Chapter 5.

6. Summing Up

Democratic Federalism has been offered as an alternative to Economic and Cooperative Federalism and in four important respects accomplishes what we had hoped. First, Democratic Federalism will provide a level of national public goods and spillovers that closely approximates that preferred by the representative from the median, most likely median-income, legislative district. In the special case in which national mean and median preferences and incomes are equal, the median legislator's choice will be economically efficient. In the more realistic case in which mean preferences and income are greater than median preferences and incomes, legislative politics creates offsetting biases. Median preferences less than mean preferences imply a demand for too little of each national public good, but median incomes less than mean incomes implies a tax subsidy from richer to poorer taxpayers leading to a demand for too much of a each public good. Exactly where the median legislator sets national public goods will then be uncertain, but it is not likely to lie too far from the efficient level, and in any case near that provided under Economic Federalism, where policies are set by the national median (typically median-income) presidential voter. Both Economic and Democratic Federalism are likely to dominate the national public goods performance of Cooperative Federalism.

Second, compared with Economic and Cooperative Federalism, Democratic Federalism is likely to provide more, and more responsive, channels for representation and thus for greater democratic participation. Our empirical analysis finds that voter turnout both in the United States and internationally is slightly higher in federal rather than in unitary democracies. Perhaps more importantly, Democratic Federalism provides a participatory channel not available to either Economic or Cooperative Federalism—called the personal vote. The personal vote provides the opportunity for citizens to communicate directly with their representatives to the national government over the level and allocation of national and local goods and individual income transfers.

Third, Democratic Federalism is likely to provide better protection for individual rights and liberties than either Economic or Cooperative Federalism, provided four conditions are met: (1) rights are mutually recognized as beneficial; (2) violating rights is costly to the majority of citizens; (3) all citizens take the long view when evaluating the benefits of protecting rights; and (4) legislators are willing to cooperate, provided others cooperate, in the protection of those rights. While there will be examples in which these assumptions are violated and legislative protections are not enough, on balance Democratic Federalism's rights performance is seen to dominate that of either Economic or Cooperative Federalism.

Fourth, the distribution of national incomes and the access to national public goods are likely to be at least as fair under Democratic Federalism as under Economic Federalism, and both are likely to dominate the equity performance of Cooperative Federalism. In the provision of local public goods considered "meritorious" or essential for achieving one's life prospects—most notably, education—allocations under Democratic Federalism are likely to be more equitable than those of either Economic or Cooperative Federalism. In contrast to Economic and Cooperative Federalism, which finance such goods from a local and inequitably distributed tax base, Democratic Federalism, with policies decided by a U legislature, will finance local goods from a shared national tax base. Increased equity in the provision of local public goods as merit wants is the likely result.

For all its virtues, Democratic Federalism has two weaknesses. First, from the sharing of costs of localized public goods through the national tax base, national legislators are likely to overspend on local public goods. The resulting inefficiencies can be significant, perhaps as much as 3 to 6 percent of a typical family's income, and in the limit, as in Brazil, bankrupt the national treasury. Second, for all its ability to protect minority rights and to provide redistributive goods and services, Democratic Federalism only succeeds for all citizens when all citizens are represented within the legislature. There is little reason to believe, however, that an existing national legislature will voluntarily open its doors to the disenfranchised. Correcting these two weaknesses will require extralegislative institutions. This is our agenda for Chapter 5.

5

Democratic Federalism

THE SAFEGUARDS

1. Introduction

The central institution of Democratic Federalism as envisioned by James Madison is a locally elected national legislature. The legislature is to set national policies for protecting the new republic, for managing the national economy, for resolving disputes between the local governments, and perhaps most importantly, for ensuring the constitutionally defined rights of all citizens. But as Madison and Alexander Hamilton both appreciated, all is not perfect. Governance by a single, locally elected national legislature runs the serious risk of abusing the national tax base by favoring local over national policies and, unless all citizen interests are represented and influential within the legislature, may create majorities that ignore or even actively deny the rights, liberties, and future opportunities of politically isolated minorities. A national legislature is a start toward constructing Democratic Federalism, but it cannot be the end.

Achieving the goals of efficiency, representation, and ensured rights and liberties will require additional institutional safeguards beyond those provided by a national legislature. Only then might we hope to have, in Jenna Bednar's (2009) words, a truly "robust federation." The formal (constitutionally based) institutions we consider here are those advocated by Madison in *Federalist* No. 51 and elaborated on throughout *The Federalist Papers* by Madison and Hamilton. They include a second legislative chamber called a senate, a nationally elected president, and an appointed supreme court. We also follow the counsel of William Riker (1964), who urged the contribution of competitive political parties as an additional, informal (organically derived) safeguard for a robust federation. When taken together with a national legislature, a senate, a president, a supreme court, and competitive political parties provide the full structure for Democratic Federalism. It is a structure that retains the virtues of a national legislature as a voice for local interests and minorities while providing a sequence of checks for when those voices ask for too much or fail to listen to the less vocal, or the unheard, before speaking.

Section 2 describes how the three constitutionally created institutions might strengthen the performance of the national legislature. Section 3 then considers the ability of independent political parties to improve legislative performance. Section 4 evaluates the potential gain in economic efficiency, representation, and the protection of rights from these safeguards. Section 5 concludes.

2. Madison's "Auxiliary Precautions": Senate, President, and Supreme Court

While the contributions of a popularly elected legislature were well appreciated by the Founding Fathers, so too were its weaknesses. Madison in *Federalist* No. 48 worried that "the legislative department is everywhere extending the sphere of its activity, and drawing all power into its impetuous vortex" (Hamilton, Madison, and Jay, 1982, pp. 250–251). For Madison, this inevitable appetite for influence and resources was not a reason to abandon a locally elected, national legislature, but rather a motivation to design institutional protections against the legislature's *impetuous* overreaching. In *Federalist* No. 51, the essay that outlines the full structure of Democratic Federalism, Madison stresses that "dependence on the people is no doubt the primary control of government" but also that "experience has taught mankind the necessity of auxiliary precautions" (Hamilton, Madison, and Jay, 1982, p. 262).

Madison's Virginia Plan, presented at the opening of the U.S. Constitutional Convention, offered three such safeguards: a second legislative chamber, the *Senate*, directly representing state governments; a nationally elected *president* to administer all approved statutes; and an independent *Supreme Court* to ensure that the legislature and the president adhere to the Constitution and its amendments. All funding for government activities will originate in the popularly elected national legislature, but the Senate must also approve any national law, policy, or budget. The Senate therefore has veto power over national legislature's policies. The president will administer all legislation, although the Senate must approve all important administrative appointments. In addition, the president can also be granted veto powers over any legislation approved by the national legislature and the Senate, although the veto may be overridden if both the national legislature and the Senate subsequently approve the law with two-thirds majorities in each chamber. Finally, the Supreme Court can invalidate any law or administrative action that, in the opinion of the justices, violates the Constitution and its amendments. Members of the Supreme Court will be appointed by the president, subject to the approval of the Senate. In the end, each branch of the national government will have been assigned constitutionally protected powers independent of the other branches and, within those powers, come to hold an institutional check on the other's actions. Understanding how these auxiliary checks might work in practice to improve the performance of the locally elected, national legislature is our task here.[1]

Adding a Senate

As a second chamber in a bicameral legislature, the Senate will have effective veto powers over policies approved by the national legislature. While both chambers need to approve any national policy, the Senate is designed to ensure direct representation to the national government of geographically wider jurisdictions composed of multiple congressional districts. For the United States this will be states; for Canada, provinces; for Australia, states; for Switzerland, cantons; and for Germany, länder. To take a U.S. perspective, states facilitate coordination among local communities and congressional districts for the provision of local public goods with spillovers or with economies of scale that exceed the capacity of local communities. They also represent wider, regional interests that might not be well represented by more locally focused district legislators. Each state sends at least one representative to the Senate, either directly elected or appointed by the state legislature. Madison hoped that the Senate, in addition to serving wider regional interests, could be a more reflective legislative chamber to counterbalance the immediate and pressing local interests represented in the national legislature.[2] To this end, Madison

1. Our focus is on how each new institution checks the popularly elected national legislature. However, each branch also checks the others. See de Figueiredo, Jacobi, and Weingast (2006) for a complete survey of the political economy of checks and balances.

2. Debates within U.S. constitutional law have assigned a third role to the U.S. Senate, that of protector of local government policy responsibilities within the institutional structure of federal governance. Wechsler (1954) hoped that the Senate, as the more farsighted legislative chamber, might stand as a check of national government intrusions. It remained for Kramer (2000, sec. 3) to offer a complete theory of the Senate's role in the U.S. federal system by tying

proposed six-year terms with one-third of the chamber up for reelection every two years.[3]

How many senators should represent each state is the final matter to be decided. Representation proportional to population was favored by Madison in his original Virginia Plan, presented to the U.S. Constitutional Convention. Small states naturally objected, however, and favored the alternative New Jersey Plan, which gave each state, large or small, two representatives to the Senate. Madison's proposal creates a particular difficulty for representation. If the smallest state is to have at least one representative and the ratio of large to small state populations is ten to one, for example, then the largest state will have ten senators and all other states some number between ten and one. With proportional representation, the total number of senators can become very large very quickly, with the risk of undermining Madison's hope that the Senate would be a small, deliberative chamber capable of checking the larger national legislature. To that end, the Constitution could recognize only a few large states of approximately equal populations, but at the possible cost of sacrificing original state boundaries. This was likely to be politically very difficult and would prove to be an administrative nightmare over time as state boundaries were redrawn. Further, large state boundaries would likely severely limit the legislative influence of minorities. Though not without its own potential problem of a "small state bias," the writers of the U.S. Constitution chose to use uniform representation—two senators—from each state.

With each state given an equal number of senators, how then might the Senate make policies and operate as a potential check on the overreaching and economically inefficient national legislature? Jowei Chen and Neil Malhotra (2007) provide the framework needed to answer this question. As Madison suspected, policy outcomes turn crucially on the ratio of the number of representatives in the national legislature (for the U.S., the House of Representatives) (N) to the number of senators (S).

Where Senate control will be most beneficial is in checking the locally elected national legislature's propensity to inefficiently overspend on local public goods

---

the election of senators to locally organized political parties and local financing of Senate campaigns. On the importance of local political parties, see below at Section 5.3.

3. Riker (1955) found that the originally appointed senators were rarely disciplined by their state legislatures when they voted against state interests and in favor of national policies. The Seventeenth Amendment, passed in 1913, finally allowed for the direct election of U.S. senators.

financed from the national treasury, as argued in Chapter 4. What is needed is for the individual legislators to recognize the negative fiscal externalities they impose on other legislators. Chen and Malhotra argued that the Senate can do so by internalizing the fiscal externalities between local representatives, at least *within* each state. Intuitively, the senator from each state must win the support of his or her median voter from the state as a whole. One means for doing so is to promise state citizens a more efficient use of national resources by consolidating all the small projects from the individual state legislative districts into a more efficient "total" project that is shared equally among the individual districts. Residents of each district get less of the statewide project than what they might have gotten without consolidation, but their individual savings in less national taxation may more than compensate them for their loss of project benefits. *Importantly, however, all other senators must agree to behave in a similar way to reap the full benefits of smaller projects and lower national taxation.*

As was necessary for the national legislature, the Senate must also solve the problem of cycling among policy alternatives. Like the legislature, the Senate has two choices: minimum winning coalition (MWC) or universalistic (U) politics. Fortunately, both lead to a beneficial outcome. Chen and Malhotra get cooperation by having an MWC agenda-setter propose a set of more efficient statewide budgets as an all-or-nothing choice to the full Senate. A majority of senators get a project for their state, a minority get nothing, and the more efficient Senate budget is approved. An alternative version of Senate voting would allow all senators to submit their own preferred, more efficient state budget, provided all other senators do the same. This is the Senate's version of universalism. Like the U legislature, a U Senate will need a Senate committee capable of assembling and then enforcing the cooperative, more efficient omnibus budget for state goods. The U.S. Senate has such a committee, the Appropriations Committee, which checks the legislature's spending bill. The committee then combines the individually more efficient state goods budgets into a single omnibus budget bill for a single Senate vote. All states get some state goods with the U Senate budget, but fewer than proposed with the original U legislature. Against the alternatives of no state goods or accepting the inefficient U legislature's budget, the U Senate will unanimously support the more efficient Senate budget. In both versions of Senate voting, the Senate approves a more efficient state budget.

The efficiency gain from Senate budgeting for local goods when Senate votes as a U Senate is shown in Figure 5.1, a reproduction of Figure 4.3. The typical resident's marginal benefit from a local public good is curve *MB*, and

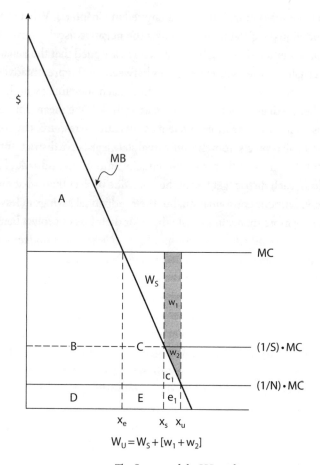

FIGURE 5.1. The Senate and the U Legislature

the average cost curve to a district's average resident is $(1/N) \cdot MC$. For these district benefits and costs, the district's legislator will prefer x_u for the residents of his or her district. But the level of each of the district's local public good that the state's senator prefers will depend on the tax cost of local goods to the average statewide resident. The reality of state politics has the senator assuming a statewide perspective when buying a local public good for residents in each of the state's legislative districts. If the legislator votes in favor of more of the local good for one state resident, he or she will need to vote for more for all other state residents. The senator will therefore internalize the fiscal costs of one more unit of any one district's local good as the cost to the entire state. Within a U Senate, the marginal tax cost of any local good received by the state will be $(1/S) \cdot MC$, where S is the number of all states sharing the aggregate tax burden associated with supplying that local good.

Since senators will want to do as well as they can for their average citizen, they will propose x_s, where the average state resident's marginal benefit equals his or her statewide marginal tax cost: $MB = (1/S) \cdot MC$. If there are fewer senators than legislators, then $S < N$ and therefore $(1/S) \cdot MC > (1/N) \cdot MC$. As a result, $x_s < x_u$. The typical senator prefers less of the state good for state residents than what his or her own district legislators would have preferred for their district residents. As S falls relative to N, x_s moves closer and closer to x_e, and efficiency improves. By focusing on the benefits and costs to all residents in his or her state, the senator internalizes some of the fiscal inefficiencies each of the state's legislators had ignored by representing only a small fraction of state residents. It is this more inclusive perspective, one that grows in importance as S falls relative to N, that encourages the Senate to adopt a more efficient provision of local goods.

The potential efficiency gain from the U Senate's reduction in the local good is the shaded area $[w_1 + w_2]$ in Figure 5.1. This area is equal to the tax savings that all citizens enjoy by paying less for the state good—area $[e_1 + c_1 + w_1 + w_2]$—minus the economic benefits now lost because of the reduction in the level of the state good provided—area $[e_1 + c_1]$. The net gain is area $[w_1 + w_2]$. Area $[W_S]$ still remains as an economic inefficiency.

Three comments are in order. First, the smaller the Senate is relative to the national legislature, the greater the reduction in x_s relative to x_u and the greater the potential efficiency gain from adding a Senate chamber to legislative deliberations. Second, senators from larger states with more legislative districts will internalize more within state fiscal externalities, reduce x_s even more than shown in Figure 5.1, and therefore offer even greater overall efficiency gains. In contrast, senators from smaller states with few legislative districts will reduce x_s less than average, and thus offer less efficiency gains. In the extreme, if the state has only one legislative district—Alaska, Delaware, Montana, North and South Dakota, and Wyoming in the United States—the senator will have the same incentives to provide the state good as the national legislator, and $x_s = x_u$. The result is the "small state bias" in the Senate provision of state goods.

Third, to achieve the full efficiency gains shown as the shaded area $[w_1 + w_2]$, all senators must cooperate and agree to collectively trim their state spending from x_u to x_s. If one senator alone were to cut his or her state's spending, that state's citizens would continue to lose all the associated benefits of area $[e_1 + c_1]$, but gain in return only the state residents' share $(1/S)$ of the overall tax savings, or area $[e_1 + c_1 + w_1 + w_2]$. There is a small net surplus of the area

$[w_2]$ for the state from being so publicly minded, though perhaps not large enough to persuasively appease state citizens directly harmed.

There is a final question: Since both chambers must agree, will the national legislature accept the smaller, more efficient local goods budget proposed by the Senate? The answer will turn on the ability of each state's senator to convince that state's district representatives that the efficiency gains are substantial and that the political credit for those gains can be jointly shared when running for reelection. Here Madison relies on his hope that senators can "refine" the private interests of the popularly elected legislators to support legislation in the public interest.[4] A politically more realistic view in today's politics might turn to the use of local political parties as an organizing agent, as Larry Kramer (2000) suggested. Either on merit or by strategically sharing local political gains, the national legislature will then accept the Senate's more efficient budget. If so, the Senate is decisive, and Madison's hope that the Senate could check the "impetuous" lower chamber will be realized.

What is the evidence? Does the Senate reduce local goods spending in bicameral legislatures, and will decreasing the number of "states" or senators lead to a larger reduction in government spending? The answer to both questions is yes. Requiring the approval of a smaller Senate has been shown to constrain spending by the larger, locally elected legislature in most U.S. states.[5] The results are consistent on two points. First, testing as to which of $(1/N)$ or $(1/S)$ is the decisive tax share in determining the level of state spending for local goods finds that it is only the share related to the size of the upper chamber, $(1/S) \cdot MC$, and not that of the lower chamber, $(1/N) \cdot MC$, that significantly affects state spending. Second, holding fixed the size of state population, reducing the size of the Senate reduces the level of state goods spending. This is what would be expected when there are more citizens represented by each senator, and thus each senator has the ability to internalize more of the "common pool" of fiscal externalities associated with local goods budgeting. Finally, the reduction in spending from having fewer senators is greatest where the potential problem of fiscal externalities with large legislatures is most pronounced—that is, the spending declines increase as the ratio N/S increases. The Senate provides the most discipline, when discipline is most needed.[6]

4. Beer (1993, p. 115).

5. See Gilligan and Matsusaka (1995, 2001), Primo (2006), and J. Chen and Malhotra (2007).

6. Small state bias could in theory offset the efficiency gains. The extent of the bias is typically small, however; see Atlas et al. (1995), Lee (1998), Ansolabehere, Gerber, and Snyder (2002), and Inman (2010).

Adding a President

As he had for the Senate, Madison, along with Alexander Hamilton, made the case for a nationally elected and institutionally strong president as a further check on the powers of the locally elected, national legislature. In *Federalist* No. 73, Hamilton argued for the importance of a president elected from a national constituency, separate from the direct influence of either the national legislature or the Senate, and with the power to veto legislative actions found unacceptable given the national electoral mandate. The veto would serve two important functions: first, as a "shield" to protect the presidency and the judiciary from "intrusions" by the legislature into their constitutionally assigned powers, and second, to provide "an additional security against the enaction of improper laws" (Hamilton, Madison, and Jay, 1982, p. 372). On the last working day of the Constitutional Convention, the delegates choose a two-thirds majority as the legislative threshold needed to overturn a presidential veto.

With only a two-thirds legislative threshold for an override, however, Madison in *Federalist* No. 51 feared that the veto "would be neither altogether safe, nor alone sufficient" (Hamilton, Madison, and Jay, 1982, p. 263). Confronting a universalistic national legislature, this concern is well founded. A U legislature would have no difficulty in overriding the veto and has every incentive to do so. Madison's solution was to give the president the responsibility to appoint all judges, to "execute" (that is, administer) all laws approved by the two legislative chambers, and to serve as the single commander in chief of the national military. Madison and Hamilton hoped that the positive powers of appointment and administration might be leveraged with the negative power of the veto to influence legislative decisions in the best interest of the national population.[7]

How the president's positive powers might be joined with veto powers to constrain an overreaching national legislature is seen in Figure 5.2.[8] Area $[W_u]$ measures the resulting social waste in each legislative district created by the incentives inherent in a U legislature's decision-making. A president with "positive powers" of appointment and administration can fashion a more efficient budget and, importantly, benefit politically.[9] The "negative power" of the veto can then be used to

---

7. See Beer (1993, p. 289) and *Federalist* No. 73.

8. The analysis here for presidential control of the U legislature follows that in Fitts and Inman (1992). McCarty (2000) reached similar conclusions but for presidential control of an MWC legislature.

9. In an important series of articles on legislative oversight of the executive branch, McCubbins, Noll, and Weingast (aka "McNollgast"; 1987, 1989) have argued that the legislature can

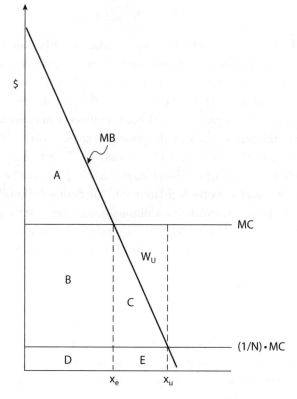

FIGURE 5.2. The President and the U Legislature

leverage presidential positive powers and thereby lower the costs to the president of politically beneficial reform policies.

Here's how. Presidential influence begins with information. The president will be presenting a coalition of legislators with a sequence of "all-or-nothing" bargains to persuade each to join a presidential reform coalition to vote down the initially inefficient budget of x_u in favor of a smaller budget spending x_e for coalition members and perhaps other districts as well. To propose this more efficient budget, the president will need to know x_e. Of course, if asked, legislators have an incentive to lie, saying x_u is efficient.

Who then provides the required information? Here the president has a significant institutional advantage that arises from his or her constitutional

---

significantly constrain the president's use of his or her positive powers by structuring the administration of the laws to favor legislative oversight. In response, Moe and Wilson (1994) argue that significant discretion remains within the executive branch.

powers to administer legislative policies. First, the administering agencies may have direct contact with the residents of legislative districts and often work directly with the district legislators to be sure residents get what they need and want. Second, the permanent bureaucracy of the executive branch has significant accumulated knowledge of the costs and impacts of legislative policies, and it is relatively easy to go from impacts to plausible estimates of constituent benefits. Finally, the president has access to outside experts. Importantly, this informational advantage lies with the executive alone, leading Cass Sunstein (2016) to call the executive branch the "most knowledgeable branch" and to recommend significant deference to presidential decision-making in the formation and implementation of government policies. With knowledge of district MB curves, and thus x_e, the president can begin to form his or her more efficient legislative coalition.[10]

First, the president uses his or her positive powers to offers to an individual legislator discretionary funding, or an equivalently valuable regulatory favor, treaty provision, or judicial or rule-making appointment, equal to just a "bit more" than the resources within area $[C+E]$. Area $[C+E]$ measures the benefits that the legislator's constituents now enjoy from the overprovision of the district's local public good from efficient (x_e) to inefficient (x_u) provision. The "bit more" can be called the district's "sweetener," denoted by s dollars. The sweetener first compensates for the difference in value between the good the legislature approved, presumably a "first choice" for the district's constituents, and the value of the policy favor that the president might be able to offer. The sweetener also compensates for the risk associated with the president actually paying the promised compensation, most likely to occur after the legislator has lost some of his or her district's favorite project and voted for reform. The required sweetener will be less, the more discretionary resources available to the president and the more trustworthy the president is when offering legislative deals. When offered the final compensation of {area $[C+E]+s$}, the legislator then agrees to request only the efficient level of his or her state's service.

The president builds a full reform coalition by repeating this bargain, legislator by legislator, until he or she has the majority coalition needed to pass reform. Once the majority is reached, the president then uses his or her agenda powers to submit a policy that imposes the efficient levels on all legislators, including the minority not in the president's majority coalition. Those legislators in the minority do not receive compensation for their district's lost

10. The actual process of bargaining is outlined in E. Thompson (1968).

benefits from the reform, nor do they receive the sweetener. How does the reform help the president? If successful, national taxes can be cut by the costs of the inefficient district policies, thereby saving the country as a whole area $[W_u + C + E]$ in national taxation.

There is a final question. While the president can propose an efficient policy, will the inefficient U legislature pass the reform? After reading the president's reform proposal, all legislators will then know the efficient level of each district's preferred policy. Why not now create a new legislative majority, different from the president's reform majority, whose members retain their inefficient policies, but that imposes efficient projects, or even less, on the minority? To do so would return the legislature to voting cycles among different "inefficient" majorities and the need again to choose between an MWC and a U legislature. If, in this legislative environment, a U legislature would be the likely outcome, the choice for members of the president's original reform coalition becomes: return to the inefficiencies of a U legislature *or* stay in the president's reform coalition and pass reform. With district compensation and sweetener plus a share of the tax savings from reform, the reform majority will prefer reform. It's a political win-win. The president is able to claim he or she has made the economy more efficient, and each of the majority legislators can return to their district with a share of the aggregate benefits of reform, an attractive presidential favor, and maybe even a presidential visit.

Having a veto enhances the likelihood of presidential reform. Rather than having to build a majority coalition of M $(=.5 \cdot N + 1)$ legislators, now the president will need to build only a veto coalition of V members where, if the legislature needs a two-thirds vote to override a veto, $V = .33 \cdot N + 1$. As before, the president offers compensation of $\{$area $[C + E] + s\}$ to the members of his or her veto coalition. Needing to compensate fewer legislators, the reform will therefore be less expensive in presidential resources. The president still needs a majority for approval of the reform, however. This means adding $.17 \cdot N$ legislators $(= M - V)$ to the reform coalition. He or she does so by allowing these legislators to keep their inefficient projects while still sharing in some of the reform's aggregate efficiency gains—for example, through national tax cuts. Given a reform majority, the president then imposes the efficient policies, x_e, on all remaining minority districts as before. But will this veto-based reform policy survive legislative consideration? The alternative for members of the veto-based reform majority is a choice between legislative cycling and gridlock, or a continuation of the inefficient U legislature, or reform. The president's majority will prefer reform. We again have a more efficient government, with access to a veto encouraging presidential reform of inefficient legislative policies.

Having created the institutional environment conducive to reform, the next question to ask is, Will the president find it in his or her political interest to pursue reform? The president will not act unless there is an election incentive to do so. This will depend on whether legislative overreach—the size of inefficiencies created by the U legislature—is large enough that "controlling government waste" becomes part of a compelling national platform. Estimates (from Chapter 4) suggest that, at least for the U.S. economy, efficiency losses can be significant, perhaps 3 to 6 percent of average incomes. Limiting the incentive for reform are term limits or a significant probability of losing in a future election for some noneconomic reason. The pursuit of economic efficiency is an ongoing job requiring both the institutions to control excesses and the incentives to do so. Again, what is the evidence?

Inman (1988) has estimated the effect of the Reagan presidency on national spending for local public goods (grants-in-aid) and found his budgets were as much as 22 percent below the historical trend expected from the prior decades, arguably set by a U legislature.[11] President Reagan achieved similar efficiency gains in his landmark tax legislation, called the Tax Reform Act of 1986, through his control of local district tax loopholes or "tax expenditures"; see Box 5.1.

The application of presidential powers for the control of legislative overreach is not unique to the 1980s or to the United States. Inman and Michael Fitts (1990) present evidence from the U.S. historical record that U.S. presidents considered politically "strong" from their successes outside domestic politics used that accumulated influence to discipline U legislatures. Spending on state goods and targeted tax favors was less by an average of 4 percent of GDP over a strong president's term of office. Torsten Persson and Guido Tabellini (1999) reach the same conclusion in their cross-country analysis of aggregate government spending in forty developed and less developed economies. After controlling statistically for economic and social determinants of government spending, they find that a presidential, rather than a strictly legislative, form of governance reduced aggregate national government spending by from 9 to 12 percent of GDP against a sample mean of 29 percent.

---

11. Reagan adopted the same approach for his reform of the federal funding of local dams, levies, and harbors. He again succeeded in cutting federal spending, here by as much as 16 percent of the prereform levels; see DelRossi and Inman (1999).

Box 5.1. Presidential Powers and the Tax Reform Act of 1986

Tax policy requires two decisions—first the tax base, then the tax rate. Both were at issue in the Tax Reform Act of 1986 (TRA86) when President Reagan used his veto and administrative powers to fashion major reforms of both for the U.S. federal tax code. Taxable income for households and firms is measured as earned income—wages, interest, and profits for households, and interest and profits for firms—less the expenses needed to earn that income and less deductions and exemptions. Importantly, as the taxpayer's use of deductions and exemptions increases, his or her final tax payment falls in relation to taxable income and the tax rate that is applied to that income. The product of the tax rate and volume of deductions for favored activities is labeled as "tax expenditures." Activities that qualified for federal tax deductions or exemptions at the time of TRA86 included state and local government income taxes, property taxes, and sales taxes; interest paid on local government borrowing; charitable contributions; home mortgage interest; and, on the business side, targeted job credits, investment tax credits, deductions for business meals and entertainment, and losses from business activities not actively managed (called "passive" activities). The level of tax expenditures had nearly doubled in the decade before TRA86, growing from $700 per person in 1975 to $1,290 per person by 1985.[a]

President Reagan's reform proposal was to remove or limit deductions and exemptions and to return the savings from reduced tax expenditures to citizens and firms as reductions in their tax rates. To achieve passage of his reform, Reagan built a reform coalition by (1) the selective use of continued tax favors allowing some coalition members to keep their local tax breaks; (2) using the "negative powers" of the presidential veto to block any proposal that did not ensure his commitment to a maximum tax rate target of 28 percent for individuals (down from 50 percent before reform) and 33 percent for corporations (down from 40 percent); and finally, (3) using the presidential "positive powers" of the budget to target spending outside tax policy to those on the fence in their support of tax reform; see Birnbaum and Murray (1987) and Inman (1993). In the end, TRA86 succeeded in reducing the level of local tax expenditures by 40 percent, to $800 per person, by 1990 and in lowering individual and corporate rates to Reagan's targets. Reagan enjoyed a significant bump in his Gallup Poll overall approval rating, particularly among lower-income households, which enjoyed the greatest gain in after-tax incomes. Economic evaluations of the reform have been universally favorable.

---

[a] "Revenue Losses Estimate for Selected Tax Expenditures by Function," U.S. Office of Management and Budget, *Special Analyses, Budget of the United States Government*, various years.

Importantly, almost all of the reduction was observed in less spending for local, rather than national, public goods or on programs of social insurance.

Finally, who gets the savings from more efficient national budgets? From the historical U.S. evidence, almost all of the savings from reduced spending on local public goods and local tax favors are returned to taxpayers as reductions in national taxation. This is just what we might hope for from a more

efficient national budget. The international evidence shows the same allocation from presidential efficiencies; fiscal savings from more efficient budgets
are returned both in lower current taxes and in lower future taxes as government debt is repaid and deficits are reduced.[12] In a large international study,
Jose Antonio Cheibub (2006) found that presidential governance reduced the
national average tax rate by 7 to 10 percent per annum and the annual deficit
as a share of country GDP by 1.5 percent a year. Consistent with our analysis
here, presidential influence came from the positive power to set the national
fiscal agenda and from the negative power of having a presidential veto. Finally,
Cheibub estimates that these powers are most effective when the national
legislature is most divided among fragmented political parties—that is, when
the legislature is decentralized and thus most likely a U legislature.[13]

Adding a Supreme Court

While Madison relied on the Senate and the president as the most effective
checks on the overreaching tendencies of the popularly elected national legislature, Hamilton in *Federalist* No. 78 outlined a theory for how a Supreme
Court might act as an additional constraint on legislative behavior. Both Madison and Hamilton expected the Court to "umpire the constitutional balance"
between the legislature and the executive branches and between the national
government and the states.[14]

Against the Senate's co-powers for setting the budget and the president's
executive powers for implementing policies, the Court's constitutionally assigned powers pale in comparison. To enforce the Constitution's "parchment
barriers" of responsibility, the Court has only reason and judgment on its side.
The Court will therefore need the support of some power capable of standing
up to those of the popularly elected legislature. For Madison and Hamilton

12. See, for example, Roubini and Sachs (1989a, 1989b) for the impact of presidential governance in OECD countries and Stein, Talvi, and Grisanti (1999) for evidence from Latin
America.

13. A study by Hankla (2013) examines the forty-seven presidential countries in the Cheibub
sample and updates the analysis to 2007. He concludes (1) that party fragmentation (or U legislatures) increase spending but (2) that presidents can control such spending by fashioning
legislative coalitions using presidential powers as measured by Cheibub (2006).

14. Beer (1993, p. 302). For contemporary legal scholars studying federalism, the Court is
seen as essential to protecting the federal bargain; see Friedman and Delaney (2011,
pp. 1147–1149).

that power would have to come from the citizenry at large through their ability to discipline or even replace their elected representatives. To ensure that the Court's argument can be persuasive to the general public, it is essential that the justices be independent from the direct influence of either the legislature or the executive branches of government.

If popularly supported, the Court's resistance to legislative transgressions serves two purposes. First, the Court may overturn statutes that violate the principles of the Constitution; and second, it may discourage the passage of such laws in the first place. If the Court is to have an effective veto over legislative overreaching onto state activities, then it will need the wide support of the national citizenry. Citizens will support judicial review of legislative, or executive, actions and thus the judicial decisions that follow from that review if citizens' expected welfare is greater with the review than without. Since the full consequences of any one judicial decision will typically not be known at the time of the decision, the perspective of the citizens is necessarily forward-looking. Do we, the citizens, think we will be better off, or not, by allowing judicial review and a possible veto of legislative action? If so, then the Court has the citizens' support for that review and the Court's decisions will be potentially binding on legislative or executive decision-making. If not, the legislature and the executive will be able to operate on their own, ignoring any judicial review and subsequent Court decision. Citizen support is contingent on the importance of the policies being reviewed, how accurately the Court can separate beneficial from harmful federal policies, and how often the national legislature or executive approves legislation that might be overruled with a Court review; see Box 5.2.

If we, as citizens, support judicial review, we expect the Court to distinguish truly national goods with national benefits from state and local goods with state or local benefits only. Ideally, that review will limit the national legislature to the policies it does best—that is, the financing and provision of national goods. Citizens will support judicial federalism review when (1) the national legislature or executive has strong political incentives to overreach and provide services or regulations citizens view as best managed by state or local governments; (2) the benefits from correctly overturning an inappropriate national policy are large and the costs of incorrectly doing so are small; and (3) the Court has the ability, either from the Constitution or from accepted prior Court decisions, to infer citizen preferences for what policies are best provided and funded nationally and what policies are best provided and funded locally. When any one of these three conditions does not hold, then the expected

Box 5.2. When Will Citizens Support Judicial Review of National Overreach?

To earn citizens' support for the review of "overreach," the Court must be able to successfully evaluate the impact of national legislative or executive decisions on citizens' preferred allocation of policy responsibilities between national or state and local governments. Citizens will approve of review if the Court can successfully distinguish good national policies—those that are efficient, or promote political participation, or protect fundamental rights—from those that would have best been left to state and local governments. Consider, for example, a Court review of a national public policy that involves potential fiscal overreach (say, area $[W_u]$ in Figure 5.2) or discourages political participation, or one that limits individuals' rights and liberties. Such national policies may impose a loss on the average citizen of L dollars when compared with state and local policies. A successful Court review would reject that policy. The Court, however, might get it wrong. Perhaps the national policy truly is a national public good, or promotes valued political participation, or protects an important right or liberty, each of which provides a net benefit above that available from state and local governments of B dollars. Then those benefits will be lost if the Court were to overturn the national policy. When will citizens want the Court to evaluate the national policy as a constitutionally valid, or invalid, policy?

As a safeguard, the only Court decisions that make a difference are ones that prevent the implementation of the national policy.[a] What, then, are the expected benefits of getting it right (that is, the Court denies the national policy when it should deny it), and what are the expected costs of getting it wrong (that is, the Court denies the policy when it should be allowed)? Expected benefits from a Court decision to deny when it should deny will be $(1 - \pi) \cdot \rho \cdot L$, where $(1 - \pi)$ is the chance the national government policy is an inappropriate policy best left to state and local governments, ρ is the chance the Court successfully identifies the national policy as inappropriate, and L is the loss saved by denying the inappropriate national policy. The expected costs from a Court decision to deny the national policy when it should be allowed will be $\pi \cdot (1 - \rho) \cdot B$, where π is the chance the national government policy is an appropriate national policy, $(1 - \rho)$ is the chance the Court wrongly identifies the national policy as an inappropriate national policy, and B is the national benefits lost because a valid national policy has been denied.

Court oversight of national policies thought to affect state and local governments will be preferred, and thus supported by citizens, when

$$\textit{Expected Benefits of Review} = (1 - \pi) \cdot \rho \cdot L > \pi \cdot (1 - \rho) \cdot B = \textit{Expected Costs of Review.}$$

This will be so when (1) the national government often approves policies that should be best managed by the state and local sector—that is, when $(1 - \pi)$ is close to 1 and π is close 0; (2) the Court is good at identifying those national policies best managed by the state and local sector—that is, when ρ is close to 1; and (3) the losses saved by successfully overruling an inappropriate national policy (L) are large relative to the losses incurred (B) when the Court denies a valid national policy.

In other words, citizens' expected benefits from Court review will be relatively large compared with its expected costs, and thus citizens support a Court review of "overreach," when the

Continued on next page

Box 5.2. (*continued*)

national government actively "overreaches" onto state and local policies, the losses from this overreach are large, and the Court has a workable and effective test—a judicial "bright line"—that successfully distinguishes between federally appropriate and inappropriate national policies.

[a] The alternative is having the Court accept all decisions, equivalent to having no Court review. The analysis here of citizens' support for a Court review of federal "overreach" follows from the more general analysis of citizens' acceptance of judicial decision-making as presented in Stephenson (2004).

costs of allowing judicial review will be too high, citizen support will be absent, and the national legislature and executive will be able to ignore the Court and pursue their own agenda without judicial oversight.

How well have the U.S. courts, and courts elsewhere, done in meeting these three conditions for successful judicial review of nationally provided or funded public services? The recent U.S. experience is instructive, and it has been mirrored in the experiences of courts in other federal unions.[15] The difficulty has been in finding a compelling theory that separates national and local responsibilities that the Court could apply and that citizens would readily accept.[16] In *National League of Cities v. Usery*, the U.S. Supreme Court proposed such a standard, the "traditional state function" test, where the Court specified protected state functions as those "traditional" to state sovereignty.[17] Justice Blackmun in his concurring opinion sought to give some content to the guideline of "traditional" by suggesting a "balancing approach" where national government policies would be allowed when the national interest was greater than the state or local interest or where state compliance with imposed federal standards would be essential to achieve the national policy's objective. Even with Blackmun's guidance, the "traditional state function" test proved unworkable, however. In each of a series of federalism cases as disparate as the regulation of age discrimination, railroads, land use, and state utility rates, the Court always favored federal regulation over state autonomy.[18] Finally, in *Garcia v. San*

15. For an analysis of judicial decisions affecting the enforcement of the federalism principle of subsidiarity in the European Union, see Bermann (1994, 1999) and Vandenbruwaene (2013). On the decline of federalism review in Canada, see Swinton (1992) and Bednar (2009, pp. 140–143).

16. See Corwin (1950). For a historical review of the search from the Marshall Court of 1801 to the Reagan Court beginning in 1986, see Eskridge and Ferejohn (1994).

17. *National League of Cities v. Usery*, 426 U.S. 833 (1976).

18. On federal regulation of work rules, see *EEOC v. Wyoming*, 460 U.S. 226 (1983). On federal regulation of railroads, see *United Transportation Union v. Long Island R.R*, 455 U.S. 678

Antonio Metropolitan Transit Authority, the Court abandoned *Usery* altogether and declared its "traditional state function" test "unworkable."[19]

Ten years later, in *United States v. Lopez,* and then later in *United States v. Morrison,* the Court offered a new standard.[20] The new test would divide state activities into those that are commercial or economic and thus open to regulation by the federal government under the U.S. Constitution's Commerce Clause and those activities that are "noneconomic" and thus not open to Commerce Clause review. The Court reasoned that since commerce is nationwide and potentially affects all citizens, policies that regulate or affect commerce "must" be national in scope as well. Noneconomic policies cannot have such spillovers and thus can remain the protected domains of state and local governments. In *United States v. Lopez,* the Supreme Court ruled that the possession of guns near local schools was a "noneconomic" activity, as was, in *United States v. Morrison,* violence toward women. Under the logic of *Lopez* and *Morrison,* both activities may be worthy of regulation, but such policies should be decided by an overseeing state or local government. Finding a workable definition of what is "economic" or "noneconomic" has proved difficult for the Supreme Court, however, and this standard has now been abandoned.[21]

More promising has been the Court's efforts to create a process, rather than an outcome, standard for judicial review of national legislation. Two decisions in the 1990s, *New York v. United States* and *Printz v. United States,* held that federal legislation cannot compel state governments to implement federal government regulations or programs without acceptable compensation, a doctrine known as the *anti-commandeering* principle.[22] The virtue of this process standard is its clarity in implementation. A federal requirement on state or

---

(1982). On federal regulation of land use, see *Hodel v. Virginia Surface Mining and Reclamation Ass'n,* 452 U.S. 264 (1981). On federal regulation of state utility rates, see *FERC v. Mississippi,* 456 U.S. 742 (1982).

19. *Garcia v. San Antonio Metropolitan Transit Authority,* 469 U.S. 528, 543–545 (1985). In its conclusion to the *Garcia* decision, the U.S. Supreme Court abandoned its efforts to find a workable and acceptable standard and argued that U.S. federal governance should rely on the ability of the executive and the Senate to police federalism's borders. Legal scholars have been skeptical that these protections will be sufficient; see, for example, Rapaczynski (1986), Kramer (2000), Baker and Young (2001), and McGinnis and Somin (2004).

20. *United States v. Lopez,* 514 U.S. 549 (1995); *United States v. Morrison,* 529 U.S. 598 (2000).

21. Feeley and Rubin (2008, p. 135). See also Schapiro (2009, chap. 10) for a comparable critique.

22. *New York v. United States,* 505 U.S. 144 (1992); *Printz v. United States,* 521 U.S. 898 (1997).

local governments to implement a regulation or a program will be clear in the national legislation, and compensation will, or will not, be available. Its limitation is the ease with which it can be satisfied by national legislation affecting state and local governments. First, the standard only applies to how a state or local government alone regulates or provides a service; it does not preclude federal regulation of states and localities under a general law—such as the Fair Labor Standards Act—that also regulates similar behaviors by private firms or citizens. Second, it only applies to national legislation that *mandates* states and localities to actively regulate or spend; the doctrine does not preclude national statutes that *prohibit* state and local regulations or programs. Finally, and most importantly for our analysis, the anti-commandeering doctrine does not prevent the federal government from offering clearly stated financial incentives to lower jurisdictions to adopt a particular national policy.[23] As now specified, the U.S. anti-commandeering doctrine is likely to do little to prevent overreach by the national legislature. Indeed, one of the best ways to fund economically inefficient national policies is to provide nationally financed intergovernmental transfers for state and local policies whose beneficiaries are local residents only.

Holding more promise as a process standard against overreach is the *clear-statement* requirement advanced in *Gregory v. Ashcroft*.[24] At issue was a provision in the Missouri state constitution that all judges, other than municipal judges, retire at the age of seventy. Judge Gregory sued the state for continued employment, arguing the constitutional provision was in violation of the federal Age Discrimination in Employment Act's provision that no employee over the age of forty may be fired because of his or her age. The U.S. Supreme Court ruled in favor of the Missouri state constitution over the federal requirements in the act by requiring that all federal provisions that directly affect the state as a "sovereign entity" specifically include a clear statement of purpose to so regulate. If there is any ambiguity as to the reach of the regulations, the Court will nod in the direction of protecting state sovereignty, as it did in *Gregory*.

Gregory's clear-statement process review has three virtues. First, it provides some protection for states from overreaching national policies by requiring the national legislature to state explicitly that it intends to regulate states as states, thereby alerting state political officials and their constituents and potentially raising extralegislative hurdles for final passage. Second, it removes the Court from a task it does not do well, that of drawing a bright line between

23. See *South Dakota v. Dole*, 483 U.S. 203, 207–211 (1987).
24. *Gregory v. Ashcroft*, 501 U.S. 452 (1991).

national and state and local policies for the promotion of federalism goals. Third, the clear-statement approach has a good chance of being accepted by citizens and their representatives to the national legislature and thus of being relevant to federal decision-making. The national legislature must explicitly state its preferences for regulating states and localities, and in so doing encourage a wider, and perhaps deeper, discussion of the implications of the national statute for federalism values.[25]

3. Riker's *Auxiliary Precaution*: National Political Parties

William Riker (1964, chap. 5) was doubtful that Madison's constitutional safeguards would be enough to protect federal governance from becoming unitary governance over time. For Riker, what matters most for democratic decision-making are not the formal institutions of democratic federalism but rather the incentives and ability of elected officials to use those institutions to protect the federal bargain. After detailed case studies of federal governance in the major federal unions, Riker concluded there was "one institutional condition that controls the nature of the [federal] bargain . . . and [t]his is the structure of the party system" (1964, p. 136).[26] But not all party structures will provide protection for federal governance. To do so, *the party system must be decentralized in its representation, yet centralized in its organization.*

Contemporary scholars from political science and the law have developed Riker's insight more fully. Larry Kramer (1994, 2000) stresses the importance for national political parties to be decentralized, bottom-up organizations. Elected state and local officials provide politically tested, quality candidates whom the national party needs to win national legislative elections. In return, national parties provide local candidates with campaign funds, campaign workers, and a valuable brand name that conveys the policy position of the candidate at low cost. Jonathan Rodden (2006) and Mikhail Filippov, Peter Ordeshook, and Olga Shvetsova (2004) provide compelling case studies of party governance in federal unions. Political parties in Canada, India, Germany, and Australia rely on locally tested candidates and national party resources; as a result, both national and local interests play important roles in policy design and implementation. In contrast, political parties in Brazil are

---

25. For how this deeper discussion might be engaged, see Chapter 6.

26. In addition to the United States, the other federations he examined include Canada, Australia, India, Argentina, Brazil, Germany, and the Soviet Union; Riker (1964, chap. 5).

decentralized, with little ability to control national policies, while those in Mexico over most of its history have been highly centralized, with little allowance for local choice and implementation. Political parties in the United States have always been decentralized in their representation but have vacillated in their ability to control national policies.

How might political parties affect federal policies chosen in Democratic Federalism? The key to political party protection of the federal bargain is for the party to control locally elected legislators' behaviors as they decide national policies. To do so, the national party will need to align representative interests with party interests and then align party interests with a national interest in maintaining the federal bargain and limiting overreach.

Parties as Organizations

Why would a local representative ever choose to join a national political party, particularly if the national party might ask the representative at times to vote against the obvious interests of his or her local constituents? The answer lies in party-provided resources, both monetary and nonmonetary, that help the local representative get elected to national office.[27]

The "contract" between legislators and their party is relational. To be effective, the relationship must be ongoing. Deviation from the contract by the legislator will mean the loss of party resources in the future. Deviation from the implicit contract by the party will free the candidate to pursue his or her own policy agenda if elected. It is essential that party resources be gathered from donors *outside* the legislature. If not, a legislative coalition of non–party members could vote to "take" the party's legislative resources, and then legislative decision-making would cycle from policy to policy or become universalistic and overreaching. To ensure passage of its favored policies, the political party will need to control a majority of the legislature.[28] Finally, successful parties are those that can be sustained in the long run through their reputation for passing or administering policies favored by their donors and national electorate.

Party resources from outside the legislature include donated funds and the donated time of campaign volunteers. But the party's most valuable outside resource is its "brand name," represented by the party's platform of national

27. See Jenkins and Roscoe (2014).

28. See J. Schlesinger (1984) for an overview of parties as organizations. On the importance of incentives to control party member voting within the legislature, see Olson (1965, chap. 6).

policies. The party's brand name helps local candidates in three ways. First, the strategic choice of the party platform can be used to deter entry into any local election by a competitive third candidate.[29] Second, the party's brand name provides "rationally ignorant" voters with valuable information; endorsements by an established political party with a reputation for policy performance and quality candidates provide valuable information to local voters. Third, the party's brand name is a self-selection device that the party can use to guarantee that the preferences of its local candidates align with the party platform.[30]

Parties then allocate their outside resources across local candidates for the national legislature. The party's objective is to win a majority of the legislative seats. To do so, parties first select candidates whose underlying preferences align closely with the party's policy platform. The parties' choice of platform, once advertised, then provides each party with its "natural," or platform, advantage in the local district election and can be thought of as the candidate's share of votes if the competitive parties were both to allocate the same level of monetary resources to the election. In some districts the party's platform alone may be sufficient to guarantee election; in others the platform may be such a disadvantage that even the best-funded candidate could not win election. Increasing the attractiveness of the party's platform nationally will raise the natural advantages of the party's candidates and increase the party's probability of being the majority in the legislature. Once the platform has been selected, the party allocates its outside monetary resources, first to its safe seats to "lock in the advantage" and then to the closely contested seats so as to prevent the opposition from overcoming any platform disadvantage. The party with the more attractive national platform will have more safe seats and thus a higher probability of controlling the national legislature. The more attractive platform is also likely to attract more outside donors. In the end, parties with platforms that appeal to the most voters nationally will have the best chance of controlling the national legislature.[31] The important question for us is, *Will promoting an efficient, more equitable, and more participatory federal bargain constitute an attractive feature of a national political party's platform?*

A key issue for federal governance is the potentially adverse economic and participatory effects of national policies and regulations chosen by a decentralized universalistic national legislature. First, the national budget is too large.

---

29. See Callander (2005).

30. See Snyder and Ting (2002).

31. See Snyder (1989), particularly his Proposition 4.2, and Corollaries 4.1 and 4.2.

Second, because the national government is providing local services, often with national regulations, local policies may be "displaced" and local democratic choice diminished. A national party platform that promises stronger federal governance by constraining legislative overreach and restoring local control over local services and regulations may have appeal to national voters, both as taxpayers and as citizens participating in local governance. If so, the task for the successful national party will be to deliver on a promise of stronger federal governance and increased local policy responsibility. To do so, the national party must control voting by its local representatives in the national legislature.

Parties in the Legislature

Having elected a majority to the national legislature on a promise of effective federalism, the party will need to adopt policies that constrain national legislative overreach. The instincts of individual legislators, however, are likely to stand in opposition to the efficient and democratic federal bargain. Legislators want to do things for their local constituents, even at the national expense. To deliver on the federal governance agenda, the party must check these motivations. It can do so by allocating party resources in ways that benefit the reelection prospects of locally elected representatives, but only when they are supportive of the party's federalism agenda.

Party resources come from both outside and inside the legislature. *Outside* resources are donated funds and volunteer time under the control of the party and, perhaps most importantly, the party's endorsement of the candidate for election by allowing the candidate to use the party label.[32] *Inside* resources come from the majority party's control of the legislature's voting rules that govern the consideration of policy. A legislative rules committee under the control of the majority party is given responsibility for deciding when (if ever) a policy will be considered and how (for example, with or without amendments) the policy will be decided by the full legislature. By controlling the legislative rules, the majority party has agenda control, and with agenda control, the party can determine which policies will be adopted. In addition to controlling voting rules, the majority party also controls the design of policies

---

32. For evidence that outside resources matter, see A. Gerber (1998) and Levitt (1994). For evidence that donors expect a return on their outside money, see Snyder (1990, 1993) and Stratmann (2005). Finally, that citizens find the party label valuable when deciding how to vote for their national representatives, see Bartels (2000).

through its control of policy committees that review and propose legislation. Membership spots on these legislative committees are valued appointments. Party control of these inside resources is an additional lever of control over the voting behavior of party members. Together, outside and inside resources are used to control party member voting to approve party-proposed policies.[33]

How, then, might the party use its majority to control policy overreach and promote the federalism agenda? In two ways. First, under majority party rule, only districts represented in the majority party will receive a nationally financed local public good. Without a national subsidy, residents in minority districts will pay the full cost of their local goods encouraging greater local political participation and, as a result, a better balance of local marginal benefits against local marginal costs and thus improved economic efficiency.

Second, districts represented in the majority party will continue to receive a nationally financed level of their district's preferred local good, but the level will now be controlled by the party through its agenda powers. It will be in the interest of the party leadership to control *within-party* spending by asking all members to recognize the added costs they impose on other party members when making their requests for district local goods.[34] If so, then when asking for another dollar for their own district, members will internalize that request and assume their colleagues have a right to another dollar as well. The cost *to the party* of the request will not be one dollar but rather M dollars, where M is the number of districts in the majority party. Of course, these dollars will be paid by all taxpayers in all N districts of the legislature. Thus the *party's* share of any dollar a majority member spends will be (M/N) dollars. It is this share of dollars that matters to the party leaders. Party members will still receive district local goods from the national treasury, but they will be allocated by the party leadership at a party price of $(M/N) \cdot MC$, where MC is the marginal cost of another unit of a district's local good. Since (M/N) is greater than $(1/N)$, the effective price for district goods is higher with political parties than under the fully decentralized U legislature. As a result, spending for district goods, even in the majority party districts, is less, shown as x_m $(<x_u)$ in Figure 5.3.[35]

---

33. Kam (2014) calls evidence from the party's control over outside and inside resources "party discipline." For evidence on party control over member voting behaviors in the U.S. Congress, see Snyder and Groseclose (2000) and Ansolabehere, Snyder, and Stewart (2001).

34. See Kramer (2000, esp. pp. 278–287).

35. For evidence that majority party members do receive more of the district good than minority party members, see Levitt and Snyder (1997) and particularly Albouy (2013).

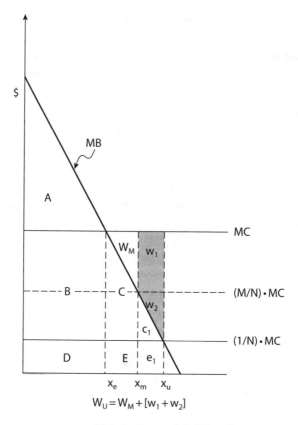

FIGURE 5.3. Majority Party and the U Legislature

The aggregate welfare gain from having a majority party set local goods spending comes, first, from the decision by the majority party to no longer use the national treasury to provide district goods to minority party districts. Those districts can still buy the local public goods locally at the efficient price of MC and purchase x_e. This reduction of spending on local public goods provides a net benefit to the national taxpayer of area $[W_M + w_1 + w_2]$. Second, the majority party cuts nationally financed spending in each of the majority party districts from x_u to x_m. This saves area $[e_1 + c_1 + w_1 + w_2]$ in national taxes. Subtracting the lost benefits from the lost consumption of the local public good— area $[e_1 + c_1]$—shows an additional net gain in economic efficiency of the shaded area $[w_1 + w_2]$. Area $[W_M]$ still remains as an economic inefficiency in each majority party district, however. In the end, the majority party gains by being able to claim credit for the net benefits of the national tax cut and for restoring local governance over local policies.

The most direct test for the impact of political parties on government spending and taxes is from an analysis of budget policies in U.S. states by David Mayhew (1986), updated by David Primo and James Snyder (2008). Over the 1957–1980 period, thirteen of fifty states had traditional parties. Their impact on state budgets was to reduce annual state spending by 10 to 16 percent and average state taxes by about the same percentage. Using an updated sample, Primo and Snyder also find a significant effect on state spending: a 7 percent reduction for Mayhew's sample years and a 4 percent reduction when the sample is extended to 2000.[36] Nationally, the Republican Party has had its moment (1994–2000) too. The result was a constraint on federal requirements for local budgets and decentralization for the financing and implementation of U.S. welfare policies; see Box 5.3.

The international evidence leads to much the same conclusion for the impact of strong parties on national fiscal overreach. For a sample of fifty democracies, Torsten Persson, Gerard Roland, and Guido Tabellini (2007) find that majority-rule party governments reduce the share of central government spending in GDP from a sample mean of 48 percent to 32 to 39 percent. For a Latin American sample, Ernesto Stein, Ernesto Talvi, and Alejandro Grisanti (1999) find that reducing the number of parties in the governing coalition from four to one reduces the share of spending in GDP by 6 percentage points. So too for OECD economies. Reducing the number of parties in the ruling coalition from four or more to one reduces the share of spending in GDP from 2 (Kontopoulos and Perotti, 1999) to 8 percentage points (Roubini and Sachs, 1989b).

Encouraging Political Party Competition

A legislatively strong political party may not by itself deliver on the promise to protect the federal bargain, however. As argued by Alberto Diaz-Cayeros (2006, chaps. 3, 4), the long national governance of Mexico by the Partido Revolucionario Institucional evolved into a hierarchical organization managed from the center. State and local governments became administrative arms of that dominant political party. Though federal by constitutional design, single-party dominance may lead to unitary governance in fact. Mexico, Russia, and Venezuela are all examples.

---

36. Inman and Fitts (1990) find a similar impact over the years of legislative dominance by the Democratic Party (1933–1950), with reduced national spending on local public goods and local tax expenditures of 12 and 10 percent, respectively.

Box 5.3. The Passage of UMRA and PRWORA

The passage in the United States of the Unfunded Mandates Reform Act (UMRA) of 1995 and the Personal Responsibility and Work Opportunity Reconciliation Act (PRWORA) of 1996 are both examples of how party influence can affect the federal bargain. Both bills sought to increase control by state and local governments over domestic policies. UMRA hoped to do so by requiring the Congressional Budget Office to estimate the direct costs to state and local governments of complying with any proposed mandatory federal regulation or program whose national budget exceeded $50 million. Those costs estimates were to be given to Congress before consideration for passage of the regulation or program. Regulations or programs without the cost review could be denied consideration by the full legislature. Regulations and programs where participation is voluntary are excluded from review. It was hoped that PRWORA would increase local control of welfare policies by removing a requirement that state governments "match" federal money given to the state for the financing and administration of income support for lower-income households. After PRWORA, federal financial support for welfare services became a pure fiscal transfer with no strings attached. In addition, states were extended greater latitude in how federal dollars could be spent to assist qualifying households. Funds could be spent on direct income transfers (as before PRWORA) or on programs to train and assist households to find employment.

The passage of both UMRA and PRWORA depended on a Republican Party majority in both the U.S. House and Senate. The party's platform, known as the Contract with America, placed a strong emphasis on returning policy responsibility to state and local governments in what was called its federalism agenda. The agenda was strongly supported by elected state and local government officials, particularly Republican governors, who conveyed their support for both bills to their locally elected members of the House and Senate.[a] To obtain control over elected representatives, party leaders mobilized both *outside* and *inside* legislative resources. Outside resources came from increased campaign funding provided by Representative Newt Gingrich's political action committee, called GOPAC, and by Republican senator Trent Lott's political action committee, called the New Republican Majority. Inside legislative resources such as favored committee assignments were provided by the Office of the Speaker of the House, a position held by Gingrich. Gingrich and Lott used their control of outside and inside party resources to control party member votes and achieve passage of both reforms.[b]

The final impact of both bills on the balance in U.S. federalism policy has been mixed. UMRA had little impact. There have been 10,932 UMRA cost reviews by the Congressional Budget Office, of which 1,357 were identified as having unfunded mandates, of which 107 proposed bills were in violation of UMRA guidelines.[c] The majority were still approved. What is not known is how many additional federal mandates have been set aside for fear of an adverse review. PRWORA has returned responsibility for the details of U.S. welfare policy to state governments, and the evidence suggests that those policies are now more responsive to the preferences of the states' median (median-income) voter. As a result, the real value of state support for lower-income families has declined. The hope that states now unconstrained in their spending of federal monies would be more experimental in their design of income transfer policies, and that successful experiments would be replicated, has not been realized.[d]

[a] See Conlan, Riggle, and Schwartz (1995) and Katz (1996, pp. 324–334).
[b] See Drew (1996, chap. 2).
[c] See Dilger and Beth (2016, table 1).
[d] On both points, see Gelbach (2016).

Having political parties, then, is not enough to protect federal governance. There must be party competition between at least two parties, with each party having sufficient resources to compete effectively against the other for the election of local and national candidates. Two competitive parties seems best.[37] Two-party competition can be guaranteed by a constitutional requirement for the election of local district representatives by majority rule, or by what are known as "first past the post" elections. In this case, a regularity of electoral politics known as Duverger's Law predicts that the equilibrium outcome will be two competitive political parties.[38] Five conditions are necessary to ensure Riker's locally based, national political parties are competitive:

R1: Both parties must be free to select their own candidates without fear that once selected, the candidates will be subject to reprisals—loss of contracts, loss of jobs—or, in the limit, fear of imprisonment for their political beliefs;

R2: Both parties must have equal access to the institutions for implementing the party's platform, including important regulatory bodies such as the national bank, supervising agencies, and the national courts;

R3: Both parties must have open access to the media for the communication, evaluation, and discussion of party platforms and the qualifications of party candidates;

R4: Both parties must have equal access to the campaign resources needed to promote the party's platform and its candidates, though better-performing parties and those with more promising platforms and candidates should be allowed to receive greater resources as a reward for past and future performance;[39] and,

37. Better still will be two parties that can strike Coasian deals within the legislature to control even across party policy externalities; see Wittman (1989) and Acemoglu (2003).

38. See Cox (1997, chap. 5) for the argument and Fujiwara (2011) for evidence in support of Duverger's Law. For an argument as to how two *national* parties will emerge as an equilibrium in multidistrict elections for a *national* legislature, see Callander (2005).

39. Public funds that match private donations may be needed to overcome the inherent free-rider problem in donations by individual contributors. Public funding for parties has the added advantage of removing the national government from the task of deciding which individual candidates should receive funds. Two proposals for how public funding of campaigns might be structured are found in Ackerman and Ayres (2002; called *patriot dollars*) and in Lessig (2011; called *democracy vouchers*). Arizona and Maine are two states that have introduced significant public financing for legislative campaigns, and both show increased competition for legislative seats and a greater chance to defeat incumbent party candidates; see Mayer, Werner,

R5: While campaign funding should be unconstrained, campaign spending need not be, as campaign spending beyond some level can be socially wasteful or act as a barrier to entry by qualified candidates.[40]

When listed side by side, the requirements for competitive political parties look much like the Founding Fathers' requirements for a functioning Federal Democracy: competitive and periodic elections for the legislature and executive, legislative control over regulatory and judicial appointments, a free press, and open and fair legislative elections. From the U.S. record at least, with these rules in place and respected, single-party dominance and de facto unitary governance is unlikely. The average tenure for one party's control of the U.S. House of Representatives has been four consecutive elections (eight years) and that for party control of the U.S. Senate, five consecutive elections (ten years). Contrary to what the Founding Fathers may have feared in *Federalist* No. 10, competitive national political parties need not be inconsistent with an efficient and politically responsive federal democracy.

4. Evaluating the Safeguards

Democratic Federalism's locally elected, national legislature offers important advantages in federal governance. But for all its virtues, the national legislature has two important weaknesses. First, there is legislative overreach—a strong preference by locally elected, national legislators to favor national financing of local public goods and national regulations of local spillovers. Second, while the rights and liberties of minorities can be protected by the incentive to form blocking coalitions in the national legislature, this is possible only if the threatened minority already has significant legislative representation. Those without representation are not protected. Might Madison's three institutional safeguards and Riker's locally based, national political parties successfully address these weaknesses?

---

and Williams (2006). Finally, all parties and candidates should have equal access to donated campaign labor.

40. When introduced for U.S. state legislative elections, spending limits have reduced incumbency advantages and encouraged the entry of new candidates into elections. See Besley and Coate (2003a) and Stratmann and Aparicio-Castillo (2006, 2007). *Citizens United v. FEC*, 558 U.S. 210 (2010) has removed limits on campaign spending in U.S. national elections.

Controlling Overreach

From the analysis and evidence presented here, we know that each safeguard—a smaller Senate with veto powers, an independently elected president with administrative and appointment powers, an independent Court with powers of legislative review, and locally based political parties funded by national resources—has the ability to improve the economic and participatory performance of Democratic Federalism. Ability is one thing; there must also be an incentive to do so. That incentive comes from the national benefits created by controlling overreach by the locally focused national legislature. Those national benefits—increased incomes, greater political participation, increased personal security—can be significant. Using their institutional resources and then taking credit for national benefits, senators, the president, and political parties can be elected to national office. Motivation for the national Court will be in having its decisions favoring local governance accepted as national law. We conclude that each safeguard, as part of the full structure of Democratic Federalism, can contribute to securing a preferred division between national and local governance, just as Publius had hoped in *The Federalist Papers*.

Extending the Franchise

To be a truly preferred structure of national and local governance, however, all residents must have a voice in the federalism debates. To this end, the institutions of Democratic Federalism must ensure the franchise and personal liberties for all the nation's residents. The theory is that within that legislature, no majority would approve exploitive legislation for fear that an affected minority might join with others to form a new majority to "exploit the exploiters." The resulting legislative stalemate would then protect all represented minorities. But nonrepresented minorities lack this security. Given the vested interest of incumbent representatives in their own reelections, initially excluded minorities may remain excluded. The histories of U.S. slavery, the fight for full women's rights, and the abuse of indigenous peoples in the federal democracies of Australia, Canada, and the United States make this clear. The starting point for rights protection in a federal democracy must then be with the right to vote and to have elected representation—that is, the franchise. Only with the franchise can individual rights be protected. Here we ask, Might the additional safeguards of a Senate, a president, a Court, or political parties achieve full suffrage when the locally elected national legislature might hesitate?

The challenge for Democratic Federalism to extend the franchise is in overcoming the vested interests of those now elected to restrict the vote to their current supporters. If the national extension of the franchise is to occur, it will need to come from motivations beyond those of currently elected representatives. From the U.S. experience, a nationally elected president and national political parties offer the best chance for this possibility.[41] Three conditions seem necessary. First, the disenfranchised minority's preferences for policies must align with those of the current majority supporting the president or the majority political party. Second, the minority must be large enough and diffused enough across legislative districts and states that their support, once enfranchised, will be sufficient to assist the president and party in retaining national office. Third, the costs to the current majority of organizing the minority as an effective voting bloc must be relatively low.

There have been two important moments in U.S. history extending the franchise, and in each case these three conditions were satisfied.[42] The first occurred during the period 1800–1850. At the formation of the federal union, Article 1, Section 2, of the U.S. Constitution assigned responsibility for deciding who would be allowed to vote in local, state, and national elections to U.S. states. In 1790, ten of the original thirteen states required property ownership or the payment of taxes to be eligible to vote. By 1855, only three of the thirty-one states had a wealth requirement, and in those states the requirement was limited to immigrants (Rhode Island), African Americans (New York), and new residents (South Carolina).[43] The franchise was a state decision decided by state politics. The central tension around extending the franchise arose from the political conflicts between urban industrial interests favoring extension and rural agricultural interests opposed to it. Since most major policy

41. A separately elected Senate and an independent Supreme Court are the two other institutions of Democratic Federalism that might be used to extend the franchise. Neither, however, is likely to have sufficient incentives or the national resources to overcome a local bias against the disenfranchised. The Senate is constrained by senators' private interests to continue their reelection. The Supreme Court must rely on constitutional provisions and existing legal precedents and then the acceptance of its decisions as beneficial for a majority of citizens nationally. For the inability of the U.S. Supreme Court to initiate a significant rights revolution on its own, see Scheingold (1974).

42. In addition to the two examples here, the United States has extended voting rights to women with the passage of the Nineteenth Amendment and to its Native American peoples as part of the passage of the Voting Rights Act of 1965. Both are best viewed as "one-time events" unrelated to the institutions of federal governance.

43. See Keyssar (2009, appendix, tables A.3 and A.9).

choices affecting the economic interests of citizens were, at the time, state choices, state political parties were the crucial institution defining the franchise decision. New urban voters were organized and became the foundation of the popular, mass-based Democratic Party that came to dominate state and local elections and, with the election of Andrew Jackson (1828–1836) and Martin Van Buren (1836–1840) as president, national politics as well.[44] By 1850, there had been a significant expansion of eligible voters to include the urban poor and working class, and they voted. The number of voters nationally increased by more than 150 percent from 1824 to 1828 and voter participation more than doubled from 27 percent to 55 percent. By 1840, the number of eligible voters was 50 percent higher yet again, and the rate of voter participation was 80 percent.[45] The consequence was to shift state and national economic policies toward the needs of urban centers with a significant expansion of federal public works favoring the expansion of urban commerce.

While the election of Democratic Party governors and presidents meant policies favoring the newly enfranchised working-class voters, disenfranchised African Americans continued to be ignored and denied their basic rights. The first matter was overturning slavery. The Civil War alone did not resolve the issue. While Congress did pass the Thirteenth Amendment on January 31, 1865, disallowing the practice of slavery, it was not until the passage of the Fifteenth Amendment that citizens could not be denied the right to vote on "account of race, color, or previous condition of servitude" (the Fourteenth Amendment had granted citizenship to all individuals born or naturalized in the United States or subject to U.S. laws).

The passage of the Fourteenth and Fifteenth Amendments was due in substantial part to the leadership and support of the national Republican Party. While congressional Republicans felt suffrage for the newly freed black citizens was morally just, there was significant benefit for the party in national politics as well. Extending and protecting the vote for African Americans helped to ensure Republican Party electoral success in the South and continued political support from civil rights proponents in the North. With federal government protections, one million new voters entered the electorate. Black voter turnout in the 1880 presidential election averaged 60 percent across the Confederate states, comparable to the national rate of voter turnout in that election. By the end of the 1870s, nearly two thousand black men had been elected to federal, state, and local offices in the former

44. See Aldrich (2011, chap. 4).

45. U.S. Census Bureau, *Historical Statistics of the United States: Colonial Times to 1970*, Series Y 27–78.

Confederate states. As a result, laws were passed that allowed for equal school funding for black children (Arkansas), integrated schools (Louisiana) and a state university (South Carolina), funding for black colleges (Georgia, Mississippi, and Texas), protection of worker rights to wages, and the extension of civil and judicial rights.[46]

Protections were not to last. By 1880, the Republican Party, perhaps taking its southern state successes for granted, turned its organizing efforts toward western states. The Democratic Party filled the vacuum in the South and built a political coalition around white voters disaffected with Republican policies. The result was the passage over the next thirty years of a series of state laws placing barriers between black voters and the vote: literacy tests, poll taxes, and residency requirements.

Neither a president nor a Supreme Court intervened on behalf of black voting rights until the 1960s with the passage of the Civil Rights Act of 1964 under Lyndon Johnson.[47] Again, along with the moral justification for the act, the political support for the Democratic Party from African American voters in the North proved an important motivation. The act banned discrimination in employment and public accommodation based on race, color, religion, sex, or national origin. But what was not ensured was the guarantee of suffrage for African Americans. That protection came with the passage of the Voting Rights Act of 1965. The act has since been renewed in 1970, 1975, 1982, and 2006, with the last renewal to hold until 2031.[48] In each instance, the primary *political* beneficiary of the renewal has been the Democratic Party. The primary *economic* beneficiaries are African American residents in communities and states where they are pivotal to candidates' election prospects.[49]

46. See Valelly (2004, chaps. 2, 4) and Foner (1993).

47. The Court had several opportunities over the intervening years to rule in favor of black voting rights, or to move such a case into the federal Courts, but it never did so. In *Giles v. Harris*, 189 U.S. 475 (1903), Justice Holmes explained that if major changes in rights protection were to be sustainable, they had to come from the political process.

48. The act has not been without legal challenges. In *Shelby County v. Holder*, 570 U.S. 529 (2013), the Court ruled five to four that Section 4 of the 2006 renewed Voting Rights Act was unconstitutional. Section 4 defined the states and counties to be subject to federal regulatory supervision of any changes to state or local voting rules. In her minority opinion, Justice Ginsburg was skeptical. Indeed, released from federal supervision, the states of North Carolina, Indiana, Wisconsin, and Texas introduced new laws that adversely affected voting by minorities; see Charles and Fuentes-Rohwer (2015, p. 150).

49. C. Cameron, Epstein, and O'Halloran (1996) find that in the South, majority-minority districts will be needed to ensure black legislator representation. See also Epstein and O'Halloran (1999), who find that for South Carolina legislators, black voter influence is

Since the passage of the Voting Rights Act, African Americans have been elected as mayors of major cities with significant (>35 percent) black populations: Atlanta, Baltimore, Birmingham, Charlotte, Cleveland, Cincinnati, Detroit, Gary, Houston, Memphis, Milwaukee, Newark, New Orleans, New York, Oakland, Philadelphia, Raleigh, Saint Louis, and Washington, DC. Black voter influence is most direct when the minority is a majority, as is the case in predominantly black, smaller communities.[50]

Outside of urban centers or small rural communities, however, it remains that blacks and Hispanics are a political minority. In the 2017 Congress, for example, African Americans and Hispanics held eighty seats in the House of Representatives (18 percent) and seven seats in the Senate (7 percent). Minorities (blacks, Hispanics, and Asians) hold 8 percent of all state legislative seats and less than 3 percent of all local elected positions.[51] Even so, once in the legislature, minority representatives can have influence. In a U legislature, a significant minority share of legislative seats can be pivotal for approval of distributive public goods benefiting minority residents. For example, neighborhood services in Philadelphia improved significantly in black neighborhoods when three prominent white members of city council (out of seventeen total members) were convicted in the Abscam scandal of 1980 and replaced by African American representatives from the majority-black council districts.[52] Similarly, southern counties in states regulated by the Voting Rights Act have seen a significant increase in state spending compared with counties not regulated by the act. For every 1 percent increase in registered black voters, there has been a corresponding 1 percent increase in state aid to the counties with the increased registration; black voters are now being given the same level of state assistance that had been given to white voters.[53] These spending increases have been directly attributed to the

---

maximized when the black share of voters is 45 percent (table 4). Elected white officials can represent black voter interests if the percentage of voters who are black is important to reelection prospects; see Overby and Cosgrove (1996).

50. In these local communities, street paving and lighting, trash collection, and police and fire protection have been improved in the predominantly black neighborhoods; see Keech (1968) and Button (1989). This is an outcome that for Gerken (2010, 2012) "makes the case" for judicial protection of state and local governments.

51. See Brown-Dean et al. (2015, figs. 13, 14).

52. See Inman (1995).

53. See Cascio and Washington (2014).

increase in black representation in the affected state legislatures.[54] Further, legislative influence for black legislators increases with their tenure in office, affiliation with the majority party, and service on important legislative committees.[55] The ability of political minorities to obtain favorable policies turns on their ability to elect representatives sensitive to their interests. After that, it appears to be politics as usual.[56]

What is most important for the protection of minority rights in Democratic Federalism is the extension and protection of the franchise for all citizens. Then, given the franchise, minorities must elect legislators and an executive who finds it politically beneficial to protect their interests. This is how the "safeguards" of Democratic Federalism can best protect minority rights and liberties. None of these gains would have been possible, or as "easily" obtained, had the U.S. government been a unitary state.

5. Summing Up

The institutions of Democratic Federalism begin with local governments being assigned responsibility for government services whose provision entails only limited economies of scale and little or no spillovers across neighboring communities. The benefits of this assignment are the matching of citizen preferences to service provision (that is, "responsiveness"), increased democratic participation, and the protection of individual rights and civil liberties. While local governance has much to recommend it, the analysis in Chapter 2 revealed two important weaknesses. First, local governments cannot efficiently provide goods and services with significant economies of scale in production or for which there are significant spillovers across jurisdictions. Second, if minority citizens are not mobile from community to community, there is the risk of local exploitation by local majorities.

Economic Federalism addresses the first issue with the democratic election of a strong president to allocate national public goods, but with the consequence that

54. See Fitts and Inman (1992) and Johnson (2010). The ability of minority members of the legislature to influence policy has been observed at the federal level as well. Ferejohn (1986) has documented the famous logroll for the support of food stamps between minority legislators representing inner cities and farm state legislators.

55. See Preuhs (2006).

56. Nor is this "truism" limited to U.S. legislatures. Pande (2003) documents the same impact of minority influence on legislative outcomes in India following the imposition of required minority representation in state legislatures.

local interests must give way to a majority decision. Cooperative Federalism guarantees that local interests will be fully respected when allocating national public goods, but with the consequence that many allocations will go undone. Democratic Federalism: The National Legislature offers a middle road of a *locally* elected, *national* legislature to allocate national public goods, but with the consequence that this legislature may be tempted to overreach its mandate and use its national powers to supplant local policies. Finally, none of these alternatives adequately address the potential rights abuses of immobile minorities by local governments.

In this chapter, we explained how Democratic Federalism: The Safeguards hopes to address each concern. It does so by keeping significant policy roles for both local governments and a locally elected national legislature. But then it adds the institutions—federalism's "safeguards"—of an elected smaller Senate, a nationally elected president, an independent Supreme Court, and competitive political parties to police the border of assigned responsibilities between local governments and the national legislature. Finally, each safeguard provides a further benefit by helping to protect the fundamental rights of locally immobile citizens. The safeguards of a president and political parties both have an incentive to extend the franchise to unrepresented minorities. Given the franchise, the national legislature and the Senate as argued by Madison have the incentive and the ability to approve protections for minority rights and liberties. Finally, the Court has the powers and incentives to enforce the nationally approved protective regulations.

It is only through the political interplay of all institutions of Democratic Federalism that the full economic, democratic, and protective benefits of federal governance can be achieved. Each institution has built within it the ability to affect both local and national policies and the incentive to find a citizen-preferred balance between local and national interests. How we might help to define that balance becomes the agenda for Chapters 6, 7, and 8.

PART II

Encouraging the Federal Conversation

HAVING MADE the case for Democratic Federalism as a framework for governance of a diverse society, its ultimate success as a working constitution turns on its acceptance and support by the citizens it governs. That acceptance begins with an understanding of how federal institutions and resulting policies are likely to affect their daily lives. Understanding begins in turn with an informed conversation about the relative merits of local, state, and national governments when setting policies, a conversation not in the abstract but rather over the details and consequences of individual governmental decisions.

Chapter 6, "FIST: Having the Federal Dialogue," proposes a framework for having that national conversation, a framework we call a Federalism Impact Statement, or FIST. FIST will be required of all national policies likely to have a significant impact on the performance of state and local governments. FIST reviews provide a seven-step checklist against which to measure a policy's impact on the three valued outcomes of federal governance: economic efficiency, political participation, and the protection of individual rights and liberties. FIST reviews can be done by an independent commission—for example, India's Finance Commission or South Africa's Financial and Fiscal Commission—or by "competing" offices of evaluation in the executive and legislative branches of the national government. A FIST review provides information only; it does not make a recommendation. We envision FIST as the basis for an open, transparent, and reason-giving democratic dialogue about federal governance.

Practical guidelines for doing a FIST review are provided in Chapters 7, "Fiscal Policy in the Federal Union," and 8, "Regulation in the Federal Union."

Chapter 7 outlines how federal governments might best finance and then provide public goods and services. The focus is on how to allocate (assign) policy responsibilities among the three levels of governance—national, state or provincial, and local—to best achieve the three valued outcomes of federal governance. The chapter first evaluates which level of government will be the most efficient and equitable *provider* of public services. When services can be efficiently provided to relatively small populations, when there are no significant spillovers of benefits or costs across jurisdictions, and when taxes can be efficiently collected on jurisdiction residents, then local assignment of service responsibilities and taxation will be efficient. But significant economies of scale, spillovers, or an inability to locally administer resident-based taxation each argues for centralized provision and taxation. It may be best to separate responsibilities for spending and taxation; Chapter 7 provides guidance as to how best to make this separation. If such a separation is required, intergovernmental transfers from national to state, and from state to local, governments will be needed. Chapter 7 then provides FIST guidelines for how such transfers might best be specified and financed. Finally, as Greece, Puerto Rico, and Detroit have made clear, debt financing in federal systems can be abused. Chapter 7 outlines the principles and associated FIST rules for such financing—in particular, incentives to minimize fiscal bailouts and to establish enforceable balanced budget rules. Chapter 7 provides examples of three FIST reviews: one for recent reform of U.S. welfare policies, one for the reform of corporate taxation in the European Union, and a third for the decision to bail out the Greek government from its excessive national public debt.

Chapter 8 reviews how best to regulate market activity in a federal union. As for fiscal policy, the focus of a regulatory FIST review is how best to allocate (assign) regulatory responsibilities among national, state, and local governments. The assignment of regulatory responsibilities for the protection of rights and liberties is straightforward when those rights are universal and absolute; in this case only national regulation is appropriate. Matters are more complicated when the outcome to be regulated is contextual. Local regulation may be appropriate in some circumstances, state regulation in others, and national regulations in still others. We begin by examining the appropriateness of local regulation when the objective is economic efficiency. There may be a "race to the top" when local governments each provide a regulation appropriate for its own circumstances or a "race to the bottom" when the efficient regulation requires cooperation between local governments. Efficient local regulations managed by a race to the top have the added advantage of encouraging local political participation. A FIST evaluation of state regulation of corporate governance is one example. Or a local regulation may be preferred for reasons of political participation even if there is evidence of a race to the bottom, but with only modest consequences for aggregate economic efficiency. Our FIST analysis of U.S. antitrust enforcement of state business regulation provides an example in this case. Finally, inefficient local regulation may be preferred if the political incentives implementing national regulation are even more ineffi-cient. In such cases, searching for an alternative to politically supervised na-tional regulation is appropriate. Our FIST analysis of U.S. national environ-mental policy provides an example in this case, where national regulation through market supervision, known as cap and trade, is the preferred assignment.

6

FIST

HAVING THE FEDERAL DIALOGUE

1. Introduction

In a fundamental sense, federalism is an unnatural state of affairs for national governance. On the one hand, there are significant pressures for all ethnic, religious, or economic minorities to retreat into a safe enclave of those who are similar to themselves. The vote by the citizens of the United Kingdom to leave the European Union is only the latest example.[1] On the other hand, if the advantages of collective action are recognized and a federal union established, administrative and police powers and economic resources may gravitate to the center because of economies of scale in management, safety, and tax collection. It is easy to see why political decision-making and final control over policy might follow. The wealth contained in the national "common pool" tax base may prove irresistible, to both democratic and dictatorial coalitions alike.[2]

For all its potential virtues—economic efficiency, democratic participation, and the protection of rights and liberties—Democratic Federalism will be a fragile institutional equilibrium. Chapter 5 offered a number of safeguards for Democratic Federalism, but as we argued there, each requires that a majority of the voting population prefer federal to either unitary or fully

---

1. Preceded by the examples of the Soviet Union's dissolution into fifteen separate countries; Yugoslavia into Croatia, Serbia, Slovenia, Kosova, Macedonia, and Bosnia-Herzegovina; Czechoslovakia into Slovakia and the Czech Republic; and Sudan into Sudan and South Sudan. Secessionist tensions remain in Canada, Iraq, Belgium, and the United Kingdom.

2. Acemoglu and Robinson's (2006) analyses of Brazil's and Argentina's military coups offer a theory as to why the elites and the military might prefer unitary over federal governance.

decentralized governance. For this to be true, voters must be reminded of, and persuaded by, the net benefits of federalism. That, we believe, requires an ongoing public dialogue as to why federal governance might be preferred, both "in the large" and "in the small."

The "large" debate is at the constitutional stage: Do we want independent states and local governments with their own revenues and policy responsibilities coequal to a national government with its own revenues and responsibilities? The decision to ratify the U.S. Constitution in the winter and spring of 1787–1788 was exactly such a conversation.[3] While the Constitutional Convention was convened in secrecy, the ratification process was "open, legal, and certainly as the word was understood in those days, democratic" (Rossiter, 1966, p. 296). Today the United States is engaged in a sequence of "smaller" federal conversations over the financing of public services (the Unfunded Mandates Reform Act of 1995), support for lower-income families (the Personal Responsibility and Work Opportunity Reconciliation Act of 1996), educational policy (the No Child Left Behind Act of 2002), macroeconomic stimulus during recessions (the American Reinvestment and Recovery Act of 2009), and national health insurance (the Patient Protection and Affordable Care Act of 2010).[4] What is emerging is a new view of federal governance, what Keith Whittington (1998) and other political scientists have called "creative federalism," and what Heather Gerken (2014b) and her law colleagues have labeled the "new nationalism."

But how to have these federal conversations? Federal deliberations should be *open* to all citizens and groups with an interest in the final outcome, *transparent* to those outside the conversation, *reason-giving* in its arguments, and *relevant* to the legislative and executive decision-making process setting the parameters of federal policies. We view such a federal conversation as an application of the principles of deliberative democracy as outlined by Amy Gutmann and Dennis Thompson (2004, chaps. 1–3). Integral to the deliberative process will be information regarding the likely consequences for the

3. As was the drafting and ratification of the federal constitution for the Republic of South Africa in 1996; see Ebrahim and Miller (2010, pp. 133–139).

4. See Conlan, Riggle, and Schwartz (1995) and J. Dinan (2004) for the public debate surrounding the passage of the Unfunded Mandates Reform Act; Katz (1996) for the political history of the Welfare Reform Act of 1996; K. Wong and Sunderman (2007) for that of No Child Left Behind; Conlan and Posner (2011) for the passage of the American Recovery and Reinvestment Act; and J. Dinan (2011) for the passage of the Affordable Care Act.

federal bargain of the proposed policies. Here we propose a framework for providing that needed information, which we call the Federalism Impact Statement, or FIST.[5]

We envision FIST to be required of all federal statutes and executive orders likely to affect the allocation of policy responsibilities among federal, state, and local governments or the ability of state and local governments to set policies in response to citizen preferences. FIST may also be applied to evaluate state policies that affect the state's local governments or its neighbors. Exempt from FIST review will be federal policies agreed to (or constitutionally specified) as exclusively national in scope—for example, national security, foreign affairs, and monetary policy. Also exempt will be policies whose consequences for the state and local sectors are financially (say, less than $50 million) or substantively (say the Liberace museum) trivial. FIST's role will be to evaluate the implications of any proposed federal statute or executive order against the metrics of economic efficiency, citizen participation, and individual liberties and rights. Importantly, FIST will make no recommendations.

2. Specifying FIST

While this perhaps is not a Bruce Ackerman (1991) "defining constitutional moment" for the structure of federal governance, current U.S. policies continue to have important implications for the allocation of responsibilities among the federal, state, and local levels of government. President Bill Clinton's reform of the U.S. welfare system (Personal Responsibility and Work Opportunity Reconciliation Act), President George W. Bush's signature domestic policy to reform U.S. education (No Child Left Behind Act), and President Barack Obama's fiscal stimulus in response to the Great Recession (American Reinvestment and Recovery Act) and his extension of national health insurance (Patient Protection and Affordable Care Act) each made significant use of state and local governments. It is safe to say that none of these

---

5. A name not without its precedents. Named after environmental impact statements, we first used FIST in Inman and Rubinfeld (1997) to describe our proposal for evaluating national preemption of state law regulations. President Clinton's 1999 Executive Order 13132 also adopts the term "federalism impact statement" to describe the order's requirement for evaluating the impact of federal regulations on state policies. In her analysis of the courts' role in monitoring preemption, Sharkey (2009) recommends the use of a federalism impact statement, which she calls FIS.

important federal initiatives could succeed without state and local revenues and, most importantly, state and local policy expertise.[6]

National regulatory policies have also relied heavily on state and local governments for their implementation. The U.S. Environmental Protection Agency, for example, negotiates with states for the enforcement of in-state violations of the Clean Air and Clean Water Acts. The federal government and the states share responsibility for regulating immigration, low-level radioactive waste, energy usage, the protection of endangered species, and offshore drilling.[7] Even portions of the Dodd-Frank Act regulating national financial institutions retain a role for state governments, both in an advisory capacity for the previous state regulatory domains of consumer protection and insurance and in continued regulatory responsibility for state-chartered banks and financial institutions.[8] Thinking carefully about how best to allocate federal and state or local responsibilities for deciding and implementing government policies has been a central concern for economists, political scientists, and legal scholars.[9] We offer one approach—FIST—here.

The aim of FIST is to facilitate the public conversation about *which* level of government can best do *what* public services or regulations. FIST is a *process* recommendation in which the *consequences* of any federal arrangement are given primary attention. We are not the first to make such a recommendation. The Treaty of the European Union, in its Article 5(3), advanced the *principle of subsidiarity* to govern all union legislation affecting the member states: "Under the principle of subsidiarity, in areas which do not fall within its exclusive competence, the Union shall act only if and in so far as the objectives of the proposed action cannot be sufficiently achieved by the member states, either at central level or at regional and local level, but can rather, by reason of the scale or effects of the proposed action, be better achieved at Union level."

---

6. On the important role that state and local governments have played in the implementation of the Personal Responsibility and Work Opportunity Reconciliation Act, the American Reinvestment and Recovery Act, and the Patient Protection and Affordable Care Act, see Metzger (2011). For an evaluation of the role of state and local governments in No Child Left Behind, see Dee and Jacob (2010).

7. Ryan (2011, sec. 2).

8. Metzger (2011).

9. Among economists, Boadway and Shah (2009), Oates (1999), and Wellisch (2000) provide excellent summaries of the literature; among political scientists, see Treisman (2007) and Weingast (2009); and among legal scholars, see Rapaczynski (1986), Shapiro (1995), and Feeley and Rubin (2008).

Subsidiarity reserves for the member nations all policies that (1) have not been assigned by the treaty as exclusive competencies of the union government;[10] (2) do not entail significant economies of scale in production or do not have significant spillovers across member nations; and (3) cannot be provided by regional or local agreements. Our FIST proposal will do the same. Further, under the treaty's *principle of proportionality* (Article 3[b]), if the EU does propose to act within the guidelines of subsidiarity, the policy must be designed to show maximum respect for the interests of the member nations while still achieving the objectives of the treaty. The EU's governing body, the European Council, may request of the EU's executive branch, the European Commission, a report on how best to implement the principles of subsidiarity and proportionality for each piece of EU legislation.[11] In cases in which the "maximum respect for the interests of the member nations" may be in conflict with the subsidiarity's interest in utilizing community-wide economies of scale or controlling spillovers, the European Council may turn the decision over to the primary EU legislative body, the Council of Ministers.[12] Like a subsidiarity analysis, FIST will be performed by a professional independent administrative agency and, in case of recognized conflicts between the efficient policy and policies promoting other outcomes valued by member states, the final policy choice will be the task of the recognized legislative process. In contrast to subsidiarity analysis, FIST will be required.

U.S. legal scholars Thomas Odom (1987, sec. 3), Ernest Young (2001, sec. 1B), and most recently Catherine Sharkey (2009, sec. 3) have each proposed a review process similar in spirit to subsidiarity and our proposed FIST review.[13] Odom

10. Exclusive EU competencies include (1) maintenance of a customs union; (2) establishment of competition rules for the functioning of the internal market; (3) monetary policy for members belonging to the (euro) monetary union; (4) common fisheries policy; (5) common commercial policies; and (6) enforcement of international agreements if provided for by a legislative act of the union or if necessary to enable the union to exercise its internal competencies.

11. Detailed guidelines for how the report should do its analysis are provided in *Adaptation of Community Legislation to the Subsidiarity Principle* (COM(93) 545 Final). According to the adaptation report (p. 1), the report must define the "need for each new initiative" against the guidelines of the principle of subsidiarity, as well as "what is essential" using the principle of proportionality; see Bermann (1994, pp. 369–371).

12. Bermann (1994, p. 381).

13. Gardbaum (1996), Executive Order 13132 (1999), and Hills (2007) have also offered a variant of a FIST review. Baird (1986, pp. 514–515) has proposed creating permanent congressional committees in both the House and the Senate to review all legislation directly affecting state and local governments. Gardbaum (1996) proposes the Court as the appropriate watchdog

(p. 1681) would require Congress to make specific statements in the introduction to any new federal legislation as to the likely impact of the legislation on existing state laws and to list state laws so affected. Laws that affect private parties would be exempted, as would existing legislation. The specific findings of such a review would include detailing the direct impact of the proposed federal legislation on state laws, a statement of current federal and state policy responsibilities now covered by the proposed legislation, an analysis of possible statutory alternatives that might minimize the impact on current state laws, and balancing of "long-term structural effects of intrusion, contrasted with short-term policy gains." Young's review is similar in structure to Odom's, though he would, first, strengthen federalism review by requiring oversight not just of new statutes but also of executive regulations affecting state laws; second, require the review to precede the introduction of new statutes and regulations; and finally, require that the review be widely distributed to citizen groups affected by the state laws or proposed national law or regulation. Sharkey extends the Odom and Young reviews by requiring an explicit solicitation of comments from the affected parties and by specifying the courts as the preferred means to enforce the review process. On all these points, our FIST proposal will agree.

FIST is a seven-step review of a proposed federal statute or regulation as outlined in Figure 6.1. The seven steps are designed to ensure that the public discussion of any proposed statute or regulation is *reason-giving*.

Step 1: Sovereignty Test is to ensure that state and local governments remain as politically and economically independent governmental units after the enactment of the federal statute or regulation. It would apply the criteria of Andrzej Rapaczynski (1986, p. 416) and ask explicitly: (1) Does the statute or regulation interfere with the highest state legislative or executive branches so as to undermine the overall autonomy of the political processes within the

---

of federalism's goals, applying as a standard for review the U.S. Constitution's Necessary (does the legislation rationally "promote a legitimate federal end," p. 820) and Proper (is the legislation appropriate "concerning the competing claims of uniformity on the one hand and federalism . . . on the other," p. 824) requirements. Executive Order 13132 proposed its own "federalism summary impact statement" (Section 6.c.2) as part of the order's consultative process. The regulation or legislation would be evaluated on the basis of "fundamental federalism principles." Hills (2007, pp. 35–36) proposes something like FIST's public dialogue "to advance democratic values in the same way that competitive elections do, by increasing the public's awareness and political knowledge through the promotion of lively conflict." As does Gerken (2014b, pp. 120–121), when endorsing Hills's use of the Court's anti-commandeering doctrine "as a means of creating the right conditions for federal-state bargaining."

Step 1 Sovereignty Test: *Does the federal legislation or executive order threaten the ability of state and local governments to function as politically and economically independent organizations within the federal system?*

If yes, legislation or executive order is rejected   If no, proceed to Step 2

Step 2 Efficiency Test: *Is the service a national public good, entail cross-state spillovers, or national merit good?*

If yes, proceed to Step 3   If no, proceed to Step 6

Step 3 Efficiency Test: *Are efficient agreements across state or local goverments possible?*

If yes, note efficient local agreements and proceed to Step 6   If no, proceed to Step 4

Step 4 Efficiency Test: *Is the service a national public good, entail cross-state spillovers, or national merit good?*

If a public good, proceed to Step 6   If entails spillovers or a merit good, proceed to Step 5

Step 5 Efficiency Test: *Do state or local governments have an informational advantage in the provision of the spillover or merit good?*

If yes, note bilateral contracting and proceed to Step 6   If no, proceed to Step 6

Step 6 Participation Test: *Will state and local government provision encourage increased citizen participation?*

If yes, note and proceed to Step 7   If no, note and proceed to Step 7

Step 7 Rights and Fairness Test: *Does national provision protect individual rights and/or enhance economic fairness?*

If yes, note and proceed to summary table   If no, note and proceed to summary table

Summarize

FIGURE 6.1. FIST Guidelines

state; (2) does it interfere with the state electoral processes, insofar as it is not clearly related to the protection of individual rights; (3) does it subordinate state police forces or state courts to a federal command structure that would cripple the states' ability to enforce their state policies; and finally, (4) does it radically limit the states' ability to tax so as to make states' fiscal solvency a matter of federal policy? In answering this checklist, state institutions and policies are understood to include all local governments and policies chartered and allowed by state governments.

Steps 2–3: Efficiency Test are meant to establish the institutional necessity for national policy to internalize the consequences of state or local policies that significantly affect the citizens of other state or local governments. Public goods are defined by a production process with significant economies of scale not fully captured by any individual state. Examples include national defense, monetary policy, the regulation of interstate transportation and commerce, and basic research. Spillover goods arise when the activities of one state or local government significantly affect the welfare of citizens in another state. Examples include air, water, and noise pollution. Merit goods are individually consumed private goods that are collectively valued by others for their contribution to the welfare of the private individual consuming the good. Examples might include K–12 education, guaranteed access to health services to ensure physical functioning, basic shelter, and physical safety. While public goods and spillover goods are defined by their technologies, merit goods arise from a collective judgment as to what is needed by all citizens to lead a "rewarding" life, a concept first introduced to the economics literature by Richard Musgrave (1959). How that collective judgment is to be derived is left unspecified, but it transcends individual preferences and efficient market allocations.[14] For us, what is a merit good is ultimately the outcome of public deliberation, most likely at the constitutional stage or in Ackerman's (1991) constitutional "moments" when protected rights and ensured capabilities are defined. Many U.S. state constitutions, for example, guarantee a "thorough and efficient" education for all children. Chapter 2 of the Constitution of the Republic of South Africa guarantees all citizens a right to a basic education, an environment "not harmful to their health," adequate housing, health care, and "sufficient" food and water, and to have their "dignity respected and protected."

Steps 4–5: Efficiency Test are designed to identify services or regulations that might qualify as "concurrent." Concurrent services and regulations are interstate spillovers or national merit goods whose financing and provision are most efficiently done through a cooperative agreement between national and state or local governments. Typically, the national government finances the service while state and local governments provide the service or implement the regulation. This division of responsibility uses the comparative advantages of the two levels of government most efficiently—broad-based taxation at the national level and preference and production expertise at the state and local levels. Bilateral contracts, which may vary from local government to local government, define the efficient federal provision of the good or regulation.

Step 6: Participation Test asks whether state and local governments' provision of the service or regulation, whether directly or concurrently, enhances citizen participation. The evidence summarized in Chapters 1 and 2 suggests that this is likely to be the case for services or regulations that have their largest impact at

---

14. Merit wants are defined not by the usual (narrowly defined) self-interested consumer preferences expressed through markets but rather by a wider reflection on what one needs to live a full and rewarding life, defined, for example, as in Rawls (1971, pp. 92–95) or Sen (1999, pp. 74–76).

the level of the local community. Policies that provide venues for direct public commentary, particularly at the community level, are likely to facilitate political participation.[15] In a FIST evaluation, the presumption will be to favor state and local government provision for reasons of democratic participation.

Step 7: Rights and Fairness Test asks whether the national government's provision of the service or regulation, again whether directly or concurrently, acts to protect an individual right or liberty or is more equitable than financing or provision by state or local governments. In FIST, there should be no presumption in favor of national or state or local governments on matters of rights and fairness. Policies that strengthen state and local governments will strengthen their ability to offer protection to abused, but mobile, minorities; see Rapaczynski (1986, p. 416). Mark Pauly (1973), for example, has argued that citizens who value fairness and opportunity may do so locally in ways that a less egalitarian national taxpayer might not. But abused citizens may not be mobile, and poor communities may lack the resources needed to achieve significant gains in equity. Here national policies will be needed. Each federal, state, or local policy will have distributive consequences.

Answers to the seven-step FIST analysis provide the "scorecard" for evaluating the federalism impact of any proposed national government policy or, as well, any proposed state government policy. The FIST scorecard should then be made publicly available to legislators and all interested parties to the proposed legislation. Democratic deliberations then follow. FIST is what Heather Gerken (2014b, p. 119) has called "second-order" policing of the federal bargain. FIST sets the ground rules for a dialogue about a proposed policy's implications for federal governance; it *does not* unilaterally prescribe the boundary lines between federal and state or local responsibilities.

Table 6.1 shows how the final deliberations might resolve the assignment of a service or regulation. Assume, first, that the answer to Step 1 is no; the proposed statute or regulation does *not* fundamentally affect the ability of state or local governments to serve as seats of democratic governance. We then move to Steps 2–5, the Efficiency Test. The resulting analysis will conclude that the good, service, or regulation is best managed nationally, concurrently, or locally for economic efficiency. FIST then turns to the analyses required by Steps 6 and 7. If the efficiency analysis favors national provision and the participation analysis favors local provision (Step 6, yes), then there will need to be a balance of the competing goals of efficiency and participation. FIST will offer no

15. See Delli Carpini, Cook, and Jacobs (2004).

TABLE 6.1. FIST Evaluations

	Efficient national provision*			Efficient state/local provision**		
Step 6: Participation Test	Step 7: Rights and Fairness Test	Recommendation	Step 6: Participation Test	Step 7: Rights and Fairness Test	Recommendation	
(1)	(2)	(3)	(4)	(5)	(6)	
Yes	No	Discuss	Yes	No	State/local provision	
Yes	Yes	Discuss	Yes	Yes	Discuss	
No	Yes	National provision	No	Yes	Discuss	
No	No	Qualified national provision	No	No	Qualified state/local provision	

*The Efficiency Test in Steps 2–5 prefers national government provision or regulation. The good or service has a national public goods technology, entails spillovers, or promotes a meritorious national objective that requires national government financing for its efficient provision (Step 2, Yes), *and* no agreements between state or local governments are possible or expected for its provision (Step 3, No), *and* the good is a pure public good displaying significant economies of scale in its production (Step 4, pure public) *or* is a spillover good or a merit good that can be locally supplied or regulated (Step 4, spillover or merit good) and there is no comparative informational advantage favoring state or local government provision (Step 5, No).

**The Efficiency Test in Steps 2–5 prefers state or local provision or regulation. The good or service does not have a national public goods technology, does not entail spillovers, nor does the good promote a meritorious national objective that requires national government financing for its efficient provision (Step 2, No) *or* the service or regulation does have a national public goods technology, does entail spillovers, or does promote a meritorious national objective (Step 2, Yes) *and* agreements between state or local governments are possible or expected for its provision (Step 3, Yes), *or* is a spillover or merit good (Step 4, spillover or merit good) and there is comparative informational advantage favoring state or local government provision (Step 5, Yes).

conclusion of its own. FIST's recommendation is to discuss the policy's pros and cons for all affected parties. Perhaps tipping the balance in favor of a national assignment might be a strong relative performance for the policy against the metric of rights protection or fairness (Step 7, yes), but FIST again only recommends discussion. National provision will only be recommended if there are no demonstrated advantages to democratic participation (Step 6, no) and there are clear rights or fairness gains with national assignment (Step 7, yes). There will also be a presumption in favor of national provision when, again, there are no participatory gains (Step 6, no) and no clear national equity gains either (Step 7, no). In this case, the efficiency advantages alone may be decisive.

Alternatively, the efficiency analysis of Steps 2–5 may favor local or concurrent provision. In this case, if there are gains in participatory democracy (Step 6, yes) and no clear gains in fairness or rights (Step 7, no), state or local assignment will be recommended by FIST. But if there are gains in fairness or rights with national provision (Step 7, yes), FIST again reveals a possible conflict between federalism's three goals, now efficiency and participation balanced against fairness. The FIST recommendation will again be to discuss. So too does FIST recommend discussion when local provision is more efficient and there are no clear gains in participatory democracy (Step 6, no) but national provision better protects rights, fairness, and the provision of merit goods (Step 7, yes). Finally, there will be a presumption in favor of state or local provision when the efficiency analysis points to local provision, with no clear offsetting gains in participation (Step 6, no) or rights and equity (Step 7, no).

When FIST recommends discussion, we imagine a process of deliberative democracy as specified by Gutmann and Thompson (2004, chaps. 1–3) and championed by Sunstein (1988) and Michelman (1988) as proponents of a "republican revival" in government policy-making. FIST discussions are valuable for two reasons. First, they can improve our understanding of a policy's impact on state and local governments as institutions and on citizens as they receive the benefits of, or pay the costs for, the policy. Second, FIST discussions can reveal the relative importance of potentially competing federalism values and thereby allow compromise when necessary. Deliberations should be reason-giving, transparent, open, and relevant.

To ensure that FIST deliberations are *reason-giving*, the initial FIST evaluation should be done by a technically competent, politically independent, and trusted government agency. In the United States, this might be the Congressional Budget Office, or perhaps an independent government agency modeled after the Federal Trade Commission or the Securities and Exchange

Commission. To ensure *transparency*, all FIST evaluations should be formally included as part of the proposed legislation or regulation and, by giving notice, be easily available to all interested parties, including all affected state and local officials and their affiliated professional associations. The underlying methodologies and data should be included in the published FIST evaluation.

While we imagine that most FIST discussions will take place primarily through the usual channels of representative government—legislative floor debate, committee hearings, and informal advocacy (for example, lobbying)—an *open* deliberation will require direct invitations for comment by all parties likely to be affected by the legislation or regulation. Comments might include a discussion of the methodology of the "official" FIST, an alternative FIST analysis, or the explicit advocacy for one of the competing federalism values. There will be a requirement that all contacted parties to the FIST deliberations be listed in an appendix to the original FIST evaluation.

Finally, to ensure that the FIST analysis and subsequent discussion are *relevant*, the FIST evaluation should be completed within a fixed time limit (say thirty or sixty days) after a preliminary recommendation of the legislation or regulation by the relevant legislative committees or executive agencies and before final approval. Legislation or regulations passed with a (sunset) provision for renewal might also require a postscript FIST evaluation of the initial successes and failures of the policy.

How will FIST be enforced? This will be the role of the courts as envisioned in the U.S. Supreme Court's ruling in *Gregory v. Ashcroft*, requiring a clear statement by Congress of its intent to regulate the states.[16] FIST clarifies exactly what such a "clear statement" might entail. Consistent with *Gregory*, the Court's review of the FIST requirement is a *process*-only review asking, Did the process for approval of the statute or regulation meet the requirements of a FIST review? But while *Gregory* requires that in regulating the states, the statute or executive order

---

16. *Gregory v. Ashcroft*, 501 U.S. 452 (1991). We propose that the Supreme Court enforce adherence to the FIST *process*; see Ely (1980) generally and later Dorf (2005) in response to Ely's critics of the process approach to constitutional law. To ensure potential Supreme Court review, we suggest that a FIST review be required by the FIST-enabling statute. New federal constitutions could, of course, include FIST provisions directly in the constitution, as do the EU Treaties' principles of "subsidiarity" and "proportionality" for governing federal-state relations; see Henkel (2002). The European Court of Justice has shown great deference in the specific evaluation of subsidiarity and proportionality, however, requiring only that the process of a FIST-type review has been adhered to when considering legislation, an approach with which we agree; see Moens and Trone (2015).

only say that "it intended such an exercise,"[17] the FIST review demands reasons for the legislation or regulation and that the deliberative process for approval be transparent, open, and relevant. Enforcement by the courts requires that the FIST process has been followed and work completed within the prescribed time frame. We prefer that the timing of judicial enforcement be based on provisions outlined in an enabling statute for a required FIST review.

How will FIST be implemented? We prefer a statutory rather than a constitutional specification of FIST and its triggers. Constitutional specifications can be both too broad and too narrow. Difficulties in enforcing a broad guideline to government responsibilities are well illustrated by the aborted legal history of the U.S. Constitution's Tenth Amendment guaranteeing that "the powers not delegated to the United States by the Constitution, nor prohibited by it to the States, are reserved to the States respectively, or to the people." Drawing a bright line between what are national and what are state or local responsibilities by this constitutional standard has proved elusive, however, leading Justice Stone to conclude, "The amendment states but a truism that all is retained which has not been surrendered."[18] In contrast, the federal constitution for the Republic of South Africa illustrates the limitations of too fine a constitutional standard. The Constitution lists explicitly those activities (security, international affairs and treaties, central bank) and taxes (income, VAT, general sales, customs duties) reserved for the national government alone and then those reserved for provincial and local governments only (for example, libraries, liquor licenses, beaches and amusement parks, fencing and fences, billboards, and street vending). All other governmental activities and most of the important policies (environment, health care, education, transportation, infrastructure, trade, urban development, welfare services) are classified as shared responsibilities. In both cases, the Constitution provides little useful guidance on how to actually allocate most governmental functions.[19]

---

17. *Gregory v. Ashcroft*, 501 U.S. at 464.

18. *United States v. Darby Lumber*, 312 U.S. 100, 124 (1941). Efforts by U.S. constitutional scholars to find alternative judicial strategies for federalism enforcement include Gardbaum (1996) and Jackson (1998) using the Constitution's Necessary and Proper Clause, by Merritt (1988) using the Constitution's Guarantee Clause, and by Cooter and Siegel (2011) using the Constitution's Article 1, Section 8, clause stating that Congress shall have the power "to provide for the common defense and general welfare of the United States."

19. The German and Canadian federal constitutions are more precise. The German Constitution explicitly favors national regulation (1) where the legislation of an individual state "cannot be effective"; (2) where the action of one state might "prejudice the interests" of another state;

As an exercise in deliberative democracy, there may be those who doubt either the usefulness or the feasibility of a FIST review.[20] First, as a process review, our FIST proposal explicitly refuses to make a recommendation. Completing Steps 1–7 satisfies the requirements of FIST. The policy itself may well result in economic segregation or wide inequities in the distribution of income and meritorious public services, true, but Steps 6 and 7 will require all such consequences of a policy to be explicitly considered and publicly debated. It is at this post-FIST stage that policy-makers, not FIST, decide the policy. Second, FIST may look democratic, but it can easily be captured and used to give "cover" for special interests' policy recommendations. Again, true, but FIST can minimize this danger of capture by requiring an independent agency or commission to provide the evaluations, not the administering federal agency or legislative or executive's staff.[21] And there are explicit requirements in FIST for its wide distribution and open commentary. Violations of those provisions give interested parties and the enforcing court a clear signal that favoritism is the intended consequence of the proposed policy. Third, by revealing the important and possibly competing outcomes of the policy, won't FIST make reaching a decision more difficult? It is true that conflicts will be revealed, but by getting the facts right, FIST can also narrow the range of disagreement. Further, if conflicts are clarified but overcome by democratic deliberation and agreement, then enforcement of the approved policy may become less costly. Finally, won't FIST itself be costly? A concern that evaluations will be costly has arisen in the enforcement of environmental impact statements for

---

and (3) where the maintenance of legal and economic unity necessitates regulation. The Canadian Constitution provides explicit protection for provincial responsibilities that include (1) exploration for nonrenewable natural resources within the province; (2) protection of forests and natural resources within the province; and (3) the generation and production of electrical power. See Blumstein (1994, p. 1280, n. 123, 124).

20. See Gutmann and Thompson (2004, pp. 40–63).

21. A complaint by pro-regulatory environmental, labor, and consumer groups of the analyses by the Office of Information and Regulatory Affairs (OIRA) in the president's office was that the consistently negative OIRA reviews became an excuse to table regulations that did not fit the pro-business agenda of the president, specifically Presidents Reagan and George H. W. Bush. "These feelings were especially justified in the early days of OMB [Office of Management and Budget] review, when OIRA was the place good regulations went to die" (Revesz and Livermore, 2008, pp. 24–30, 189). Subsequent leadership of OIRA under Presidents Clinton and George W. Bush managed the regulatory review process with a more even hand, leaving to the political process—not the process of review—the task of choosing policies (Revesz and Livermore, 2008, p. 44).

evaluating federal environmental regulations. Appropriately designed and implemented, however, FIST can avoid large costs.[22]

FIST's biggest hurdle will be in convincing the national legislature to approve a FIST statute. We are asking the legislature to regulate itself.[23] In 1999, the U.S. Congress had this opportunity with Senate Bill S. 1214 (Federalism Accountability Act of 1999) and House Bill H.R. 2960 (Federalism Preservation Act of 1999). The Senate bill required any new statute or regulation to (1) state explicitly its intent to preempt a state or local law (Section 6); (2) provide a "federalism assessment" of the impact of the legislation on the state and local sector and to give reasons for such intrusions into local policy-making (Section 7); (3) consult with state and local officials regarding the impact of the legislation and to seek ways to minimize its impact on those governments (Section 7); and finally if approved, (4) for each federal agency to appoint a "federalism officer" to oversee the implementation of the bill's requirements (Section 7). House Bill H.R. 2960 sought to put congressional weight behind an already existing executive order from President Ronald Reagan, Executive Order 12612. The bill required all federal agencies or departments to implement congressional statutes and executive regulations according to guidelines in the executive order. That order required (1) all national legislation and regulations affecting the states to have a clearly stated "national scope" not "merely common" among the states (Section 3-c); (2) the implementing agencies to "identify the extent to which policy imposes additional costs or burdens on the states" (Section 6-c-3); and (3) the Office of Management and Budget to oversee the implementation of the order (Section 7).

Both proposals failed to become U.S. law; the environmental lobby and the social service lobbies were opposed, as was the business lobby.[24] Their concern

---

22. Much of the early litigation over environmental impact statements arose because of the lack of guidelines for when in the policy process the statements were required and exactly how they were to be completed; see Sharkey (2009). We are clear on both points; see Section 3 on implementing FIST.

23. Though self-regulation has occurred in U.S. fiscal policy. Congress has done so on two prior occasions—the passage of the Congressional Budget and Impoundment Control Act of 1974 and the Gramm-Rudman-Hollings Balanced Budget Act of 1985. Sadly for those who favored the legislation, both were largely ineffective in their attempts to control congressional spending and ensure a more rational budgetary process. A redeeming feature of FIST, however, is that it does not require an explicit outcome, but rather a process. For this reason, FIST may have a better chance at success than balanced budget rules.

24. See J. Dinan (2004). Absent a FIST-like process, U.S. legal scholars have turned instead to using existing national statutes and executive orders for review of legislative or executive

was for losing the legislative and administrative convenience of centralized government policies. Rather than coming only to Washington, DC, to fashion a nationally uniform policy to preempt state policies, affected parties would need to work with fifty state governments and comply with fifty state policies.[25] Finding a resolution of this problem is exactly the public debate FIST wishes to promote.

3. Implementing FIST

Completing the seven steps of a FIST analysis may appear daunting. It is not. Step 1's Sovereignty Test is a rule-driven test and only requires noting whether the federal statute or regulation meets Rapaczynski's four criteria for protected state and local sovereignty: (1) inhibits the ability of the state legislature or governor to perform their elected duties; (2) interferes with the election process, other than to protect individual rights; (3) subordinates the state police or courts to federal supervision; or (4) limits the state's ability to raise revenues. Providing a FIST evaluation under criteria (2) and (3) is relatively straightforward, at least for U.S. policies. The U.S. Supreme Court has set the ground rules for (2) in its "anti-commandeering" decisions in *New York* and *Printz* disallowing federal laws that require states to implement federal regulations and for (3) by its fifty years of supervision of the Voting Rights Act of 1965. Evaluating a federal action by criterion (1) or (4) of the Sovereignty Test will involve a judgment as to whether a federal policy impedes the ability of state and local officials to set or fund state policies. For example, a national regulatory standard or spending policy that *explicitly disallowed* state supplementation would clearly violate (1) of the Sovereignty Test. Less obvious is whether a national standard or level of spending that allows supplementation but "crowds out" state policy is a violation. We would say no and allow FIST to proceed.[26] The analysis in Steps 2–7 might make

---

actions affecting state and local governments. See Metzger (2008) and Sharkey (2007, 2009).

25. See Elliott, Ackerman, and Millian (1985). Teske (2004, p. 21) makes the same point more colorfully: "Better to have one 500 lb. gorilla in charge of regulating the industry its lobbyists reckoned, than with 50 monkeys on steroids."

26. The U.S. Supreme Court faced this question in its decision to disallow the regulation in the Affordable Care Act that threatened to take away all preexisting Medicaid funding if a state did not accept the new regulations for the expansion of Medicaid coverage. In *National Federation of Independent Business v. Sebelius*, 132 S. Ct. 2566 (2012), a 7-2 majority of the Court ruled that even with the additional funding, the loss of current funding for noncompliance was so

a strong case against such a national policy, however, which is the point of a FIST review. Finally, when implementing (4) of the Sovereignty Test, we need to ask, Would states have sufficient revenues of their own if the national government were to outlaw state access to important taxes, even if compensated with national aid? We would allow such restrictions provided that at least one significant, broad-based tax remained under the direct control of state and local governments. For example, our use of the Sovereignty Test would allow the nationalization of all profits, income, and sales taxation and perhaps state borrowing provided that state and local governments retained the use of property and land taxes and user fees. It would then be the task of Steps 2–7 of FIST to clarify the potential costs and benefits of such a national policy.

Implementing Step 2 of FIST is a technical exercise. Knowing whether an economic activity is a national public good requires knowledge of economies of scale in the provision of the good. If the average cost per person in providing a given level of services declines as the population exceeds that of the average state or province, and certainly so for the largest state, then the good would qualify as a national public good. For economic efficiency, that good or service is most cheaply provided at the national, or perhaps regional (cross-state), level. Knowing whether an economic activity entails cross-state spillovers (that is, externalities), either as a benefit or as a cost, requires measurement of how the activity of one state affects residents in other states. Measurement may include monitors of environmental flows and predictions as to their sources, as well as of the mobility of residents and how individual attributes—skills, health—affect the attributes of other states' residents.[27] Identifying a good or

---

onerous that the new regulation took away meaningful choice for the states to participate—and thus violated the Court's anti-commandeering principle. For the courts to set such a policy threshold may discourage the national legislature from using states in future policies. We prefer the legislative process to set such a threshold, but with full information from a FIST review as to its consequences for efficiency, participation, and fairness. We would say no to the Sovereignty Test and to allow the full FIST analysis to proceed.

27. There are two definitions of externalities common in the literature, one of which is based on technology and the other of which is based on market consequences; see Myles (1995, pp. 313–314). The technological definition asks, Does a good or service provided by one state directly affect the welfare (utility or profit) of residents in another state? The second definition asks whether a good or service provided by one state affects its neighbors through its impact on the prices in a shared market. It is only in the first case that a national government policy might be recommended; see Myles (1995, pp. 315–331). The second case involves what economists call a pecuniary externality—say, when one state's purchase of nurses for its state hospitals raises the wage of nurses in a neighboring state.

service as a potential national merit good requires the revelation of resident preferences as to whether those in one state care about the well-being of residents of another state, beyond any direct impact on their own well-being. Knowing that the education and health of a child in Alabama is important to a Pennsylvanian, even though they may never meet, defines that child's education and health as a national merit good. If so, private markets or individual state governments are not likely to provide these goods and services efficiently; there is then a need for national government provision or regulation. The presence of merit good preferences might be revealed by donations for that child's education, by citizen surveys, or by constitutional commitments.[28]

Implementing Step 3 returns us to the analysis in Chapter 3: When are efficient intergovernmental agreements likely to occur? There we identified seven conditions for when this might be true: (C1) participation is voluntary; (C2) bargaining reflects citizen preferences; (C3) community property rights are respected; (C4) preferences are known; (C5) bargaining is (nearly) costless; (C6) there is agreement on the division of costs and benefits; and (C7) agreements are enforceable. The validity of each condition can be observed directly or inferred by past behaviors of state and local governments. Failing any one of these conditions, the bargain will either not occur or be economically inefficient.

Step 4 of FIST repeats the informational requirements of Step 2. Implementing Step 5 requires an evaluation of the state or local government expertise in providing the merit good or in providing or regulating the externality. This expertise will most likely be available if state and local governments have already been providing the service or regulating the activity. Local teachers and health professionals know their clients. State regulators know the technologies and behaviors of their regulated providers. If state or local expertise is evident, then a bilateral agreement or contract between the national government and the state or local government is appropriate. Such agreements will typically involve national government financing or standard setting and state and local government provision and enforcement. Terms of the agreements may vary across governments by local conditions. How we might specify such agreements is presented in Chapter 7 as "contract federalism."

---

28. The key distinction between externalities and merit goods is the underlying source of citizen interdependencies. Externalities are interdependencies based on technologies. Merit wants are interdependencies based on preferences, including perhaps preferences as seen from behind a Rawlsian veil when we act for our better selves; see Besley (1988).

Steps 2–5 conclude with an estimate of the aggregate efficiency gains of the proposed policy.[29] Policies may (1) create new state and local institutions (for example, special districts or merge governments); (2) alter the financing of state and local government services by offering federal aid or altering the national tax code; or (3) use state and local agencies to enforce national regulatory standards on the private sector. In each case it will be necessary to, first, predict the impacts of the proposed policy on valued public and private outcomes and, second, provide estimates of how citizens value those outcomes. All outcomes should be measured by their value added above that available to citizens without the policy. Outcomes can be valued by market prices when market alternatives are available, or by "hedonic prices" as revealed from market purchases of goods "bundles" (for example, a home), or by willingness-to-pay surveys of affected citizens when market or hedonic prices are not available.[30] The costs of providing the valued outcomes should be measured by the opportunity costs of the required inputs, in most cases best measured by market prices. When valuations of outcomes are possible, aggregate net benefits of the policy should be computed as aggregate benefits less aggregate costs. When valuations of outcome benefits are not available, cost-effectiveness ratios should be provided. Finally, when benefits and costs are ongoing following the introduction of the federal policy, future benefits and costs should be discounted into today's dollars at an accepted interest rate. Efficiency evaluations should be reported in the FIST summary.

When implementing Step 6 of FIST, we prefer a broad definition of citizen participation to include all legal actions "through which ordinary citizens of a political system influence or attempt to influence political outcomes;" see Jack

---

29. See the U.S. Office of Management and Budget's Circular A-4 for a practical guide to how the efficiency performance of a FIST might be conducted. Circular A-4 was developed as a guide to U.S. federal agencies for meeting the requirements of Executive Order 12866 (Section 3-f-1) to provide a regulatory impact analysis for new federal regulations. Circular A-4 reads much like our FIST proposal. The analysis should be "clearly stated" (p. 2), "seek the opinions of those who will be affected by the regulation" (p. 3), "be transparent" (p. 3), and "provide references to all sources of data, appendices with documentation of models (where necessary), and results of formal sensitivity . . . analyses" (p. 3). Like our Step 6, the analysis should provide information on all "non-monetized benefits and costs" (p. 27). Like our Step 7, the analysis should "provide separate descriptions of distributional effects" (p. 14).

30. For benefits estimated by market prices, see Willig (1976) and Hanemann (1991). For benefits estimated by hedonic prices, see Epple (1987). For benefits estimated by surveys of users' willingness to pay, see Carson (2012).

Nagel (1987, p. 1). Participatory actions include voting, debating, marching, picketing, contributing, and passive resistance. Step 6 of FIST requires that we be able to measure access to, and utilization of, the means for participation. *Access to* includes regular and competitive elections and referenda, open and transparent legislative and executive deliberations, free mobility across states and communities, and a free press and media. *Utilization of* includes voter participation, formation of and participation in community and political action groups, the creation of and relocation to new communities, switching political parties, and campaign donations of time and money. The implications of the proposed policy for political participation should be reported in the FIST summary.

The implementation of Step 7 of FIST requires a specification of protected individual liberties and rights, standards for economic fairness, and the metrics for their measurement. The specification of protected rights and a commitment to economic fairness may come from the original federal constitution or from the federal statute to be evaluated. Step 7 may require a separate metric for each valued outcome, measured with and without the proposed policy.[31] Metrics should be reported in the FIST summary.

Based on the FIST summary, deliberative discussions within the institutions of Democratic Federalism will debate the balance of the efficiency, participation, and rights outcomes and then choose to implement, or not, the proposed policy. If not, FIST deliberations may suggest possible reforms that would make the policy more attractive to those deciding the balance of national, state, and local responsibilities.

4. Locating FIST

Locating the responsibility for doing the FIST analysis is a matter of institutional design. The aim is to locate the FIST evaluation in the institutional setting most conducive to a transparent, open, and relevant democratic dialogue. There are three choices: within the legislature as an advisory committee to the legislative majority, within the executive branch as an office of evaluation, and finally, as an independent commission providing analyses to the legislature, the executive, and the general electorate. In each case, those

---

31. Ideally each outcome metric could be summarized by individuals or households, ordered by age or by income, and perhaps grouped by race and sex if that is relevant to the stated objectives of the federal policy. It should be recognized that the choice of each metric for aggregating individual outcomes will not be value-free; see Sen (1973).

responsible for FIST evaluations will provide information to, and be supervised by, the legislature, the executive, or, in the case of a commission, to, and by, the general citizenry.

At first glance, the commission approach may appear the most attractive as a vehicle to encourage a deliberative dialogue over federalism policies. By design it can be required to hold open hearings, to be transparent through the dissemination of its rulings, and, with the support of a professional staff, to be reason-giving. Commissions have generally proved ineffective, however. The issue is relevance.[32] The U.S. experience with its federal commission, known as the Advisory Commission on Intergovernmental Relations (ACIR), is instructive.

Created by Congress in 1959, ACIR's mandate was to provide expert advice when asked by Congress or the president; to comment generally on the overall state of U.S. federal, state, and local relations and policies; and most importantly, to review and recommend proposed legislation on federal governance. The commission included representation from each level of the U.S. federal hierarchy: Congress and the executive branch, governors, mayors, county supervisors, and private citizens. In the end, the impact of ACIR on substantive U.S. federalism policy was limited—for two reasons. First, the commission lacked focus. It was asked both to evaluate and recommend policies and to be responsive to the immediate policy demands from Congress, the president, and state and local officials. Second, rather than provide information only, as FIST does, the commission was explicitly required by its enabling legislation to make recommendations on federalism policy. When addressing substantive policies, commission recommendations were the result of partisan lobbying.[33] As a result, the commission lost its credibility as an independent evaluator; and policy-makers turned to their own analysts for information regarding the likely consequences of federal, state, and local policies. ACIR evaluations and

---

32. Much like the judiciary, a FIST commission is an evaluative body without a specific policy portfolio or enforcement powers. And much like the judiciary, relevance of a FIST commission will depend on the acceptance by the general electorate of its rulings. Support will be forthcoming only when (1) the policy being reviewed is salient to the national electorate; (2) the commission is seen as capable of distinguishing beneficial from harmful policies along each of the dimensions—efficiency, participation, and rights and fairness—of federal policy; and (3) the benefits of avoiding a bad policy or adopting a good one are significant to the electorate. See Box 5.2.

33. See McDowell (1997, pp. 117–124).

recommendations were then ignored. The commission's enabling legislation and funding were not renewed in 1997, and the commission was disbanded.

Two commissions, the Finance Commission (FC) in India and the Financial and Fiscal Commission (FFC) in South Africa, have had more success contributing to national deliberations over substantive policies affecting state or provincial and local governments. Both commissions were established as part of the countries' original constitutions with specifically assigned, and therefore focused, evaluative responsibilities.[34] As constitutionally required, their roles are limited to evaluating the allocation of nationally collected tax revenues for the provision of constitutionally assigned national public goods, social insurance, and provincial or state and local services. In both countries, the constitution requires significant revenue sharing from the center to the states and localities. In addition to specifying an aggregate share of revenues for the three levels of government, both commissions also recommend how the assigned state and local shares might be allocated across the individual states and provinces, with allowance for differences in population, average income, age distribution, and rates of poverty.

Over time, both commissions have come to offer recommendations on policies beyond the allocation of national revenues among the tiers of government. India's FC has made recommendations for extending taxing powers to state and local governments and for improving fiscal discipline—the "hard" budget constraint—for national, state, and local borrowing.[35] South Africa's FFC has also recommended increasing tax autonomy for provincial governments and proposed ground rules for provincial and municipal borrowing.

Both the FC and the FFC have made substantive contributions to national federalism policy since their inception, and both continue to be active advisers on national policies affecting state, provincial, and local governments. Unlike the ACIR, the FC and the FFC have remained focused on *national* policies affecting each country's lower-tier governments. The commissions have not been drawn into the details of running state and local governments and have not publicly endorsed policy positions.[36] When the commissions have publicly advocated for a specific federalism reform, they have been ignored; in

---

34. See Article 280 of the Indian Constitution and Chapter 13, Sections 220 and 221, of the South African Constitution.

35. See Rao and Singh (2006).

36. Though, on one important policy matter, the FFC went too far, criticizing the national government's proposed macroeconomic policy in a published FFC document. The minister of

both countries, national politics determines federalism policy. Finally, both the FC and the FFC have become formally integrated into the national budgetary process deliberating federal finances.[37] These are the important institutional lessons learned for the successful location of FIST: the need to remain focused, apolitical, and integral to the policy process.

The alternative to the commission structure is to institutionally embed the FIST analysis directly in the legislative or executive branch, or perhaps in both as a way to encourage public dialogue and the competition of ideas. But to do so places FIST evaluations directly in the path of political decision-making. Within the legislature as a FIST committee, members will be legislators appointed and supervised by the legislative majority. Within the executive branch, the evaluative office will be appointed and supervised by the elected president. The FIST committee or office will then provide information to its supervising elected official. Officials will then use the FIST evaluation to adopt, or reject, the proposed federal policy. A FIST committee or staff cannot change the proposed policy, but it can significantly influence the attractiveness of the policy to the elected official by the content of its analysis. Knowing officials' preferences, it may "tilt" the evaluation to alter the attractiveness of the policy. Credible (that is, accepted) information is power. A damaging FIST report can kill a policy, while a favorable report can encourage its adoption. In this sense, the legislative committee or executive office administering the FIST review becomes a "gatekeeper" to the adoption of new federalism policies.[38]

Which settings, then, legislature or executive, is more conducive to providing an informed and impartial FIST analysis? There are two important cases. The first is when all parties—legislators, the executive, and the evaluators—are equally well informed as to the likely consequences of the proposed federal policy, the case of *symmetric* information. There are no experts—no one legislator, executive, or staff person has better information than any other as to the likely consequences of the policy before the evaluation is to be done. The second case, called *asymmetric* information, allows for experts. Using experts

finance withdrew the document and publicly reprimanded the FFC as overstepping its constitutional mandate; see de Visser and Ayele (2014).

37. The institutional history of the FC is reviewed in Rao and Singh (2006), and that of the FFC is reviewed in de Visser and Ayele (2014).

38. The gatekeeping powers of FIST evaluators arise from their informational advantage; see Gilligan and Krehbiel (1990).

saves on the costs of new and detailed FIST evaluations, but with this risk. Experts often come to the analysis with strong preferences for particular allocation of federal responsibilities, and thus with a bias in favor of specific assignments.

Who, then, should be appointed to do the FIST evaluation? In the case of symmetric information and no obvious expert, the appointing legislature or executive will want someone whose preferences for the assignment, financing, and administration of government policies most closely approximates their own. In this case, the only issue for the location of FIST evaluations is how closely the legislature's or the elected executive's preferences approximate those of the general electorate.[39]

In the case of asymmetric preferences, the value of expertise may dominate the advantage of having a like-minded agent in charge of FIST. Here the choice must weigh the value of information from policy expertise against the risk that the expert doing the FIST analysis will be biased in his or her reporting of a policy assignment. A biased FIST analysis leads to bias away from the legislature's or executive's preferred outcome. The legislature or executive will prefer an expert-run FIST (1) the greater the policy uncertainty; (2) the greater the cost savings from using an expert; and (3) the closer the expert's and decision-maker's preferences.[40] In the case of the legislature, expert FIST committees will be staffed, and experts chosen, by legislators from the majority party. The elected executive has more latitude and can choose the director of the FIST office from a pool of nationally available experts vetted for possible evaluation bias.

Between locating FIST in the legislature or executive branch, we prefer the executive branch for four reasons. First, FIST evaluations will typically entail a wide range of federalism issues, both new policies and the reform of existing policies. With a broad agenda, uncertainty over consequences and (particularly) citizen preferences regarding consequences seems likely. It is doubtful that there will be a single level of expertise useful across all evaluations.[41] As a result, the case of symmetric information seems more compelling. With

---

39. See Gilligan and Krehbiel (1990, p. 546 and appendix A).

40. See Gilligan and Krehbiel (1990, pp. 552–553 and appendix B).

41. Within the executive branch, we prefer centralizing the FIST evaluation rather than assigning FIST to individual agencies supervised by the executive for two reasons. First, a FIST analysis done within an agency will miss, or inadequately evaluate, policies affecting the outcomes outside their domain of expertise. Second, each agency will seek to protect its own domain and thus will be likely to provide biased FIST analyses; see Mendelson's (2008a, pp. 2169–2170) evaluation of the Environmental Protection Agency's efforts at environmental impact analyses.

symmetric information about individual policies, evaluators should be chosen to mirror the preferences of the appointing legislature or executive. Second, legislative preferences will be the result of either universalistic deal making or strong party politics representing the median position of the dominant party. Either way, legislative preferences are likely to be biased away from those of the national median voter.[42] In contrast, the general election of the executive will typically pull the winner's preferences toward the national median.[43] As an exercise in deliberative democracy, presidential elections seem to us the more responsive mechanism to engage and decide the broad issues of federal, state, and local government responsibilities.[44] Third, if there is a role for expertise, it is better to select from a wide pool of trusted experts. Here too, the executive has the advantage. Fourth, if FIST reveals a preferred policy, a strong president has the resources needed to implement that policy. Locating FIST evaluations within the executive branch has one risk, however. FIST analyses may become the "private property" of the executive branch alone. It is essential, therefore, that the enabling FIST legislation or constitutional provision require all FIST evaluations to be publicly distributed in a timely manner.

There is a fourth alternative: competing legislative and executive evaluations as now exist for the design of U.S. national fiscal and regulatory policies. On matters of fiscal policy, the president has the Office of Management and

42. See Poole and Rosenthal (1997, chap. 4) for evidence on the separation of legislators' voting behaviors by political party (liberal vs. conservative) over time. This evidence, coupled with the analysis of Cox and McCubbins (2007) arguing that strong party leadership controls legislative outcomes—and presumably would control our FIST analysis—suggests a bias away from the national median with strong party governance.

43. While presidential candidates will be pulled toward the median position of the party's electorate, they are pulled back toward the national median by the need to win the national election. Evidence for the influence of presidential preferences on national policy from Cameron's analysis of veto bargaining between the legislature and the president indicates that the president pulls congressional proposals or "concessions" toward the president's positions when there is divided government. Conservative Republican proposals are pulled toward the median by more liberal Democratic presidents, as are liberal Democratic proposals by more conservative Republican presidents; see C. Cameron (2000, chap. 6).

44. Certainly this has been the case in U.S. presidential elections since 1932; see Scheiber (1978) generally and J. Schlesinger (1984) for Franklin D. Roosevelt and the New Deal, McDowell (1997) for Dwight Eisenhower's and Reagan's commitment to state governments, Beer (1976) for Richard Nixon and revenue sharing, Weaver (2000) for Clinton and welfare reform, and Metzger (2011) for Barack Obama and the use of state governments within the Affordable Care Act and the American Reinvestment and Recovery Act.

Budget. Within that office, the Office of Information and Regulatory Affairs evaluates regulatory policies.[45] The U.S. Congress has access to the same evaluative capacity through its Congressional Budget Office (CBO). CBO was created as part of the Congressional Budget and Impoundment Control Act of 1974 in response to the legislators' desire for independent evaluations of presidential budgetary requests. The director is to be a nonpartisan appointment nominated by the House and Senate budget committees to serve a four-year term. CBO's primary responsibility is to the budgetary and tax committees of Congress, but the other committees of Congress can ask for policy evaluations by the CBO staff as may be necessary or appropriate. CBO analyses have proved to be an effective counterweight to the informational advantages provided to the president by the Office of Management and Budget.[46]

When tried, has FIST worked? The most prominent application of a FIST procedure has been the implementation of the European Union's founding principles of subsidiarity and proportionality when deciding union policy. For the EU, subsidiarity requires that union policies be limited to only those circumstances in which member-country policies, or negotiated regional policies, cannot achieve a union-wide objective or in which that objective can, for reasons of economies of scale, be more efficiently achieved by union policies. Proportionality requires union policies to be no more extensive than needed to achieve the valid union objective. The European Commission has been charged with implementing these two principles as part of the EU's legislative process; the commission's proposed procedures correspond closely to our seven-step FIST analysis.[47] Like our proposed application of FIST, the commission's procedure is designed to be transparent, open, and reason-giving. For any new legislation or regulation affecting member nations, the commission is to submit a FIST-style analysis to all national parliaments for their

45. Also within the executive branch, under the Office of Domestic Finance in the U.S. Treasury, is the Office of State and Local Finance, whose agenda includes the regulation and supervision of the U.S. municipal bond market but also general matters of state and local finance.

46. See Joyce (2011, pp. 123–127, chap. 8, and p. 211). Requiring FIST analyses by both the president and CBO will not require a new agency or a new bureaucracy. At the moment, the Office of Information and Regulatory Affairs provides such analyses in the president's office and CBO currently has a staff charged with evaluating the costs to state and local government of all federal policies and regulations costing the federal government more than $50 million. The central issue for both offices will be to add a sufficient number of qualified staff; see Sharkey (2012, p. 593) and Inman and Rubinfeld (1997, p. 1293 n. 296).

47. See Moens and Trone (2015, pp. 86–89, 95–96).

review and comment. Parliamentary commentaries that challenge the commission's subsidiarity conclusions, called reasoned opinions, are returned to the commission and shared among all member nations. After commission commentary, one-third of the member nations may require reconsideration of the proposed legislation on the grounds that it violates subsidiarity, a procedure called the yellow card (for Americans, akin to a warning for a soccer violation). At this point, if the commission wishes to continue with the legislation, it will be reviewed again, and if one-half of the parliament's member nations still object, the legislation is tabled for violations of subsidiarity, an outcome known as the orange card.

The commission's process of subsidiarity review has had a significant impact on policy-making within the union. While the orange card has not been used, in at least one important instance the yellow-card procedure proved a sufficiently high hurdle that the commission withdrew a proposed regulation of cross-border labor actions. The process of subsidiarity review has also been instrumental in moving the commission's harmonization policies away from the use of "regulations" and toward an expanded use of "directives." Regulations require member nations to adopt a commission-specified approach to policy harmonization. Directives leave member nations free to decide how to best achieve an EU-wide policy goal. More generally, the commission's use of FIST reviews, coupled with the fact that national parliaments are now formally part of the review process and, with the yellow-card procedures, have a forum through which to coordinate and express their concerns, has led to a significant reduction in commission proposals that raise subsidiarity concerns. Commission proposals "entirely inconsistent with subsidiarity . . . are now . . . rare."[48]

Less successful have been efforts to embed effective FIST reviews within the offices of the U.S. president. The structure for an executive FIST review has been provided by President Clinton's Executive Order 13132 requiring all federal government agencies to provide a FIST-style review whenever an agency's proposed regulation or policy is expected to have "substantial direct effects on the States, on the relationship between the national government and the States, or on the distribution of power and responsibilities among the various levels of government" (Section 1[a]). The difficulty has been in enforcing agency compliance. Executive Order 13132 and its predecessor from President Reagan (Executive Order 12612) have either been ignored completely or, when

---

48. See Cooper (2006, p. 268).

an agency review has been submitted, done in only a perfunctory manner and typically denying any impact on state or local governments.[49]

The Environmental Protection Agency (EPA) has been the one significant exception to the U.S. reluctance to use FIST-style reviews. Catherine Sharkey (2009) suggests two reasons for the EPA's more responsive approach to federal and state regulatory policies. First, the enabling legislation for the EPA explicitly mandates the cooperative enforcement of EPA rulings with state agencies, and second, EPA regulators have come to rely heavily on the technical and political expertise of their state counterparts. The EPA's superior procedural performance aside, however, Nina Mendelson's (2008a, p. 2169) review of the EPA's federalism analyses finds them "impoverished." While EPA staffers understand environmental policy, they have little expertise on matters of federal governance. And perhaps more importantly, as the federal agency responsible for environmental policy, the EPA has little incentive to turn over the implementation of that policy to regulators over whom it has no direct control. To empower FIST analyses, both Sharkey (2009, p. 2174) and Mendelson (2008a, pp. 2171–2174) strongly support our proposal: congressional legislation that requires and codifies FIST analyses by the president and by CBO for significant regulations and policies affecting the responsibilities of federal, state, and local governments.

5. Summing Up

For all its virtues, federal governance is a fragile political institution. While constitutional safeguards can be constructed, as we reviewed in Chapter 5, they will only work if citizens are committed to the benefits of shared powers among local, state, and national governments. At any moment and for any one policy, concentrating powers centrally or locally may seem appropriate, only for it to be discovered later that the decision has significant adverse consequences for one of federalism's valued outcomes at a later date—for example,

---

49. See Mendelson (2004, pp. 783–784), Sharkey (2009, pp. 2138–2143). The General Accounting Office's review of agency compliance with Executive Order 12612 found that of the 11,414 agency rulings issued from 1996 to 1998, 3,016 mentioned the requirements of the executive order for review, but only 5 provided such a review; see L. Nye Stevens (1999, fig. 1). In her own survey of agency compliance, Mendelson (2004, pp. 783–785) sampled six hundred agency regulations over a three-month period and found that only six provided the required federalism impact statements.

bailing out one "worthy" state in fiscal distress today may lead to sizeable nationwide deficits tomorrow.

We have proposed a public dialogue as a means to ensure that all citizens are informed of the federal consequences of such decisions. The dialogue is to be open to all, transparent, reason-giving, and relevant. To facilitate that conversation, we have offered a seven-step review, called FIST, of each major national policy likely to significantly affect the performance of state and local governments. Successful FIST reviews must be constitutionally or statutorily required and located either in a protected independent commission or within the executive office at the presidential level. That said, a politically independent office of policy analysis reporting directly to the legislature can be a valuable counterweight to these executive evaluations; the U.S. CBO is an example.

The question that now remains is, How should we *do* a FIST evaluation? Offered as primers for FIST evaluators, Chapters 7 and 8 provide some guidance for two important areas of national policy-making: fiscal policy and regulatory policy.

7

Fiscal Policy in the Federal Union

1. Introduction

A central role for government in a democracy, whether unitary or federal, is to improve the allocation of national resources for the benefit of all citizens. The first order of government's business is to establish and protect private property rights and to adjudicate contract disputes so as to ensure well-functioning private markets. Yet even with efficient ground rules, private markets will typically not guarantee the full potential of the national economy. If so, what will be needed is a nonmarket mechanism to reveal citizen preferences for those activities external to the market and a way to provide those allocations that are beneficial to citizens given their revealed preferences. In a democracy, that mechanism is voting and that institution is government. Government can achieve a new, and hopefully more efficient, allocation of society's goods and services by direct provision, by changing the incentives of market participants, or by simply regulating or prohibiting inefficient market activities. In this chapter we focus on government's direct provision of public goods and services in a federal public economy using the fiscal policies of spending, taxes, and debt. Chapter 8 evaluates regulatory policy.

2. Spending in a Federal Union: Grants and Contracts

When providing local public goods and services, local and state governments may themselves adopt policies that significantly affect their neighbors. Examples are not hard to find. One local government decides to save money and not treat its wastewater, or to tax nonresidents, or to offer subsidies or tax breaks to lure business away from another community or state. Left alone, such decisions may result in outcomes that the citizens of all local and state governments, collectively, agree are not what they would prefer. What is needed is a decision in a larger forum to correct these externalities. Here that larger forum is the national government and the decision is to design a national policy that encourages local and state governments to fully recognize the wider benefits and costs of their fiscal decisions. In fiscal unions, that national fiscal policy will be intergovernmental grants decided by the national government.

Managing Fiscal Externalities: Matching Aid

The first objective is to have provincial, state, and local government decision-makers meet the same standard for economic efficiency that we require of private market decision-makers: Does the social marginal benefit (SMB) of their decision equal or exceed the associated social marginal cost (SMC)? While this is often the case, it need not always be. Local government decision-makers, like those in the private market, will pay attention only to the private marginal benefit (PMB) and private marginal cost (PMC) of their decision. If, for any reason, private marginal benefits and costs do not equal social marginal benefits and costs, then local government decision-making will be inefficient. When might this occur? In two instances. First, when the benefits of the local government policy extend to citizens outside the local decision-maker's political coalition; in this case, the local government will be spending too little on its local service. Or second, when the costs of the local policy fall on those outside the decision-maker's coalition; in this case, the local government will be spending too much on its local service.

Appropriately designed intergovernmental grants can correct both problems. In the case in which the local decision-maker neglects benefits outside his or her coalition, then the social marginal benefit will exceed the private marginal benefit by an estimated markup of φ: $SMB = \varphi \cdot PMB$, where $\varphi > 1$. Those outside the decision-maker's coalition may live outside the local jurisdiction or live within the jurisdiction but be an ignored minority. The analysis applies equally to both cases. If the social marginal cost still equals the private marginal cost, then the local decision-maker will provide too little of the service when he or she balances private benefits and costs. To encourage an expansion of local services, a centrally provided intergovernmental grant that matches local spending at the rate of $m = 1 - (1/\varphi)$ will do the job, where $m > 0$ as $\varphi > 1$.[1] Now setting the private marginal benefit equal to the private marginal cost net of grant subsidies

1. The case for matching grants as the best central government policy for addressing the problem of fiscal externalities was first made by Oates (1972) in his important treatise on fiscal

will give the efficient allocation: $PMB = [PMC - m \cdot PMC] = [(1-m) \cdot PMC] = (1/\varphi) \cdot PMC$, which becomes $SMB = \varphi \cdot PMB = PMC = SMC$.

Alternatively, in the case in which the local decision-maker ignores the costs he or she may impose on those outside the coalition, then the social marginal cost will be greater than the private marginal cost, perhaps at the estimated rate ρ, where $SMC = \rho \cdot PMC$ and $\rho > 1$. If the social marginal benefit equals the private marginal benefit, the local decision-maker will provide too much of the local service when he or she balances private benefits and costs. The decision-maker needs to be discouraged. Now a centrally designed "surcharge" on the provision of the local service at the rate of $s = \rho - 1$ will give the socially efficient allocation. Setting the private marginal benefit equal to the private marginal cost plus the surcharge, implies $PMB = [PMC + s \cdot PMC] = (1+s) \cdot PMC = \rho \cdot PMC$, which becomes $SMB = PMB = \rho \cdot PMC = SMC$. Again, we have social efficiency, but now with a nationally imposed intergovernmental surcharge.[2]

Figure 7.1 illustrates the advantage of using matching aid to influence the fiscal choices of state and local governments, as seen from the perspective of national taxpayers. Panel (a) shows how a positive matching grant paid at the efficient rate m will affect a local government's fiscal choice. Local officials will choose to make citizens as well off as possible, represented by the citizens' indifference curves, shown by V in Figure 7.1, by choosing the best allocation possible subject to available resources, represented by the budget line $I_0 I_0$ with a slope equal to the local cost (PMC) of buying local public goods. Before matching aid, the local government chooses to provide g_0 in local services and leave y_0 in after-local-tax income to reach its highest local resident indifference curve of V_0. A matching grant lowers the price of local services and allows local officials to buy more services along the new budget line, $I_0 I_m$, with a slope equal to the new price, $(1-m) \cdot PMC$. Now local officials provide g^* in Panel (a) and citizens have an after-local-tax income of y^*. In the case in which $PMC = SMC$ and m is the efficient matching rate, g^* is the socially efficient level of local spending. The cost of the matching grant to national taxpayers will be the new level of local spending times the efficient matching rate, or $m \cdot (PMC \cdot g^*)$, shown in Figure 7.1 as the dollar amount, Z.

---

federalism. Lockwood (1999) places Oates's original analysis within the contemporary perspective of efficient mechanism design.

2. With both positive benefits ($\varphi > 1$) and cost spillovers ($\rho > 1$), the required matching rate for federal efficiency becomes $m = 1 - (\rho / \varphi)$. See Dahlby (1996).

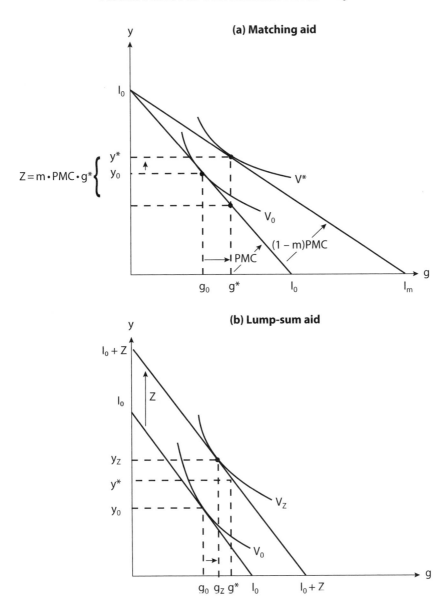

FIGURE 7.1. Matching versus Lump-Sum Aid

Panel (b) shows how an equal-cost lump-sum grant of Z would influence the local coalition's decisions to buy more local services. Now there is no matching grant, so local services are charged the private marginal cost for each unit purchased. If the national taxpayers were to give the ruling local coalition a lump-sum grant (Z) equal to what had been the cost of the matching grant, then Z would equal $m \cdot (\text{PMC} \cdot g^*)$, as shown in Panels (a) and (b). Now the local decision-maker increases local spending on the fiscal externality to only g_Z, less than g^*. Why? Just as consumers might divide an unconstrained grocery coupon between vegetables and cupcakes, so too will the local government divide its Z service "coupon" between the fiscal externality and favored other local services ("cupcakes"). To reach the socially efficient level of the local fiscal externality at g^*, national taxpayers will need to offer a lump-sum grant of $Z^* > Z$ (not shown), potentially far more costly than the matching grant. While national taxpayers clearly prefer the lower-cost matching grant to correct the local government inefficiency, residents of the local community will prefer the nonmatching grant that allows national resources to be spent as the local community most desires. This conflict between the preference of national taxpayers for an efficient matching grant and the desire of local political leaders for an unconstrained lump-sum grant is a constant tension in the design of intergovernmental fiscal policies.

Building Unions and Regional Insurance: The Role for Lump-Sum Aid

There are two circumstances in which lump-sum or unconstrained transfers will have an independent and important role to play in federal fiscal policies: first, when building or expanding a democratic federal union, and second, when insuring local governments against the consequences of adverse economic shocks to their regional economies.

When creating a federal union, the political players in each of the new provincial governments may be unknown to each other. Learning the craft of democratic governance and compromise may be easiest when "dividing a pie" of free money, where everyone can win, rather than first taxing and then allocating provincial monies, with possible losers and winners.[3] Further, unconstrained lump-sum grants are also useful when expanding an existing federal union. A potential new union member with "outside options" may be reluctant to join the union without sharing in the benefits that a larger union affords to current member states. Unconstrained, lump-sum aid provides the greatest direct benefit to a new member and therefore will be the least costly transfer for those in the federation hoping to attract the new member.[4]

---

3. This was an important motivation for the use of lump-sum aid to provinces in the early years of the new democracy in South Africa; see Chapter 10.

4. See Le Breton and Weber (2003). The European Union used lump-sum aid for just this purpose as it expanded its membership in southern and eastern Europe; see Chapter 9.

The second important role for lump-sum aid from the central government to state or local governments is as part of a national social insurance policy to ease the consequences of adverse economic shocks to regional economies. Ideally, the opportunity to move to new, more economically viable locations will provide the residents of the fiscal union with the "insurance" they might need when faced with adverse local economic events, whether temporary (cyclical) or permanent (structural). Labor mobility is both economically and emotionally costly, however. Even in federal unions with high rates of labor mobility, such as Canada and the United States, the adverse consequences of a negative local labor market shock can remain for many years.[5] Absent full labor mobility, one option for residents of an adversely affected local economy is to have their local government borrow from national financial markets and to use those funds to maintain essential public services or to provide direct income insurance for residents. Lacking a local option to borrow (for reasons outlined in Section 3), local governments will then look to their national government for assistance using national fiscal insurance. Relief could be paid directly to individuals, but if local or state governments know best who is most affected and how to pay compensation and maintain local services, then the preferred policy will be a nationally funded lump-sum transfer to the affected local government sufficient to cover temporary resident income and budgetary losses. The grant should be administered by the national government and paid for either by national taxation or by possibly offering less aid to state or local governments that have benefited from a favorable economic shock. If all state or local governments are adversely affected, then aid financed by an increase in national debt will be appropriate, repaid when the aggregate economy improves.[6]

Such a national policy of fiscal insurance for local governments faces two problems. First is the problem of *moral hazard*, which arises when the central government cannot precommit to a precise insurance formula based only on the attributes of the local economy. For example, the local government can

---

5. See Obstfeld and Peri (1998). Estimates for Canada and the United States show that after an initial exogenous 1 percent decline in regional employment, nearly one-fifth of the affected residents are still unemployed or have dropped out of the labor market after five years. It takes from ten to fifteen years for there to again be full employment of regional residents, and this is achieved only by workers leaving the local economy for jobs elsewhere. For every regional job lost initially because of an adverse economic shock, only half of a job returns.

6. See Bordignon, Manasse, and Tabellini (2001, Proposition 2).

invest in public activities that improve the income and job performance of the local economy—perhaps job training or public infrastructure—and does so in part to reduce the adverse consequences of future economic shocks; national fiscal insurance will discourage these local investments. Knowing they will be covered for bad events, local governments have an incentive to under-invest in their own cost- and risk-reducing activities. Lump-sum aid conditional on local economic circumstances is still the correct transfer policy, but in this case payments must be less than full coverage, where the reduced level of federal transfers seeks to strike a balance between income and budget protection and the need to maintain incentives for the local government to still invest in its own risk-reducing activities.[7]

The second problem for the design of regional income insurance arises when the national government cannot accurately measure the income and the budgetary losses to be compensated. In this case, the local government has an informational advantage. How bad, really, is local unemployment? What is the true decline in the local tax base? The national government wants to cover local losses that actually occur, but it must rely on the local government to report what those losses are. This is the problem of adverse selection. To get local governments to reveal their true losses, the national government needs a transfer policy that will encourage each local government to reveal its true "type."

The appropriate policy comes in two parts: a lump-sum transfer for insurance and a matching grant tied to the fiscal behavior of local governments that encourages each government to reveal the true state of its underlying economy. For example, a province very sensitive to, or at risk of, adverse economic shocks is likely to value risk-reducing and redistributive services more highly than a province less sensitive to such shocks. If the national government were to offer a policy that subsidized such programs at a common matching rate, the more at-risk provinces would always buy more of those services than provinces that are less at risk.

The preferred policy will be to offer all local governments a choice of a full-insurance lump-sum grant that covers only the losses of the low at-risk government (Z_L^*) or a matching grant at rate θ that covers a share of the costs of redistributive services. The matching rate would be chosen so that the localities at low risk will always prefer their full-insurance lump-sum grant to the

7. See Persson and Tabellini (1996, Proposition 3). In practice, intergovernmental transfers have offered less than full insurance; see Bayoumi and Masson (1995), Sorensen, Wu, and Yosha (2001), and Mélitz and Zumer (2002).

matching grant. Alternatively, the localities at high risk that need redistributive services will always prefer the matching grant to the modest lump-sum grant. With an appropriately specified two-part policy of Z_L^* and θ, localities will reveal their true, at-risk types.[8] This insurance policy that uses both lump-sum and matching aid (Z_L^*, θ) will always be more efficient than offering a single lump-sum transfer or a common matching rate to all local governments.

Protecting the Federal Compact: Equalization Aid

Creating a federal union will almost always lead to rich and poor states. Assigning policy responsibilities to state and local governments will favor residents of richer localities. They have a larger tax base. The stability of the federal compact may require adherence to a principle of horizontal equity: equal treatment of equals irrespective of geography. Both the Canadian and South African constitutions have an explicit commitment to this objective.[9]

Implementation requires a working definition of horizontal equity: if two provinces choose to buy the same level of public services, then residents in the two provinces with the same tax base should make the same tax payment. "Equals" will be national residents with identical tax bases and "equal treatment" who will be paying identical taxes for identical levels of local public services. Intergovernmental transfers that equalize cost-adjusted tax bases across all provinces and local governments will achieve this outcome; see Box 7.1.

For national fiscal policy to implement a common, cost-adjusted provincial or local tax base, each locality will need to be given sufficient aid so that when applying its chosen tax rate to its actual cost-adjusted tax base, it receives the same services that it would if it had a common, national target cost-adjusted base. The appropriate per-capita grant, denoted as AID/N in Box 7.1, will be the transfer needed so that each local resident can buy a common bundle of local public services for the same local tax payment, no matter in which locality they may reside. Ineffective or high-need, high-cost, low-tax-base localities will have a relatively low cost-adjusted tax base per resident and will qualify for positive aid. In contrast, effective or low-need, low-cost, high-tax-base localities will receive less aid and may even be asked to contribute to the national treasury to finance positive transfers to the less well-endowed local governments. Full

8. See Lockwood (1999) and Bordignon, Manasse, and Tabellini (2001).

9. See the Canadian Constitution of 1982 at Subsection 36(2) and the Constitution of the Republic of South Africa at Chapter 13, Section 214, 1(b) and 2(e–g).

Box 7.1. Horizontal Fiscal Equity and Equalization Aid

To satisfy the principle of horizontal fiscal equity in the provision of provincial, state, or local public goods, the central government will need to ensure that residents in each locality can buy their public services from an equal *cost-adjusted tax base per resident*, $\bar{I}^*$. To do so, the national government must specify (1) how local government tax bases, input costs, and service needs affect the ability of resident taxes to provide resident services; (2) the fiscal rule that must be met to achieve horizontal equity for residents; and (3) how nationally funded equalization aid can satisfy the rule for horizontal equity.

Resident Taxes and Resident Services

A resident with a local tax base of I will pay taxes equal to Tax $= r(g) \cdot I$, where $r(g)$ is the local tax rate needed to provide services, g. The total cost for the local government to provide g will be $k \cdot X$, where k is the average cost of buying X units of an input sufficient to provide g. Finally, each public input will be shared by the local government's N residents, so that $g = \gamma \cdot (X/N)$, where γ is a measure of the relative effectiveness of, or "need" for, public inputs in providing public services in that local jurisdiction.

The Rule for Horizontal Equity

Horizontal equity will require all residents with identical tax bases to pay the same amount in taxes for the same level of services received. Given the jurisdiction's total tax base, $\bar{I} \cdot N$, the tax rate must be sufficient to cover the costs of producing g, where $\bar{I}$ is the average tax base per resident. Therefore, $r(g) \cdot \bar{I} \cdot N = k \cdot X$, or $r(g) = (k \cdot X/\bar{I} \cdot N)$. The resident's actual tax payment will be $r(g) \cdot I = [(k \cdot X/\bar{I} \cdot N)] \cdot I = \{[I/\bar{I}] \cdot [k/\gamma]\} \cdot g$ as $X/N = (g/\gamma)$. Horizontal equity therefore requires equalizing $\{[I/\bar{I}] \cdot [k/\gamma]\}$ across all local jurisdictions to ensure that all taxpayers of income I will have the same tax payment for the same level of local services. To do so requires setting each local government's cost-adjusted tax base per resident—$\bar{I} \cdot (\gamma/k)$—equal to a common target base per resident of $\bar{I}^*$. Once equalized, each citizen's tax payment becomes $r(g) \cdot I = [I/\bar{I}^*] \cdot g$ and horizontal equity is achieved. All citizens with an income I will have the same tax payments for the same level of local services.

Intergovernmental Aid for Full Horizontal Equity

For national fiscal policy to implement a common, cost-adjusted local tax base, each jurisdiction will need to be given sufficient intergovernmental aid (AID) so that, when applying its chosen tax rate $r(g)$ to its own cost-adjusted tax base, the jurisdiction raises the same revenues that it would if it had the target cost-adjusted base. That is,

$$r(g) \cdot [\bar{I}(\gamma/k) \cdot N] + AID = [r(g) \cdot (\bar{I}^* \cdot N)], \text{ or}$$

$$AID = [r(g) \cdot (\bar{I}^* \cdot N)] - r(g) \cdot [\bar{I} \cdot (\gamma/k) \cdot N], \text{ or}$$

$$AID/N = \{1 - ([(\gamma/k) \cdot \bar{I}]/\bar{I}^*)\} \cdot [r(g) \cdot \bar{I}^*].$$

AID/N is the required intergovernmental transfer that needs to be paid to each local government so that each resident can buy a common bundle of public services for the same tax payment, no matter in which jurisdiction they may reside. A local jurisdiction's AID/N is greater the lower the jurisdiction's actual tax base per capita ($\bar{I}$ declines), the less efficient the community is in the use of local inputs (γ declines), and the higher the costs the jurisdiction pays (k rises) to buy its public service inputs. Further, AID/N rises as the local government raises its tax rate, $r(g)$.

Administering Equalization Aid

Implementation of AID/N requires the national government to assign an index of input costs (k), an index of input effectiveness (γ), and an average tax base ($\bar{I}$) to each jurisdiction. The national government must then select a target *cost-adjusted tax base* ($\bar{I}^*$). Given $\bar{I}^*$, AID/N for each local government follows from the application of the equalization aid formula. It is possible that some local governments will be required to contribute to (AID/N < 0) rather than receive (AID/N > 0) aid as their cost-adjusted tax base is greater than, or less than, $\bar{I}^*$. Relatively rich, low-cost, and efficient jurisdictions receive less equalization aid. Higher values of $\bar{I}^*$ result in greater intergovernmental aid for all jurisdictions.

---

equalization aid will also be a "matching grant" with aid payments rising as local governments increase their tax rates and spending.

Though achieving horizontal equity, fully equalizing aid raises three concerns. First, a local jurisdiction that pays higher costs for its public inputs or whose inputs are used less efficiently in providing government services will receive more intergovernmental aid per capita. As a result, equalizing aid may encourage local governments to pay too much for local inputs (particularly public employees) or to use those inputs inefficiently. The solution is to select *exogenous* indicators of input costs and government performance applied uniformly to each jurisdiction.

Second, if jurisdictions are free to choose their own local tax rates, the matching rate implicit in full equalization aid will create an incentive to overspend on local services. To control this inefficiency, the equalization aid formula will need to preselect a value for the local tax rate beyond which no additional aid should be given. That exogenous local tax rate creates a *representative tax system*. Local governments now receive the same revenues as available to a jurisdiction with a representative tax base per resident, applying a representative tax rate.[10] As a result, local choice no longer determines equalization aid, and thus aid becomes a de facto lump-sum grant. There are two consequences of this respecification. First, since there is no additional aid

---

10. See Smart (1998) for an application to the Canadian equalization formula for grants-in-aid.

for additional spending, there will be no adverse incentive to overspend on services. That's the good news. But second, by "capping" equalization aid, taxpayers in rich and low-cost provinces will again be able to buy additional services beyond the limit for less than taxpayers in poor and high-cost jurisdictions. Full horizontal equity no longer holds. And in the limit, if we wish to remove all adverse spending incentives, then the spending cap should be set at the *lowest* service level among all local jurisdictions. If so, equalization aid's ability to reduce horizontal inequities will be significantly reduced. That's the bad news.

Third, whether full equalization aid or aid paid in response to a representative tax, relatively poor jurisdictions will receive more aid than relatively rich jurisdictions. That, of course, is the point. But there may be political resistance by the losing governments to such a scheme, and particularly so if some governments are asked to contribute to the national treasury. There are two possible responses. First, raise the spending limit for aid so that even the richest jurisdictions receive assistance. This will be very expensive, however, when there are very rich localities. Or second, the aid policy can impose a constraint that no locality can be "taxed" by the policy—that is, "receive" negative aid. But then again, full horizontal equity will be lost. Residents in rich or low-cost localities will still be better off than their less favored citizens.

Specifying an equalization grant for horizontal equity will inevitably involve economic and political trade-offs. Full horizontal equity can be achieved, but at the cost of inefficient overprovision of local public goods and high national taxation. Partial equalization can be achieved, but then the low-cost, low-need, rich localities will remain in a favored fiscal position when financing local services.

Contract Federalism: Project Aid

The boundary between national and local government responsibilities is not always bright. It may be that neither level of government is fully efficient in the provision of a government service. Typically, the national government has a comparative advantage in financing and coordination across governments, but local governments have a comparative advantage in service provision because of local expertise. To take full advantage of both efficient financing and efficient service provision will require the national government and the state and local governments to cooperate. Federalism scholars from political science and the law have called the resulting joint governance by national and local governments "cooperative federalism," the "new federalism," "polyphonic federalism," or the "new nationalism."[11] We prefer the label "contract federalism," since it is a formal contract between the two levels of government for the joint financing and provision of services that is at the heart of this new form of federal governance.

A federalism contract that shares powers between national and state and local governments has four important features. First, the contract is a bilateral contract between the national government and each state or local government and is unique to local circumstances. Such contracts provide national financing known as "project aid" in return for service provision by the state or local government. It is now common for all U.S. states and most large cities to have offices in Washington, DC, whose primary function it is to apply for, and negotiate the terms of, such bilateral federal project grants.

Second, the process of bargaining begins with an offer by the national government of a fiscal contract that will pay money to the state or local government for the provision of state or local services. The national government values those services, and the state or local government is the efficient provider. The national government will therefore be the "principal" and the state or local government the "agent" in the contracting relationship.

Third, while the national government "controls" the terms of the contract, the local government has the right to reject the contract. No local government is required to join the contract if its provisions are unacceptable to local residents—a requirement that contract theorists call the participation constraint. In U.S. federalism, the participation constraint is enforced by the Unfunded Mandates Reform Act of 1995 and the "anti-commandeering" rulings of the U.S. Supreme Court in *New York v. United States* and *Printz v. United States*. Both seek to limit the ability of the national government to unilaterally impose costly service or regulatory mandates on local governments.

Fourth, the contract must address the fact that local governments have a potential informational advantage. That advantage comes in two forms: asymmetric information and moral hazard. First, only local officials know local tastes and local costs when providing the good or service with regional or national spillovers. This is asymmetric information. The national government prefers a high matching rate for those local governments with low own

11. Hills (1998) and Sharkey (2009) call the new form of governance "cooperative federalism," Metzger (2008) the "new federalism," Schapiro (2009) "polyphonic federalism," and Young (2001) and Gerken (2014a) the "new nationalism."

demand for, or high own-cost technologies of, the spillover good. But a high matching rate is preferred by all local governments, no matter their demands or costs. Thus, all local governments will announce they are low demand and/or high cost. As a result, the national government will overpay intergovernmental aid, resulting in an inefficient overprovision of the local spillover good for some governments. Second, the national government may know local demands and local technologies but not be able to judge the effort made by local officials in providing the spillover good. This is moral hazard. Local officials may have a private incentive to be lazy or corrupt, appear to be high cost, and thus be "rewarded" with a high matching grant. While federal contracts can be written to address both problems, the contracts will be less than fully efficient.[12]

What should the national government do when there is an asymmetry of information? The analysis will be the same if we focus on differences in local demands or costs, so let's focus on differences in demand. We assume that the national government knows what level of the spillover good the high-demand local government would provide for a given matching rate and also what level of the good a low-demand local government would provide for the same matching rate. What the national government does not know is which local governments are in fact high or low demanders. It does know, however, that the high-demand local governments will always demand more of the spillover good than the low-demand local governments for the same incomes and matching rates. The best strategy is to offer two contracts, one appropriate for a high-demand local government and a second appropriate for the low-demand local government. If specified correctly, the high-demand governments will prefer the contract appropriate for their economic circumstances and the low-demand governments will opt for the contract appropriate for theirs. Neither government will prefer the other's contract. If so, the two contracts define a "separating equilibrium," which represents the best the national government can do given that it does not know everything about every local government.

What are the key features of the two contracts? The contract meant for the low-demand government has the higher matching rate consistent with what would be needed for the efficient provision of the local public good by the low demander. The contract meant for the high-demand government will have a lower matching rate consistent with what would be needed for the efficient provision of the local public good by a high demander. If that were all that

12. The analysis that follows is based on the arguments, though simplified here, presented in Boadway, Horiba, and Jha (1999).

would be offered, the high demander would conceal its "true identity" as a high demander, announce it is a low demander, and receive the high-matching-rate contract. What, then, can the national government do to discourage such behavior and still reveal true identities?

The answer is to add some additional funding to the low-matching-rate contract meant for the high demander in the form of an exogenous lump-sum grant that is just sufficient to induce the high demander to prefer the combined contract with a low (but still efficient) matching rate *plus* the additional lump-sum funding, but not so much lump-sum funding that it would encourage the low demander to opt out of its efficient high-matching-rate contract. Appropriately structured, the low demander takes the high-matching-rate contract and the high demander accepts the low-matching-rate plus lump-sum-aid contract. By accepting the latter contract, the high-demand local government earns an "informational rent" equal to the lump-sum aid needed to have the government reveal its true demand for the spillover good. When in place, the required separating equilibrium will be reached and local allocations with aid will be efficient.[13]

Knowing local demands and technologies, however, may not be enough for an efficient intergovernmental contract. With moral hazard, corrupt or just lazy local officials may misappropriate the national grant for their own purposes, a common problem in developing economies.[14] Though local government "effort" cannot be accurately measured, government outcomes often can. The national government may know whether the downstream water is clean, whether roads are built, and whether the children of the community can read and do basic mathematics. In such cases, the national government will want to design an intergovernmental contract that stresses performance and will prefer a federal contract that encourages high effort.[15]

Such contracts should include a "pay-for-performance" clause in the form of a matching grant that rewards local expenditures that lead to measured

---

13. The formal details for designing such separating contracts are presented in Bolton and Dewatripont (2005, pp. 52–56).

14. See Boadway and Shah (2009, chap.16) and Bardhan and Mookherjee (2006).

15. For how the courts might enforce such contracts between governments, as distinct from contracts between private parties, see Fahey (forthcoming). Lacking judicial enforcement, enforcement will turn on political monitoring; see McCubbins and Schwartz (1984). Reinikka and Svensson (2004) provide a fascinating study of the control of local corruption in the spending of school aid in Ugandan villages, best achieved by informing the women in the villages of how much in school resources their children *should* receive.

higher outputs of local spillover goods. But local officials may resist a performance-only contract. If they make large expenditures or a large "effort" but experience a bad event that reduces the measured outcomes—such as heavy rains, damaging freezes, or flu on the school testing day—they may lose money. To ensure participation, local governments will need a contract that guarantees at least some payment independent of performance outcomes. That protection can be provided by including a lump-sum grant as part of the federal contract. To both protect the interests of the national government against the problem of moral hazard and ensure the participation of local governments, therefore, the federal contract must be of the form $Z + \mu \cdot g$, where the grant Z is a lump-sum payment for participating in the contract and μ is the matching rate of performance reimbursement, measured in dollars per unit of observed service outcomes, g.

The federal contract's exact value for lump-sum aid and the matching rate will jointly depend on the extent of national or regional spillovers from the local good—that is, the local good's social marginal benefit—and the local government's outcome uncertainty and tolerance for risk. Both are likely to be unique to each local government, and the negotiated federal contract will be unique as well. The larger the social marginal benefit from the provision of the local public good—that is, the greater the spillovers—the more willing the national government will be to offer a performance matching grant, and so the greater the negotiated matching rate (μ) will be. The more risk averse the local government or the greater the uncertainty that local effort will translate into improved local outcomes, the greater the lump-sum aid (Z) paid to ensure that the local government participates in the contract must be.

Contract federalism is the new reality for much of intergovernmental finance. The enabling national legislation will set broad parameters of intergovernmental fiscal policy and then leave the details of policy implementation to a supervising national agency.[16] The agency uses its best estimates of the spillover benefits from a state or local government service and each government's own demands for the local service to set an "opening offer" for a matching rate for the provision of the local service. For contracts tied to local performance with uncertain outcomes—children's test scores, pollution abated, roads paved—the agency will need to guess the local government's "enthusiasm" for participating in the federal contract, conditional on uncertainty in outcome

16. For an example of how such contracts have actually been negotiated, see Chernick's (1979) study of national water and sewer grants paid to local governments.

performance and local officials' risk aversion to a bad—that is, locally expensive—outcome. The national agency may need to offer a lump-sum grant to ensure local participation in the contract. The local government then accepts or rejects the agency's proposed contract; if rejected, negotiations may move to a second round. The final outcome will be a contract between the national government and the local government for the provision of a spillover public good, unique to each government.[17]

A FIST Evaluation: Welfare Aid Reform

The ability of intergovernmental transfers to achieve their full value as policy instruments in a federal union turns crucially on the willingness of the central government to use the policies for the objectives for which they have been designed: matching aid for spillovers, lump-sum aid for fiscal stabilization against adverse regional shocks, and equalization aid for horizontal equity. The record of performance for U.S. intergovernmental aid has been mixed, however. As stressed in Chapter 4, representation of state or provincial governments in the national legislature will create pressure to focus on local rather than national interests. As seen in Figure 7.1, the preferred local policy will be unconstrained, lump-sum aid rather than an efficient targeted, matching grant. Here is where a FIST evaluation might be useful. As an example, consider the passage of the Personal Responsibility and Work Opportunity Reconciliation Act of 1996 (PRWORA), a reform for the intergovernmental financing of U.S. welfare policy.

PRWORA changed the U.S. national government's means for financing state-provided, lower-income assistance. Funding went from using a matching grant, Aid to Families with Dependent Children, to using a uniform lump-sum grant per eligible recipient, Temporary Assistance for Needy Families. In so doing, PRWORA shifted U.S. poverty funding away from a nationally specified entitlement for eligible participants to a discretionary income transfer set by state policies. The legislation stressed two new objectives: first, the return of responsibility for the design of income support policies to elected state and local officials, and second, the encouragement of state and local

---

17. An example of when state or local governments rejected a federal matching program because of wider political risks is the decision by eighteen states to reject a financially attractive expansion of federal matching aid for lower-income health-care services (Medicaid) as part of President Obama's American Recovery and Reinvestment Act. What was missing from the negotiations was the use of lump-sum aid to encourage program participation.

experimentation in program design and implementation. Funding for the reform reduced national welfare funding by $55 billion over the first five years.

The consequences of the PRWORA reforms have been significant. One objective of the original Aid to Families with Dependent Children funding formula was to control a "race to the bottom" in the state-provided welfare services. Taxpayers will exit high-welfare, high-taxation states, just as lower-income residents are attracted to those states.[18] Relocation continues until after-tax incomes for both groups are equalized among all locations.[19] The consequence will be an inefficient location of workers and firms across jurisdictions—a negative spillover—perhaps as large as ten to twenty cents for every extra dollar in state revenue raised to support increased welfare spending.[20] The efficient fiscal solution to manage the spillovers of state-provided income support is a matching grant that pays for state transfers to lower-income households.

Fairness measured by access to, and the level of support for, transfers to lower-income families may also suffer. Replacing a matching grant that pays a fraction of each additional dollar of income support with a lump-sum grant that may be spent more widely removes an important incentive to concentrate federal and state spending on transfers to lower-income families. At the time of passage, Chernick (1998) estimated that aggregate spending for income support would decline by 35 percent with PRWORA reforms. In fact the decline has been much greater, perhaps as much as 70 percent.[21] Funds "released" from state welfare budgets have gone into general state spending, tax relief, and the repayment of outstanding state debt. The result is a U.S. welfare system that now provides only modest income protection for lower-income families, an outcome particularly evident during the recent Great Recession.[22] The primary beneficiaries of these changes in the structure of U.S. funding for welfare services have been middle-class taxpayers, the core political constituency of the governors managing the new reforms.

While PRWORA's structure of intergovernmental finance has had adverse effects for economic efficiency and economic fairness, there have been benefits with respect to local responsiveness to citizen preferences.[23] The evidence

---

18. See Helms (1985) and Haughwout and Inman (2002).
19. See Feldstein and Wrobel (1998), Gelbach (2004), and Baicker (2005).
20. See Wildasin (1991, 1999).
21. See Gelbach (2004) and Baicker (2005).
22. See Ziliak (2016, table 4.5, fig. 4.4.B) and Bitler and Hoynes (2016).
23. See Gelbach (2016).

suggests that the preferences of middle-income state voters (especially lower-skilled workers) were being heard when setting the new levels of welfare funding.[24] Following the passage of PRWORA, state spending shifted away from services for the poor and toward more spending for middle-income services and tax relief. Finally, at the time of the reform, there was also hope that the reform would stimulate state policy innovations as conjectured by Justice Brandeis. In fact, the record is mixed at best.[25]

Figure 7.2 outlines a possible FIST analysis for PRWORA. From Step 1, the proposed reforms did not seriously threaten the political or economic independence of state governments from national policies; on the contrary, state policy responsibilities were increased. From Step 2, the evidence suggests significant tax spillovers from state financing and potential spending spillovers, as evidence of a "race to the bottom" in state welfare policies. Further, revealed preferences from national charitable contributions for local disasters show that residents of one state care about the economic welfare of the less fortunate in other states, although survey evidence suggests that this "goodwill" is limited to the "deserving poor." There is no evidence that states have sought to coordinate their welfare policies to address these spillovers. Thus, from Step 3, national policies for welfare services are appropriate. From Step 4, welfare services as national public goods show no significant economies of scale in service provision. Thus state and local governments can "produce" the service efficiently; the issue of whether there should be national financing for those services remains. In Step 5, we observe that there is a likely informational advantage in using state and local governments to reveal relevant facts for the provision of welfare services as local economies and social environments differ—who is poor, what will work. As policy circumstances are often unique to each locality, local policies and national financing should vary by locality. This is best done by bilateral contracting coupled with national oversight of local policy variation. From Step 6, there is significant variation in local preferences for redistribution; the decentralization of policy responsibility and the increased use of lump-sum aid have allowed that variation to be expressed through local policies. From Step 7, PRWORA's decision to replace matching

---

24. Moffitt, Ribar, and Wilhelm (1998); Moffitt (1999).

25. See Carlino and Inman (2016) and Grogger and Karoly (2005, chaps. 6, 7). PRWORA did include "maintenance of effort" requirements, but enforcement has been difficult; see Germanis (2016) and Semuels (2016).

Step 1 Sovereignty Test: *Does the federal legislation or executive order threaten the ability of state and local governments to function as politically and economically independent organizations within the federal system?*
No, proceed to Step 2

Step 2 Efficiency Test: *Is the service a national public good, entail cross-state spillovers, or national merit good?*
Yes: *Evidence of tax spillovers in financing and spending spillovers in benefits.*
Proceed to Step 3

Step 3 Efficiency Test: *Are efficient agreements across state or local goverments possible?*
No: *No evidence of shared state agreements for welfare financing or provision.*
Proceed to Step 4

Step 4 Efficiency Test: *Is the service a national public good, entail cross-state spillovers, or national merit good?*
Yes: *There is evidence of state taxation spillovers and a "race to the bottom" in services.*
Proceed to Step 5

Step 5 Efficiency Test: *Do state or local governments have an informational advantage in the provision of the spillover or merit good?*
Yes: *Local informational advantage in service provision favors bilateral contracting and national oversight.*
Proceed to Step 6

Step 6 Participation Test: *Will state and local government provision encourage increased citizen participation?*
Yes: *Evidence that state welfare policies vary with citizen preferences but little evidence of replicable innovations.*
Proceed to Step 7

Step 7 Rights and Fairness Test: *Does national provision or financing protect individual rights and/or enhance economic fairness?*
Yes: *Evidence that matching (AFDC) aid is significantly more protective of basic economic security than lump-sum (TANF) aid.*

Summarize

FIGURE 7.2. A FIST Evaluation for PRWORA

aid with lump-sum financing was predicted to have, and has had, significant adverse effects on the economic safety net for lower-income households.

In summary, a FIST analysis for PRWORA would have likely revealed a significantly lower safety net for lower-income families after reform and, by dropping the matching rate in favor of lump-sum assistance, less efficiency in the location of labor across states. In return, PRWORA gave greater control to state and local residents for the allocation of welfare spending, allowing national welfare policies to be more responsive to the preferences of the median-income residents of participating states. The decision to approve PRWORA should reflect the balancing of these (here) competing objectives of federal governance.

3. Raising Money in a Federal Union: Taxation

The benefits of federal governance arise from local choice. Citizen choice is likely to be most meaningful when citizens' own economic resources are directly at stake. Paying local and state taxes creates the incentives needed for effective citizen supervision of their elected local and state officials. The goal for the assignment of state and local taxation is to encourage the efficient allocation of public and private resources and to conform as closely as possible to societal agreed-to norms of economic fairness. From the perspective of economic efficiency, the Founding Fathers had it right. Differential local taxation of mobile economic factors of production may create two economic harms. First there is the danger that local taxes will disfavor those working in one state but residing outside the state.[26] Second, tax competition between state and local governments may discourage local taxation of mobile factors of production.[27] State and local tax assignment should seek to avoid both problems, or at least minimize their consequences.

Federal Principles for Efficient State and Local Taxation

Broadly defined, there are two types of state and local taxes. First are *resident-based* (also known as *destination-based*) taxes on residents' labor and capital incomes, on the consumption of residents, and on the value of locally owned property. Second are *source-based* (or *origin-based*) taxes, which tax the returns

26. James Madison in *Federalist* No. 42 summarizes his concern that states would tax the economic activities of nonresidents to the benefit of residents and the harm of nonresidents: "It must be foreseen that ways would be found out to load articles of import and export, during passage through their jurisdiction, with duties which would fall on the makers of the latter, and consumers of the former.... The desire of the commercial States to collect in any form, an indirect revenue from their uncommercial neighbors, must appear not less impolite than it is unfair; since it will stimulate the injured party ... to resort to less convenient channels for their foreign trade" (Hamilton, Madison, and Jay, 1982, p. 214).

27. After making the general argument for customs duties as the preferred tax, Alexander Hamilton, in *Federalist* No. 12, worried that there may be a "race to the bottom" if collecting the tax were left to the states alone: "The difference between a direct importation from abroad and indirect importation, through the channel of a neighboring State, in small parcels, according to time and opportunity, with the additional facilities of inland communication, must be palpable to every man of discernment. It is therefore, evident, that one national government would be able, at much less expense, to extend the duties on imports, beyond comparison further, than would be practicable to the States separately" (Hamilton, Madison, and Jay, 1982, pp. 58–59).

to factors of production in the location where the factors are employed and the consumption of goods and services where they are purchased. Examples include capital income and property taxation of local firms, and nonresident wage, sales, and natural resource taxes. As a general proposition for efficient taxation, it is best to avoid the taxation of factors of production or source-based taxation and to tax the final consumption of goods and services.[28] In the federal economy, that advice favors resident-based taxation.

Resident-based taxation may not always be fully efficient, however. Like all taxes, resident-based taxation can have adverse effects on the labor, investment, and consumption decisions of residents. The inefficiency of the residential tax—also known as its "excess burden"—arises because the tax raises prices and thus reduces the residents' consumption of valued goods and services. Alternatively, the tax lowers returns and thus reduces the residents' supply of valued factors of production. The loss in economic value will be small when the taxed commodity is inelastically demanded as prices rise—the residents really need the good—or is inelastically supplied as after-tax returns fall—the residents really must offer the factor of production. In general, as tax rates rise, the adverse impacts on consumption or factor supply increase, and so does the average excess burden of taxation per dollar of revenue raised.[29]

The most efficient resident taxes are taxes on residents' work decisions, on income, and on their consumption of necessities like food and clothing. For a typical state or local community, the estimated excess burdens of these residential taxes are relatively modest, given that they are inelastically suppled or demanded. Plausible estimates of the average excess burden per dollar of revenue raised from a residential tax on labor income or residential consumption is only about five cents on the dollar. Slightly higher is the average excess burden per dollar of revenue for the residential property tax. When appropriately viewed as a tax on housing consumption, the excess burden per dollar of revenue raised is close to ten cents.[30] Best of all of residential taxes, since it will

28. As shown by Diamond and Mirrlees (1971).

29. Our estimates of excess burden will be the *average* excess burden per dollar of revenue raised. This is the appropriate measure when choosing between taxes. In the simplest case, with no income effects, the average excess burden per dollar of revenue raised will be: Excess Burden / Revenues $= E = .5 \cdot \tau / \{(1 / |\varepsilon_D|) + (1 / \varepsilon_S)\}$, where τ is the tax rate, $|\varepsilon_D|$ is the absolute value for the elasticity of demand for the taxed good, and ε_S is the elasticity of supply of the taxed good.

30. $E = .05$ for values of $\tau = .10$, $|\varepsilon_D| = 1.5$ and $\varepsilon_S = 2$ for residential labor and residential consumption. For residential housing consumption $E = .10$ for values of $\tau = .33$, $|\varepsilon_D| = 1.0$ and

be inelastically supplied, is a tax on the value of land inclusive of the present value, if any, of the land's mineral rights.[31] When making choices for spending on state and local public goods, local officials should recognize the full cost of taking resources from the private sector and thus include both the revenues collected and the excess burden imposed on the private economy by their local taxes. To lower the overall cost of government, local officials should prefer low-excess-burden taxes.

Though the estimated tax inefficiencies of residential taxes are relatively low at the local level, these taxes may create a tax inefficiency at the national level that is unique to fiscal unions. It arises when local governments share a tax base with the national government, thereby creating a "vertical tax externality" between the union's lower and upper tiers of government. If national and local governments share the same residential tax base, then an increase in the residential tax rate by any one government will raise all governments' combined tax rate, and thus the excess burdens all governments now face when deciding taxes. The resulting increase in the excess burden of taxation of the shared tax base will be a negative tax externality borne by all other governments when they purchase public services. The final tax choices of all governments, and thus the combined tax rate and the ultimate degree of fiscal inefficiency, will depend on the final outcome of their joint tax decisions.[32] An increase in the rate of one level of government may discourage the use of the tax by the other, or alternatively, the preferred tax rates of all governments may rise together. The efficiency consequences will be worse if the rates move in tandem, and this is what the evidence suggests.[33] If so, the resulting vertical tax externality will increase the social marginal cost of taxation for each level of government

---

$\varepsilon_S = 2.0$. A tax on housing value is equivalent to a tax on housing consumption of $\tau = (r \cdot V / \rho \cdot V) = (r / \rho)$, where r is the property tax on home value, ρ the rental rate for housing services, and V is the value of the home. For a local property tax rate on value of .02 and rental rate for housing services of .06, then $\tau = .33$.

31. If the elasticity of the supply of land in a jurisdiction is perfectly inelastic, then $\varepsilon_S = 0$ and thus $E = 0$. Importantly, the value of the land must be measured in its "highest and best use"; see Oates and Schwab (1997).

32. For how these joint tax decisions might be made, see Keen (1998); see also Keen and Kotsogiannis (2002).

33. For evidence of state or provincial and national taxation from Canada, see Esteller-Moré and Solé-Ollé (2002); from the United States, see Besley and Rosen (1998), Esteller-Moré and Solé-Ollé (2001), and Devereux, Lockwood, and Redoano (2008); from Switzerland, see Brülhart and Jametti (2006).

above each government's perception of its own private marginal cost—that is, $PMC = \lambda \cdot SMC$, where $\lambda < 1$. Local governments will ignore these added national tax inefficiencies from the shared tax base and will tax too much.[34] Fortunately, there is a national policy response that continues to allow for local choice and the use of a local residential tax but can correct for this national tax inefficiency. It will be for the national government to impose a tax surcharge on the use of the local tax shared with the national government.

In principle, local residents' incomes, consumption, and assets will be the preferred tax bases for state and local governments in a federal economy. In practice, however, collecting such local taxes may be difficult if residents work, consume, and own assets outside their taxing jurisdictions. Resident taxation requires detailed records by location for all taxed activities. While this may be possible in developed economies with the records and addresses required of national transactions, it is certainly not so in developing economies. As a consequence, many residential taxes may not be administratively feasible at the local level. Far easier to collect are source-based taxes as, by definition, the taxed activity—work, consumption, and investment—takes place within the local jurisdiction. State and local governments often prefer to tax activities "where they work," not "where they live." Unfortunately, source-based taxation introduces two economic inefficiencies arising from their *direct* and *indirect* revenue effects.[35]

The *direct* revenue effect of a source-based tax arises from the revenue that the tax raises from nonresidents. Examples include taxation of the profits of firms owned by nonresidents, taxation of the wages of nonresidents who work within the jurisdiction, and taxation of the sales of goods to nonresidents, including, perhaps most importantly, natural resources sold to firms outside the state or locality. The political attraction of source-based taxation for local jurisdictions is obvious. Revenues collected from nonresidents are monies that will pay for services consumed by residents. The national efficiency consequences of these taxes can be sizeable, however.

Figure 7.3 illustrates the consequences for resource allocations from source-based taxation when one state or local government taxes a mobile factor of

34. See Dahlby (2008, chap. 9), who estimates that for the most likely responses of national and local taxation using a shared tax base, $PMC = .75 \cdot SMC$.

35. For the foundational theoretical analysis of source-based taxation in a federal economy, see Gordon (1983), and for a review of the subsequent literature and extensions, see Inman and Rubinfeld (1996).

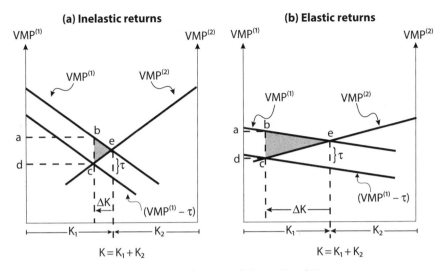

FIGURE 7.3. Tax Inefficiency with Source-Based Taxation

production—say, capital—while the other local governments do not. The two downward-sloping curves in both panels represent the value of the marginal productivity of capital in the taxing jurisdiction 1 as $VMP^{(1)}$ and in all other jurisdictions as $VMP^{(2)}$. Panel (a) illustrates the case of relatively inelastic factor returns in each jurisdiction, while Panel (b) is the case of elastic returns. The net returns to the factor, here capital, will equal VMP less any taxes. The factors locate between jurisdictions to equalize after-tax returns. Without taxation, the equilibrium allocation will be at point e in Panels (a) and (b), with K_1 units of capital locating in jurisdiction 1 and K_2 units in other jurisdictions. Together, total capital in the economy is $K_1 + K_2 = K$ and is assumed to be fixed. Both panels begin with the same allocation of capital between the jurisdictions and the same rate of return when there is no taxation.

What will be the allocation of capital if jurisdiction 1 imposes a source-based tax of τ? The after-tax return to capital in jurisdiction 1 falls to $(VMP^{(1)} - \tau)$. Capital will now relocate from jurisdiction 1 to all other jurisdictions to restore equality in after-tax returns. The new allocation of capital will have $(K_1 - \Delta K)$ units in jurisdiction 1 and $(K_2 + \Delta K)$ units in the other jurisdictions. Capital will have moved from the taxed to the untaxed jurisdictions, with consequences for the efficient allocation of taxed factor. Each unit of capital that leaves jurisdiction 1 "costs" society a return of $VMP^{(1)}$, along the line segment from e to b in both panels, and "gives back" the return of $VMP^{(2)}$, along the line segment from e to c. Since $VMP^{(1)} > VMP^{(2)}$, lost returns are greater than those gained; the shaded triangle Δbec in both panels measures the size of the resulting economic excess burden or inefficiency. The rectangles $[abcd]$ measure the revenue that is collected in jurisdiction 1 by the tax: Revenue $= \tau \cdot (K_1 - \Delta K)$. The inefficiency per dollar of revenue collected is the ratio of triangle Δbec to the rectangle $[abcd]$. The efficiency consequences of the tax are much larger when the taxed factor is equally productive (that is, not specialized) and mobile between jurisdictions, as in Panel (b). The analysis of Figure 7.3 applies to any source-based tax, whether on capital, nonresident (commuter) labor or nonresident (tourist) consumption.

In deciding the tax rate for a source-based tax, local residents will use the tax to the point where their private marginal cost of the tax inclusive of the tax's excess burden is just equal to their private marginal benefit of using those revenues. For resident-based taxes, all costs and benefits are borne by residents within the taxing jurisdiction—as it should be for local fiscal efficiency. For source-based taxation, however, some of the burden of the tax is borne by nonresidents. If $\lambda < 1$ is the fraction of revenues of the tax that is paid by residents, then residents' private marginal cost will be less than the tax's social marginal cost, both inclusive of the tax's excess burden. In deciding local tax policy, residents will set their private marginal cost equal to the private marginal benefit of spending that dollar. In the simple case in which private marginal benefit equals social marginal benefit—that is, no spillovers—then $\lambda \cdot SMC = PMC = PMB = SMB$, or finally, $\lambda \cdot SMC = SMB$. But since $\lambda < 1$, it will be true that $SMC > SMB$. As the result of the direct revenue effect, the source-based tax is overused.[36] As seen in Figure 7.3, the efficiency consequences of source-based taxation will be most significant when the taxed activity is highly mobile between jurisdictions. The tax will be most attractive to local jurisdictions when the share of local taxes borne by nonresidents is high—that is, when the direct revenue effect is large.[37]

Recent estimates of the adverse efficiency consequences of the direct revenue effect, measured by the average excess burden per dollar of revenue raised from the source-based tax, show how damaging these taxes can be to the national economy. For capital taxation in the federal economies of Australia, Canada, and the United States, the excess burden per dollar of revenue raised ranges from a low of ten cents to perhaps as high as fifty cents per dollar

36. See Arnott and Grieson (1981) and Dahlby (1996).
37. See McLure (1981) and Courant and Rubinfeld (1978).

of local revenue, with the higher estimates relevant for higher elasticities of demand for capital across jurisdictions.[38] The excess burden estimate for Philadelphia, which uses a source-based nonresident wage or "commuter" tax, equals twenty cents per dollar of revenue.[39]

The taxation of natural resources by resource-exporting states raises the price of the natural resource to the importing states, thereby reducing resource consumption by residents and firms in these other states. Estimates of the efficiency loss from the taxation of coal by U.S. western states suggest the resulting inefficiencies may be as large as fifty cents per dollar of tax revenues.[40] Estimated tax inefficiencies are lower for source-based taxes on consumption (that is, tourist taxes)—around ten cents per dollar of revenue raised—as nonresident purchases are typically a small fraction of local sales, tax rates are relatively low (since residents bear the burden too), and the taxed goods (alcohol, tobacco) often have very low elasticities of demand.[41]

The *indirect* revenue effect, the second source of tax inefficiencies from the use of source-based taxation, arises from the impact of the local tax on the location of factors of production. All else equal, mobile factors of production will seek the lowest-taxing jurisdiction. The jurisdictions with the lower tax rate then benefit. First, the entry of the mobile factor provides additional tax base and additional public revenues for the low-tax jurisdictions. Second, if the increased use of one factor of production increases the marginal productivity of the other factors, the returns to other factors will increase as the mobile factor enters the jurisdictions. For example, a relatively high profits or property tax elsewhere will increase the flow of capital to the low-tax jurisdictions, thereby raising the marginal product of labor and thus wages in low-tax jurisdictions.[42] For both reasons, the indirect revenue effect creates a positive spillover for residents in the low-tax jurisdictions.

As a result of the indirect revenue effect, the private marginal cost of taxation in the high-tax jurisdiction, having ignored the positive tax spillovers created in other jurisdictions, will be greater than the national social marginal cost of that local tax; now, $PMC = \theta \cdot SMC$, with $\theta > 1$. Citizens in the

---

38. See Dahlby (2008, table 7.5).

39. See Haughwout et al. (2004).

40. See Kolstad and Wolak (1983, 1985).

41. See Christiansen (1994) and Asplund, Friberg, and Wilander (2007).

42. Mendoza and Telsar (2005) estimate that these local tax spillovers may be worth as much as 3 percent to annual resident consumption.

high-tax jurisdiction will continue to set the private marginal cost of their local taxes equal to the benefit of their public spending. Assuming that the private marginal benefit of local spending is equal to the social marginal benefit of spending, then $SMB = PMB = PMC = \theta \cdot SMC$, and therefore, $SMB = \theta \cdot SMC$. But, from the positive tax spillovers ($\theta > 1$) from the indirect revenue effect of the local source-based tax, it will be true that $SMB = \theta \cdot SMC > SMC$. Because of these positive tax externalities from the indirect revenue effect, the taxing jurisdiction will now underutilize the local tax and provide too little local services.[43] These neglected positive benefits can be significant, perhaps as much as thirty cents per dollar of local revenues from the source-based tax.[44] The importance of these indirect revenue effect turns, as for the direct revenue effect, on how responsive factor locations across jurisdictions are with respect to higher local source-based taxation. Capital and firm profits are most responsive.[45]

National Policies for State and Local Taxation

Every effort should be made to move local taxation as close as possible to full resident-based taxation. Taxation by provincial, state, and local governments in federal unions should be limited to the taxation of residents' incomes, properties, and consumption. National policy can help by sharing the required records of residents' income, savings, and estimates of consumption needed to impose residential taxes. The most direct and perhaps easiest way to do so is to offer local jurisdictions the chance to "piggyback" their administration of local tax collection onto national tax collection. When filing their national taxes—say, a national income or consumption tax—citizens report their local address and their local and state taxing jurisdictions. Local and state jurisdictions report their chosen tax rates to be imposed on residents. The national government then collects the required local and state taxes along with national taxes, and returns to local and state government all revenues collected on their behalf, perhaps less a small fee for the costs of tax collection.[46] Local

---

43. See Zodrow and Mieszkowski (1986).

44. See Wildasin (1989).

45. See Zodrow (2010), Mintz and Smart (2004), and Suárez Serrato and Zidar (2016).

46. The central government could play a similar role as a clearing house for cross-jurisdiction credits and debits for a coordinated system of state or provincial value-added taxes; see Keen and Smith (1996), McLure (2000), and Bird and Gendron (2000).

jurisdictions that might wish to use a different definition of tax base could do so by allowing residents to apply to the jurisdiction for a direct payment of a local tax credit.

If local, source-based taxes must be used, then just as for spending externalities, the national government should use matching grants applied to local revenues to internalize tax-created fiscal externalities. In the case of positive externalities that arise from the indirect revenue effects of source-based taxation—$PMC = \theta \cdot SMC$, $\theta > 1$—the matching rate (m) should be $m = [1 - (1/\theta)]$.[47] With this specification, the local jurisdiction would be encouraged to use more of the beneficial local tax by setting its local private (equal to social) marginal benefit equal to its subsidized private (now equal to social) marginal cost: $SMB = PMB = PMC \cdot (1 - m) = SMC$. In the case of the negative externalities that arise with the direct revenue effects of source-based taxation—$PMC = \lambda \cdot SMC$, $\lambda < 1$—the matching rate (m) should be $m = [1 - (1/\lambda)]$. Since $\lambda < 1$, the matching rate becomes a tax surcharge—that is, $m < 0$.[48] With this specification, then the local jurisdiction would be discouraged from using the harmful local tax by setting its local private (equal to social) marginal benefit equal to its now penalized private (now equal to social) marginal cost: $SMB = PMB = PMC \cdot (1 - m) = SMC$. The same specification for a negative matching rate, or tax surcharge, on local revenues should be applied when local jurisdictions raise their marginal tax rates, and thus the excess burden faced by the national government from the vertical tax externalities of a shared national tax base. In this case, λ measures how much the cost of local jurisdiction taxation underestimates the excess burden added to national taxation because of the higher shared tax rate.[49]

For tax fairness in federal unions, see Box 7.2.

47. See Wildasin (1989), who estimates that a positive matching rate of .33 ($\theta = 1.5$) might be appropriate for the local taxation of business property.

48. In the case of natural resource taxation, the surcharge could be as high as 100 percent ($m = -1.0$, $\lambda = .5$), as recommended by Boadway and Flatters (1982) for their intergovernmental grant for the efficient location of mobile factors across jurisdictions when states or provinces have access to natural resource taxation.

49. When the same source-based tax has both a direct and indirect revenue effect, national policy should first apply a surcharge ($m < 0$) to the local use of the tax to internalize its negative externalities from overuse, and then a positive ($m > 0$) matching rate to internalize the positive externalities from the underuse of the tax. The appropriate overall "matching" rate is approximated by the sum of the negative surcharge and the positive matching rate.

Box 7.2. Vertical Fiscal Equity in Economic Unions

The received wisdom of economists has been that redistribution should be a national policy, for two reasons. First, societal norms may require all citizens to be treated fairly, and this can only be uniformly enforced by national government policies. Second, efforts by state or local governments to reduce inequities are likely to be undone by the mobility of the rich to escape taxation and by that of the poor to receive higher transfers.

In democracies, societal norms of fairness and their implications for fiscal policy are to be found in citizens' beliefs as to what is a fair or just society. Citizens may view economic fairness as fair economic outcomes and favor a system of national tax and transfers that achieves a final distribution consistent with their democratically preferred norm of fairness; see, for example, Mirrlees (1971) and Rawls (1971) and see Saez and Stantcheva (2016) for an application. Progressive national income taxation and transfers are the usual outcome. Or citizens may favor a view of fairness defined by a just economic process and fair rules of exchange, promoting a government agenda for equal economic opportunities for those of equal abilities; see Nozick (1974) and Roemer et al. (2003) for an application.

Efforts by state and local governments to introduce progressive taxation and to offer significant transfers to lower-income residents are limited by the mobility of the rich from, and the mobility of poor to, those jurisdictions pursuing progressive policies. Pauly (1973) details the conditions required for successful state and local income redistribution. First, taxpayers in the state or local jurisdiction must wish to make transfers to the less well off. Second, taxpayers must be the democratic majority that decides the transfer policy. Finally, the mobility of the rich and poor across jurisdictions cannot undermine the long-run sustainability of the local tax base funding locally preferred transfers. In the United States, the third requirement is a significant constraint on local preferences for income redistribution. The U.S. Supreme Court in *Shapiro v. Thompson* (394 U.S. 618 [1969]; striking down a one-year waiting period before receiving low-income benefits) and *Saenz v. Roe* (526 U.S. 489 [1999]; declaring as unconstitutional a California state law limiting in-migrants' payments to those in their previous state of residence) legally guaranteed the mobility of the poor and their access to local transfers. In response, the poor have moved to local jurisdictions with pro-poor income policies; see Gelbach (2004). Taxpayers, even those initially supportive of income transfers, have also moved, but now out of the jurisdiction with the redistributive income policies; see Feldstein and Wrobel (1988). The result has been a decline in the tax bases of those states pursuing their own pro-redistribution policies, and an increase in the share of citizens qualifying for income transfers. The response of states has been to reduce their support for their own lower-income transfers, an outcome known as the "race to the bottom" in state welfare spending; see Baicker (2005).

The preferred national policy response is a matching grant paid to the states to support states' preferred levels of redistribution. In the United States, such grants have come through two separate policies. The first is a matching grant for the direct support of the marginal dollar spent by states for income and in-kind transfers. The second has been the use of the federal tax code to allow the deduction of state taxes when computing federal income tax liabilities. Deductibility becomes an implicit matching grant to encourage higher state taxation, revenues from which can be used to support lower-income transfers. Both policies are *national* matching rate inducements to adopt *locally* preferred transfers to lower-income households. Recent national policy reforms, first as PRWORA (see Section 2 of this chapter) and more recently as the 2017 Tax Cut and Jobs Act dropping deductibility of all state and local taxes, have removed both incentives for state-supported lower-income transfers.

A FIST Evaluation: EU Corporate Tax Policy

In October 2016, the European Commission submitted to the European Parliament and the Council of Ministers a proposed reform of corporate taxation in the European Union. There were three issues. First, the business community had been directly affected by the administrative costs of filling separate and very different tax returns in all the EU countries in which they did business. Second, tax burdens could be shifted from high- to low-tax jurisdictions by the strategic assignment of firm overhead, favoring larger firms and firms doing business in multiple jurisdictions. Third, as a source-based tax and because of significant differences in country tax rates, corporate taxation had significant adverse effects on the efficient allocation of capital across member countries (see Figure 7.3, Panel [b]).

There are three possible policy responses. First, the EU-wide ("national") government can adopt a common tax base (known as the common consolidated corporate tax base) and then impose a common EU-wide tax rate on that base, a policy called full tax harmonization. Aggregate revenues could then be spent by the central government or returned to each of the member countries according to a sharing formula. If all taxed EU businesses do almost all of their business within member countries and are largely owned by EU residents, then such a tax system will approximate the residency principle of taxation.

Second, the EU can administer a common consolidated corporate tax base but leave to the individual Member States the right to tax that common base at a country-decided corporate tax rate. The common consolidated corporate tax base will consist of two parts: (1) a common corporate tax base computed for each firm and (2) a common formula apportionment to allocate the common base to individual countries. Specifying a common tax base removes the incentive for profit shifting across countries, reduces tax competition through the definitions of tax base, and increases transparency in corporate taxation for tax-paying firms and citizens alike.[50] The share of each firm's union-wide common corporate tax base is then allocated to each member country by that country's common apportionment formula. Apportioned firm profits for all

---

50. Without requiring a common base, local jurisdictions will compete not only by tax rates but also by their tax base definitions; see Gordon and Wilson (1986). For empirical evidence of such competition, see Goolsbee and Maydew (2000) and Gupta and Mills (2003). There has been no effort by the U.S. courts to discourage tax base competition; see *Moorman Mfg. Co. v. Bair*, 437 U.S. 267 (1978).

firms doing business in a country are aggregated to specify the country's total corporate tax base. The country is then free to tax that allocated base at its own chosen corporate tax rate. Under this policy of base harmonization, the apportioned tax base is still taxed at the country level and the tax remains a source-based tax.

Third, subsets of the member countries can be encouraged to form cooperative agreements among themselves for tax or base harmonization. The most likely coalition will be among Member States most competitive with each other for the location of business capital, most likely the advanced economies of central Europe. In this case, the central government's role would be to enforce, and perhaps administer, the cooperative agreements.

Two studies have simulated aggregate EU gains and country-specific GDP and citizen welfare for each of the three policy options.[51] The best policy, both for increases in GDP and for citizen welfare, is full tax harmonization. The gain in GDP occurs because capital is more efficiently allocated across member countries, aggregate investment rises, and more workers are hired. Citizen welfare also increases with full tax harmonization. However, welfare gains are less than GDP gains, as workers have to give up leisure—which they freely choose to do—for their increased incomes. Base harmonization alone also improves GDP and welfare performance, but the benefits are lower. Countries that gain the most under full tax harmonization are those with relatively high pre-reform tax rates (Austria, Belgium, Denmark, France, Italy, Netherlands, Luxembourg, and the Czech Republic), while those that lose are the countries with low pre-reform tax rates (Ireland and the newer members from eastern Europe), as capital exits from the initial low- to the high-tax-rate economies. Finally, there are clear benefits from full harmonization agreement for a group consisting of the fifteen original EU members, but their gains in GDP come at the expense of a small decline in GDP for those who do not participate as capital relocates from the excluded to the included economies.

Given this analysis, what would a FIST evaluation say regarding the proposed reforms? See Figure 7.4. From Step 1, there is no threat to the overall federal structure of EU governance from the adoption of either full or base harmonization of the corporate tax. Individual countries will continue to have

---

51. Brøchner et al. (2007) provide estimates for each policy for a coalition of the original fifteen EU members. The authors simulate the economy of the twenty-five EU members at the time of their study; Bettendorf et al. (2010) do the same for the twenty-seven EU countries at the time of their study.

Step 1 Sovereignty Test: *Does the federal legislation or executive order threaten the ability of individual country governments to function as politically and economically independent organizations within the federal system?*
No, proceed to Step 2

Step 2 Efficiency Test: *Is the service a national public good, entail cross-state spillovers, or national merit good?*
Yes: *Lost economic efficiency due to tax spillovers from differential corporate tax rates and definition of tax bases.*
Proceed to Step 3

Step 3 Efficiency Test: *Are efficient agreements across state or local governments possible?*
No: *No EU inter-country agreements for coordination of corporate tax policy. US tax agreements have not been enforced.*
Proceed to Step 4

Step 4 Efficiency Test: *Is the service a national public good, entail cross-state spillovers, or national merit good?*
Yes: *EU evidence of corporate tax inefficiencies and US evidence of a "race to the bottom" in rates.*
Proceed to Step 5

Step 5 Efficiency Test: *Do state or local governments have an informational advantage in the provision of the spillover or merit good?*
No: *Information required to centrally administer an EU corporate tax policy; required EU institutions not in place.*
Proceed to Step 6

Step 6 Participation Test: *Will state and local government provision encourage increased citizen participation?*
No: *No evidence of citizen interest in setting corporate rates and other country taxes available.*
Proceed to Step 7

Step 7 Rights and Fairness Test: *Does national provision or financing protect individual rights and/or enhance economic fairness?*
Yes: *Revenues from an EU corporate tax can be allocated for distributional services or transfers.*

Summarize

FIGURE 7.4. A FIST Evaluation for EU Corporation Tax Reform

unconstrained access to significant revenue instruments. The answer to Step 2 is yes; the analysis confirms the likely inefficiencies that now exist within the decentralized EU corporate tax structure. At Step 3, a cooperative agreement among the original fifteen EU countries would show clear winners and losers in welfare and revenue, but making such cooperative agreements is difficult given the small overall economic benefit of cooperation.[52] The answer to Step 3 is therefore no. The economic analysis suggests that FIST's answer to Step 4 is yes. There

---

52. U.S. state efforts to organize voluntary agreements for base harmonization have generally failed as well; see Clausing (2016).

is an efficiency argument for the full tax harmonization of the EU corporate tax; the efficiency evidence in favor of base harmonization is less compelling.

The challenge is implementation at Step 5. While the central government has an informational advantage in administering both full and base harmonization, full harmonization will require political institutions capable of setting a uniform corporate tax rate and allocating the proceeds among member countries. Current EU treaty rules require unanimous agreement within the Council of Ministers, after consultation with the European Parliament. Given the significant distributive consequences of full harmonization, unanimous agreement is unlikely. Base harmonization may win approval and is best administered centrally. Finally, from Steps 6 and 7, there are no clear advantages to decentralizing corporate taxation, either from the perspective of political participation or from the perspective of fiscal equity. EU members have access to resident-based taxes for their own services and for local redistribution, and fiscal fairness can be enhanced by the centralization of the corporate tax and the redistribution of tax revenues. To sum up, the FIST analysis will likely see little to favor with the continued decentralization of EU corporate taxation. As a matter of implementing the FIST recommendation, however, the EU's current lack of a majority-rule institution for tax policy makes reform very difficult.

4. Raising Money in a Federal Union: Debt

State and local governments may also be granted the right to use long-term (longer than the fiscal year) debt for the financing of jurisdiction services. There are two instances when this may be desirable: tax smoothing for the financing of large expenditures, and aggregate demand creation in response to adverse economic shocks. Only tax smoothing, we will argue, is a compelling reason, however, and even here we prefer to limit long-term borrowing to the financing of expenditures that can be easily monitored. Generally, this will be for capital projects only. The risk is that local borrowing privileges will be abused. National policies will then be needed.

The Role for State and Local Debt

As we have explained, taxes on residents and firms for the provision of government services can create significant market inefficiencies. The higher the tax rate, the greater the tax inefficiencies will be; doubling the tax rate will more than double the total excess burden of the tax. It will therefore be efficient to avoid one big jump in the tax rate if a sequence of smaller tax rate increases spread over time can raise the same revenues. This can be achieved by borrowing the funds needed to pay for the one-time large expenditure, and then repaying the loan over time with small increases in the tax rate. Of course, nothing is free. To spread the initially large tax increase over time requires the government to pay interest to those lending the funds for the large one-time payment. Still, if the future (discounted) excess burdens from the extra taxes needed to pay interest and principal are less than the initial large excess burden of the original tax increase, then it is efficient for the local government to spread its tax payments over time. Long-term government debt is the financial instrument that allows this "tax smoothing."[53] Government debt is therefore the appropriate way for local jurisdictions to finance large, one-time expenditures— for example, local government capital investments.

A second argument advanced for long-term debt financing of state and local spending is the Keynesian argument that in periods of economic recession and stagnant aggregate demand, local governments can borrow money and spend the proceeds on outlays likely to stimulate private market demand for unemployed labor and idle capital. Government debt provides the resources needed for an income multiplier. Once the economy has returned to full employment, the debt can be repaid. There are two reasons to be skeptical of this argument.

First, as a matter of economic policy, the ability of state and local governments to affect their local economies with local debt is limited. Debt-financed increases in local aggregate demand will be spent in part in economies outside the borrowing local jurisdiction, thereby reducing the local impact and thus the benefits for local residents of the debt-financed increase in local spending. And even if the demand for locally produced goods increases, workers from other states may migrate into the state and again dilute the aggregate demand benefits of local deficits for local residents. In both instances, the beneficiaries of the local debt, which local residents will need to repay, will include residents of neighboring states. Like any policy with positive spillovers, local governments will underprovide the efficient level of debt to finance an expansion in aggregate demand.[54] This is the argument first made by Musgrave (1959) and Oates (1972) for assigning the debt-financed aggregate demand stimulus to

53. See Barro (1979) for the details of this argument.

54. For evidence on the importance of employment spillovers from local debt, see Carlino and Inman (2013) for U.S. states and Beetsma and Giuliodori (2011) and Auerbach and Gorodnichenko (2013) for OECD economies.

the national government. State and local governments will have a role to play in such policies, but there may be inefficient spending of the proceeds of the national, not local, debt.[55]

Second, as a matter political economy, the Keynesian argument may become a convenient excuse for local officials to use local debt for current accounts spending. Job creation by local governments is difficult and expensive—by recent U.S. estimates, costing more than $100,000 per local job created in the most favorable of circumstances.[56] Arguments for a "local multiplier" from current accounts spending are without foundation. Only capital projects have the potential for a positive economic return capable of justifying the use of local debt, and even here the benefits for residents will be from services provided, not jobs created.

The only argument to justify the use of state and local debt is tax smoothing, and the only efficient use of local debt will be capital investments. That said, giving state and local governments the right to borrow, and limiting that right to capital outlays, does not guarantee that they will not abuse the privilege.

Local Borrowing May Be Abused

In a federal economy with multiple jurisdictions, local residents can shift the burden of repaying local debt to those outside their jurisdiction. First, current residents can move to a new jurisdiction before the full burden of the local debt falls due, leaving new residents as future taxpayers with the obligation to repay the remaining debt. Second, current residents can default on their ability to repay outstanding debt, leaving bondholders or, if there is a bailout of what is owed, national taxpayers with the obligation to repay remaining local debt.

---

55. This was the strategy adopted by the Obama administration in response to the Great Recession of 2007. The American Recovery and Reinvestment Act borrowed $797 billion nationally and allocated those revenues to $381 billion for federal tax relief and unemployment compensation, $98 billion for direct federal government spending, and $318 billion for state and local government spending on infrastructure, wages for local teachers, and most importantly, additional state spending for lower-income health-care services (Medicaid). The act is estimated to have increased aggregate income by 1.8 percent over the no-growth path and to have increased national employment by 1.3 million jobs. If the act had adopted the most efficient combination of policies—national tax cuts and federal matching aid for lower-income transfers and health care only—output would have grown by 2.6 percent over the no-growth path and jobs by 1.85 million; see Carlino and Inman (2016).

56. See Carlino and Inman (2016) for a survey of the evidence.

In both instances, current residents receive a subsidy for current spending from "future" citizens, whether local or national taxpayers or bondholders. As tax exporting with source-based taxation, only a share of the burden of current spending by the jurisdiction will then be borne by current residents. If so, we will again see too much local spending, now financed by too much local debt. Because of debt exporting, local debt is overused.

The share of debt financing borne by current local residents will depend on which of the two strategies—move or default—current residents find more attractive. If residents move, new residents may demand compensation for their added tax burden from past local debts. If so, the price of homes and businesses can be expected to fall by the full burden of the unpaid debt, an outcome known as debt capitalization. With full debt capitalization, there will be no shifting of debt burdens onto future taxpayers, and thus local debt financing will be efficient. But absent full capitalization, local fiscal inefficiencies remain.

If residents remain, default is their second strategy. With default, either of two things may happen. First, the national government can decide to offer a "bailout" that will pay the obligations of some or all of the defaulted debt. In this case the local debt burden will be shifted onto national taxpayers. Or second, if there is no bailout, the local government can declare bankruptcy and seek debt relief from the national courts. If the court offers full or partial relief, then nonresident bondholders will bear the burden of local debt through reduced payment of their principal and interest payments owed. But if there is no national bailout or if bankruptcy relief is not offered, there is no shifting of debt burdens onto national taxpayers or bondholders, and jurisdiction financing again will be efficient. What, then, is the evidence for debt capitalization, bailouts, and bankruptcy relief?

First, there are good institutional and theoretical reasons, supported by the U.S. evidence, to be skeptical that the local land markets will be a sufficient control for inefficient local borrowing. Efficiency requires that those purchasing land within the local jurisdiction know the future obligations of all outstanding debt. Discovering those obligations may be very difficult. Local governments borrow using multiple debt instruments and multiple budgets when they borrow; the most difficult to monitor are underfunded public employee pensions to pay for local labor services.[57] As a result, discovering the true stock of local debts will be

57. Discovering the actual debt liability of a public pension can be very difficult and, even if measured, open to controversy as to the preferred method for computing debt obligations; see Novy-Marx and Rauh (2011).

costly.[58] Further, the required information may be a public good. Potential residents who discover the true cost of future obligations will discount their offer prices for land and property in the local jurisdiction by the sum of those obligations. Others may then be able to "back out" that cost from their observed offer prices. All market participants therefore have an incentive to have others discover the true value of local debt obligations, wait to see the offer prices, and then infer the value of unfunded debts. As with any public good with free riders, the required information will be underprovided by the market.[59]

Second, what will be the likelihood of a national bailout of state or local debts? In this case, the burden of repaying local debts becomes an obligation for national taxpayers, and again there is shifting of the local debt burdens. Certainly, this would have been a reasonable expectation in the 1990s for the residents of the major provinces of Argentina and Brazil and perhaps for the EU residents of Greece, Portugal, and Spain following Europe's Great Recession of 2009. In each instance, local jurisdictions went to the national government, or in the case of Greece, Portugal, and Spain, to their fellow EU member countries, hoping for debt forgiveness or debt bailouts. For the provinces of Argentina and Brazil and for Greece within the EU, bailouts were forthcoming. In the cases of Spain and Portugal, no relief was granted.

The bailout decision by the national government turns on a balance between the cost of a debt bailout to national taxpayers—equal to the cost (D)

---

58. Private firms can provide this information, but how the firm should be reimbursed for its services is not obvious. An "issuers pay" pricing model makes the information available to all market participants, with the cost of collecting the information borne by the local jurisdiction. However, this model, which is used by U.S. credit-rating agencies, creates an incentive for local jurisdictions to "shop" across credit-rating agencies for the most favorable evaluation of their deficit position. Outcomes have not always been optimal; witness the New York City fiscal crisis (Morris, 1980, p. 224) and the 1980s savings and loan crisis and the 2010 mortgage-backed securities crisis (L. White, 2013).

59. An argument first offered by S. Grossman and Stiglitz (1980). The best test of the debt capitalization hypothesis has been Robert C. MacKay's (2014) study of the impact on home values of the 2004 public announcement and extensive news coverage of San Diego's large pension liabilities. Before the public announcement, home values had been growing at an average rate of 10 percent per year for the previous five years. After the announcement, the rate of growth fell by 2 to 4 percentage points within the jurisdiction of San Diego, with no effect on appreciation in neighboring communities. The estimated dollar impact of the announcement, $4,000 to $8,000 per household, bounds the estimated $6,000 per household in unfunded pension liabilities. Once the market has a credible estimate of debt obligations, market prices reflect those obligations. As stressed by Grossman and Stiglitz, however, the problem is in providing a market incentive to discover those true obligations.

of the debt outstanding—and the national benefits that debt relief provides. There are two benefits from the bailout. First, by paying local debt outstanding, a financial crisis with a potential economic cost of F dollars may be avoided. Financial recessions, or worse yet bank runs and a financial collapse, can have significant long-run adverse consequences for the national economy.[60] This was certainly the motivation for the bailouts of provincial debts in Argentina and Brazil and for the restructuring of Greek debt held by banks within the EU.[61] Second, residents in the local jurisdiction being asked to repay the debt may be economically disadvantaged, or alternatively politically favored, so that a debt bailout from the national government redistributes national tax dollars to disadvantaged or favored local residents. The net benefit from this redistribution will be worth V dollars to the national government. A bailout will occur when the benefits of the bailout $(F + V)$ are greater than the costs of the bailout, D. Only when $(F + V)$ is less than D can we be confident that no bailout will occur. The task for controlling bailouts will therefore be to keep financial and redistribution costs as low as possible.[62]

Minimizing the financial consequences of a state or local jurisdiction default requires that the jurisdiction's debt be a small portion of any one bank's portfolio, so that if a local default occurs, it will not threaten the financial viability of the bank. For mature financial systems capable of evaluating the risks of individual securities, Barry Eichengreen and Charles Wyplosz (1998) recommend a threshold of 5 percent of the bank assets as a sufficient margin for bank holdings of any one local jurisdiction's debt. In less mature financial systems susceptible to financial contagions, a single debt default may signal weakness for other local government debts. In this case, bank thresholds for local debt holdings may need to be lower, perhaps only 2 or 3 percent of bank assets. It was the risk of a possible contagion from a Greek default to the debt of the other at-risk economies that led the European Union, the European Central Bank, and the International Monetary Fund to fashion a partial bailout of Greek debt.

Minimizing the adverse distributional consequences of a jurisdiction default requires the national government to have available alternative redistribution policies to meet the needs of jurisdiction residents adversely affected by the default. A debt bailout is a lump-sum grant to the defaulting jurisdiction. However, such grants are an inefficient policy for aiding specific jurisdiction residents.

60. See Reinhart and Rogoff (2014).
61. See Webb (2003) and Rodden (2003).
62. See Inman (2003).

Rather than a bailout of the local government, direct national transfers to the individuals harmed by the default or matching aid to the jurisdiction to support essential local services will be more efficient policies.

Together, national bank regulations limiting the exposure of the financial system to the consequences of local defaults and national redistributive policies targeting adversely affected local residents are the preferred policies to a national bailout. With both policies in place, the national government can say no to bailouts.

Third, assuming no capitalization and no bailout, the final path for relief from its debt obligations is for the local jurisdiction to petition for bankruptcy in the national courts. The court must reach two decisions. First, is the sum of all legal claims against the jurisdiction greater than the ability of the jurisdiction to pay those claims—that is, is the jurisdiction insolvent?[63] Second, if insolvent, whose claims on the debt—unpaid contractors, contractual public employees and retirees, and bondholders—should be paid? The court must then balance the claims of those owed money against the ability of the residents of the jurisdiction to meet those obligations. Claims can be met by selling local government assets—say, the city's art and art museum—or by raising taxes. If the court rules against the claimants and in favor of residents, then residents are relieved of their obligations.

Two standards might be applied by the courts to allocate debt obligations: that of a "fair and equitable" distribution of available jurisdiction resources and that of the "best interest of the creditors." The first entails dividing a fixed pie of jurisdiction resources among all claimants, with each claimant having to approve the court's proposed distribution. The fair-and-equitable standard was used by Judge Steven Rhodes in settling the Detroit bankruptcy petition in 2014.[64] In contrast, the standard of the "best interest of the creditors"

---

63. The ability of the jurisdiction to pay all claimants depends on its ability to (1) raise additional taxes, recognizing the fact that taxed activities can leave the jurisdiction and thus avoid taxation; (2) sell government assets; (3) obtain contractual revenues from private or other public entities; and possibly (4) continue to borrow to meet current obligations. This last source of funding may only add to the problems, but it was the strategy the court chose rather than to grant a bankruptcy petition to Bridgeport, Connecticut, in its proposed default; see *In re City of Bridgeport*, 129 B.R. 332 (Bankr. D. Conn. 1991).

64. Under this standard, bondholders of the most favored general-obligation debt received 74 percent of what was owed, revenue bondholders only received 41 percent of what was owed, and bondholders with no preassigned claims to city revenues received 13 percent of what was owed. Among other claimants, pensioners received 96 percent of their proposed pensions but lost their cost-of-living increases and saw a significant reduction in promised health-care benefits.

requires all bondholders with a valid contractual claim to be paid in full. This standard seeks to ensure the efficient use of future local borrowing powers by placing the full obligation for past debts on the shoulders of the local residents who approved the borrowing. Whichever standard is adopted, bankruptcy legislation may need to grant the courts the right to impose taxes; reduce unnecessary public spending, including negating costly public employee contracts and pensions; and sell jurisdiction-owned property.[65]

In the end, four institutions are required to ensure the efficient use of public debt by local jurisdictions. First, to ensure full capitalization, an active market for local assets (typically land) will be required with market participants well informed of jurisdiction debts. Second, to reduce the financial motive for nationally funded debt bailouts, bank holdings of local jurisdiction debt should be regulated. Third, to reduce the redistribution motive for nationally funded debt bailouts, national redistributive policies capable of minimizing the adverse consequences of a fiscal crisis should be in place. Fourth, to ensure that local borrowers bear the full cost of their local debt, the national bankruptcy code should first protect the financial interests of valid creditors. Lacking one or all of these institutions, national regulation of local borrowing known as balanced budget rules (BBRs) may be required.[66] The EU seeks to provide such discipline through its Stability and Growth Pact.

A successful BBR requires that all spending for the delivery of current-period services, including the maintenance of existing infrastructure and contributions to ensure fully funded public employee pensions, be paid from current-period revenues.[67] The rule will allow local government borrowing for reasons of tax-smoothing policy—say, for spending on large infrastructure projects. To encourage current savings in anticipation of a temporary economic downturn or natural disaster, the BBR might require small current account surpluses from each fiscal year to accumulate in a "rainy day fund" equal to perhaps 5 to 10 percent of local current spending.[68] To be a successful regulation of budget behavior, BBRs must be enforced at the end (ideally, one

65. See McConnell and Picker (1993, pp. 474–476).

66. It is useful to ask at this point whether an informed bond market can prevent inefficient local borrowing. The bond market will set interest rates to reflect the risk of default, but where those risks include the chance that the defaulted bonds will be bailed out; see Rubinfeld (1973). Thus risk-adjusted rates will not by themselves prevent local debt abuses.

67. For specifying an appropriate "current accounts" budget for efficient fiscal policy, see Buiter (1985) and Bohn (1992).

68. See Zhao (2014).

quarter before the end to allow adjustments) of each fiscal year as an ex post requirement. Deficit "rollovers" from one fiscal year to the next should not be allowed. The BBR should be constitutional, not statutory, and enforced by a politically independent institution—say, the courts or outside agency. Finally, the right to bring a violation of the BBR should be available not just to a national regulator but to outside watchdog groups as well.[69] If appropriately structured, BBRs can be a valuable complement to the four institutions recommended earlier for efficient local borrowing.

A FIST Evaluation: Preventing the Greek Debt Crisis

August 2007 marked the beginning of the global financial crisis. In tandem with the major central banks of western Europe and the United States, the European Central Bank slashed short-term interest rates and provided needed euro-denominated liquidity to private banks. Despite these efforts, EU countries found it necessary to rely on external financing to balance their budgets. Greece was the most deeply affected. In October 2009 the newly elected Greek government revised upward the 2009 budget deficit forecast to 12.7 percent of GDP along with a ratio of public debt to GDP of 129 percent. By the beginning of 2010, interest rates on Greek ten-year bonds had risen by over 300 basis points.

Fear that Greece could not repay its debts prompted a refinancing of Greek debt, funded by the European Central Bank, the International Monetary Fund, and the general EU budget. What began as a debt restructuring in 2010 became debt bailouts in 2012, 2015, and 2017.[70] Greek debt had become economically unsustainable.[71] Consistent with the International Monetary Fund's bailout policy, private creditors were "asked" to absorb a reduction in the present value of private debt owed beginning with the 2012 International Monetary Fund loans.[72] The resulting losses to private lenders equaled 65 percent of private debt outstanding.[73]

Accompanying the bailouts was a requirement for the Greek government to balance its budget to satisfy the EU's Stability and Growth Pact guidelines to reach an annual deficit no larger than 3 percent of GDP. To meet this target,

---

69. See Bohn and Inman (1996) and Inman (1997).

70. For the political history of the Greek economic crisis, see Pisani-Ferry (2011).

71. See House and Tesar (2015).

72. See Lane (2012).

73. See Zettelmeyer, Trebesch, and Gulati (2013, table 3).

the government struck a political compromise with unions and the elderly to place most of the burden on a 3 percent increase in the value-added tax, the tax least susceptible to evasion. Cuts in pensions, public employment, and public wages were modest. Though politically viable in the short run, the resulting fiscal policies proved economically disastrous for the longer run. By 2013, unemployment had risen to 27 percent, annual private investment had dropped by 75 percent, and GDP had fallen by 27 percent.[74]

The Greek fiscal crisis of 2010 should not have been a surprise. The bulk of state spending went to public pensions, to support the military, and for public-sector jobs and wages. EU grants for growth-promoting infrastructure were allocated to transfers to retirees and public employees. Tax evasion, both by individuals and by corporations, was widespread. Private firms were granted monopolies and protected by national regulations and trade restrictions. Workers with jobs were protected by high minimum wages and regulations that made layoffs or firings difficult.[75] Deficits were financed by short-term borrowing primarily from private banks in Belgium, France, and Germany at euro-zone average interest rates of less than 5 percent. History might have provided a warning. Before 2010, the Greek government had experienced three prior fiscal crises, each financed by external borrowing followed by defaults and "haircuts" for private lenders.[76]

Given this analysis, would FIST have helped anticipate the Greek debt crisis and perhaps have mitigated its efficiency and distribution consequences? See Figure 7.5. From Step 1, a FIST evaluation of state budgets will not limit the ability of states to set their own budget priorities. The FIST evaluation is only of budget balance and will not require specific spending cuts or tax increases. From Steps 2 and 4, preventing a fiscally induced, union-wide financial crisis is clearly a national public good. At Step 3, there is no evidence that credible voluntary monitoring agreements had been reached or would have been respected by union members. At Steps 5 and 6, member governments and the citizens of those governments have an informational advantage in providing a FIST-required budget evaluation, but there is no reason to think the provided information will be accurate. Finally, in Step 7, to the extent the FIST

74. See Gourinchas, Philippon, and Vayanos (2017). The Greek experience with an austerity budget is consistent with the historical experience in other countries; see Alesina, Tabellini, and Trebbi (2017).

75. See Thimann (2015).

76. See Reinhart and Trebesch (2015, table 2).

Step 1 Sovereignty Test: *Does the federal legislation or executive order threaten the ability of individual country governments to function as politically and economically independent organizations within the federal system?*
No, proceed to Step 2

Step 2 Efficiency Test: *Is the service a national public good, entail cross-state spillovers, or national merit good?*
Yes: *Evidence for a fiscally induced banking crisis impacting all major EU economies indicates a public good.*
Proceed to Step 3

Step 3 Efficiency Test: *Are efficient agreements across state or local governments possible?*
No: *There is no evidence that Union members would voluntarily agree to outside monitoring of own finances.*
Proceed to Step 4

Step 4 Efficiency Test: *Is the service a national public good, entail cross-state spillovers, or national merit good?*
Yes: *Information sufficient to prevent a Union-wide financial crisis is in the interests of all Union members.*
Proceed to Step 5

Step 5 Efficiency Test: *Do state or local governments have an informational advantage in the provision of the spillover or merit good?*
No: *Member states have an informational advantage, but state incentives are to not report the deficit evaluation truthfully.*
Proceed to Step 6

Step 6 Participation Test: *Will state and local government provision encourage increased citizen participation?*
No: *Local monitoring may emerge, but whether the provided information will be credible remains in doubt.*
Proceed to Step 7

Step 7 Rights and Fairness Test: *Does national provision or financing protect individual rights and/or enhance economic fairness?*
Yes: *To the extent the provided information clarifies the distributional impact of austerity budgets, fairness may be promoted.*

Summarize

FIGURE 7.5. A FIST Evaluation of Greek Deficits

evaluation of state budget balance either prevents a fiscal crisis or provides evidence as to who exactly loses under any proposed austerity budget, then distribution objectives are promoted. Together Steps 1–7, coupled with an outside BBR review of Greek budgets, would have provided a strong case for an EU policy evaluation, independent publication, and then supervision of Greek budgets before the economic collapse of 2009.

5. Summing Up

This chapter has outlined the management of fiscal policies for an efficient and equitable provision of public services by state and local governments. The efficient assignment of spending powers allocates those public services that involve relatively small, geographically local spillovers to communities and geographically wider, but not national, spillovers to states. But the geography of public services will not always match state and local government boundaries. The activities of one state or local jurisdiction may affect the residents of another, and if so, then national policies to coordinate service provision across boundaries may be needed. The appropriate spending response will be nationally funded and administered intergovernmental grants-in-aid. Positive matching aid as a "price" incentive is the preferred policy to encourage the efficient provision of local goods with positive interjurisdictional spillovers, while a negative matching rate (that is, a "tax" on local spending) is the appropriate incentive when a jurisdiction's spending adversely affects the residents of another jurisdiction. Matching aid will also be the preferred policy when the national objective is horizontal equity in the financing of state or local services. The matching grant equalizes the tax burdens of residents with identical incomes across communities for the provision of a common level of services. Lump-sum grants, as a pure transfer of income, will be preferred in three instances: first, as a direct transfer to share the aggregate benefits of the fiscal union, perhaps to induce a valuable but reluctant jurisdiction to join, or stay within, the union; second, as fiscal insurance to compensate residents who have suffered an adverse local economic shock or natural disaster; third, as an inducement to encourage a strategic jurisdiction to accept an efficient matching grant when the national government does not know that government's true policy responses.

The efficient assignment of taxing powers allocates "resident-based" taxes, those whose burden falls only on residents or immovable assets, to state and local governments. These taxes include residential income, consumption and property taxes, and land taxes. The assignment ensures that residents pay for their own state or local services and therefore have a vested interest in efficient government performance. Implementation of resident-based state and local taxation must solve several problems, however. First, a residential tax base shared with the national government creates a vertical tax externality from local tax rates to national rates. The appropriate national policy will be a surcharge on state and local governments for their use of the shared tax base.

Second, it may be difficult to administer a resident-based income or consumption tax at the state or local level. If so, allowing local taxes to be collected as an "add-on" to the collection of a national resident-based tax will be appropriate, a strategy called piggybacking. Locally collected "source-based" taxation of nonresidents and mobile factors of production should be avoided. The local incentives are to overtax nonresidents and mobile factors and to overspend on local public goods. Both consequences are inefficient. The solution is again a nationally administered matching grant (when there are positive spillovers) or a national administered surcharge (when there are negative spillovers) on the use of the local source-based tax. Finally, it will be the task of the national government to ensure the equitable allocation of local goods and services and the equitable allocation of citizens' after-tax and transfer incomes.

The efficient assignment of borrowing powers will allow state and local debt, but only for "smoothing" over time of tax payments required to fund large, one-time expenditures. Local residents may be tempted to abuse their local borrowing powers, either by borrowing for current-period services and then moving from the jurisdiction before debts fall due or by defaulting on those obligations. Three national policies will encourage efficient local borrowing. First, the national government should provide credible and verifiable information as to the true funding status of state and local government budgets so that new residents and lenders can evaluate them and therefore demand compensation for risky local borrowing. Second, the national government must say no to local requests for debt bailouts. Third, the temptation to seek relief from the national courts through bankruptcy must be checked by a bankruptcy standard that stresses the "best interests of creditors." Lacking these institutions, the national government will need an independently evaluated and enforced balanced budget requirement for all states and major local governments requiring current-period services to be financed by current-period revenues.

With matching and lump-sum grants to correct interjurisdictional spillovers, resident-based taxation for the financing of local services, local borrowing limited to tax smoothing, and a national government to provide national public goods and horizontal and vertical fiscal equity, Democratic Federalism will have all the fiscal tools it needs, and their appropriate assignment, to provide public services efficiently and fairly.

8

Regulation in the Federal Union

1. Introduction

Government regulations set the ground rules for citizen interactions, both in the public forum and in the marketplace. How best to assign regulatory responsibilities in federal unions is the agenda for this chapter. For some assignments the task is straightforward, as for the protection of individual rights deemed by the Constitution as both universal and absolute. In this case, the only regulatory assignment that has the potential to achieve uniform compliance is to the national government. Here we focus on outcomes that are contextual, where a regulation might be best assigned to local governments in some circumstances, to the national government in others, or perhaps to shared regulatory responsibility in still other settings.

We begin in Section 2 with an evaluation of assignment when measured against the most commonly used metric for performance: At which level of government will regulatory decisions be most efficient? If there is a regulatory "race to the top," then assignment should go to local governments. In this case, economic efficiency will be achieved when each local jurisdiction sets its own regulation to best meet the needs of its own citizens. However, if a local regulation imposes substantial costs or benefits on citizens in other jurisdictions, then local assignment may result in a "race to the bottom" and assignment should instead go to the national government in hopes that the external effects of regulation can be minimized.

Deciding whether there is a race to the top or to the bottom, however, only begins the analysis. Regulatory assignment in Democratic Federalism must balance the comparative advantage of each level of government in meeting the valued objectives of economic efficiency, political participation, and democratic stability, as well as the protection of individual rights and liberties.

Section 3 applies our FIST framework to engage this broader evaluation of regulatory assignment.[1] We illustrate how FIST might assist in the decision to assign regulatory responsibility with three applications. The first considers the assignment for regulating corporate governance. On all dimensions of our FIST analysis, we conclude that there is a race to the top and that decentralized assignment is likely best. Our second application evaluates the assignment with respect to the regulation of business strategies. For reasons of political participation and local efficiency, we conclude that decentralized assignment is best *unless* the strategy creates substantial out-of-jurisdiction monopoly rents—negative spillovers—earned at the expense of nonresidents who had no say in the approval of the local regulation. If so, national antitrust regulation will be needed to ensure that local jurisdictions "stay in their lane" in the local regulatory race. Our third application is to the regulation of environmental quality. Again we find a race to the top favoring local regulation decided by local participation, but environmental effects must remain localized. If there are significant interjurisdictional spillovers, then national regulation is preferred for its efficiency benefits. National regulation by U.S. politics has not always cleared this hurdle, and may in some circumstances be worse than reliance solely on local regulations. If so, we need to look for an alternative means for national supervision. One encouraging possibility is national regulation not by politics but by markets, using cap and trade. Section 4 sums up.

2. Race to the Top? Race to the Bottom? How to Decide?

Those responsible for local government regulation in a federal system inevitably face the questions, Will my neighbors follow my regulatory lead, and do my citizens care? If I, as governor, choose to regulate the workplace environment to improve worker safety for my citizens, might my state's current or future firms leave for a neighboring state that offers regulations that are free of most regulatory cost burdens? If so, my workers are safe, but now unemployed. Perhaps the right decision is to protect their jobs, and let the workers decide whether they want to bear the risk of workplace accidents. Reasonably priced insurance might be available. So too for environmental regulation. Do I regulate air quality, raise the costs of doing business in my state, and lose firms and

---

1. A framework we feel might help Stewart (1986) and Sunstein (1987) find their preferred national vs. local balance in U.S. administrative law, where regulatory assignment is an essential consideration.

jobs to my neighbors? Or do I not regulate, protect state jobs, and therefore reduce the quality of my state's environment? But better yet, perhaps the neighboring governors will agree that workplace safety and environmental quality are valuable goods for their citizens too and, best of all, follow my lead.

In the first case, in which local regulations have adverse economic consequences when others do not follow, there is a risk of a race to the bottom in local regulatory policy. Local regulations that all citizens might value—for example, worker safety and clean air—may not be put in place. In the second case, in which local regulations, perhaps with adverse consequences, are adopted by all governments because local benefits outweigh costs, there may emerge a race to the top in local regulatory policy. If local regulation leads to a race to the bottom, then national regulation should be considered. With a common national regulation, job losses will be minimized and the benefits of regulation achieved. Alternatively, if there is a race to the top, national regulation will not be necessary, and may even be counterproductive if common standards preclude beneficial local choice. In this case, it will be best to allow local regulations. As a first step in deciding regulatory responsibility in federal unions, we need an answer to this question: Is there a race to the top, or a race to the bottom?

Race to the Top

As first argued by Charles Tiebout (1956) and for a precisely specified economic environment (see Chapter 2), competitive local governments can be efficient in their provision of local government services. As separately argued by William Fischel (1975) and Michelle White (1975), that same economic environment may also lead to efficient local regulation. Tiebout's efficient environment is defined by six conditions, specified now for local regulatory policies:

T1: Local regulatory policies can be efficiently provided by each local government.

T2: There are many local governments, each capable of providing efficient regulation.

T3: Households and firms are mobile between local governments.

T4: Households and firms understand the benefits and costs of local regulations.

T5: Households and firms can be excluded from the community by zoning.

T6: Local regulation creates no spillover costs or benefits for citizens of other governments.

As in the case of local public services, the same six conditions, when generalized to the provision of local regulations, are sufficient to ensure local efficiency in regulatory policies.

First, Condition T_1 requires there be no significant economies of scale in regulating activities within the community. Small communities or states are just as efficient in controlling bad outcomes as are large communities or states. Competitive governments (T_2) and mobile (T_3) and informed (T_4) citizens and firms ensure an efficient matching of preferences and profits to local regulatory standards. Condition T_5 guarantees that no firm or household will be able to exploit any existing community; specifically, residents pay for the administrative costs of regulation and firms compensate residents for any adverse consequences from relaxed regulatory standards. Finally, from Condition T_6, local regulatory standards create no benefits and impose no costs for those outside the regulating jurisdiction.

If Conditions T_1–T_6 apply, then residents in each community will choose those regulatory standards that maximize their benefits over costs, and firms will earn their required, competitive rate of return after conforming to the regulation. Failure to meet the regulatory standard will require firms to compensate residents for the residual harm they may impose. Compensation is paid as a "fine" for a violation of the standard, or as an "impact fee" for the privilege of locating in the community. Communities that place a high relative value on the regulated activity—clean air or worker safety—will set a high standard or require payment of a high, compensating impact fee. Only firms that meet the cost of the standard or value the location sufficiently to pay the impact fee will locate in the "high-standard" community. Alternatively, communities that place a low relative value on the regulated activity will set a low standard or demand only a low impact fee. Firms that find it costly to meet a regulatory standard will locate in those communities. In the end, there will be an efficient matching of resident preferences for the regulated activity to the firms' abilities to conform to the regulation.

This Tiebout regulatory economy of competitive communities will provide efficient regulation. But is this realistic? In a much-cited article on the regulation of environmental quality, Wallace Oates and Robert Schwab (1988) extend the Fischel-White analysis to allow local governments to be responsible for local services as well as regulation and to use a wider set of local taxes, not just impact fees and fines. Three assumptions are central to their argument. First, the regulated activity—say, emissions or worker safety—is assumed to be linked by a fixed technology to the use of a locally taxed input. Second, the taxed input is in fixed supply within the community. Third, owners of the taxed input decide regulatory policy. For Oates and Schwab, that fixed factor is residential labor, which has a direct one-to-one production relationship with the regulated activity, and finally, resident workers decide local regulatory policy. The local government regulates the level of emissions or worker safety and thus the technology that each firm adopts. Firms are free to locate in any community, even those with no regulations, and when markets are in equilibrium, they all earn a competitive rate of return. Each firm hires the profit-maximizing number of workers accounting for both the productivity of the workers and the costs associated with adopting the regulated technology. Workers who otherwise would have been paid a wage equal to the value of their productivity are now paid that wage less the costs of the technology needed to meet the required emissions or other regulatory standard. Resident workers prefer the regulatory standard that just balances the extra benefits of the regulation—clean air or safer work environments—against the fall in wages required to ensure the firm's competitive rate of return. Other things equal, a higher standard will mean lower wages, and conversely, a lower standard allows the firm to pay a higher competitive wage to resident workers—a wage that compensates for the loss of regulatory benefits. Competition between localities for firms will again lead to a race to the top as long as local regulation is decided by those affected by the regulated activity and those affected fully enjoy the benefits and bear the costs of a higher regulatory standard.[2] Importantly, the

---

2. In Oates and Schwab, workers are in fixed supply and wages are determined by each (identical) firm's demand for labor. Each firm pays the value of the worker's marginal product (VMP) less the costs of the worker's effort diverted to meeting the regulatory standard. The regulated activity is measured by hours of worker effort linked to the fixed labor input L, where α is the share of the worker's effort that must be diverted to meeting the chosen regulatory standard and $(1 - \alpha) \cdot L$ is the effort remaining to produce goods and services. The (net of regulation) VMP of labor that earns money for the firm is therefore $(1 - \alpha) \cdot \text{VMP}$. Equilibrium in the labor market ensures that resident-workers are paid $w + \tau_L$, where τ_L is the tax on labor income and the firm pays the net VMP: $w + \tau_L = (1 - \alpha) \cdot \text{VMP}$. The local community sets the tax to pay for residential services; it is a benefit tax. How is the regulatory standard decided? From equilibrium in the local labor market, $w + \tau_L = (1 - \alpha) \cdot \text{VMP}$ and the local labor tax is fixed at τ_L. Thus, any increase in the local regulatory standard, $\Delta \alpha$, must be paid for by a fall in the local wage of $\Delta w = -\Delta \alpha \cdot \text{VMP}$. Resident-workers pay the full cost of a higher regulatory standard in

preferred regulatory standard is very likely to vary across localities according to how each government's residents balance the economic benefits and costs associated with the regulated activity.

Race to the Bottom

Losing any one of the six Tiebout conditions will undo the race to the top. While assuming many local jurisdictions (T2) and mobile firms and households (T3) seems reasonable, at least in the longer run, Conditions T1 for local efficiency, T4 for full information, T5 for efficient exclusion, and T6 requiring no spillovers are each open to question. If not true, an inefficient race to the bottom in local regulatory policy may be the result. State or national regulation may then be justified. While imperfect information as to the benefits and costs of regulation is surely important, particularly so for the regulation of complicated economic activities, there are strategies other than direct centralized regulation that may be appropriate.[3] We focus here on the problems created by the loss of Conditions T1 (economies of scale), T5 (no exclusion), and T6 (spillovers).

LOSING T1, ECONOMIES OF SCALE

Figure 8.1 illustrates the difficulties created for efficient local regulation when implementing a regulatory standard entails significant economies of scale. For example, the efficient technology for keeping a river clean or disposing of radioactive waste may use a technology whose average cost of cleanup, shown as $c(q)$ in Figure 8.1, falls significantly when local regulation requires increasing levels of environmental quality (q). The reason for the falling average cost is that each unit of improved environmental quality (q) shares the fixed costs of a large cleanup facility. Also shown in Figure 8.1 is the low constant marginal cost, $mc(q)$, of the use of the facility, perhaps the transportation costs of

---

lower wages; they select α so that the marginal benefit of a higher standard equals each worker's marginal cost in lower wages. As a result, the chosen regulatory standard in each community is economically efficient.

3. A potentially attractive alternative solution to national regulation when Condition T4 no longer holds is for the national government to provide the needed information as to the benefits and costs of alternative regulatory technologies and then allow local regulatory competition to set policies.

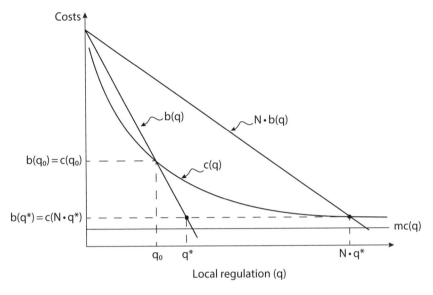

FIGURE 8.1. Economies of Scale in Local Regulations

moving waste to the treatment site. If each local community or state were to set its own standard and be required to pay the average cost of cleanup, it would choose a level of q_0, where the community's demand for a cleaner environment, shown as the marginal benefit curve $b(q)$, just equals the average cost to provide q_0: $b(q_0) = c(q_0)$. If all N local communities, assumed identical in Figure 8.1, were to separately regulate to q_0, then the *aggregate* costs of meeting the q_0 standard would be $N \cdot c(q_0)$.[4]

But what if the communities were to cooperate and share the efficient cleanup technology—for example, by providing for a common waste site or a large and efficient water treatment plant? In this case, total demand could be efficiently satisfied at $N \cdot b(q^*) = c(N \cdot q^*)$, where $N \cdot q^*$ is the aggregate level of preferred cleanup.[5] By sharing the common technology, citizens in each of

4. The analysis generalizes to the case in which demands are variable. Communities with lower demands provide lower levels of q and pay higher average costs; the converse is true for communities with higher demands. Communities with demands that lie below the average cost schedule for q will choose $q = 0$.

5. Three comments are in order. First, the aggregate demand for the regulatory standard will be the "horizontal" (across) summation of the individual community demands. With N identical local governments, the aggregate quantity demanded will be $N \cdot q(b)$. Second, there may be a simpler technology that is more efficient than the cooperative technology for low levels of

the N communities benefit, first from the lower costs of doing what they had been doing because of economies of scale—$c(q_0) > c(N \cdot q^*)$ in Figure 8.1—and, second, from a decision to now provide addition cleanup ($q^* > q_0$) because the average cost of providing environmental quality has declined. The efficient outcome is only possible because the N communities agree to share the costs of the common, efficient cleanup facility. The efficient outcome will not be possible if communities decide policy individually and provide only q_0. Locally chosen regulatory standards will be less stringent and cost more to implement. We then observe a race to the bottom. National regulation and the national sharing of the efficient technology may be required.[6]

Efforts to store both low-level (medical, research, industrial) and high-level (nuclear) radioactive waste in the United States provide two examples of how acting individually may undo joint efficiency. U.S. national policy has required each state to regulate locally produced radioactive waste to meet national standards for public safety. For both low-level and high-level waste, states are free to choose how the national standard should be met. The efficiency advantages of cooperation for storage of both forms of radioactive waste are significant. Accounting for the costs of storing low-level radioactive waste among a possible consortium of thirteen southern states showed that cooperation among the states could reduce the cost of storage by over 300 percent. Were each state to build its own facility, the average annual breakeven cost of storage (price equal to average total cost) would be $400/cubic foot of waste—$c(q_0)$ in Figure 8.1—excluding transportation costs to the state site. Were the thirteen states to cooperate and build only five sites in mutually convenient, cost-minimizing locations, the breakeven annual average cost could be reduced to as little as $150/cubic foot, now including transportation costs.[7]

Even more dramatic savings are possible for the cooperative provision of a single (or perhaps two) national site for the storage of high-level radioactive waste. High-level waste is most efficiently and safely stored underground in solid rock. For the United States, the low-cost and safest site is in the Nevada

---

cleanup, but more expensive when all local governments share the efficient, large-scale technology. Third, the choice of q^* is the efficient point using average cost pricing. Marginal cost pricing is preferred in general, but it requires independent taxation to finance the fixed cost of the shared facility.

6. Rather than national regulation, regional regulation might also provide significant benefits. Regional regulation, however, will require the cooperation of each local government as part of a regional compact. For reasons detailed in Chapter 3, we are skeptical.

7. For the analysis, see Coates, Heid, and Munger (1994).

desert at Yucca Mountain. The site can accommodate all existing and future (to 2050) defense and civilian nuclear waste at an annual average cost of approximately $1,035/cubic foot. If each of the thirty-five states with nuclear facilities were to adopt this safest technology on its own, the annual average cost for each state would jump to $21,400/cubic foot![8] The nearly twentyfold increase in average annual storage costs occurs because each state must pay the very large fixed costs of replicating the safety and storage capacity of a Yucca Mountain—even if it had one.

Given these large cost advantages, have the U.S. states, either regionally or through national legislation, adopted the efficient shared technology for the storage of radioactive waste? After more than forty years of trying, the answer remains no. The Low-Level Radioactive Waste Policy Act of 1980 provides for regional compacts, and the Nuclear Waste Policy Act of 1982 directed the U.S. Department of Energy to help states find a single efficient national site for the disposal of high-level waste. Eleven regional compacts have been established, but none have achieved cooperation among the member states for the siting of a low-level waste disposal site. No state has volunteered to be the site without compensation, and all other states in the compact have been unable to agree on sufficient compensation.[9] A similar failure to act has been the response to the siting for disposal of high-level radioactive waste. Analysis by the Department of Energy identified Yucca Mountain as the most efficient disposal site. Selecting Nevada as the site, however, requires an act of Congress and the cooperation of a majority of states. Members, even those representing

8. The estimate by the Blue Ribbon Commission on America's Nuclear Future (2012, pp. 31, 43) of the total lifetime cost of using Yucca Mountain for disposal of the anticipated (by 2050) 122,000 tons of high-level waste is $96 billion, of which $57 billion is the fixed cost of site construction and $39 billion is the lifetime variable cost of transportation, storage, and security. Each ton of waste occupies approximately thirty-eight cubic feet. Thus the average lifetime cost will be $20,700/cubic foot, the lifetime average fixed cost will be $12,300/cubic foot, and the lifetime average variable cost will be $8,400/cubic foot. Assuming a .05 rate of interest, the annual average cost will be $1,035/cubic foot, the annual average fixed cost will be $615/cubic foot, and the annual average variable cost will be $420/cubic foot. To estimate the cost for each individual state to provide secure storage comparable to Yucca Mountain, we assume the state will need to duplicate the lifetime fixed cost of $57 billion. Each of the thirty-five states with nuclear sites is assumed to have produced 3,500 tons of high-level waste by 2050. Ignoring variable costs, this implies a lifetime fixed cost of $428,000/cubic foot or (again, at .05 interest rate) an annual cost of $21,400/cubic foot.

9. Site selection has become a prisoner's dilemma among the states, a game popularly known as "not in my backyard," or NIMBY.

states unaffected by the siting or by transportation of waste to the site, would not vote in favor of the site unless representatives from Nevada accepted the legislation.[10] Efforts to reassure the citizens of Nevada have been unsuccessful. Yucca Mountain has now been abandoned as the preferred site for disposal of high-level waste.[11] While there is still widespread agreement that building one or two sites remains the economically efficient strategy, which state will be the location of that site remains unresolved. Efforts among the states to find efficient solutions for the disposal of radioactive waste have failed. In the end and for the regulation of both low and high level radioactive waste, the outcome has been a race to the bottom in the provision of environmental quality and citizen safety.[12]

LOSING T5, NONEXCLUSION AND INEFFICIENT TAXATION

Essential for the efficient provision of local public goods, and here the efficient provision of local regulation, is the requirement that the regulating government have the ability to exclude individuals or firms, most commonly through zoning, not willing to pay the local costs of services or regulation. Exclusion controls free riding by requiring firms and households to pay at least the marginal cost imposed on current residents. Those costs will include the added expense of providing local services and compensation for any environmental burdens in increased congestion or pollution imposed on local residents. New residents and firms will only pay those marginal costs if the benefits of local services or regulations provided by the community just equal or exceed the payment. If so, local taxation becomes efficient benefit taxation. But if local governments cannot exclude, then benefit taxation is no longer guaranteed and the location of households and firms will typically be inefficient.[13] When taxes and regulation both affect the economic decisions of new residents, then understanding how the two policies interact to affect local economies and resident welfare becomes important.

---

10. Yet another example of a U Legislature setting an inefficient national policy; see Chapter 4.

11. See Walker (2009) for the political history of the failed efforts to locate the high-level waste disposal site at Yucca Mountain.

12. In contrast, the unitary governments of Finland, Sweden, and France have successfully managed the construction of national sites for the disposal of their radioactive waste.

13. Oates and Schwab (1988) do not explicitly allow for exclusion and benefit taxation in their analysis, but they achieve the same result by assuming a fixed supply of labor in their local communities and using a per-worker tax—equivalent to a head tax—to pay for services.

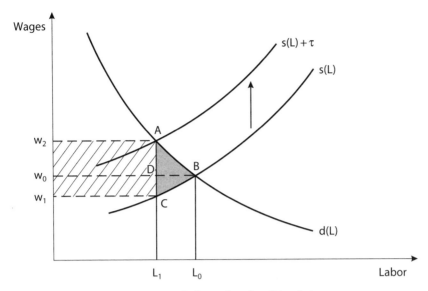

FIGURE 8.2. Tax Spillovers from Local Regulations

John Wilson (1996) has provided the analysis.[14] Here's the argument for the case in which all firms are identical.[15] Local governments are assumed to use a tax on resident labor incomes to finance their local services, as shown in Figure 8.2.[16] The local market demand for labor is shown as curve $d(L)$, and the supply of local labor by residents is $s(L)$. The labor market balances firms' benefits and the cost of hiring workers. Without a tax, this will be at point B, where the market wage is w_0 and the labor hired by local firms is L_0. When the local government assesses at tax at rate τ on workers, the tax must be added to the supply curve so that the after-tax wage will still equal $s(L)$. With the tax, the new before-tax wage will now be w_2, the after-tax wage w_1, local labor hired L_1, and government revenues equal to $\tau \cdot L_1$, shown as the hatched area. The resulting falls in take-home wages from w_0 to w_1 and labor hired from L_0 to L_1 have important adverse effects on the local economy. First, fewer workers will have been hired. While those not hired do have more leisure time (home production, if you wish), the gain in leisure will not compensate for the lost benefits

14. The formal development appears in Kim and Wilson (1997).

15. For a more complete analysis of the market-wide effects of taxes and labor demand and supply, see Pindyck and Rubinfeld (2018, chaps. 8, 14).

16. Local government could tax capital, but with capital mobile across locations, the labor tax will typically be the preferred, more efficient tax; see Bucovetsky and Wilson (1991).

from the fall in income. Workers therefore lose ΔDBC in economic benefits. Second, firms lose too. They hire fewer workers, which saves them money, but they also lose the value of the output that those workers would have produced. As a result, firms lose ΔABD in valued profits. Together the workers and the firm jointly lose $\Delta DBC + \Delta ABD$, shown as the shaded area, called the excess burden of taxation. While the local government has raised revenues, it has created an economic inefficiency—the excess burden of the tax.

What will a neighbor's regulations mean for this government using inefficient taxes? As Wilson points out, some businesses are likely to leave the regulating community and move into the original (nonregulation) community using labor taxes. This increases the demand for labor by community firms. The community continues to tax at rate τ, but with the higher demand for labor, employment increases (not shown in Figure 8.2). The resulting increase in employment provides two beneficial *tax spillovers* to the community gaining the inflow of businesses. First, local revenues generated by taxes on each firm are increased as new firms enter the community. Increased revenues will mean more local public goods. Second, the newly hired workers are paid a higher after-tax wage, which more than compensates them for the leisure they now lose from rejoining the local workforce. This net gain in direct worker benefits is a tax inefficiency "gained back" because of increased employment.[17]

What does all of this mean? When local governments use inefficient local taxes, most likely taxes on labor, and regulated capital is mobile across jurisdictions, then an increase in one jurisdiction's regulations will create positive tax spillovers for those communities with low regulatory standards as beneficiaries of the influx of new capital. The resulting positive spillovers on its neighbors from local regulation of business are ignored by the regulating communities. There will be too little regulation and thus, again, a race to the bottom.[18]

The taxation of local labor will be common among larger local governments, and certainly so among state, province, and national governments. The importance of the tax spillovers just described depends on the responsiveness

17. Note that if the labor supply curve is perfectly inelastic, there are no tax inefficiencies and no tax spillovers. Thus regulation has no net consequences for tax policy. This is the assumption of Oates and Schwab and why their analysis finds no race to the bottom with local regulation.

18. From the point of view of local governments, the positive revenue effect and the positive tax efficiency effect create incentives for the government to want to reduce local regulations. In terms of aggregate social welfare, however, only the gain in tax efficiency from increased employment should be considered; see Kim and Wilson (1997).

of the local labor supply to changes in local after-tax wages and the responsiveness of local capital to changes in local regulatory policy. Labor elasticities are largest among competitive local communities and neighboring states where workers can find job opportunities as firms leave.[19] Likely to be more important is the mobility of capital in response to local regulations.

Empirically estimating the causal impact of local regulations on capital's decision to move from high to low regulatory environments is not easy. The best studies—those that look at capital flows before and after regulation—uniformly conclude that firms will seek low regulatory environments, all else equal.[20] Estimated impacts are largest for environmental regulation. Studies of the impact of changes in federal air quality standards from the 1977 Clean Air Act found that U.S. counties required to increase their air quality standards relative to their neighbors suffered a 26 to 45 percent decline in new plant births in the industries most affected by the new standards. The end result was the loss of 590,000 jobs in those counties and $75 billion in firm output. The 1990 amendments to the act increasing regulatory standards led to further job and earnings losses in the most affected locations. Foreign direct investments in U.S. states have been similarly affected; states with higher compliance costs for firms saw a decline in investment and the number of locating firms from 1977 to 1994. Finally, studies of the location of European firms across EU countries have shown similar adverse effects of higher environmental standards, with the effects strongest for firms in polluting industries. It is for environmental regulations that location effects are greatest, and that is thus the area where these tax spillovers from inefficient exclusion are most likely to induce a regulatory race to the bottom.[21]

LOSING T6, INTERCOMMUNITY SPILLOVERS

The most obvious potential inefficiency when local communities regulate their economies is when a local regulatory decision, or indecision, affects the welfare of residents in neighboring communities or states— that is, an economic spillover. Spillovers may follow from a regulation that provides a direct

---

19. See Haughwout et al. (2004).

20. The results for the impact of environmental regulations on firm relocation summarized here and references for the relevant studies are found in the excellent surveys by Levinson (2003) and Carruthers and Lamoreaux (2015, sec. 3.2).

21. See Carruthers and Lamoreaux (2015) for a valuable summary of the evidence.

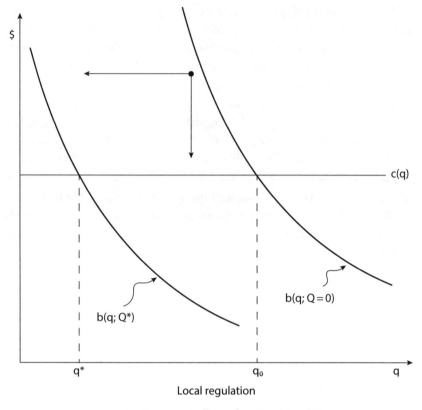

FIGURE 8.3. Economic Spillovers from Local Regulations

benefit, such as requiring clean water or clean air, or from a regulation that imposes a direct cost—for example, allowing the sale of guns with minimal background checks. In either case, there is a potential role for national policy to check a race to the bottom with too little of the "good" regulation or too much of the "bad."

Figure 8.3 illustrates both the cause of the economic inefficiency from spillovers and their economic consequences for the case of "good" regulations. The figure shows how positive regulatory spillovers from neighbors can affect the regulatory decisions of a local community. Shown are two benefit curves for a single local jurisdiction from its decision to provide local environmental regulation providing q units of environmental quality. The higher benefit curve, shown as $b(q; Q=0)$, traces the marginal benefits to community residents from spending money to improve the community's own environmental quality (q) when its neighboring jurisdictions provide no spillover benefits, where $Q = 0$ is the environmental quality provided by the neighbors. In this case, the community is on its own, so its own investments in improved quality will have very high benefits. Also shown in Figure 8.3 is the horizontal line, which represents the marginal cost of improving local environmental quality, $c(q)$. With no spillovers and thus each community on its own, each community provides q_0 in local environmental quality where local marginal benefits equal local marginal costs.

The second benefit curve, $b(q; Q^*)$, shows the benefits that the local community enjoys when there are positive spillovers from its neighbors. Now the environmental cleanup provided by its neighbors benefits the local community. If so, there is less need for local spending. With positive spillovers of Q^* the benefits from the community's own spending will decline, now shown by the lower own-benefit curve of $b(q; Q^*)$, where now Q^* measures total spillovers from other communities. The lower benefit curve following spillovers implies less need for local own investment. Again setting local marginal benefits equal to local marginal costs, the community's own provision of local environmental quality will equal q^*. If we assume all communities have similar costs and benefits from environmental quality, then in equilibrium each community provides q^* $(<q_0)$ and the spillover benefit to each will be $Q^* = (N-1) \cdot q^*$ where $(N-1)$ is the number of neighboring communities providing benefits. When there are positive spillovers, there is the potential for a race to the bottom.

What is the likely outcome of this race as the number of neighboring communities increases? As $(N-1)$ increases, the positive spillovers benefiting each community increase, holding fixed the original regulatory standard of each community. But the analysis in Figure 8.3 shows that local standards are likely to decline with increasing regulatory spillovers. As the aggregate number of communities increases, and thus the equilibrium aggregate level of regulatory spillovers $(N-1) \cdot q^*$ increases, each community's own best standard q^* declines. Since in equilibrium all identical communities will choose the same regulatory standard q^* and more communities are providing spillover benefits, the quality of the regulatory standard in each community must decline. The race to the bottom becomes worse in terms of declining overall regulatory standards as the number of affected communities increases.[22]

22. A point first emphasized by Olson (1965) in his classic analysis of spillovers and voluntary (decentralized) decision-making. The analysis presented here was first offered by

The finishing line for the race need not be zero standards, however. Most likely all communities will provide some positive level of regulation, even as N gets very large.[23] That said, the race will still be economically inefficient. In equilibrium, each community sets its marginal benefit from a small increase in its level of regulation to its marginal cost of providing that regulation, given the benefits from regulations by all other communities: $b(q^*; Q^*) = c(q) = c$ in Figure 8.3. Because of the spillover benefits of local regulations, that last small increase in regulation by any one community provides benefits to all other communities too. The increase in total benefits will therefore be $N \cdot b(q^*; Q^*)$ which is clearly greater than $b(q^*; Q^*) = c$.[24] When making its decisions on its own, each community ignores the benefits to its neighbors of its regulatory improvements and thus underprovides regulation. Even when there are positive standards, the social benefits of additional regulation by any one community will exceed the added costs of providing that regulation. With positive regulatory spillovers, too little of a beneficial regulation is provided. There is a race to the bottom.

Intercommunity regulatory spillovers appear most important for environmental policy. In a valuable series of papers, Hilary Sigman (2002, 2005, 2014) carefully documents, both for U.S. states and internationally, the presence of environmental spillovers, and given spillovers, the propensity for local governments to underregulate their local environment.[25] While the U.S. Clean Water Act of 1972 sets national standards for water quality, qualified states have been authorized by the national government to enforce these standards on their own. Using exogenous variation in state authorization, Sigman (2005) then compares water quality across self-regulated (authorized) and nationally

---

Chamberlain (1974) for the provision of public goods. See Cornes and Sandler (1986) for the most careful general exposition of economic behavior with spillovers.

23. A zero regulation cannot be an equilibrium outcome. If $q^* = 0$ for a very large value of N, then all communities will return to providing q_0. In this case the levels of regulation will cycle between some local regulation and no local regulation.

24. For identical communities $N \cdot b(q^*; Q^*) > b(q^*; Q^*) = c$. Assuming communities are identical simplifies the presentation, but the argument for inefficiency with spillovers generalizes for communities with different benefits and costs. See Inman (1987).

25. Sigman's work has two important advantages over other studies seeking to identify spillovers between governments. First, and most importantly, having measures of both upstream and downstream water quality allows her to compute direct measures of spillovers from one jurisdiction to another. Second, her studies employ panel data that include variation in jurisdiction policies and environmental outcomes over time and across jurisdictions, thus allowing for more confident identification of the impact of policy on outcomes.

regulated (unauthorized) states. She finds that water quality is significantly lower, all else equal, in downstream states when the upstream state is allowed to self-regulate. Water quality for within-state rivers, however, is unaffected by a state's federal regulatory status. Sigman concludes that (1) there are significant spillovers between states sharing interstate rivers and that (2) states with the freedom to enforce national standards do so less carefully when the consequences of lax enforcement fall on out-of-state residents.[26] Similar conclusions follow from her studies (2002, 2014) of pollution in international waterways. Consistent with the conclusion that centralized policy may help mitigate a race to the bottom is her result that European rivers flowing across borders are significantly less polluted when regulated by the European Union. Regulatory standards appear capable of checking a race to the bottom, but only when centrally enforced.

How to Decide?

Participation in the regulatory "race" is a decision made by local officials hoping to maximize the economic welfare of their residents. The outcome of the race will determine resident welfare, and perhaps the welfare of residents in other jurisdictions as well. A race to the top improves aggregate economic performance; a race to the bottom does not. A race that improves aggregate welfare should be supported by national policy and allowed to continue; a race that does not should be redirected by national policy or stopped.

Observing a policy race among local jurisdictions is by itself insufficient evidence as to the final outcome of the race. Local governments may mimic the policies of their neighbors or set policies in opposition to those choices, but such policy interactions tell us nothing about the value for citizens in all communities of the final outcomes. Indeed, observing no race at all may simply mean that all local jurisdictions have found their own best policies. Rather than just observing a race, evaluation requires a careful accounting of the benefits and costs created by the final allocation of each jurisdiction's inputs and outputs. Specifically, do Conditions T1–T6 hold for the local governments' regulatory policies in a federal economy? If so, there is a race to the top and no need—from the perspective of economic efficiency—for national policy. If

---

26. Interestingly, these conclusions hold independent of residents' expressed preferences for national environmental policies. A state's decision to regulate its own environment is unaffected by voters' environmental preferences as measured by the support of the state's congressional delegation for national environmental policies.

not, there is a race to the bottom and a potentially valuable role for national policy to improve the economic performance of all local jurisdictions.

Conditions T1, T5, and T6 deserve the closest scrutiny. Condition T1 will be violated if there are significant economies of scale in the implementation of a local policy or regulation. Our example was the storage of hazardous radioactive waste. Condition T5 will be violated when there is an inefficient interaction between local regulatory policy and local fiscal policies, in particular the impact of local regulation on the efficient use of local taxes.[27] Condition T6 will be violated when a local regulation provides unpriced spillovers, whether as benefits or costs, on residents in other jurisdictions. In many cases, as for local environmental regulations, spillovers can be easily observed, then measured, and finally evaluated for their economic impacts. In other cases, such as the local regulation of contagious diseases or of local market competition, perhaps less so. In all instances, however, estimates of the magnitude of a local regulation's economic spillovers will be needed, as well as an evaluation of the spillovers' economic benefits or costs for nonresidents.

When, then, might national regulation in a federal union be appropriate? Lacking a clear violation of Conditions T1–T6, we would argue that local regulatory policy is very likely to be economically efficient—that is, we have a race to the top—and national regulation superseding local policies will not be necessary. Observing a violation of T1–T6 will mean that local regulatory policy is inefficient—we have a race to the bottom—and thus national regulation *may* be appropriate. But we emphasize *may*. Finding a race to the bottom is a conclusion as to economic inefficiency only. As we have stressed, Democratic Federalism requires the assignment of public policies to weigh not just efficiency in the balance but also the assignment's impact on political participation and democratic governance and on the protection of individual rights and liberties, including an equitable distribution of economic resources. Our FIST analysis provides that scale. The next section offers three FIST applications from U.S. regulatory policy.

3. Assigning Regulatory Policy: A FIST Analysis

While finding a regulatory race among local jurisdictions—whether to the top or to the bottom—provides important information for the assignment of regulatory responsibilities in a federal union, it is not decisive by itself, nor

---

27. Economists will recognize this interaction as an example of the very general problem of designing the use of multiple policies in a world of the "second best."

should it be. There is a need not only to measure the economic costs and benefits of any regulatory race but also to engage a wider discussion of how assignment might affect other important societal values beyond economic efficiency—values such as political participation and the protection of individual rights and liberties. Evidence as to spillovers between states because of state gun regulations illustrates the importance of such a conversation. The analysis of Brian Knight (2013) summarized in Box 8.1 provides convincing evidence that state gun regulations, or lack thereof, have important consequences for neighboring states. Lax gun laws allow criminals to purchase weapons in one state in order to commit crimes in a neighboring, more strictly regulated state. The effects can be very significant, particularly for geographically small and close states. The evidence might suggest the need for national gun regulations for economic efficiency, but strict national regulations will have consequences for other valued outcomes: rights, local political participation, and, given that spillovers are greatest for poor communities, equity as well.

Having a public dialogue on how to balance these possibly competing values is therefore a first-order task for deciding regulatory assignment. Our FIST framework offers guidance for how to have such conversations. As examples, we provide a FIST analysis for three important regulatory assignments: (1) state regulation of business incorporation, (2) state regulation of market competition, and (3) state regulation of environmental quality.

A FIST Evaluation: State Regulation of Corporate Governance

In contrast to owner-managed businesses, the modern corporation separates ownership from management control. Shareholders desire a return on their invested capital, and managers are hired to apply their expertise—in production, finance, and marketing—to maximize that expected return. However, shareholders have neither the time nor the expertise to closely supervise their managers, and thus they face an "agency problem." What is the best way to design a relationship of shareholder supervision and management reward that maximizes the economic returns to the shareholders' invested capital? That relationship will involve both formal (written) and informal (implied) contracts between shareholders and management. It is the task of corporate governance to supervise the administration of those contracts. In the United States, both historically and today, it has been state governments that have taken the lead in writing and administering the regulations for corporate governance. The issue here is, Will state supervision of corporate governance lead

Box 8.1. Interstate Spillovers from Gun Control

The regulation of guns in the United States has largely been the responsibility of state governments. The U.S. Congress approved and President Bill Clinton signed the Brady Handgun Violence Prevention Act in 1993, and it is still in place in 2019. The Brady Bill requires background checks for all firearm purchases from a federally licensed dealer, manufacturer, or importer. However, the impact of the law has been modest at best; only .6 percent of all pending sales have been denied. States provide the primary regulation of gun sales in the United States, and regulations vary significantly across states. Knight (2013) has provided a careful study of the impact of these state laws on gun sales and on the flow of purchased guns between states. Knight's first question: Are there regulatory spillovers in gun sales between states? The answer is yes.

States with strong regulations employ extensive background checks on sales at all outlets (including gun shows), require permits for gun purchasing, limit purchases on behalf of others ("straw" purchases), require reporting of lost or stolen guns, and permit strong local regulations. Because of variation in state regulations, there has emerged a significant secondary market in gun sales that is largely unregulated. Prices of guns in the secondary market of strong-regulation states are often four times the prices of guns in the primary market of weak-regulation states. As a result, there is a strong economic incentive for gun traffickers to move guns from weak- to strong-regulation states. Knight explains this substantial flow between states by various determinants of the demand for guns by honest gun owners in each state, by distances between states, and by the relative strength of state regulation of gun sales in the primary market. He finds strong evidence that guns flow in this secondary market from states with weak to states with strong regulations and that the effects are strongest for flows among states that are geographically close.

Knight then asks the important second question: Do states with strong regulations that are surrounded by neighbors with weak regulations see this inflow of guns from the secondary market being used in criminal activity? Here too, his answer is yes. Comparing the use of imported guns in armed robberies between strong- and weak-regulation states, Knight finds that strong states would see a significant decline in the criminal use of imported guns if all other states were to adopt their stricter regulatory standard. Conversely, weak-regulation states would see an increase in the criminal use of imported guns if all other states were to adopt their weaker regulations. Here is what Knight finds for the six states with the strongest and the six states with the weakest regulations.

Percentage change in criminal gun use with strong uniform regulations		Percentage change in criminal gun use with weak uniform regulations	
District of Columbia	−26.9	Vermont	12.2
Connecticut	−16.1	South Dakota	11.0
New Jersey	−14.0	West Virginia	9.2
Rhode Island	−13.7	New Hampshire	6.2
Iowa	−12.2	Montana	6.1
Massachusetts	−11.6	Maine	5.8

to an efficient (race to the top) or inefficient (race to the bottom) allocation of shareholder capital?

Today's race has a clear frontrunner—it is Delaware. To be an exchange-traded firm and attract equity capital for investments, a company must be incorporated in a U.S. state and have its management supervised by shareholders according to the incorporation rules of the state. Incorporation in a state does not require the firm to have a significant production or management presence in the state. All that is typically needed is to have legal representation in case there are governance disputes. Thus, it is relatively inexpensive for firms to incorporate in one state and, importantly, to "reincorporate" if alternative rules for governance in another state seem advantageous for managing shareholder assets. As a result, there is an active "market" across states for the rules of corporate governance.[28] Delaware, a very small U.S. state, is far and away the market leader. It currently supervises the corporate governance of 56 percent of all U.S. exchange-traded firms, and its dominance extends to firms in all industries, to new firms, and to the merger of existing firms.[29]

The important questions for federal governance is whether this regulatory race between the states is economically efficient. And if efficient, whether there are consequences, good or bad, for other valued objectives of governance. There are detractors and there are promoters for the decentralization of governance regulation. Among the leading detractors have been William Cary (1974) and Lucian Bebchuk (1992); leading promoters are Ralph Winter (1977) and Roberta Romano (1985). Cary argues that state officials are particularly tempted by the fiscal advantages of within-state incorporations and easily manipulated by the political influence of management. As a result, incorporation rules will be biased in favor of lax supervision that places shareholder value at risk. Regulations will allow management to allocate corporate

---

28. The active U.S. market for incorporation is in sharp contrast to that in the European Union. EU countries require firms to be incorporated in the country or province where the firm has its most important production or management operations. For firms to be incorporated in a new location will therefore require the firm to move major operations, raising significantly the cost of relocation, thereby discouraging competition across jurisdictions in the rules of corporate governance.

29. See Daines (2001, table 5). Delaware incorporates the majority of stock-traded firms in manufacturing (55 percent), retailing (54 percent), services (55 to 70 percent), and exploration (66 percent), and most firms in finance (46 percent). Among new firms, 61 percent of all initial public offerings are incorporated in Delaware, as are 81 percent of firms undergoing mergers or a leveraged-backed acquisition.

resources toward their own private returns—large salaries, expensive emoluments, or being just plain lazy or incompetent. There emerges a race to the bottom. For Cary, only national regulation of firm incorporation can protect shareholder value. Bebchuk also worries about lax supervision, but he argues that even if rules of governance do maximize shareholder value, that singular focus will ignore the interests of other socially valued stakeholders in the governance of corporations. If regulations promote only the interests of shareholders, then the interests of both large and small creditors, employees, and the communities where firms are located will be ignored. The rules of governance and their enforcement need to consider the consequences of corporate decision-making for these stakeholders as well. For this to be true, national rules for incorporation will be needed.[30]

Promoters of state incorporation argue for a race to the top. Competition in state incorporations allows each firm to find that set of regulations for supervising manager-investor relationships that allows the best return for shareholders conditional on the investment alternatives available to the firm. A state's rules for corporate governance define how management's performance will be monitored.[31] With state competition, the shareholder-manager relationship will be governed by an efficient (mutually preferred) contract, one that first pays the managers a fixed salary and then pays a performance bonus based on firm profitability. Payment of the bonus requires monitoring of firm performance. Successful monitoring in turn requires (1) access to verifiable (audited) information on firm costs, sales, and profits; (2) appointment of independent supervisors of management performance, typically a majority-elected board of directors; and (3) means for shareholders to directly (by election) or indirectly (by board decision) both appoint and dismiss management if performance goals are not met. Corporate takeovers provide a further, outside discipline of management performance, as do large investors (pension and equity funds) through stock price performance. Strict rules for corporate governance are not always best for shareholders, however. Winter (1977)

---

30. Rules of governance in EU states do require the interests of workers, creditors, and local communities to be considered along with those of shareholders. As a result, there is typically a requirement for the firm to hold a significant economic presence in the state of incorporation.

31. The most important of these rules are those governing share ownership by members of the board, the legal responsibility of board members for firm performance, stockholder votes on merger decisions, allowance for outside appraisals, and outside takeovers. See Romano (1985, pp. 233–242) and Daines (2001, table 4).

argues that firms should be free to incorporate in those states where the rules of governance are most suitable to the firm's business needs. Entrepreneurial firms in innovative industries may need greater management discretion to seize profitable opportunities when they arise. Firms in technologically complicated industries such as natural resource extraction may wish tighter controls to reassure investors that funds are being allocated as promised. State competition in corporate governance allows for an efficient matching of governance structures to firm, and thus shareholder, needs.

Romano's analysis (1985) completes the argument. Not only must states' rules provide for efficient governance, they must be consistently enforced. That will require both knowledgeable administrators who are expert in the purpose of the rules of governance and committed to reliance on precedents, typically the state's judiciary, and a state legislature committed to rule stability. Further, deviations from reliance on precedents and rule stability must be costly to the state. Romano sees that cost in the adverse consequences for state revenues when firms exit (reincorporate) to another state. Incorporation revenues come from state franchise fees. If the state does not enforce its laws in a consistent manner, firms will leave the state for incorporation elsewhere—as indeed they did when New Jersey changed its incorporation rules in 1913 and as have firms today when California adopted strict anti-takeover regulations. Romano sees Delaware as a model for the enforcement of corporate governance. In contrast to other states, Delaware has established a specialized court to resolve disputes over governance, known as the Chancery Court, and judges on the court specialize in the law of corporate governance. To minimize the chances of self-serving changes in state rules, Delaware has also insulated its legislature from lobbying by firms subject to takeover bids. Finally, the state has structured its revenues so that franchise fees are a significant portion of all state revenues, never less than 10 percent and often over 20 percent.

The ultimate test for the relative efficiency of state regulations will be the impact those rules have on shareholder value. Given the dominance of Delaware in the state race for incorporations, a test for efficiency has been to examine the difference in stockholders' returns between firms incorporated in Delaware and those incorporated in other states. If Cary is right, firms are in Delaware because the rules and enforcement favor managers over shareholders. If Winter and Romano are right, firms are in Delaware because Delaware's incorporation regime maximizes shareholder value. The preponderance of the evidence and the most carefully executed study both support the

Winter-Romano argument for a race to the top. After controlling for firm size, industry, firm management structure, riskiness of firm investments, accounting returns on firm assets, and common yearly shocks to all firms' profitability, firms incorporated in Delaware had a statistically significant 10 percent higher shareholder return on invested capital than firms incorporated in other states.[32] At this point in time, it seems clear that Delaware has won the race, and the race enhances shareholder value.

Knowing that the winner of the race in corporate governance has contributed to shareholder value is important—we can reject the concern that management waste leads to a race to the bottom—but we do not yet know that the race is overall socially efficient. Perhaps we might do better with national regulation that mimics Delaware's rules and enforcement performance but then solves one or more of the three weaknesses of any regulatory race: economies of scale (T1), inefficient tax competition (T5), and policy spillovers (T6). This seems unlikely, however, for three reasons.

First, economies of scale in rule enforcement may be important, since expertise and judicial specialization have value, but Delaware has achieved this scale at an annual cost for the Chancery Court estimated to be $3.9 million, or $4/resident. It will not be difficult for other states to replicate the court, apply the case law, and match Delaware's judicial expertise.[33] Second, any adverse effects for other states' tax policies from firm relocations—here reincorporations—are likely to be minor. The capital entailed with relocations will be law offices, the labor gained will be corporate lawyers, and the taxes affected will be economically efficient franchise fees. Finally, policy spillovers from decentralized regulation of governance have largely been positive. Delaware, for example, has been an important innovator in the rules of governance

---

32. See Daines (2001, table 4), where shareholder returns are measured by a 10 percent higher value of the ratio of the firm's stock market value to the replacement cost of the firm's physical capital, known as Tobin's Q. The study's sample included 349 of the Fortune 400 firms between 1984 and 1991. In addition, Daines provides a review of all previous studies, the overwhelming majority of which also conclude that Delaware's incorporation rules favor shareholder value. Daines's own study uses the most complete sample of large firm incorporations.

33. There may be concern that Delaware's dominance generates monopoly power in the enforcement of governance. This is unlikely, given the relatively low costs of replication. Further, Roe (2003) has argued that the "threat of entry" by the federal government into governance litigation has served as a constraint on Delaware's dominant position and, further, has been a stimulus for valuable innovations in Delaware's regulations.

as the monitoring needs of shareholders have changed with the increasingly entrepreneurial nature of firm investments.[34]

While the efficiency benefits of decentralized regulation seem clear, might an evaluation from the perspective of federalism's other values tilt the scales toward national regulation? For the goal of political participation, decentralization seems to again have the advantage; state politics will generally be more responsive to voter preferences than national politics.[35] If there is a potential advantage to national supervision therefore, it will have to be in the protection of the rights and economic interests of nonstate residents when setting or enforcing regulations, as, for example, when deciding to allow mergers or takeovers. By focusing on the manager-shareholder relationship, state regulations leave out of consideration any adverse impacts those decisions may have on firm employees, creditors, and residents of communities where the affected firms reside.[36] The national government can best alleviate these impacts, however, through fiscal, not regulatory, policy. Affected workers can be protected by national unemployment insurance and retrained through nationally funded training grants; creditors can be protected by national bankruptcy regulations; and affected communities can be protected by nationally funded community redevelopment grants.

Figure 8.4 summarizes our FIST analysis for corporate governance. From Step 1, federal regulation of corporate governance will not adversely affect state governance. From Steps 2–4, there is no evidence that local corporate

34. For the application of the general argument to corporate governance, see Romano (1985, sec. 3.1). The one important exception might be the adverse consequences generally of inadequate state regulation of firm accounting for costs and assets in high-risk industries. The two largest corporate bankruptcies, those of Enron and WorldCom, both in 2002, occurred because of inadequate monitoring of corporate assets and liabilities. In response, the U.S. Congress approved and President George W. Bush signed into law the Sarbanes-Oxley Act, which set stricter national regulations for financial and cost accounting and tougher penalties for violations. It is worth noting, however, that at the time of their bankruptcies, Enron was incorporated in Oregon and WorldCom in Georgia.

35. See Chapter 2 generally, and specifically for the formation of regulatory policy, see Inman and Rubinfeld (1998). For example, Delaware has only 710,000 registered voters and 62 state legislators; U.S. national politics is decided by 153.1 million voters and 535 legislators.

36. See Bebchuk (1992, sec. 3). One could imagine state regulations that did take into account the interests of workers, creditors, and communities, but then such a structure would need to require incorporation where the firm had significant production and management capacity, much as does EU incorporation law. Such requirements would significantly raise the cost of firm relocation and thus severely limit the ability of states to compete, however.

Step 1 Sovereignty Test: *Will the proposed federal regulation threaten the ability of individual state or local governments to function as politically and economically independent organizations within the federal system?*
No, proceed to Step 2

Step 2 Efficiency Test: *Is the regulation to address a national public good, cross-state spillovers, or national merit good?*
No: *There is no evidence that a national financial crisis would be caused by inadequate state administered rule of corporate governance.*
Proceed to Step 5

Step 3 Efficiency Test: *Are efficient agreements across state or local governments possible?*
Yes: *Such agreements are possible, but there are no significant interstate spillovers or economies to require such agreements.*
Proceed to Step 5

Step 4 Efficiency Test: *Does the regulation provide a national public good, curtail cross-state spillovers, or promote a national merit good?*
No: See Step 2, and **Proceed to Step 5**

Step 5 Efficiency Test: *Do state or local governments have an informational advantage in the provision of the regulation?*
Yes: *States can develop an expertise and do so efficiently for the drafting and enforcement of regulations for corporate governance.*
Proceed to Step 6

Step 6 Participation Test: *Will state and local government regulation encourage increased citizen participation?*
Yes: *Revenues (franchise fees) encourage local oversight to ensure the efficient performance of corporate regulation.*
Proceed to Step 7

Step 7 Rights and fairness Test: *Does national regulation of corporate goverance protect individual rights and/or enhance economic fairness?*
Yes, but: *There are alternative national fiscal policies that can more efficiently protect those rights and promote fairness.*

Summarize

FIGURE 8.4. A FIST Evaluation of Federal Regulation of Corporate Governance

governance will encourage a national financial crisis, nor is there any evidence of significant cross-state spillovers from, or national merit goods adversely affected by, state regulation. On the contrary, state variation in the rules of corporate governance is likely to be efficiency enhancing. Step 5 reveals a significant local informational advantage in the administration of local rules for corporate governance. From Step 6, local political participation and local governance will be enhanced by the decentralization of the design and enforcement of the rules for corporate governance. While there are potential advantages for redistributive objectives from the nationalization of corporate governance enforcement, there are other national policies that can achieve this objective more efficiently. We conclude, then, both for the positive benefits of economic efficiency and political participation and because of the availability of more effective national fiscal policies, that regulatory responsibility for corporate governance in the United States is best assigned to states.[37]

A FIST Evaluation: State Regulation of Business Strategies

Successful firms in a market economy provide goods and services to consumers, make returns sufficient to compensate workers and investors, and allocate the remaining cash flow to the owners of the firm as profits. Profit-maximizing strategies include providing new or improved products, using technologies that lower costs below the competitive market price, and designing a market strategy that advantages the firm relative to its competitors. By U.S. federal competition law, the last may well be anticompetitive and, indeed, may be illegal. Yet almost by definition, state and local government regulations that restrict market behaviors will be anticompetitive. As noted by Frank Easterbrook, "A collision between federal rule in favor of competition and state rules supplanting competition is almost inevitable" (1983, p. 24). Under the Supremacy Clause of the U.S. Constitution, whereby federal law trumps state law when there is a conflict, federal competition law will win. If so, all state regulations that do not meet the standards for efficient competition as specified by (among others) the Sherman Antitrust Act (1890), the Federal Trade Commission Act (1914), or the Clayton Act (1914) might be disallowed. Indeed, with a very strict interpretation of state business regulations, there would be no state race to the top, or race to the bottom, only national, or nationally permissible, business regulations. For nearly a century, U.S. courts have sought to find a policy arena where state business regulations might survive, even thrive, alongside U.S. competition law. For U.S. federalism, the boundaries of that arena have been defined by what is now known as the "state action doctrine" of U.S. competition law. The doctrine balances two of our aims for federal governance—that of economic efficiency and democratic governance through the promotion of local political participation.

---

37. For a similar analysis and a conclusion favoring decentralization for the assignment of security regulation, see Romano (2002). For assignment of regulation for insurance, also favoring decentralization, see Butler and Ribstein (2008).

In 1890, when Congress passed the Sherman Antitrust Act, there was no thought that the act's restraints on business behavior would have implications for regulation by states or political units within the state.[38] The issue first presented itself in 1943 when the U.S. Supreme Court was asked to consider California's Agricultural Prorate Act as a possible violation of the Sherman Act. Under the Prorate Act, ten or more suppliers of an agricultural product could petition the state's Prorate Advisory Committee to implement a restrictive market program. If 65 percent of all growers of the product agreed to the program, it would be implemented. The program was challenged by a California producer of raisins on the grounds that it violated the anticompetitive provisions of the Sherman Act.

After first noting that the program would violate the Sherman Act had it been implemented by a private coalition of producers, the Court in *Parker v. Brown* allowed the program to stand as a legitimate act of the state legislature, ruling that "in a dual system of governments in which, under the Constitution, the states are sovereign, save only as Congress may constitutionally subtract from their authority."[39] The Court was careful to emphasize, however, that the sovereignty of the state was defined by the democratically elected state legislature, and it was only the legislative passage of the Agricultural Prorate Act that provided the national regulatory immunity for California raisin producers. The Court did recognize that California raisins were consumed by citizens living outside California, but since the U.S. Congress had not actively sought to regulate that market, California was free to do so in the best interests of its citizens. By so ruling, the Court allowed a monopoly pricing scheme for the raisin producers of California. The producers supplied 95 percent of the national raisin market at the time. In the interest of promoting participatory state governance, the supervising national Court allowed the potential state-created monopoly to stand. The only limitation was that the regulatory decision be made by a democratically elected state legislature.

Since *Parker*, the Court has issued further rulings seeking to clarify the exact boundaries of state sovereignty over business regulations, the most important of which is arguably the 1980 decision in *California Retail Liquor Dealers Association v. Midcal Aluminum*.[40] At issue was the involvement of a

38. See Hovenkamp and MacKerron (1985, pp. 725–728).

39. *Parker v. Brown*, 317 U.S. 341, 351 (1943).

40. *California Retail Liquor Dealers Association v. Midcal Aluminum*, 445 U.S. 97 (1980). A series of earlier rulings by the Court denied state-action immunity for regulations not

state agency in a per se violation of national antitrust laws—supporting a resale price maintenance scheme for wine distributors. The Court denied immunity for the agency under *Parker*, and having lost immunity, the regulation was found in violation of the price-fixing provisions of federal antitrust law. Though the state legislature created the pricing agency, the legislature did not review or approve the prices set by the agency.

By its ruling, *Midcal* expanded the test for state regulatory immunity to now include both (1) the requirement from *Parker* that the regulation be clearly articulated and affirmatively expressed as state legislative policy, and now (2) the requirement from *Midcal* that the policy be actively supervised by the legislature when implemented. From the perspective of promoting political participation in the setting of state regulatory policy, both requirements make sense. By first requiring "clear articulation" of the regulatory policy, *Midcal* ensured that all potentially interested parties to the regulation know of, and have the opportunity to be involved in, the approval of the regulation. By then requiring the state legislature to "actively supervise" the regulation, *Midcal* assured all parties that the regulation would be enforced as agreed to. The second requirement gives content to the first. Since *Midcal*, the Court has strictly adhered to its requirements for state legislature approval and legislative oversight of state business regulations.[41] While the *Midcal* precedent continues to hold, the U.S. Supreme Court continues to struggle with its application, as evident by the recent decision regarding the regulation of teeth-whitening businesses; see Box 8.2.

Current U.S. federal law has now carved out a domain for state regulation of business practices. As long as citizens can actively participate in the setting of those regulations that have been promulgated by their state legislatures, the regulations are likely to be immune from oversight by federal antitrust enforcement.[42] From the perspective of federal governance, and our FIST analysis, current U.S. law gives precedence to the goal of political participation when creating space for state regulation of business strategies. While a focus on political participation is certainly appropriate, the other important goals of

---

explicitly approved by the state legislature, even those approved by municipal governments incorporated by the state.

41. Subsequent case law applying the *Midcal* test is reviewed in Inman and Rubinfeld (1997).

42. State enforcement of state competition policies remains a possibility, at least in principle.

Box 8.2. Is There Active Supervision on the Teeth Whitening Business?

In *North Carolina State Board of Examiners v. FTC* (135 S. Ct. 1101 [2015]), the Supreme Court upheld the lower court's opinion that the North Carolina Dental Board, whose membership was primarily practicing dentists, had, without sufficient supervision, made efforts to exclude nondentists from the teeth-whitening business. Relying heavily on the two-pronged *Midcal* test, while attempting to limit the holding in *Parker v. Brown*, the majority of the Court stressed the importance of the active-supervision prong of the test, especially in light of the fact that the Dental Board was not a political sovereign of the state. The vote was six to three, with the three most conservative justices in opposition. The division on the Supreme Court suggests a tension between the competition-oriented policies of the federal antitrust laws and the right of states in a federalist system to impose their own restrictions on occupations. The majority emphasizes the importance of free markets and opts to strengthen limits on state regulatory discretion, stating, "Active market participants cannot be allowed to regulate their own markets free from antitrust accountability." In its majority opinion, the Court offers guidance as to what it takes to actively supervise a regulatory activity. The supervision must be flexible and content dependent, and it must include review mechanisms that provide "realistic assurances" that any anticompetitive conduct by the board promotes the interests of the state and not the individual interests of the board and the dentists whom the board effectively represents.

Why was this a divided opinion? There are no obvious cross-state externalities here. The difference between the majority and minority opinions turns on how Court chooses to define acceptable within state political participation when setting the regulatory standard for acceptable professional practice by dentists. According to a North Carolina statute, dentistry includes removing "stains, accretions or deposits from human teeth." It is not obvious whether this applies to teeth whitening or not. The regulatory board chose an interpretation that protected dentists' market power by sending cease-and-desist letters to nondentists who offered competitive teeth-whitening services (typically at lower prices than dentists). In making this decision, was the regulatory board adequately supervised?

The board's governing statute did not explicitly authorize a role for nondentists, and the board's actions were taken without broad political participation that would have incorporated the views of nondentists. In his majority opinion, Justice Anthony Kennedy made it clear that "State agencies are not simply by their governmental character sovereign actors for purposes of state-action immunity." What about the three minority votes? Justice Alito, joined by Justices Scalia and Thomas, dissented based on a strict reading of *Parker v. Brown*. In their view the fact that the actions were taken by a state-created agency should have ended the discussion. Did nondentists have the ability to participate, monitor, and potentially object to the actions of the Dental Board? The minority dissent never tackled this substantive question. As a result, we are left with an open question as to what degree of local supervision is sufficient to justify antitrust immunity.

federalism are now being ignored, the most important of which is economic efficiency.[43]

Elsewhere we have proposed an extension of the current state action doctrine to include an evaluation of market efficiency when reviewing state business regulations.[44] Matters of efficiency arise whenever a state regulation imposes significant economic spillovers on national consumers in the regulated market. While California's prorated pricing regulation in *Parker* met the Court's initial participation test (and would also meet today's expanded test of *Midcal*), it created a cartel for California raisin producers controlling 95 percent of national production. Such market power would allow the raisin producers to set a national monopoly price for raisins. Losers would be national consumers; winners would be California raisin producers earning monopoly profits. An adverse economic spillover on national consumers is the result. This outcome is a violation of our requirement (T6) for justifying efficient local regulation and thus a reason to require an alternative national regulation or, more appropriately here, national supervision of the state regulation. U.S. antitrust enforcement provides that supervision.

To fill this gap in regulatory assignment, we have proposed a two-step spillover test that triggers a national antitrust review when a local business regulation violates Condition T6.[45] The spillover test would ask the following questions:

1. Does the state regulation create an interjurisdictional monopoly spillover with the potential to significantly harm residents outside the state?

2. If so, was the state regulation decided without effective political participation from the affected consumers residing outside the state or from other state legislatures?

To limit bringing frivolous state action cases—almost all state business regulations will affect some outsiders—we limit Step 1 of the test to *economically*

---

43. See Easterbrook (1983) and Inman and Rubinfeld (1997). Concern that protection of individual rights might also be ignored by current regulatory doctrine may be eased by recognizing that the protection of rights is arguably a corollary outcome of active political participation; see Rapaczynski (1986).

44. See Inman and Rubinfeld (1997).

45. See Inman and Rubinfeld (1997, pp. 1271–1282).

significant harm suggested by a review of U.S. merger enforcement under the Clayton Act and the Federal Trade Commission Act with respect to harmful mergers. Does the business regulation allow state firms to raise national market prices by more than 5 percent?[46] That guideline implies that all state-regulated products whose market demand has price elasticities of demand (as a measure of potential market power) less than (that is, more negative than) −2.0 would be exempt from further review by Step 1 of the proposed spillover test. State-regulated products with low price elasticities of demand and in violation of Step 1 would then have to clear Step 2. By Step 2, the test would then also exempt any market prices regulated by a legislatively decided multistate agreement, as, for example, would one state's regulation of power generation for an interstate power grid. Against Steps 1 and 2, California's Agricultural Prorate Act regulating national raisin prices would fail our spillover test and thus would be open to national antitrust enforcement.[47]

By carving out a protected domain for state business regulations, current U.S. assignment has avoided Easterbrook's worry about national dominance under federal antitrust policy. The Supreme Court has, to this point, given states substantial latitude to regulate business strategies of state firms, as long as the regulations are actively supervised by state legislatures. The virtue of this assignment is the weight it gives to local decision-making. Citizens of the state decide state regulations balancing residents' benefits and costs. Economically inefficient regulations affecting only state residents but offset by other resident benefits will be allowed to stand. When this is the case, resident decisions provide a race to the top.

Unfortunately (in our minds) current U.S. assignment allows state regulations that impose significant out-of-state inefficiencies to stand as well. A spillover test for state regulations can correct this shortcoming.[48] Elsewhere we have provided a full FIST analysis that balances the benefits of local political

---

46. The enforcement agencies, whose concern goes beyond price to include innovation and other non-price concerns, do not use a formal 5 percent rule when deciding whether or not to block a merger. However, the five percent threshold does appear on many occasions when the agencies are evaluating market definition. See the United States Department of Justice and Federal Trade Commission (2010).

47. The price elasticity of demand for California raisins has been estimated to be about −1.0. California's main competition is from Iran and Turkey; see Soltani and Saghaian (2012).

48. See Inman and Rubinfeld (1997). For a comparison of U.S. and EU competition enforcement using the framework of FIST, see Rubinfeld (2019).

participation against possibly adverse economic spillovers from the regulation of business strategies. In the end, we prefer a state-decided race to the top in the regulation of state business strategies, but one refereed by national antitrust policies when a state "goes out of its lane" and adopts a regulation adversely affecting the economic welfare of nonresidents.

A FIST Evaluation: State Regulation of Environmental Quality

Within every local, state, or provincial jurisdiction, private actions may have environmental consequences that will require government intervention. When the consequences are only local—as, for example, with local trash, smog, or lake pollution—then only a local government policy response is needed. National regulation of environmental quality will be appropriate, however, when there is a race to the bottom in local decision-making, because of significant scale economies in treatment (T1), because of the inability of communities to efficiently exclude polluting activities (T5), or because of interstate spillovers (T6). While each is important, it will be the presence of interstate spillovers (T6) that will be most important for defining the boundary of responsibility between local and national environmental regulations.[49]

National regulation of interstate spillovers will *not* be needed if contractually binding (Coasian) regulatory agreements between polluting and recipient states can be designed. Such voluntary agreements are very difficult to fashion, however, for at least three reasons.[50] First, agreements require a clear understanding of the level of pollution transmitted by each polluting state and the pollution received by each recipient state. Calibrating such

49. Our analysis here draws heavily on the research of Richard Revesz as summarized in Revesz (2000). The interstate economic consequences from violating Conditions T1 and T5 are likely to be modest. Scale economies in environmental treatment (T1) are less a question of assigning regulatory responsibility and more a matter for the national provision of a collective public good. A failure of Condition T5 rests on the availability of local tax instruments and the relative elasticities of supply and demand for the locally taxed goods. These effects are likely to be greatest for environmental regulation by local communities within a metropolitan area, but much less so for state governments nationally. Even so, the failure to meet Condition T5 is *not* an argument for national regulatory policy. Rather, it is an argument for improving the tax structures of competing local and state governments.

50. See Chapter 3 for a full discussion of the difficulties of intergovernmental bargaining as a way to solve intergovernmental inefficiencies.

baselines is often very difficult, particularly for air pollution. Second, the terms of the agreement require specifying the costs of cleanup to the polluting states and the benefits of a cleaner environment to the recipient states. Both sides to the agreement have strong incentives to conceal their true costs and benefits. Finally, as the number of parties to any regulatory agreement increases, both polluting and recipients states have an incentive to drop out of the agreement—that is, to free ride. Successful voluntary agreements to control interstate or international pollution are difficult to design and to enforce.

Thus, national policy will be needed. The U.S. experience under both the Clean Air Act of 1970 and the Federal Water Pollution Control Act of 1948 as amended in 1972 are instructive as to the difficulties in using a regulatory strategy to efficiently and fairly limit interstate spillovers.[51] Effective national regulation of interstate spillovers must address three issues: (1) how best to design regulatory standards, (2) how to enforce the standards, and finally, (3) how to win political approval of the standards by the national legislature.

Having established the economic and social benefits of regulating interstate spillovers, the first task for implementation is to define the regulatory standards that each polluting state—specifically, firms within the state—must meet. U.S. efforts to do so for the control of interstate air pollution illustrate the difficulties in setting effective standards. Effective standards seek to control the level of pollution borne by residents of the "downwind" state sent from one or more "upwind" states. Ideally, an efficient regulation will set different standards for each of the upwind states, with standards varying by industry, the state's location, and weather patterns. Setting the efficient standard will require detailed information on each dimension of upwind pollution and then a matching regulatory structure.

In contrast, the initial standards in the Clean Air Act of 1970 were simple. The act set a uniform standard for emissions by each upwind state, with three undesired consequences. First, the use of a uniform standard across polluting states was not economically efficient. Using a common standard ignores the fact that, for reasons of geography or industry, technologies for removing pollution might be much less expensive in some states than in others. The less expensive states should face a higher standard. Second, a

---

51. See Revesz (1992) for an evaluation of the Clean Air Act and Leone and Jackson (1981) for an evaluation of the Federal Water Pollution Control Act.

uniform state standard will tend to be "overly inclusive" in its regulatory impact, as it limits not only out-of-state pollution but also pollution that remains in-state—an outcome best regulated by the state alone. Third, the uniform standard may also be "underinclusive" as states seek to meet their state standards by strategically locating polluting plants and using tall smokestacks for discharging the pollution. After the introduction of uniform state emissions standards, the use of tall smokestacks for the control of within-state emissions rose from only 2 stacks over five hundred feet in 1970 to more than 180 stacks of five hundred feet or more by 1985 and 23 stacks higher than one thousand feet.[52]

Subsequent amendments to the Clean Air Act in 1977 and 1990 sought to address these problems by shifting the locus from measuring emissions by the polluting states to measuring air quality in the downwind, recipient states. These improved standards became difficult to enforce, however. In particular, how should the regulating agency, in this case the Environmental Protection Agency (EPA), allocate responsibility for the degradation of air quality in a downwind state to each of the polluting upwind states? And then, once allocated, was the pollution attributed to any one of several upwind states the "cause" of poor air quality in the downwind state? The EPA placed the burden for producing these facts on the downwind state. The difficulty of credible enforcement is perhaps best seen in the fact that the EPA has never found in favor of a downwind state seeking to enforce the interstate spillover standard on an upwind state. U.S. courts might be an alternative venue for enforcement, but the U.S. courts have typically deferred to the EPA's expertise on matters of enforcement.[53] As a result, lax enforcement of interstate spillover standards has become the norm for U.S. air quality regulation.

The last question to ask is, Why has U.S. national regulatory supervision of interstate spillovers proved so ineffective? The answer is likely to lie in the politics of national regulatory policy. Weak standards and lax enforcement appear to have best served the interests of the U.S. Congress. At the time of the passage of the Clean Air Act, the Clean Water Act, and their subsequent amendments, congressional decision-making was decentralized and meant to facilitate the local political interests of the 535 members of Congress.[54]

52. Revesz (2000, p. 52).
53. See Revesz (1996, secs. 1, 2).
54. See Chapter 4.

Institutions capable of coordinated policy-making, such as strong political parties or a strong president, with an interest in environmental policies were lacking. Because politics were local, national environmental groups had only a modest influence on the design and enforcement of policy. Their memberships were never more than a small fraction of any one district's eligible voters. No matter how well organized or persuasive, the agenda of the national environmental lobby would be second to that of local economic interests. The result has been environmental regulations whose primary beneficiaries are local constituents: both residents and firms. National environmental policies in the United States have created barriers to entry that favor older, established firms; uniform standards that advantage large firms with significant economies of scale; regulations that favor the technologies of one firm or group of firms; that actively promote the use of equipment produced by local firms in favored districts; and standards for air quality that are set to favor some districts over others in the competition for new investment.[55] There were enough "margins" on which to bestow local favors that both bills passed in the House and the Senate nearly unanimously.

The administrative structure needed to enforce the laws also protects local regulatory interests. First, as legislated, national regulations are flexible and states are allowed to design their own policies—known as Strategic Implementation Plans—to meet the standards. Second, once agreed to, enforcement of the state plan by the EPA is subject to public hearings (known to political scientists as "fire alarms") to ensure that local interests are heard. Third, to minimize any unilateral power over enforcement by the EPA, Congress has arranged to move important regulatory decisions to a "competitive" agency, the Federal Energy Administration. Fourth, Congress retains budgetary control over both agencies to ensure compliance with the locally negotiated agreements. Finally, Congress has limited the potential influence of the courts by writing flexible regulations with unclear paths for implementation. U.S. courts have typically been reluctant to impose a particular judicial interpretation on legislative rules; as a result, the courts have deferred in most cases to the supervising agencies. The agencies are supervised, in turn, by Congress.[56]

---

55. Revesz (2001, pp. 571–578) provides examples for the provisions of the Clean Air Act. Leone and Jackson (1981) do so for the Clean Water Act.

56. For the full details of the argument with an application to the Clean Air Act, see McCubbins, Noll, and Weingast (1989).

Like the enabling legislation, U.S. regulatory enforcement of interstate spill-overs best serves the local economic interests of a locally elected Congress.

The end result has been U.S. national regulation of environmental spillovers that is both weak and at times counterproductive. Fortunately there are alternatives, but they move policy away from regulation by politics and toward regulation by markets using cap and trade to meet a regulatory standard.[57] As a general rule, U.S. politics has not been receptive. Market-based regulations remove the ability of locally elected politicians to directly control the costs and benefits of regulatory policies. In contrast, environmental policies in the European Union show the advantage of decision-making by a less decentralized political process. Environmental policies in the EU are decided by the agenda powers of the European Commission and approved by the Council of Ministers.[58] The outcome has been the adoption and implementation of a system of cap-and-trade policies designed to enforce EU-wide emissions standards. The benefit for the environment has been a significant reduction in the level of EU emissions at an abatement cost far below what might be needed under traditional centralized regulatory standards.[59]

Given the current political management of U.S. national regulatory policy, Steps 5 and 6 of our FIST analysis would favor the decentralization of regulatory responsibility to states to manage in-state pollution via a race to the top; Steps 2 and 3 would recommend the nationalization of policies to manage interstate environmental spillovers and the protection of national merit wants; but Step 4 argues for a market-based regulatory strategy to replace the potential for biased national governance favoring local economic interests. Environmental policies may have implications for the final distribution of income, but by Step 7, national fiscal policies rather than environmental regulation are better suited to achieving national goals of economic fairness. See Figure 8.5.

---

57. See Revesz (2000) for one attractive cap-and-trade proposal. We favor cap and trade over a carbon tax for reasons first stressed by Weitzman (1974) and both policies over the current politicized administration of U.S. environmental policy. See Stavins (2019) for a comprehensive overview of the advantages and disadvantages of a national cap-and-trade policy as compared with a carbon tax. California, Massachusetts, and Washington have introduced their own cap-and-trade policies.

58. See Chapter 9 for the institutional details of EU decision-making and Van den Bergh (2000) for an application to environmental policy.

59. See Goulder (2013).

Step 1 Sovereignty Test: *Will the proposed federal regulation threaten the ability of individual state or local governments to function as politically and economically independent organizations within the federal system?*
No, proceed to Step 2

Step 2 Efficiency Test: *Can regulation protect a national public good, curtail cross-state spillovers, or promote a national merit good?*
Yes: *There is evidence of significant spillovers of pollutants across state borders and need for protection of environmental merit goods.*
Proceed to Step 3

Step 3 Efficiency Test: *Are efficient regulatory agreements between state or local governments possible?*
Yes: *Such agreements are possible, but they are typically less than efficient and often difficult to enforce.*
Proceed to Step 4

Step 4 Efficiency Test: *Does the proposed regulation provide a national public good, curtail cross-state spillovers, or promote a merit good?*
Yes, but: *Political incentives in a decentralized legislature encourage inefficient regulation. A market based strategy may be preferred.*
Proceed to Step 5

Step 5 Efficiency Test: *Do state or local governments have an informational advantage in the provision of the regulation?*
Yes: *States have needed regulatory and fiscal policies to efficiently regulate within state spillovers.*
Proceed to Step 6

Step 6 Participation Test: *Will state and local government regulation encourage increased citizen participation?*
Yes: *Resident welfare is impacted by within state spillovers; citizens therefore have an incentive to paticipate in setting regulations.*
Proceed to Step 7

Step 7 Rights and Fairness Test: *Does national regulation of interstate spillovers protect individual rights and/or enhance economic fairness?*
Yes, but: *There are alternative national fiscal policies that can more efficiently protect those rights and promote fairness.*

Summarize

FIGURE 8.5. A FIST Evaluation of Federal Regulation of Environmental Quality

4. Summing Up

The appropriate assignment for the regulation of economic and social activities is a central issue for a federal democracy. When the activities of residents in one jurisdiction affect the well-being of those in another, the coordination of policy between the two jurisdictions may be necessary. Coordination may occur through a mutual agreement to manage the joint activity using the institutions of Cooperative Federalism or, if mutual agreements are not possible, through democratically approved policies using the institutions of Democratic Federalism. A first-order decision for Democratic Federalism is to decide which level of government—local, state, or national—should be responsible for setting policy: the assignment decision. Here we have considered the assignment of regulatory policy.

Our theory for regulatory assignment begins from the perspective of economic efficiency. If an activity only affects residents within a local or state jurisdiction, then responsibility for any regulation of that activity should be with the residents in the jurisdiction. From the perspective of economic efficiency, it is only when local or state regulatory activities create costs or benefits for neighboring jurisdictions that centralized regulation should be considered. This is most likely to occur in three instances: (1) when there are significant economies of scale in the efficient management of a regulated activity such that sharing those costs can make residents of all jurisdictions better off, (2) when local jurisdictions adopt regulatory policies that have adverse consequences for the efficient use of fiscal policies by neighboring jurisdictions, and (3) when regulatory decisions by one jurisdiction create economic spillovers for its neighbors. In all three instances, we are likely to observe a race to the bottom in regulatory policy. For efficiency, the race will need new "rules" set by national regulatory policy.

While important, economic efficiency should not be the sole goal of regulatory policy. As with the assignment of all policy responsibilities in Democratic Federalism, other important values may weigh in the balance. For example, it may be efficient to have all waste disposal located in a low-income community, but there may also be adverse consequences for the health and general well-being of community residents. Equity might demand another location. Or it might be efficient to destroy the habitat of an endangered species or mine for minerals in the Grand Canyon, but the welfare of future generations will need consideration. Alternatively, local regulatory decisions may be inefficient, but local jurisdictions might be the preferred venue for democratic involvement. Finally, the assignment of regulatory policy, like all policies, must consider the decision-making capacity of local, state, and national governments. FIST provides a common framework to balance these competing objectives when assigning regulatory responsibilities.

We have provided three examples of regulatory assignment where FIST can provide guidance. First, for the regulation of corporate governance, both economic theory and evidence point toward a race to the top with regulatory decentralization. Competing values either support a decentralized assignment (participation) or are unaffected (equity) or best managed by other, nonregulatory national policies. Second, for the regulation of business strategies, local regulation will either be efficient (for example, local zoning) or, if inefficient, potentially supportive of democratic participation. If local participation is structured so as to ensure that all those adversely affected by a regulation have a protected path for its reform, then locally inefficient regulations should be allowed. What will not be allowed, and thus requires national regulation, are local regulations that create significant economic spillovers on nonresidents who have had no say in their initial approval. In the United States and EU, national competition policy best provides this oversight. In both places, union-wide competition policies are well managed and have provided significant efficiency gains. Third, for the regulation of the environment, both efficiency and participation favor local regulation of local environmental spillovers. Interjurisdictional spillovers, however, are best managed nationally for reasons of economic efficiency and for reasons of intra- and intergenerational equity. That said, politically supervised regulation of interjurisdictional spillovers with the current structure of U.S. national governance has been both inefficient and at times counterproductive. For this reason, a FIST analysis for U.S. environmental regulation recommends an alternative approach, that of national regulation through a cap-and-trade policy.

PART III

On Becoming Federal

THERE HAVE BEEN TWO MAJOR TRANSITIONS toward federal governance over the past fifty years. The first is Europe's efforts to establish an economic union and, for its most ardent supporters, perhaps a full political union. The second is South Africa's creation of a new democratic state, for which shared powers between elected national and provincial governments were essential for a peaceful transition from apartheid to democracy. The recent histories of the European Union and democratic South Africa are instructive as to what is needed to become a well-functioning federal democracy. Simply writing a federal constitution is not enough. Citizens must embrace Democratic Federalism as their preferred form of governance and be willing to debate and balance its benefits and costs.

Chapter 9, "The European Union: Federal Governance at the Crossroads," traces the evolution of the European Union from a six-nation compact to manage the production and distribution of coal and steel to its current configuration as a twenty-eight nation (perhaps twenty-seven after Brexit) customs and currency union. Economic Federalism provides the conceptual foundation for the union's guiding principles of *subsidiarity* and *proportionality*. Cooperative Federalism provides the institutional foundations now in place for the implementation of those principles. For the twenty-eight members of the customs union, union governance now decides policies for the funding of regional public goods, income transfer to poor regions, transfers to agricultural producers, regulation of union-wide market competition, harmonization of Member State taxation, and most importantly, the lowering of barriers to trade and the movement of people between member nations. In addition, for the nineteen Member States that also belong to the EU's currency union, known as the Economic and Monetary Union, policies also include the provision and management of a common currency (euro) and the regulation of member countries' banking and financial institutions. By most measures, the EU's customs union has been a success, adding 1 to 2 percent per year to Member States' real GDP. Less clear are the net benefits of membership in the currency union. While the common currency has lowered the cost and uncertainty of financial transactions, it has also reduced the ability of Economic and Monetary Union members to manage their aggregate GDP fluctuations, and it has introduced new temptations to abuse a now wider access to international lending. The EU's slow recovery from the global recession of 2009 and Greece's fiscal collapse and subsequent bailout are costly examples of Cooperative Federalism's inability to manage the details of running a currency union. Further, setting EU policies by the institutions of Cooperative Federalism requiring (near) unanimity among country-level officials has led to inaction on important issues and a feeling of irrelevance by EU citizens, a sense of frustration and isolation known as the "democratic deficit." Finally, Cooperative Federalism's rule by unanimity makes disciplining Member States for rights violations very difficult; Hungary and Poland are now testing the limits of EU enforcement. One proposed solution to the EU's current institutional failings is to become a full political union guided by the principles of Democratic Federalism. We are doubtful the union is ready for such a step. Successful political unions require a commitment to democratic rule and a willingness to make mutual financial and personal sacrifices for the benefits of citizens from nations other than one's own. At the moment, a majority of EU citizens lack the common political ethos necessary for such compromises. We suggest a more modest path of reforms that stays within the current structure of Cooperative Federalism.

In contrast to the culturally and politically diverse nations of the EU, most South African citizens at the time of their transition from apartheid to democracy shared a common commitment to democratic governance, a commitment personified by Nelson Mandela. After more than thirty years of unresolved armed conflict, both the African majority represented by the African National Congress (ANC) and the economic elites and white minority represented by the National Party agreed that the only path forward was democratic, with equal civil and political rights for everyone. But only if economic and racial minorities could be assured they would not be exploited by the new majority. Mandela made it clear to his ANC followers that democracy could go forward only if there could be "structural guarantees" that majority rule would not result in the "domination of whites by blacks." Chapter 10, "Mandela's Federal Democracy: A Fragile Compact," argues that those structural guarantees were to be provided by the institutions of Democratic Federalism. The new national government controlled by the ANC would set national tax and transfer policies, but provincial governments, drawn to ensure elite and minority political control of at least one or two provinces, would be constitutionally assigned responsibility to provide redistributive services financed by a constitutionally guaranteed share of national tax revenues. The result has been a "hostage game" in fiscal policy, with the majority and the elite each capable of imposing fiscal harm on the other if either deviates from the implicitly agreed-to "federal compromise" of modest taxation and efficient provision of public services. The compromise has held for the first twenty-five years of the new democracy. But it is a fragile compact and can be undone by either an impatient majority within the ANC or a less flexible and dynamic private economy exposing the elite to higher taxation. The fiscally corrupt administration of President Jacob Zuma has made clear how fragile the Mandela compact might be. Fortunately, the institutions of Democratic Federalism have provided an additional protection. The ruling Democratic Alliance of the Western Cape province has demonstrated to a national electorate the benefits of efficient and honest governance. Fearing a Democratic Alliance challenge in the 2019 national elections, the ANC leadership removed Zuma as head of the ANC in favor of a longtime Mandela disciple, Cyril Ramaphosa. Democratic Federalism has provided the institutions needed for South Africa's peaceful transition to democracy. Whether they can provide what is needed for its democratic future is less certain.

9

The European Union

FEDERAL GOVERNANCE AT THE CROSSROADS

1. Introduction

For years, the European Union has been seen as a vibrant and evolving federal system. Yet the Greek fiscal crisis, the 2016 vote by the citizens of the United Kingdom to exit the union, challenges to EU rules for democratic governance by Hungary and Poland, Italy's standoff with the European Commission on excessive government deficits, and questions relating to union policies on immigration all highlight fundamental weaknesses in the union's federal structure of governance. The union, as a formal political organization, originated with the approval of the Treaty of Paris, which created the European Coal and Steel Community. Several years later, Jean Monnet helped to create the European Economic Community (EEC) for the free movement of goods and people. The success of the EEC encouraged a still wider expansion of union responsibilities and membership through the Treaties of Maastricht, Amsterdam, Nice, and Lisbon. But will the union continue to evolve as a successful, stable federal system?

This chapter reviews the institutions and performance of the European Union through the lens of our models of Economic, Cooperative, and Democratic Federalism. We will explain that while there have been efforts over time to fashion the EU as a full political union governed by the principles of Democratic Federalism, to date member states have chosen to manage their EU affairs guided instead by the tenets of Economic and Cooperative Federalism. Economic Federalism provides the conceptual foundation for the union's guiding economic principles of *subsidiarity* and *proportionality*. EU policies are set under the governing principles of Cooperative Federalism using directly elected or appointed representatives from each member state to a forum setting policies by supermajority and, in most cases, unanimous agreements.

Section 2 reviews the current state of the political economy of the EU in light of our model of Cooperative Federalism. In Section 3 we evaluate the performance of the union against our three objectives: economic efficiency, democratic participation, and the protection of property and civil rights. While there are clear long-run economic gains from the creation of the EU, we find room for improved performance in how it manages potential fiscal and banking crises and union-wide economic downturns. The democratic performance of the union is also widely debated: Is there or is there not a failure to achieve the ideals of a democratic system? Against those ideals, there is a failure grounded in the decision-making rules of Cooperative Federalism. Finally, current EU policies offer only limited added protections for personal rights and liberties beyond member states' own protections.

Section 4 recognizes that the EU is at a crossroads. To address its current weaknesses, EU governance can move in either of two directions: continue as Cooperative Federalism but approve modest reforms to address each shortcoming of EU performance *or* create a full political union governed by the rules of Democratic Federalism. Our preferred option is modest reforms, but with the thought that if successful, institutional reforms embracing a more complete political union might then be feasible. To ensure continued economic success, even the modest reforms should include a credible commitment to a "no bailout" policy for member state fiscal crises and a self-financing union-wide fiscal insurance policy against common economic shocks. To advance toward the broader goal of increased democratic governance, we propose a general election for the president of the European Commission for a five-year term.[1] To further protect individual rights and liberties, we support the current fiscal penalties and the hope that the EU will have the will to implement them. As a final step, we advocate expulsion for those that systematically violate EU standards for individual rights and liberties.

One of the twentieth century's leading democratic theorists, Robert Dahl, sees the European Union as the first serious test case for the use of transnational organizations for the governance of human affairs. From city-states, to feudal alliances, to nation-states, each created a need to invent new institutions of democratic governance. For Dahl (1994), today's international economy

1. Eichengreen (2018a) has made a similar proposal.

governed by transnational governments is the next step in this evolution. The European Union provides the first opportunity for an in-depth evaluation of one example of this new form of governance as a full democratic *state*.[2] That is our aim here.

2. EU Governance as Cooperative Federalism

The European Union began in 1951 as a two-country treaty between Germany and France, with Luxembourg, Belgium, the Netherlands, and Italy soon to follow as signees. The agenda was to supervise the production, pricing, and free trade of coal and steel. As an economic treaty, decisions were to be made unanimously by the six member countries. The agreement was a success on three levels. First, it created allies in the shared production of military inputs between long-standing antagonists. Second, it helped to foster strong economic growth for the member countries. Third, its success demonstrated the ability of European governments to cooperate to their mutual benefit.

Encouraged by the European Coal and Steel Community's success, a wider economic alliance was proposed for the free movement of goods and people among member nations. The result was the Treaty of Rome and its eventual approval by twelve member nations forming the EEC. In specifying the treaty, it was felt that the wider policy agenda, including subsidies to agriculture (Common Agricultural Policy, or CAP) and economically backward regions (Cohesion and Structural Funds), would require a decision process more flexible than a rule of unanimity. An executive branch, the European Commission, would have sole agenda responsibility for proposing policy, but decisions would now be made by a Council of Ministers composed of one appointed representative from each member state, with votes allocated roughly (with a small-state bias) in proportion to the population of each member. In addition to the council, there would be a more representative legislative body, the Parliament, with member states also represented in proportion to population. At its inception, the European Parliament had no decision powers—only a

---

2. We emphasize *state* to distinguish the EU from transnational organizations seeking to meet specific policy objectives, such as national defense (NATO), free trade (World Trade Organization), financial transactions (International Monetary Fund), or environmental quality and the protection of human rights (United Nations). A *state* assumes responsibility for a broad range of policy objectives and has the ability to raise and spend money and to enforce agreed-to rules and regulation.

consultative role in setting policies. A majority of votes within the council would decide policy, a process known as qualified majority voting (QMV). In the face of objections by France—motivated by its fear of being in a minority—QMV was effectively overturned in favor again of an informal agreement for unanimity known as the Luxembourg Compromise. In effect, all council decisions were returned to rule by unanimity.

While the EEC did succeed in lowering tariffs among member countries, within-country special interests hoping to protect local markets often established special regulations and standards in their place. Further, barriers to the free movement of capital, goods and services, and people between countries remained. In response, the twelve member countries approved the Single European Act in 1986. The act's objectives were to standardize product and service regulations, to remove capital controls, and to harmonize member states' tax policies. Under the act, QMV was utilized by the council and the role of the Parliament was expanded. The approval of community policies would require a "cooperation procedure" whereby all council-approved policies would need a simple majority approval by the Parliament. If the Parliament were to reject the proposal, the proposal would return to the council for reconsideration. After reconsideration, it would become community law if unanimously approved by the council. The threat of a "veto" by the Parliament requiring a unanimous override by the council led the council to seek unanimous consent for all approved policies at the initial passage. In effect, the new rules of governance meant unanimity remained the norm for decision-making within the council.

While success was made in lowering barriers to free capital mobility, the resulting free flow of capital between member countries led to exchange rate instability and increased uncertainty for subsequent trade in goods and services. In response, a common currency and a common monetary policy, the European Monetary Union, was proposed and approved by the member states of the EEC in 1992 (with opt-outs for some countries) as the Treaty of Maastricht. Along with the expanded policy agenda, the treaty sought to constrain the community's powers over member states' own policies with two important institutional innovations.

First, the European Commission would be charged with enforcing two principles of policy assignment—those of *subsidiarity* and of *proportionality*:

Subsidiarity: . . . In areas which do not fall within the exclusive competence, the Union shall act only if and insofar as the objectives of the proposed action cannot be sufficiently achieved by the member states, either at central level or at regional and local level, but can rather, by reasons of scale or effects of the proposed action, be better achieved at the Union level. (Article 5(3), as amended by the Treaty of Lisbon)

Proportionality: . . . The content and form of Union action shall not exceed what is necessary to achieve the objectives of the Treaties. (Article 5(4), as amended by the Treaty of Lisbon)

Together the two principles drew a "bright line" between what can be a union policy and that which will be reserved for the national legislatures of the member states. It is the responsibility of the commission to review all commission-proposed policies against these criteria and only allow those satisfying the two principles to move forward for consideration by the Council of Ministers and the European Parliament.[3]

Second, Maastricht gave the Parliament a more direct role in the formation of policy with the introduction of the "co-decision procedure." Under co-decision, policy deliberations begin with a proposal by the European Commission. The Council of Ministers then considers the proposal. If it is rejected, the existing policy remains in place. But if approved, the proposal next moves to the Parliament for consideration. If the council's approved proposal is also approved by the Parliament, the proposal becomes the EU law. If rejected by the Parliament, the proposal is forwarded to a balanced committee composed equally of council and Parliament members. If a compromise is found, the proposal is then returned to the council for approval by QMV and to the Parliament for approval by a simple majority. If there is no agreement on a compromise proposal, the proposal is considered defeated and EU policy remains at the status quo. The central consequence of co-decision for EEC decision-making has been to reduce the agenda-setting powers of the commission.[4] Once a policy has been proposed, it is in the hands of the council and Parliament to decide the outcome. It is therefore in the interest of the commission to provide policy proposals that are likely to be jointly approved by the council and the Parliament.

3. For our approach to implementing these two principles, see Chapters 2 and Chapter 6. The European Commission is the EU institution responsible for the enforcement of these principles. National parliaments of the member states have the right to submit a reasoned opinion leading to a warning, the "yellow card," of a possible violation of subsidiarity; see Cooper (2006). Finally, the Court of Justice of the European Union (CJEU) may intervene to enforce subsidiarity or proportionality, but it has rarely done so; see Moens and Trone (2015).

4. See Garrett (1995).

The subsequent Treaties of Amsterdam and Nice made minor adjustments to the governance structure proposed in Maastricht. They led eventually to the admission into the union of the independent countries of eastern Europe: new members included the Czech Republic (2004), Cyprus (2004), Estonia (2004), Latvia (2004), Lithuania (2004), Malta (2004), Poland (2004), Slovakia (2004), Slovenia (2004), Bulgaria (2007), Romania (2007), and finally Croatia (2013). With the expanded size of the union, the Treaty of Nice also reallocated votes in the Council of Ministers roughly in proportion to country population. The Lisbon Treaty, in force as of December 1, 2009, introduced the last significant changes to the rules of governance for the EU, the most important of which was to discontinue the use of QMV for the council in favor of a two-hurdle majority rule requiring a 55 percent member state majority and a threshold of 65 percent of member states' populations.

Current treaty rules now place the Council of Ministers and the European Parliament as coequal chambers, at least constitutionally. In practice, however, it is the council that has proved decisive. Current rules advantage the chamber whose decisive voter's preferences are closest to the EU's policy status quo at the time of the decision. Since the council's and the Parliament's representatives can block each other, decisions will be made by bargaining between the two chambers. Any proposed policy that makes either the council's or the Parliament's decisive voter worse off relative to status quo policy will be rejected. Proposals that move too far from the status quo will be vetoed by the chamber closest to the status quo.

The best empirical evidence suggests that the decisive chamber has been the Council of Ministers. From the prior dominance of the council in EU policymaking, its preferences will have set the status quo. Council preferences are defined by the preferences of the national parliaments appointing each member state's representative to the council.[5] Understanding council decision-making goes a long way toward understanding EU decision-making.

5. In contrast, the preferences of the Parliament are set by separately elected members. Parliament elections give those opposed to policies preferred by dominant national parties an additional opportunity to express their preferences; see Hix and Marsh (2007). These elected representatives have voted less by country interests and more by political party interests; see Noury and Roland (2002). Because the Parliament's preferences on EU policies are likely to lie outside those of their country's council representative, the council is likely to be the pivotal chamber in the consultation committee and the decisive chamber in the setting of EU policies; see Hix (2006). For a survey of studies showing the preeminence of the council in EU decision-making, see Burns, Rasmussen, and Reh (2013) and particularly Hix and Høyland (2013). For

How, then, does the Council of Ministers set policy? Before the approval of the Lisbon Treaty, decisions were made by voting in the council. Under QMV, it was difficult to approve any policy without the unanimous support of the six largest member states. Moreover, the large states still needed to attract the support of at least nine of the remaining smaller countries to reach the required majority of fifteen member states. Without the organizing structure of supranational political parties or a strong EU president, vote cycling from one policy position to another becomes a possibility. Either there was gridlock and no decisions, or there was bargaining with side deals. Side deals within a "culture of compromise" and nearly always unanimous voting have been the result.[6] More than 80 percent of council decisions are agreed to by unanimity. If there has been dissent, it is typically by only one member state voting to abstain.[7]

As of 2019, all important EU decisions have been made unanimously, or nearly so, by appointed ministers of the member states. When there is dissent, it usually comes from no more than one or two members and is expressed not by a "no" vote but by rather abstention. As an alliance first governed by de jure and now de facto unanimity rule, we view the European Union today as the most fully developed and important example of Cooperative Federalism. An evaluation of its performance against the norms of economic efficiency, democratic representation, and the protection of individual rights and liberties will therefore provide important insights as to the potential of this form of federal governance.

3. Performance of the European Union

The European Union has had, and continues to have, no shortage of critics. The 2016 Brexit vote by the United Kingdom to exit the union is perhaps the most concrete realization of the critics' concerns. A majority of UK citizens felt removed from EU decision-making and, as a result, felt that union policies have favored union citizens from other, particularly eastern European, member

---

empirical analyses, see T. Thompson (2011) and Costello and Thomson (2013), which conclude that the council preferences are decisive.

6. See Chapters 4 and 5 for the general argument, and Häge (2012) and Baldwin and Wyplosz (2004, p. 107) for its application to EU decision-making.

7. See Mattila and Lane (2001). In addition to facilitating council decision-making, unanimity has a valuable side benefit for the enforcement of EU law. While the CJEU can identify violations, enforcement will be difficult without broad citizen support from within the country violating EU law. Unanimity ensures that each member state has at least initially supported the EU policy or regulation. See Kelemen (2016); see also Glencross (2009, esp. pp. 295–300).

states over UK citizens. The EU was perceived to have failed UK citizens. The United Kingdom's decision to exit the EU was, by all accounts, a difficult one, and to date it is still unresolved. Whatever its resolution, the issues behind the Brexit vote are fundamental for the EU as a form governance; see Box 9.1.

Box 9.1. Could the Brexit Vote Have Been Avoided?

With his appointment as prime minister of England in May 2010, David Cameron was determined not to permit the internal disagreements within his Conservative Party over Europe to sidetrack his domestic reform agenda. There was growing resentment over the effect of EU competition on domestic job growth and over the influx of European migrants from eastern Europe. In the 2015 general election to the British Parliament, the UK Independence Party received 12.6 percent of the vote, replacing the Liberal Democrats as the third most popular political party. Cameron responded to this threat by proposing a national referendum on whether the United Kingdom should stay in or leave the European Union. On June 23, 2016, by a margin of 52 to 48 percent, British citizens voted to leave the union—a *Brexit*. The table that follows examines the relative importance of the two prominent explanations for the decision by a majority of British citizens to vote to leave the EU: economic decline resulting from EU competition and cultural disaffection toward immigrants moving into Britain following the EU's inclusion of the thirteen eastern European countries.

The dependent variable is the percentage of voters preferring *Leave* in each of 397 local voting districts. Explanatory variables include the change in the district's unemployment rate (ΔUE) from 1991 (the date of the Maastricht Treaty) to 2016; the decline in the share of jobs in the district that are in manufacturing (ΔMAN) from 1991 to 2016; the change in the share of residents who are foreign born (ΔFOREIGN) from 1991 to 2011 (the most recent census year); the percentage of current residents who self-identify as Christian in 2011 (%CHRISTIAN) and its interaction with ΔFOREIGN; the percentage of district residents over the age of sixty-five in 2011 (%OLD); and the percentage of district residents with a college or university degree in 2011 (%LEVEL4).

Both explanations for the decision to vote *Leave* receive support. Districts with relatively higher rates of unemployment and a decline in manufacturing jobs were more likely to vote for *Leave*, as were districts with older and less educated residents. An increase in the share of the population that is foreign born also increased the *Leave* vote, and particularly so in districts where the share of those who identify as Christians is less than 70 percent.[a]

Explaining the Leave Vote*

Constant	ΔUE	ΔMAN	ΔFOREIGN	%CHRISTIAN	%CHRISTIAN · ΔFOREIGN	%OLD	%LEVEL4
.559	1.672	−.116	1.917	.409	−2.681	.241	−.971
(.043)	(.141)	(.077)	(.409)	(.063)	(.738)	(.112)	(.045)

*The mean value for the dependent variable, *Leave*, is .527 (standard deviation = .106). Explanatory variables include ΔUE (mean = −.041, SD = .028); ΔMAN (mean = .01, SD = .044); ΔFOREIGN (mean = .047; SD = .044); %CHRISTIAN (mean = .615, SD = .092); %OLD (mean = .19; SD = .045); and %LEVEL4 (mean = .287, SD = .080). All regression coefficients except for ΔMAN are significant at the 1 percent level. Standard errors within parentheses. The adjusted R^2 is .65.

A swing of from 2 to 3 percent of the vote (approximately 635,000 voters) from *Leave* to *Stay* would have changed the outcome. Are there any policies that Prime Minister Cameron might have introduced before the referendum to ensure a victory for *Stay*? Under the assumption that those who voted *Leave* did so for reasons of cultural disaffection and thus could not have been persuaded to change their votes, this would have left only those voters adversely affected economically as open to persuasion. While EU membership had significantly increased average UK incomes, not all regions benefited equally. London and Northern Ireland enjoyed significant economic and job growth, while the eastern and southeastern regions of England declined.

Assuming unemployed workers voted for *Leave* and employed voters favored *Stay*, Cameron would have had to find 635,000 new (permanent) jobs to have reversed the *Leave* outcome. Estimates for the efficacy of the EU's Structural and Cohesion Funds find that those economic development programs have succeeded in reducing the rate of unemployment in recipient regions by from 1 to 2 percent.[b] For the average district, this would be sufficient to reduce the *Leave* vote by 1.67 to 3.34 percent ($= 1.67 \times \Delta UE$)—roughly what Prime Minister Cameron needed to gain a majority for *Stay*. How expensive are such programs? For programs comparable to those funded by Structural and Cohesion Funds, the U.S. evidence for Great Recession policies suggests the cost per job created might range from $30,000 per job to as much as $85,000 per job.[c] At those costs, 635,000 new jobs would require UK government spending of approximately £14 billion ($19 billion) to £40 billion ($54 billion) per year, or approximately 1 to perhaps as much as 2 percent of UK GDP in 2016.

Would these investments have made economic sense for Cameron's Conservative Party in light of its desire to avoid the Brexit outcome? The answer turns on the costs of losing the referendum—the costs of Brexit. There are two Brexit strategies—the "soft" exit and the "hard" exit. Under the soft exit, the United Kingdom becomes a member of the European Economic Area and is allowed to trade freely with the EU but must also accept the free mobility of workers and make a significant contribution to the EU budget. Under the hard exit, the United Kingdom trades with EU countries on newly negotiated terms but is allowed to control immigration and no longer makes a contribution to the EU budget. Estimates at the time of the Brexit vote suggest the soft exit will cost an annual decline of 1 percent of GDP, while the hard exit will have an annual cost of 3 percent of GDP. The longer-run impact from an adverse effect on UK productivity might be significantly larger, perhaps as high as 6 percent.[d] Should Prime Minister Cameron have shared the economic benefit of EU membership by investing in a UK jobs program in hopes of blocking a future Brexit vote? He certainly should have done so to avoid the prospect of a hard exit. The lesson of Brexit is more general. In Cooperative Federalism, sharing the economic benefits of cooperation may be required to ensure continued political support for the agreement.

---

[a] The coefficient for the joint effect of ΔFOREIGN on *Leave* becomes 0 (and then even negative) as the %CHRISTIAN in the district rises to, and then exceeds, 70 percent. In districts where Christians are a large majority, foreign-born immigration is perhaps less threatening. Our results are comparable to those in Becker, Egger, and von Ehrlich (2018) and Colantone and Stanig (2018).
[b] See Becker, Egger, and von Ehrlich (2018).
[c] See Carlino and Inman (2016).
[d] See Dhingra et al. (2017).

Specifically, are the concerns of those favoring exit valid generally, and if so, what might be done to reform the EU's Cooperative Federalism?[8]

Economic Performance

By tying together the economies of central and western Europe, and now those of eastern Europe from the old Soviet Union, it was hoped that open markets with the free movement of capital and workers would neutralize any national inclinations toward military aggression. To this end, the European Union has been a success. As an economic union, however, the record is mixed. Free trade and increased economic competition have significantly increased the real (price-adjusted) incomes of EU citizens *on average*, but significant disparities in how these aggregate benefits have been distributed remain. The union's fiscal tools that might correct these disparities are (with the exception of Greece) well managed but of limited scale and reach. This limitation has also hampered the ability of the union to respond to systemic shocks. Whether its current institutions of Cooperative Federalism are up to the task of efficiently managing its current and future economic challenges is another matter.

MARKET EFFICIENCY

As a "customs union" promoting free trade between member states, the European Union has proved an impressive success in lowering market prices and benefiting its consumers. It is the largest customs union in the world and has become a role model for possible economic unions in Africa, South America, and Asia.[9] There is, however, one important adverse side effect. More competitive union-wide markets favor more efficient firms at the expense of less efficient firms and firms previously protected by high tariffs. It is not surprising

---

8. Chapter 3 outlined the seven requirements needed for Cooperative Federalism to achieve its full potential. Violations have had serious consequences for the EU. First is the requirement—Condition C4—that preferences for the benefits of collective decisions are known by all participants in the union. Second is the requirement—Condition C6—that the benefits of collective action can be fairly distributed to all citizens of the union so as to ensure their continued support. Third is the requirement—Condition C7—that all agreements can be enforced. Our analysis of the Brexit decision illustrates the consequences of failing to satisfy Condition C6. Our analysis of the Greek fiscal crisis in Box 9.2 illustrates the consequences of losing Condition C4. Finally, Box 9.3 shows the consequences for the union of losing Condition C7.

9. See Andriamananjara (2011).

that a regional trade agreement like the EU would lead to trade diversion as well as trade creation. The result has been firm closures and, at least temporarily, an increase in local unemployment or a fall in local wages.[10]

Both the gains for consumers and losses for workers have been experienced by the citizens of the European Union. Following the expansion of the union, union-wide prices fell, markets expanded, and industry concentration increased as the more efficient firms, typically from the larger EU economies, produced greater shares of market outputs. Consumers in all of the post-Maastricht economies enjoyed the benefits of lower prices, with those consumers in the smaller and originally less efficient economies—Greece, Portugal, and Ireland—gaining the most benefits initially, as much as a 50 percent increase over pre-EU incomes (Ireland).[11] But job losses in the inefficient, small economies were also significant, particularly in Greece. There were qualitatively similar economic benefits and costs associated with the union's further expansion, beginning in 2004, and indeed, there is the possibility of longer-run benefits for all EU member states. A more efficient flow of investment capital into the economies of the new eastern European member states is expected to further increase their real incomes, with the important "spillover" benefit of slowing the flow of unemployed workers from the eastern economies into those of central and western Europe.[12] Finally, larger markets help to pay the costs of new technology adoption and to encourage research and development, both of which can increase future EU incomes.

While the aggregate economic benefits of the expanded EU markets are clear, so too have been the disruptions to inefficient local regions and local firms. To win approval, the original trade agreements creating the EU and its

10. There are offsetting economic adjustments. First, if the customs union allows for the free flow of labor, as does the European Union, then unemployed workers can relocate from declining to expanding regions. Even in the best of circumstances—a common language and culture—this relocation can take time, however, up to as long as ten years for regions to find their new equilibriums; see Blanchard and Katz (1992). Second, capital can flow into those once inefficient economies to reemploy unemployed local labor at a lower market wage.

11. See C. Allen, Gasiorek, and Smith (1998, table 7).

12. The evidence since the expansion suggests that the adverse effects of immigration on local labor markets have been modest. Migrant workers have typically been skilled workers who have found employment in less skilled occupations, with no significant effect on local wages; see Kahanec and Zimmerman (2010). While the economic benefits are evident, there have been adverse social consequences, as immigrants are often isolated because of language and cultural barriers; see Kahanec and Zimmerman (2016).

expansions anticipated the need to compensate losing regions and industries. Beginning in 1958 with the Treaty of Rome, the union has designed compensating EU-wide policies to ease the adverse side effects of more competitive markets. With each new treaty and expanded membership, compensation policies have been increased and unanimously approved by current and new members of the union. Not surprisingly, however, member state governments have often sought to do more on their own to protect their citizens. Unfortunately, those national policies have included "beggar-thy-neighbor" protective regulations and product standards. Labor market regulations protecting existing employees have allowed expensive, union-negotiated labor contracts raising compensation relative to worker productivity; the result is significantly higher labor costs for the affected firms.[13] Further, the most recent World Bank (2019) survey for the "ease of doing business" ranks Denmark, the United Kingdom, Estonia, Latvia, Finland, Ireland, in the top twenty of world economies, with other EU member states ranking from twenty-two (German) to twenty-seventh (Poland) to sixty-seven (Greece). For comparison, Russia ranks twenty-ninth.

Lastly, national governments have offered significant assistance in the form of state aid to politically favored, and typically inefficient, industries and firms threatened by EU-wide market competition. The effects of such national anticompetitive regulations and industry subsidies have been higher market concentrations, higher firm profits, less investment, and lower consumer welfare in the regulating national economy.[14] By the principle of subsidiarity, however, such inefficient regulations and subsidies by member states have been allowed to stand. Only 2 percent of all such local regulations and subsidies reviewed by the European Commission have been considered in violation of EU-wide competition policy.[15]

What has become an EU-wide policy concern, however, is enforcing market competition between firms serving the EU-wide markets. Having established a customs union for the free trade of goods and services, an important next step was to ensure that the resulting trade takes place in competitive markets. Again as required by subsidiarity, the focus of EU competition policy has been on competition in markets involving trade between member states. The responsibility for administering EU competition policy has been granted to

13. See Thimann (2015).
14. See Duval and Furceri (2018) generally and Gutiérrez and Philippon (2018).
15. See McGowan (2000).

the European Commission by the Council of Ministers, with the task of implementing policy assigned to the Directorate General for Competition, managed by a director general directly responsible to the commission's competition commissioner. The directorate handles individual cases of anticompetitive behavior, reviews all mergers involving significant EU-wide market sales, supervises the implementation of settlements and court rulings, drafts policy initiatives, and coordinates with the competition authorities of member states. When there is a disagreement as to a case's resolution, the case is adjudicated by the Court of Justice of the European Union (CJEU).

By most objective measures, EU competition policy has been a success. EU enforcement of anticompetitive regulations and merger guidelines has been significantly stricter than that in the United States over the past fifteen years.[16] Importantly, enforcement of comparable anticompetitive regulations by the EU's directorate general has also been stricter than that of the competition authorities in any of the EU member states.[17] However, in an effort to encourage firm location, member states have often favored local firms in a manner that might be described as a "race to the bottom" in national competition policies. Strict EU-wide enforcement, however, has helped to ensure that these local anticompetitive behaviors do not have adverse spillover effects for consumers in other member states. Overall, EU-wide competition policies have led to lower industry concentration ratios, lower firm profits in the affected industries, greater firm investment, higher firm productivity, larger industry outputs, and finally, lower prices for consumers.[18] The result is greater consumer welfare, represented by as much as a 50 percent increase in real incomes for the original Maastricht members and as much as 30 percent for the new members from eastern Europe. Greek citizens are the only ones to have lost since Maastricht. Their incomes are estimated to have declined by as much as 20 percent since 1992.[19]

Member states have remained committed to a policy agenda of free trade and market competition. The agenda has, to date, been decided and enforced

16. See Gutiérrez and Philippon (2018, sec. 3).

17. See Buccirossi et al. (2011, figs. 3–8).

18. See Gutiérrez and Philippon (2018, sec. 6) and Duval and Furceri (2018).

19. See Campos, Coricelli, and Moretti (2014, table 3). The aggregate real income gains from 1992 to 2008 are 50 percent for Ireland; 20 percent or more for Denmark, the United Kingdom, Portugal, and Spain; and from 4 to 10 percent for Austria, Finland, and Sweden. The estimated aggregate gains in income for eastern European economies admitted after 2004 range from 6 percent (Poland and the Czech Republic) to as much as 30 percent (Latvia and Lithuania).

by the institutions of Cooperative Federalism. Though there are disparities in the final distribution of market benefits, most citizens have gained. Those thought to have lost in an absolute sense with the expanded markets—declining regions and the agricultural sectors—have been at least partially protected by EU treaty–created development funds and agricultural subsidies. The EU's version of Cooperative Federalism has served the goal of overall market efficiency well.

FISCAL EFFICIENCY

Less so, however, for the goal of fiscal efficiency. The budget of the EU is dominated by allocations to promote two broad policy objectives: (1) stability for the incomes of EU farmers achieved through CAP (the Common Agriculture Policy) and the income-guarantee program within CAP, the European Agricultural Guidance and Guarantee Fund (EAGGF), and (2) convergence of the incomes of the poorer and richer regions of the EU, promoted through the European Regional Development Fund (ERDF) and the European Social Fund (ESF) and supplemented later by the Cohesion Fund. EU revenues come from three main sources: a common EU share of national VAT taxation, a country-specific subvention to the union paid for by each member state's own taxes, and EU-wide tariffs on imports into the union. CAP was established to coordinate the disparate agricultural price support and subsidy programs, and ESF was created to facilitate income convergence among the original six member states. ERDF was established in 1975 both to strengthen EU support for regional economic development and to balance the allocation of the EU budget between the union's agricultural and industrial economies. Agricultural interests, particularly in France, formed significant political blocs whose support was essential for the final approval of the original treaty. ESF and ERDF were created to address the concern that long-term support for the union would be threatened if the lower-income or economically less competitive regions failed to share in the union's economic benefits. The Cohesion Fund was added to provide additional assistance for the construction of transportation networks to link the EU economies.

The aim of each of these major programs has been, and continues to be, to share the economic benefits of the EU so as to achieve unanimous agreement among member states. Scholars of EU fiscal policies have characterized EAGGF, ERDF, ESF, and the Cohesion Fund as the "political cement" necessary to form the union and the grease that allows the "smooth running" of an economic alliance governed by unanimity.[20] The efficiency performance of these policies—their costs in taxes, inclusive of consequences for market efficiency, balanced against program benefits—defines the "price" of the cement and the grease that allow the EU to function as Cooperative Federalism.

As required by Cooperative Federalism, both EAGGF's agricultural income guarantees and regional spending through ERDF, ESF, and the Cohesion Fund have been decided by unanimous votes in the Council of Ministers. Negotiations are chaired by the president of the European Union, a position that rotates every six months among the member states. Funds within the agreed-to aggregates are then allocated across the member states as part of separate annual budget processes chaired by the commissioner for agriculture and the commissioner for regional policy. The individual commissioners act as agenda-setters; commissioner positions also rotate among the member states. Allocations within the CAP budgets are set by agreements on the guaranteed price for each agricultural product and the quota amount each country is allowed to sell. The allocations are set by a council-negotiated formula based on the incomes of the member states; the formula favors the relatively poorer states. Though budgets require the approval of a qualified majority vote within the council, all have been approved unanimously. Rotation of the union presidency and the positions of commissioner of agriculture and commissioner of regional policy limits the influence of any individual agenda-setter and helps to enforce unanimous agreements among member states.[21] Not surprisingly, aggregate allocations for EAGGF favor agricultural states, while those for regional funds favor more industrial economies. Weighted votes within the Council of Ministers influence the annual allocation of EAGGF funds, but the treaty-negotiated economic formulas are the primary determinants for the distribution of ERDF and ESF spending. Finally, new members of the union

20. See Baldwin, Francois, and Portes (1997).

21. When chosen as the agenda-setter, each member state has the opportunity to allocate more spending to itself, subject to the approval of a qualified majority in the council. There is a potential tension between majority-rule allocations, where the majority divides all the resources among themselves, and a universalistic allocation, where each member state receives at least some spending, perhaps in proportion to its voting power in the council. The evidence strongly favors the universalistic allocation; see Aksoy (2012) and Kauppi and Widgrén (2004). The union president and the agenda-setting commissioners do capture slightly larger budget shares, but the additional funding is trivial; see Aksoy (2010) and Gehring and Schneider (2018).

have been discriminated against in the allocation of EU funding, reflecting perhaps the "price" of EU membership.[22]

The payment of CAP income guarantees through EAGGF has been both economically and administratively inefficient. The program began in 1962 to ensure "fair market prices" and a "fair standard of living for agricultural communities." Initially, common prices were set for agricultural products throughout the EU at levels significantly above world prices. As a consequence, EU consumers were hurt by the high regulated price, while EU farmers were encouraged to produce more output in response to the "subsidized" price above the world price. The extra output was purchased directly by the EU using general tax revenues, then stored, and finally sold at the world price at a loss. As a result, EAGGF created three market inefficiencies. First, consumers paid more for their agricultural products than they would if purchased at world prices. The difference between the regulated price and the world price was economically equivalent to a tax on consumers with proceeds immediately rebated to farmers as a subsidy for production. The resulting reduction in agricultural consumption by EU households subsidized the transfer to EU farmers with the added cost of the "excess burden" created by the regulated price above the world price. Second, the subsidized price encouraged farmers to produce more output. Even though the extra output could be sold at the world price, the extra production costs above that price created a further inefficiency. Finally, the extra output had to be stored before being sold on the world market, another unnecessary cost.

Ultimately, reform was motivated by external pressure from other world agricultural producers during the 1986 Uruguay Round of the General Agreement on Tariffs and Trade. To placate other world producers, particularly U.S. farmers, EAGGF was reformed in 1992 to lower EU production. These reforms lowered EU support prices to world prices and then, both to compensate EU farmers and to discourage production, paid EU farmers to take acreage and livestock out of production. Known as the MacSharry reforms, the new CAP policies offered two significant efficiency benefits for EU citizens. First, as consumers, they now paid world prices; the EU "tax" on agricultural products was removed. Second, as EU taxpayers, they no longer paid for subsidized production and storage. By removing these historic "inefficiencies," CAP subsidies today are primarily income transfers from EU taxpayers to the EU agricultural sector.

22. See Schneider (2013).

To pay these transfers, there has been an offsetting increase in EU general taxation. That cost will include not only the direct cost of the required revenues but also the added loss in citizen incomes and consumption benefits that arise from that taxation—the excess burden. Recent research suggests that a conservative estimate of that added, excess burden cost of EU revenues is €0.45 for each €1.00 of EU revenues.[23] Thus, each €1.00 of a CAP transfer costs EU taxpayers €1.45. To illustrate, in 2016 the EU economy lost €25.5 billion moving resources from taxpayers to farmers—€56.5 billion in transfers to farmers less the €82 billion in lost "incomes" to taxpayers—an example of what Arthur Okun has called the "leaky bucket" of income transfers. The overall inefficiency of €25.5 billion equals about €50 per EU citizen.

The second important expenditure within the EU budget is for the EU's three regional programs: ERDF, ESF, and the Cohesion Fund. Together the programs accounted for about 21 percent of the EU budget in fiscal year 2016. As funding is for regional economic development, the net economic benefits of these programs can be measured as the economic returns in increased incomes, minus the average economic costs of required tax revenues inclusive of the excess burden of taxation. Recent research evaluating the benefits of ERDF and the Cohesion Fund investments suggests the returns may be significant, perhaps as much as €2 in discounted future incomes for each €1 invested today.[24] In 2016, aggregate ERDF and Cohesion Fund investments were €29 billion. The estimated present value benefit of these investments is €58 billion. These investments cost EU taxpayers €42 billion, inclusive of the full economic costs of taxation. On balance, therefore, 2016 ERDF and Cohesion Fund spending could be expected to provide EU citizens a net benefit of €16 billion, or on average about €31 per citizen. In contrast to CAP, ERDF and the Cohesion Fund appear to have had a positive net return for the average EU citizen.

Together, EU fiscal policies from CAP and ERDF/Cohesion Fund spending impose a net economic cost on EU citizens as the sum of their respective net benefits, or about €19 per citizen. This overall negative efficiency performance for the EU budget should come as no surprise. Its primary purpose is to distribute the economic benefits from the integration of member states'

23. See Dahlby (2008).

24. See Becker, Egger, and von Ehrlich (2018). Becker and her colleagues find that regions that qualify for ERDF funding grow annually from 1 percent to 1.5 percent more than comparable regions that do not. There was hope that these programs might also encourage income convergence between regions, but this has not occurred; see Boldrin and Canova (2001).

economies, with a focus on those citizens likely to lose the most under the larger, more competitive economy and thus the most likely to resist economic integration. Though inefficient in the aggregate, these policies are exactly what Cooperative Federalism requires. For a stable federal union, economic winners must compensate economic losers. Even inclusive of these costs of compensation, however, the EU's customs union managed by Cooperative Federalism appears a clear economic winner. Average annual income growth from the wider EU market equals 1 to 2 percent per year, while the annual fiscal costs needed to hold the union together are currently no more than .1 percent per year.

FINANCIAL EFFICIENCY

Less obvious are the net economic benefits from the EU's decision to create a "currency union." Established on January 1, 2001, the Economic and Monetary Union (EMU), is thought to provide two direct economic benefits. First, since all transactions between the member states will be conducted in a common currency, the buying and selling of goods and services will avoid the administrative costs of managing the conversion between different currencies. Preliminary estimates by the European Commission suggested that from .25 to .5 percent of member states' GDP could be saved as a consequence of removing the need for currency conversion.[25] A second and potentially more significant benefit of a common currency is the removal of currency risk when choosing to invest in member states other than one's own. For example, without a common currency, German investors in a French company would face two risks—that of the investment itself and then the additional currency risk of turning profits earned in French francs into profits valued in German deutsche marks. Currency risk depends to a significant degree on country fiscal and monetary policies and thus country politics. A common currency removes this risk and should encourage greater investment in profitable firm activities throughout the monetary union. Estimates of improved GDP for the first years following the introduction of the euro suggest that as much as an additional 2 percent per annum has been realized.[26] The source of higher growth has been increased private-sector investment.

Monetary unions are not without their potential costs, however. In the case of the EMU, these costs became apparent with the EU's inadequate policy

25. See De Grauwe (1992, p. 61).
26. See Barrell et al. (2008).

responses to the Great Recession and the subsequent Greek financial crisis. What a country sacrifices when joining a monetary union is the ability to adjust the value of its once separate currency to country-specific economic shocks, particularly adverse shocks in aggregate demand. If not a member of a currency union, a country experiencing an adverse shock to the demand for its goods and services will be free to devalue its national currency to makes its goods cheaper for foreigners to buy, thereby stimulating aggregate demand and national income. Joining a monetary union denies the member states this policy option.

Even with the loss of the devaluation strategy, economies in a monetary (currency) union still have three alternative paths to full employment after experiencing an adverse market shock. First, as demand and prices for the country's goods decline, the country's workers can accept a lower wage, firms can then still be profitable with the same workers, and full employment can be restored. Second, unemployed workers can migrate to find work in fully employed economies. Finally, the government can adopt an expansionary fiscal policy using temporary debt financing to lower taxes, to hire unemployed workers, and to offer income and unemployment insurance, thereby restoring aggregate demand.

Though these three paths to full employment are available in principle, EMU economies have not performed as one might have hoped. First, the labor market institutions of the EMU member countries—sector rather than firm bargaining, coupled with politically strong private- and public-sector unions— significantly restrict overall wage flexibility.[27] Second, labor mobility among the member states has been very limited, certainly when compared with the United States.[28] Third, while country-specific fiscal policies have been able to stimulate aggregate demand, there has been evidence of demand spillovers between EMU trading partners, raising the risk of "beggar-thy-neighbor" fiscal policies.[29] Each country has an incentive to free ride on the deficit policies of

27. See Heinz and Rusinova (2011) for the negative effect of regulated labor market institutions on wage flexibility and Arpaia and Pichelmann (2007) for measures of the overall lack of wage flexibility among EMU economies in response to adverse economic shocks. EMU economies with the most regulated labor markets include Austria, France, Greece, Ireland, Italy, the Netherlands, and Portugal.

28. For an early study, see Obstfeld and Peri (1998), and for more current evidence, see Heinz and Rusinova (2011).

29. See Chapter 7, Section 4, for an evaluation of the general arguments and Beetsma and Giuliodori (2011), Auerbach and Gorodnichenko (2013), and Hebous and Zimmermann (2013) for EU evidence.

its trading partners, or at least to "underinvest" relative to the jointly beneficial level of deficit financing. There is a race to the bottom in setting aggregate fiscal policies. This was certainly the case at the start of the Great Recession.[30] The presence of positive fiscal spillovers argues strongly for a coordinated fiscal policy in times of mutual economic downturns. The European Commission appreciated the wisdom of this logic when it proposed its European Economic Recovery Plan in 2008 in response to an EU-wide recession brought on by the global financial crisis.[31] Constrained by the EU's commitment to rule by unanimity under Cooperative Federalism, however, the EU's resulting fiscal stimulus left to member states made only a very small contribution to the overall performance of the EU economy following the Great Recession.[32]

Nor has the EU's commitment to cooperative governance been able to adequately deal with the structural weaknesses of the EU's fiscal policies, the most important of which are excessive borrowings and induced bailout expectations. Greece is the most prominent example of this failure; see Box 9.2. Excessive deficits emerge from a classic race to the bottom in fiscal policy as member states fear having to bail out the debts of other states after they themselves have run responsible balanced budgets. The "externality" that drives an EU bailout policy is the risk of a financial crisis created by unsustainable public debt. A country that borrows "too much" may reach the point where revenues from national taxation are not sufficient to service past borrowing. If debt cannot be repaid, holders of country bonds, most likely national and international banks, will suffer a capital loss. The capital loss threatens the ability of banks to repay their depositors. Nervous depositors may then withdraw their savings. The results are bank runs and a financial crisis with potentially large losses in aggregate economic activity.[33]

What can be done? At the EU level, there are two responses: do nothing and rely on the bond market to discipline those that borrow too much *or* regulate individual member states' deficit behaviors to prevent excessive borrowing. For effective market discipline, interest rates must rise with increases in

30. See D. Cameron (2012).

31. The estimated impact of this collective fiscal stimulus was modest at best, however, adding at most €200 billion to EU incomes (1.6 percent of 2008 GDP) above what they might have been without the European Economic Recovery Plan policies; see Coenen, Staub, and Trabandt (2012).

32. The €137 billion of additional EU stimulus should be contrasted with the more than $787 billion spent by the American Recovery and Reinvestment Act over the same period.

33. See F. Allen and Gale (2007).

Box 9.2. A Greek (Financial) Tragedy

Greece officially joined the EEC on January 1, 1981, and was a founding member of the European Monetary Union, established on January 1, 2002. On the surface, at least until 2007, membership benefited Greek citizens. From 1981 to 2007, the Greek economy grew at a real annual rate of 1.8 percent, increasing average annual per capita real GDP from $18,677 to $34,054. Beneath the surface, however, lay significant structural weaknesses, finally revealed in the financial bankruptcy of 2009 followed by eight years of reductions in real GDP per capita of nearly 25 percent to a 2017 level of $23,000. While income grew from 1981 to 2007, it was sustained by excessive government debt, with debt reaching $32,800 per capita (115 percent of GDP) by 2009 just before the country's financial collapse.

As a new member of the EEC in 1981, the Greek economy was fully open to free trade in goods and services with other community members. While the increased economic competition from other EEC member countries clearly benefited Greek citizens as consumers, it placed a significant strain on the profitability and productivity of Greek firms and workers. By all measures, they did not keep up. The productivity of Greek workers lagged behind that of workers in most other EEC economies while private-sector wage growth exceeded that of its competitors.[a] As a result, Greek firms were less competitive and both domestic sales and private-sector employment declined and the current-accounts trade deficit increased. What sustained the trade deficits and allowed for continued private consumption was a constantly expanding public sector financed by government debt. Government employment as a share of total employment increased and public employee wages grew at rates faster than in any of the other EU economies.[b] For years before the 2009 worldwide financial crisis, Greece had been able to borrow at interest rates that were only 1 to 2 percentage points greater than those available to the Germany.[c] The private banks in Greece, Germany, France, and Belgium continued to lend to the Greek government at these favorable rates.

Until October 2009. The newly elected national government announced that the next year's deficit would be 13.6 percent of GDP (later confirmed as 15.6 percent), not the 6 percent that was originally projected. With a debt-to-GDP ratio of 115 percent and the economy's weak prospects for GDP growth, the financial markets finally questioned the long-run fiscal solvency of the Greek economy. By spring 2010, Greece was shut out of the financial markets. Without access to public debt, the Greek public sector turned to large tax increases, aggressive tax collection, and significantly reduced public spending. These austerity public budgets sent the economy into a deep recession; GDP per capita declining by 25 percent from 2009 to 2017.[d]

Even with austerity budgets, it was unlikely the Greek government could repay its debts. A failure to meets its debt obligations threatened the financial stability of Greek banks and raised the prospect of significant capital losses for German, French, and Belgium banks as well. There were only two options: debt default or a financial bailout. Default would mean capital losses for Greek, German, and French banks and would raise the serious possibility of contagion onto Portugal's, Spain's, and Ireland's public debt. Bailout was preferred. The International Monetary Fund, the European Union, and the European Central Bank collectively contributed €220 billion in direct transfers, low-cost loans, and loan guarantees.[e] In return for this assistance, Greek elected officials reluctantly agreed to additional austerity

Continued on next page

Box 9.2. (*continued*)

fiscal measures. It was not until 2017 that the Greek economy returned to positive GDP growth, at the modest rate of 1.4 percent per year. At this rate, real GDP per capita will not reach its 2007 precrisis level of $34,000 per capita until 2040! The ultimate economic cost of the Greek financial crisis was a 25 percent reduction in Greek GDP over the period 2009 to 2017, equivalent to an average annual income loss of $5,000 per resident each year. The distribution of this loss has been far from uniform. The Greek rate of unemployment rose from 8.5 percent in 2007 to 23 percent in 2017, with almost half of all citizens under the age of twenty-four being unemployed.

The unsustainable long-term trends in Greek public employment, public transfers, and growing government debt were publicly known before 2007. The information was ignored by both the financial markets and European Commission administrators. Hopefully not again, or elsewhere.

---

[a] See Thimann (2015, fig. 1).
[b] See Holm-Hadulla et al. (2010, table 1) and Lane (2012, fig. 1).
[c] See Inman (2013).
[d] See Gourinchas, Philippon, and Vayanos (2017).
[e] See Ardagna and Caselli (2014).

---

government deficits, and when the risk of default is sufficiently high, the wayward state must be denied additional borrowing. Such has been the historical performance of the bond market for U.S. state and local governments.[34] This clearly was not the case during the early years of the EMU. While deficit and debt levels varied significantly among EMU member states from 2000 to the 2009 financial crisis, interest rates were all within 1 to 2 percentage points of that for Germany, the EMU's best credit risk.[35] The EU bond market was not checking member state borrowing.

Why was there a failure of market discipline? For effective discipline, lenders must know the level of each government's public debts and deficits. Governments have a strong incentive to conceal their obligations, not just market-placed debt (usually known) but also pension promises to public employees and citizens, costs to repair decaying infrastructure, and unpaid bills to contractors and suppliers. All these obligations, plus spending for essential services (particularly health care), must be paid from current revenues. Accurate estimates of current spending and revenues can be easily manipulated.[36] What looks like a balanced budget to outside investors may in fact be a large hidden

---

34. See Gramlich (1976).
35. See Inman (2013, fig. 1).
36. For the argument that this has been true for EMU countries, see Frankel and Schreger (2012).

deficit. When all is finally revealed, as happened for Greece in 2009, the bond market denies new borrowing. For the bond market to function efficiently, it needs accurate information about each government's true deficit and outstanding debt.

Lacking effective market-based regulation, the alternative is public regulation. This has been the path chosen by the EU, but with mixed success. Specified as the Stability and Growth Pact, the EU's original regulation set two targets for member state budgets: an annual deficit equal to or less than 3 percent of GDP and an aggregate debt-to-GDP target of 60 percent or less. The European Commission would monitor national budgets based on fiscal data submitted by the national government. Like the marketplace, the public regulator needs accurate information of member state deficits and debts. Here the EU, using the resources of the European Commission, has an advantage over market participants. Accurate information about public deficits and debts is very costly to collect. All past borrowing must be recorded, pension promises evaluated, infrastructure status assessed, and current and future revenues projected. But once collected, a private investor's subsequently offered interest rate or even a simple willingness to participate in the market reveals the informed investor's best estimate of those debts, deficits, and revenues to other investors. The incentive for all investors is to then free ride on the efforts an informed investor. If they do so, no investor gathers the needed information. Information as to the true risks of member state debt obligations is a public good, shared by all once revealed.[37] Thus, it should be a public agency that collects the required information and shares it with the market. As part of a fiscal compact of regulations approved in November 2011, all EU member states (not just those in the EMU) must now (1) provide public accounting applied to all government revenues and spending and be subject to independent audits; (2) employ consistent accounting rules across all government activities; (3) provide a three-year, forward budgetary forecast based on realistic spending and revenue projections; and finally, (4) make all budgetary data publicly available.

In hindsight, the original Stability and Growth Pact did not succeed as a form of fiscal regulation. The problem was failed enforcement by the Council of Ministers.[38] Member states have been reluctant to vote for sanctions for those in violation of the deficit and debt limits, for fear that sanctions might

37. See S. Grossman and Stiglitz (1980).

38. For a detailed analysis of the failure of the Stability and Growth Pact, see Eichengreen and Wyplosz (1998).

be imposed on them were they ever to violate the regulations.[39] While many member states have been in violation of the deficit regulation and the debt target, Greece, Ireland, Italy, Portugal, and Spain have been the most significant abusers. Greece and Ireland both required bailouts to prevent a possible EMU-wide financial crisis.[40]

Reforms of the pact approved in 2011 (the "Six Pack") and 2013 (the "Two Pack") sought to strengthen enforcement, first by making the regulations more flexible and thus more likely to be used and then, second, by removing the requirement of unanimity in the council for enforcement. Under the new regulations, the 3 percent deficit target becomes a guideline by which to monitor a cyclically adjusted balanced budget, allowing for larger deficits in recession years provided they are repaid in expansion periods. The 60 percent debt-to-GDP target is no longer an absolute standard to be meet each year but rather a target toward which member states must show steady progress if they exceed the limit. To ensure compliance, all member states in violation are subject to an "excessive deficit procedure" and required to submit a draft budget to the commission and the council showing either compliance or a set of credible "corrective actions." Further, the 2013 reforms changed the voting rule for the imposition of sanctions to a reversed qualified majority—that is, a sanction would be imposed unless a qualified majority voted *not* to impose the fine.[41]

While most of the member states have been under budgetary review as part of the excessive deficit procedure, no fines have yet been recommended. This is not surprising; the greater flexibility in the terms of the Stability and Growth Pact also made for greater difficulties of enforcement—they made it easier for member states to reach the politically expedient conclusion that there is no problem.

Overall, adding a *currency* union (the EMU) to the EU's existing *customs* union seems to have been only slightly better than a "break-even" proposition

---

39. The exception was the Netherlands in 2003, which voted to sanction itself in an effort to give credibility to the Stability and Growth Pact. The Netherlands then balanced its budget in the next fiscal year, and, consistent with pact rules, the resulting penalty was returned with interest.

40. Surprisingly, Ireland and Spain were both fiscally well behaved, and in compliance, before the crisis.

41. The new voting rule enhances the bargaining power of the commission for enforcing the 3 percent and 60 percent rules, since the offending member state must now build a twenty-seven-member coalition (or smaller with large states included) to block review. What has happened in the past, however, and is likely to continue is for the offending state to negotiate more lenient terms for the review and possible sanction ex ante with the commission; see Baerg and Hallerberg (2016).

for the member states that have chosen to join the euro zone. Estimates for the savings from lower costs for financial transactions are from .2 to .5 percent of GDP for participating economies. The estimated increased in income growth for EMU members is 2 percent per year for the six years before 2008. Offsetting these gains have been the economic losses in lower GDP growth during the Great Recession. Finally, the EMU has exposed a fundamental weakness in the EU's ability to regulate damaging fiscal behaviors by individual member states. Greece, Ireland, Italy, Portugal, and Spain have all run excessive state deficits, threatening the underlying stability of the EU's financial system. In the case of Greece, a crisis was avoided only by a bailout. The required austerity budget that followed has had a crippling effect on the Greek GDP of (at least) 25 percent over the period 2009–2017.

Democratic Governance

The driving motivation behind each step in the development of the EU has been to use economic policies to ensure long-run peace and security for Europe. The fundamental objective of the customs and currency unions has been to tie together the economies of Europe so that all citizens have a vested interest in the security and ultimately the long-run economic success of their neighbors.

A commitment to the EU is only likely, however, if the EU's institutions are perceived by the citizens of all member states as responsive to their economic needs and rights as citizens. The concern is that the current institutional structure, that of Cooperative Federalism, is neither hearing citizen concerns nor responsive even if they are heard, leading to what has been called the EU's "democratic deficit." At least five different versions of the deficit have been offered: (1) the EU is a "superstate" now dominating policy-making for EU citizens; (2) legitimately elected national parliaments have no say in EU policies; (3) most citizens do not understand EU issues or how EU institutions make decisions; (4) the EU has been captured by global elites, favoring liberal market policies to the detriment of the social democratic agenda of most member states; and finally, (5) there are no EU institutions, including the European Parliament, that allow citizens to directly express their preferences regarding EU issues. The consensus now seems to be that only the fifth issue qualifies today as a compelling source of the democratic deficit.[42] If there is such a deficit, it is in the failure of EU

---

42. See Hix (2008, chap. 5) and Moravcsik (2008).

institutions to allow for the direct expression of citizen preferences on EU policies *before* policies are decided, a concern perhaps felt instinctively by those voting no in the Brexit referendum and most acutely in Greece, Italy, Ireland, and Portugal after the imposition of EU and Central Bank austerity reforms following the financial crisis of 2010.[43]

While both the European Commission and the Council of Ministers allow for the direct representation of the democratically elected governments of member states, the outcomes of those national elections rarely turn on EU issues. Further, council deliberation over policies largely take place behind closed doors. Citizens do vote directly for their representatives to the European Parliament, but those elections too are rarely decided by EU policies.[44] In contrast to Robert Dahl's hope that the EU's decision-making might evolve into an "enlightened democracy," it is at this moment closer to what Simon Hix (2008, p. 85), in his review of the democratic deficit, has called "enlightened despotism."

Rights Protection

Institutions capable of protecting the civil, political, and property rights of EU citizens are essential for the EU's economic success. Protecting civil liberties encourages individuals to invest in their own human capital, and secure property rights encourage investment in physical capital. As observed in Chapter 1, both are essential for an economy's economic growth. Finally, political rights ensure democratic governance and the rule of law, which in turn provide the institutional safeguards of civil liberties and property rights. These protections must be enforced union-wide.

While the political institutions of the EU have recognized the importance of protecting individual rights and liberties since the 1977 publication of the Joint Declaration on Fundamental Rights, it was not until the drafting of the Charter of Fundamental Rights of the European Union in 2000 that a working list of protected rights was fully articulated.[45] And finally, only in 2009 with the completion of the Lisbon Treaty were those rights formally recognized as

43. See Armingeon and Baccaro (2012).

44. See Hix and Marsh (2007).

45. The lack of an articulated list of protected rights was a clear limitation to rights enforcement before the adoption of the charter; see Alston and Weiler (1998). The motivation to develop the charter came from applications for admission to the union by the states of central and

binding on EU member states.[46] But the question remains, How successful have the EU institutions—the Court of Justice of the European Union (CJEU), the European Commission, the Parliament, and the Council of Ministers—been in enforcing charter rights? They are already significantly constrained by Article 51 of the charter itself; these institutions can only intervene when the rights performance of a member state directly impedes the EU's ability to administer union policies.

COURT OF JUSTICE OF THE EUROPEAN UNION

The CJEU is limited to three roles for the enforcement of the Charter of Fundamental Rights. First, the court may hear and adjudicate substantive claims involving the violation of charter-protected rights. Second, it may hear and adjudicate substantive claims as to the implications of EU legislation for the enforcement of charter rights on member state policies. Third, it may evaluate the process by which EU legislation is considered on the way to passage by asking, Does the proposed policy achieve the law's objective of having the least adverse consequence for charter rights? If not, the CJEU may encourage a deeper review of alternatives, but without a mandate to propose an alternative policy.

Not only is the court's domain of oversight restricted, so too is its ability to enforce a remedy. If a violation is found, the CJEU must rely on either the national courts or the government of the offending member state to correct the infraction or appeal to the political institutions of the EU—the commission, council, or Parliament—to enforce the right by legislatively approved sanctions. The court's own powers of enforcement of the charter are limited

---

eastern Europe and the need for standards by which to judge their qualifications as working democracies; see Merlingen, Mudde, and Sedelmeier (2001).

46. The charter's protected rights include a right to life and human dignity, free of torture, slavery, or forced labor (Chapter I); freedom of thought, religion, assembly, and expression and the right to privacy, liberty, security, and asylum (Chapter II); equality before the law and nondiscrimination (Chapter III); worker rights to collective bargaining and fair and just working conditions, and citizen rights to social security and assistance, health care, and a clean environment (Chapter IV); political rights to vote and stand for office, to access information, and for free movement and of residence (Chapter V); and finally, the right to a presumption of innocence, a fair trial, proportionality in punishment, and each administered without double jeopardy (Chapter VI). Chapter VII of the charter details the ground rules for protection, with Article 51 applying EU enforcement "only when implementing Union law."

to a call of notice to a rights violation and then the hope that the force of public argument might lead to national or EU reforms.[47]

THE PARLIAMENT, THE EUROPEAN COMMISSION, AND THE COUNCIL OF MINISTERS

Among the EU's political institutions, the Parliament has been the most active institutional voice for increased protections of individual rights and liberties. In 1977, it promoted a joint resolution to respect fundamental rights in the use of EU powers. Beginning in 2000, the Parliament had been the prime mover for the union's Charter of Fundamental Rights, which, as mentioned, was adopted as EU law in 2009. Political divisions within the Parliament have significantly limited its ability to actively promote or enforce charter rights on member states, however.[48] This has been nowhere more evident than in the limited success the EU has had in responding to recent rights violations by Hungary and Poland; see Box 9.3. As a result, any hope for the effective enforcement of the charter has fallen to the European Commission and the Council of Ministers. Here, too, success has been mixed.

The European Commission views its role as that of the watchdog for rights violations, both with regard to member state implementation of EU law and in terms of adherence to the charter when passing EU laws or directives. In 2005, the commission established guidelines for the monitoring of rights performance as part of its more general process of "impact assessments" of EU policies (in the spirit of Step 7 of our FIST analysis). Typically, however, these assessments have been done by agencies within the commission whose primary policy concern is not rights protection.[49] A more proactive role for the commission is possible, but to date such efforts have had only marginal effects on rights protection.

If there is going to be a successful intervention in support of charter rights, acceptance of the EU's policy by affected member states will be essential; the obvious institution to make this happen is the Council of Ministers. The

---

47. The CJEU is also limited in the reach of its enforcement by the threat of noncompliance by the member states; see Carrubba, Gabel, and Hankla (2008). On the court's role more generally for the protection of rights, see Dawson (2017) and Williams (2015).

48. See Dawson (2017, pp. 100–107).

49. In only 5 percent of reviews in 2013/2014 were rights mentioned as a possible reason for reconsideration. See Dawson (2017, p. 93).

Box 9.3. Hungary, Poland, and the Rule of Law

In the Hungarian parliamentary elections of 2010, Viktor Orban's party, Fidesz (Alliance of Young Democrats) won a clear majority and Orban was appointed prime minister. Orban's platform was nationalist and anti-EU. It resonated particularly with voters feeling the economic hardship of the Great Recession, left behind by the success of the educated ("elites") in the new competitive Europe, and threatened by the influx of legal and illegal immigrants from the Middle East. In the elections of 2015, Andrzej Duda, representing the Law and Justice Party, won the presidency of Poland on a similar nationalist platform. Both governments have now constrained their national courts and limited the freedom of their national media. In Hungary, the government forced the retirement of then-current judges to allow the appointment of judges friendly to Fidesz, took control of the national Media Council in charge of licensing and appointing media directors, introduced new supermajority voting rules to protect laws passed by Fidesz from future reform, and sought to influence Central Bank policy through high-level staff appointments and the threat of dismissal of bank directors for unspecified "serious misconduct." In Poland, the newly elected Law and Justice Party fired directors of state-owned companies as insufficiently loyal, passed a new law to allow party control of the national media, and approved legislation that allowed the president and the appointed minister of justice to begin disciplinary action against sitting judges and to appoint their replacements.

Citing these actions as violations of Article 2 of the Treaty of the European Union, the EU sought to reverse each of these decisions. Two approaches have been tried: first, persuasion, and then economic sanctions. Success has been limited. The European Commission for Democracy through Law, known as the Venice Commission, wrote detailed reports condemning the actions of both countries. The Special Rapporteur for the Independence of Judges submitted critical opinions to the UN Human Rights Council. The International Monetary Fund spoke out against the efforts by Hungary to influence Central Bank policies. The EU Parliament adopted a report, known as the Tavares Report, critical of Hungary's efforts to control the courts, and the European Commission threatened to invoke Article 7 for the expulsion of both Poland and Hungary from decisions by the Council of Ministers. In response, both countries submitted agendas to the Venice Commission promising reform, but the initial legislation remains in effect. Economic sanctions have been only slightly more successful. Legal proceedings against Hungary invoking an EU age-discrimination law led to the threat of fines that Hungary has avoided by appointing all previously "retired" judges to minor positions with pay raises. The only economic sanction that has succeeded was the threat by the International Monetary Fund to withhold a previously negotiated $15 billion loan to Hungary unless the independence of the Central Bank was restored. It was.

With only limited success from persuasion and fines, the EU has turned to its final disciplinary option—the application of Article 7 of the Treaty of the European Union allowing expulsion of Poland and Hungary from decision-making within the Council of Ministers. On September 12, 2018, the European Parliament voted 448 in favor, 197 against (a 69 percent majority) to begin sanctions under Article 7 against Hungary. Final approval of expulsion requires unanimous agreement by the Council of Europe (excluding the offending member state), however. Poland has not agreed, and expulsion has not gone forward.

council has embraced the charter and its legislative role to promote rights protection in EU legislation, but in most instances, and understandably so given the council's adherence to a norm of unanimity, only by showing deference to national standards. When engaging issues of charter rights in its deliberations, the council stresses subsidiarity and the need for respect of national constitutional norms. For example, when considering policies to limit a worker's right to strike so as to promote the EU goal of free mobility of labor, the measure was defeated because of opposition by member states with strong labor unions. Further, deference to member state policies has led to wide disparities in the union's enforcement of rights for the Roma people.[50] As a result, the council's—and thus the EU's—protection of charter rights has not reached beyond that provided by the member states.

RIGHTS PROTECTIONS AND ACCESSION

Rights protection for EU citizens has been constrained by, first, enforcement of EU-approved laws only and, second, by the EU's commitment to governance by unanimity. As a consequence, EU rights performance has largely been defined by the protections offered EU citizens by the constitutions and laws of each member state. How, then, might the EU affect rights protections more generally? The significant economic advantage of EU membership might be one important lever.

Table 9.1 suggests that the accession criteria defining rights and liberties for member states may have served as a useful disciplinary device, particularly for those nations from central and eastern Europe wishing to join the EU.[51] The table summarizes each member state's performance in providing for civil liberties and political rights both before and after accession. A score of 1 indicates a fully functioning democracy with complete safeguards of individual rights to assembly, association, education, and the practice of religion; a score of 2 represents some restrictions on political rights by the presence of political corruption, restrictions on the ability to form opposition parties, or voting

50. See Gould (2014) for a discussion of discrimination against the Roma people in France and A. McGarry (2012) for a discussion of discrimination in the eastern European member states.

51. Entry into the EU requires applicants to meet the standards of Article 2 of the Treaty of the European Union. They are (1) stability of democratic institutions, adherence to the rule of law, and protection of human rights and respect for and protection of minorities; (2) a functioning market economy; and (3) the administrative and legal ability to implement EU law.

TABLE 9.1. Protecting Rights and EU Accession

Country	Accession year	Civil liberties				Political rights			
		1992	Four years before accession	Postaccession	2018	1992	Four years before accession	Postaccession	2018
Belgium	1992	1.0	1.0	1.26	1.0	1.0	1.0	1.0	1.0
Denmark	1992	1.0	1.0	1.0	1.0	1.0	1.0	1.0	1.0
France	1992	2.0	2.0	1.56	2.0	1.0	1.0	1.0	1.0
Germany	1992	2.0	2.0	1.48	1.0	1.0	1.0	1.0	1.0
Greece	1992	2.0	2.0	1.67	2.0	1.0	1.0	1.26	2.0
Ireland	1992	1.0	1.0	1.07	1.0	1.0	1.0	1.0	1.0
Italy	1992	2.0	1.0	1.56	1.0	1.0	1.0	1.04	1.0
Luxembourg	1992	1.0	1.0	1.0	1.0	1.0	1.0	1.0	1.0
Netherlands	1992	1.0	1.0	1.0	1.0	1.0	1.0	1.0	1.0
Portugal	1992	1.0	1.0	1.0	1.0	1.0	1.0	1.0	1.0
Spain	1992	1.0	1.0	1.37	1.0	1.0	1.0	1.0	1.0
United Kingdom	1992	2.0	2.0	1.48	1.0	1.0	1.0	1.0	1.0
Austria	1995	1.0	1.0	1.0	1.0	1.0	1.0	1.0	1.0
Finland	1995	1.0	1.0	1.0	1.0	1.0	1.0	1.0	1.0
Sweden	1995	1.0	1.0	1.0	1.0	1.0	1.0	1.0	1.0
Mean	—	1.33	1.27	1.23	1.13	1.0	1.0	1.02	1.07

Continued on next page

TABLE 9.1. (*continued*)

Country	Accession year	Civil liberties				Political rights			
		1992	Four years before accession	Postaccession	2018	1992	Four years before accession	Postaccession	2018
Cyprus	2004	1.0	1.0	1.0	1.0	1.0	1.0	1.0	1.0
Czech Republic	2004	2.0	2.0	1.0	1.0	1.0	1.0	1.0	1.0
Estonia	2004	3.0	2.0	1.0	1.0	3.0	1.0	1.0	1.0
Hungary	2004	2.0	2.0	1.50	2.0	2.0	1.0	1.50	3.0
Latvia	2004	3.0	2.0	1.28	2.0	3.0	1.0	1.71	2.0
Lithuania	2004	3.0	2.0	1.07	1.0	2.0	1.0	1.07	1.0
Malta	2004	1.0	1.0	1.0	1.0	1.0	1.0	1.0	1.0
Poland	2004	2.0	1.0	1.14	2.0	2.0	1.0	1.0	1.0
Slovakia	2004	4.0	2.0	1.0	1.0	3.0	1.0	1.0	1.0
Slovenia	2004	2.0	1.0	1.0	1.0	2.0	1.0	1.0	1.0
Bulgaria	2007	3.0	2.0	2.0	2.0	4.0	1.0	1.91	2.0
Romania	2007	4.0	2.0	2.0	2.0	4.0	2.25	2.0	2.0
Croatia	2013	4.0	1.25	1.0	1.0	4.0	2.0	2.0	2.0
Mean	—	2.62	1.54	1.23	1.38	2.46	1.17	1.32	1.46

Notes: Civil liberties: 1 = freedom of expression, assembly, association, education, and religion; 2 = restrictions on worker rights, discrimination against women and minorities; 3, 4, or 5 = additional limitations on expression, assembly, and association, and government-protected discrimination against women and minorities; 6 or 7 = dictatorial. *Political rights:* 1 = wide range of political rights, including free and fair elections; 2 = political corruption, limits on competitive parties, flawed election protections; 3, 4, or 5 = corruption, political discrimination, and limited voting rights; 6 or 7 = dictatorial.

Source: Freedom House (2018).

irregularities, and on civil liberties because of restrictions on worker rights or discrimination against women or minorities. The highest (that is, worst) scores among EU countries are values of 3 or 4, representing clear and entrenched government restrictions on political rights and civil liberties. Countries are ordered by their date of accession into the union; those whose year of accession is 1992 are the original signers of the Treaty of Maastricht. The sample has been divided into two groups: the original member states plus Austria, Finland, and Sweden, which joined in or before 1995; and the thirteen new members, which joined in or after 2004. Included in this second group are the EU members originally belonging to the Soviet Bloc.

The original fifteen member states of the EU are clearly strong democracies that protect individual rights, as evident by the near-perfect scores (nearly all 1s) from the date of admission to the union to today. The only significant blemishes on the record of the founding members come from France for its treatment of the Roma people and from Greece for its suppression of urban riots in the early 2000s and again in 2009 during the Great Recession. These scores for the original member states contrast with those of the member states from central and eastern Europe that joined in or after 2004 (Cyprus and Malta also entered the union in 2004 with perfect scores of 1, although Malta has had problems with press freedom.) The mean scores in 1992 for all member states that joined in or after 2004 are 2.62 (2.91 excluding Cyprus and Malta) for civil liberties and 2.46 (2.73 excluding Cyprus and Malta) for political rights, leading these states to be classified as "partially free." Country scores for the four years just before accession, however, show significant improvements. Once in the EU, those states have continued to provide rights protections, with only two recent exceptions—Hungary (political rights) and Poland (civil rights). In 2018, both Hungary's and Poland's scores were no better than their immediate post-Soviet (1992) scores.

While the "carrot" of EU membership does appear to offer an inducement for improved rights performance, it is by itself no guarantee of continued protections. Once in the union, it appears member states can stray from the Charter of Rights with few direct consequences. Where is the "stick"?

4. The EU at a Crossroads

The European Union is now a reality in the economic, civic, and personal lives of the majority of European citizens. The economic gains from the free-trade customs union and the enforcement of market competition are significant.

Citizen involvement in EU policies occurs through their direct election of members to the European Parliament and the indirect election of their national representatives to the European Council, the European Commission, and the Council of Ministers. Direct citizen participation in EU affairs is similar to that in national politics. Finally, the EU has made an important difference for the protection of rights and liberties for those citizens joining the union from the previous Soviet Bloc states of central and eastern Europe.

For all of its successes, however, the EU faces significant challenges moving forward. First, while the monetary union has improved the allocation of capital across EMU member states, the single currency has made the management of temporary economic and financial crises more difficult and, in the case of Greece, encouraged a crisis on its own through lax financial supervision. Second, citizens can affect EU policies but only indirectly, creating a democratic deficit. Finally, while rights performance has improved, there is evidence of backsliding by four of the new eastern European member states—Bulgaria, Hungary, and Poland—and a need to resolve the current challenge of immigration and asylum seekers. Disciplining rights performance remains a problem for the EU.

The question that now remains is how EU performance might be improved. There are two paths the EU might follow. The first is to move toward a full political union—Democratic Federalism. The second is to retain the current institutions of Cooperative Federalism but introduce modest reforms to address each of the EU's current weaknesses. Given current realities, we prefer the second path.

A European Political Union

Moving the current institutions of the EU toward those required for a well-functioning federal political union should, in principle, not be difficult. Paralleling the U.S. federal institutions of the House of Representatives and the Senate, the elected Parliament provides a forum for the direct voice of EU citizens, while the appointed Council of Ministers provides a forum for the collective voice of each member state. The process of co-decision now treats the two chambers as coequals in deciding policies. The European Commission serves as a professional bureaucracy to implement EU policies, and an independent central bank sets monetary policies and supervises the financial sector for those member states in the monetary union. There is an independent court of justice composed of appointed justices from each of the member states.

Finally, the Treaty of the European Union provides explicit protections for the independent policies of the member states through its governing principles of subsidiarity and proportionality. All that is missing is a popularly elected executive, a president of the European Union, with agenda powers over EU domestic and foreign trade policies and the power to administer those policies through executive control of the commission.

Policy reforms to address the weaknesses of the current union could begin with the election of the president. A progressive candidate might advocate a less austere fiscal response for member states under short-term fiscal distress, educational and training subsidies for lower-income households and increased structural aid for less developed member states, and an EU-wide income insurance policy. Each policy might be financed by a progressive EU income tax. The resulting progressive fiscal union would provide further income insurance against asymmetric economic shocks. Another candidate might propose ending inefficient agricultural income supports; reducing the EU-wide VAT tax rate; harmonizing capital taxation for improved allocation of firm investments; providing an EU-managed, experience-rated unemployment insurance system; and tightening supervision of member state borrowing. Both candidates might also advocate an EU-funded and EU-supervised security force for increased rights protections (the progressive candidate) and border controls (the liberal candidate).

Of course, the election of an EU president will not by itself ensure the passage of efficient and fair EU policies. The president would need to win approval of his or her proposals from the Parliament and the Council of Ministers. To build the required majority or supermajority coalition would require resources and political agreements. It is on this crucial point that we, and others, are skeptical.[52] Without trust, the political "deals" needed for efficient and fair EU policies cannot be reached. Either there are no deals and thus no policies or there emerge rotating grand bargains of local projects that abuse the "common pool" of EU taxable incomes..

Alberto Alesina, Guido Tabellini, and Francesco Trebbi (2017) have evaluated the potential for political cooperation in the EU by asking whether member states of the Europe Union together constitute an optimal political area. They are doubtful. The issue is not the extent of religious or cultural differences of citizens across the EU member states—they are in fact no greater in Europe than in the United States—but rather one of giving up national

52. See Berglöf et al. (2003), Ash (2012), Spolaore (2013), and Eichengreen (2018b).

identities for a European identity and a willingness to make financial or personal sacrifices for the benefit of citizens from countries other than one's own. Successful political unions require a common political ethos arising from a shared political history (India, Australia, or the United States) or a dominant nationality (Canada and Germany).[53] Today's EU has neither. For this reason a successful political union seems doubtful.

Toward a Stronger Union through Modest Reforms

The alternative is to seek more modest reforms within the current structure of Cooperative Federalism. Rather than new institutions to reform policies, we suggest new policies that, if successful and embraced, might then lead to a political union in the future. We propose (1) two economic reforms, one to address the need for a more responsive fiscal policy in times of recessions, and second to ensure stronger fiscal discipline generally; (2) the popular election of the Commission President to a five-year term to address the perceived democratic deficit; and finally, (3) the introduction of an outside review of member states' rights performance with increasing financial sanctions for those states in violation of the union's Charter of Fundamental Rights.

To strengthen the economic performance of the union economies in times of economic downturns, we propose the adoption of an EU-wide and EU-supervised system of unemployment insurance. At the moment, such insurance is financed and administered by each member state. We propose a minimal or foundation level for benefits common across all member states financed by a tax to be experienced rated by industry and country, shared by employers and employees, and administered by the EU. Member states would be free to supplement the benefit foundation with an experience-rated tax or progressive income tax. Unemployed workers would be paid benefits set by the member state of the worker's place of employment. The policy would provide EU-financed income insurance against asymmetric economic shocks to member state economies. In the case of a union-wide recession, the EU could vote to supplement benefits for all member states with the understanding that any deficits in "state accounts" would be repaid after a recovery or from a surplus ("rainy day") account in the EU fund. The intent of the policy is to provide

53. See O'Leary, Lustick, and Callaghy (2001).

EU economies with a common fiscal stimulus to overcome the "free rider" incentives now present in member state fiscal policies during recessions.[54]

To control the propensity toward excessive member state borrowing, EU bailouts, and future "Greek fiscal crises," we propose the completion of an EU banking union. The EU may be tempted to bail out a member state's debts if default on those debts would lead to an EU-wide banking crisis, loss of banks' lending capacities, and finally, an EU-wide recession. In such circumstances, the costs of an EU-paid fiscal bailout may be less than the wider economic losses that follow from default. If so, a bailout follows. If a bailout is likely, then there is a temptation for member states to run large deficits. The EU should continue to regulate deficit behaviors—as it now does with the Stability and Growth Pact—but in addition seek to minimize the EU-wide consequences of country defaults. The EU banking union is designed to minimize these wider economic consequences. Two of the required three "legs" for a successful banking union are now in place: a single supervisory mechanism to monitor the capital requirements of EMU banks (leg one) and a single resolution mechanism (leg two) to allow the orderly restructuring of a failing bank. Capital requirements are designed to ensure that banks do not hold a risky level of any one member state's debt. A resolution mechanism will allow for the recapitalization of potentially successful banks suffering a temporary adverse shock, while allowing truly mismanaged banks to fail. The missing third leg provides deposit insurance so as to minimize the risk of bank runs in times of crisis, even for strong banks. Member states now provide deposit insurance up to €100,000. We recommend passage of the proposed European Deposit Insurance Scheme, which should provide further insurance for member state programs in the case of large local shocks.

With respect to the commission president, we suggest a direct EU-wide election for a five-year term. Presidential candidates would benefit from the support of EU-wide political parties, and EU-wide political parties will be encouraged. The president would retain full and primary agenda powers, supported by the professional staff of the commission. The president would have the right to appoint and replace an ineffective commissioner, with commissioners hopefully appointed on the basis of abilities, not political expediency. The Council of Europe—composed of EU heads of government—would continue its advisory role to the president and the commission. Approval of policies would still require a qualified majority vote by the Council of

---

54. See Farhi and Werning (2017).

Ministers. The council would retain the right to propose and amend policies, subject to a presidential veto, which could be overridden. To improve citizen oversight, all official legislative deliberations within the council should be transcribed and be made publicly available.[55] Deliberations should show a clear consideration of how each major piece of legislation satisfies the governing principles of subsidiarity and proportionality, using perhaps our FIST. The Parliament would still have proposal powers.

For the successful enforcement of EU citizen rights and liberties, the union has relied on national courts and the governments of member states, and it must continue to do so. While most member states have continued their commitment to EU rights and liberties, Poland and Hungary have challenged the rule of law and democratic governance; see Box 9.3. The union is struggling with what might be done to restore an independent judiciary and free and open political discourse in both countries. Financial penalties have been proposed and the CJEU has used fines with some success, but typically only when the stakes were small.[56] The remaining option is to enforce Article 7 of the EU treaty. Article 7 allows the union to suspend the voting rights of a member state if the state is in persistent breach of fundamental EU values as stated in Article 2. Article 7 does not allow direct EU intervention into the affairs of the violating state, however, nor does it require that an economic penalty be assessed.

More effective would be the proposal advanced by Müller (2015). He proposes a "Copenhagen Commission . . . with a mandate to offer comprehensive and consistent political judgments" (2015, p. 150) as to member state compliance with the Charter of Fundamental Rights. The body would be composed of legal experts and statesmen and stateswomen with proven records of considered and fair judgment. If violations of the political and legal rights of member state citizens were found, sanctions would be imposed by the Council of Europe in consultation with the elected president of the European Commission. First, the state would receive a formal warning coupled with a clear statement of the Copenhagen Commission's concerns and perhaps an outline of corrective steps. Second, a failure to respond constructively to the warning

---

55. See Berglöf et al. (2003, chap. 4).

56. Fines have been imposed to enforce EU regulations of member state environmental policies, but the policies had only modest consequences for member state economies; see Jack (2013). Large fines will be needed to enforce a change in policy. Scheppele (2016) recommends withholding CAP and Structural Fund allocations.

would trigger progressively growing economic penalties, implemented by withholding an increasing share of CAP and Structural Fund allocations. Finally, if violations continued or grew more serious, the member state could be expelled from the union with the loss for citizens and firms of all the economic advantages membership allows—"Brexit" on the EU's terms. The country could be readmitted only after showing a clear and sustained commitment to the rule of law and democratic governance. To be effective, the citizens of the country must sufficiently value EU participation to remove the current offending political leadership.

If implemented, each of these reforms has the potential to address a current weakness in EU performance. Importantly, each can be implemented using the current institutions of the union, those of Cooperative Federalism. Success over time may well engender a level of trust in EU policy-making that is now missing, and might eventually lead to sufficient trust as to warrant a full political union.

5. Summing Up

Writing just after the passage of the Maastricht Treaty creating the European Union, Robert Dahl (1994) ventured a guess as to the future of democratic governance. Democratic governance has experienced three great transformations: from nondemocratic to democratic city-states during the fifth century BC, from autocratic to democratic feudal states, and finally from feudal states to today's democratic nation-states. The challenge now is to find a means of democratic governance for nations seeking to manage the new international economy. For Dahl, the European Union as proposed in Maastricht stands as the most complete effort in this direction, and as such it now provides a unique opportunity to evaluate how well such institutions might do in resolving what he called "a democratic dilemma" of "system effectiveness versus citizen participation." This chapter has offered such an assessment.

Under the Maastricht Treaty, the EU's chosen form of governance is Cooperative Federalism. With Cooperative Federalism, the EU makes decisions by unanimity among the participating member states, each of which is represented in the Council of Ministers and advised and assisted by a professional staff called the European Commission. Leadership of the professional staff by the president of the commission rotates among the member states. Governance allows for direct citizen input through the locally elected Parliament, but the Parliament's role is largely advisory. Responsibility for enforcement of

EU laws and regulations rests with the member states, guided as needed by rulings from the CJEU, which is composed of appointed justices from the member states.

Against the criterion of economic efficiency, the union has, on balance, been a success. Its customs union enforcing free trade and market competition among member states has increased citizens' incomes on average by 1 to 2 percent per year. Gains have not been evenly distributed, however. Open markets will disadvantage protected farm interests and less competitive industries. The necessity of compensation was anticipated at the time of the signing of Maastricht, leading to the passage of the EU's two major fiscal policies, CAP subsidies for farm interests and Structural Fund allocations for declining areas. While CAP has clearly been inefficient, Structural Fund policies have helped to grow incomes in declining regions. Overall, there are fiscal inefficiencies from the EU budget, but not enough to offset the significant economic gains enjoyed from open markets.

More troublesome for EU efficiency has been the performance of the EMU. To complement the EU's customs union, the EMU established a currency union to facilitate efficient financial transactions and thus encourage greater EU-wide investments. But at a cost. The common currency denied member states access to devaluations as a means to boost local economies in times of economic decline. Further, the common currency has allowed member states to conceal a history of deficit financing, with inefficient EU fiscal bailouts as a result. The economic gains from more efficient financial transactions and investment flows have been offset by economic losses from the EU's inability to collectively manage economic downturns and from its payment of inefficient fiscal bailouts.

Less successful too has been the ability of the union's institutions to engage citizen participation, expressed as a concern for a democratic deficit. There is now only one avenue through which citizens can directly influence EU policies: by electing a local representative to the Parliament. The Parliament has been only a marginal player in the setting of EU policies.

Finally, the EU has led to improved protection of EU citizens' rights and liberties, particularly for the citizens in the new member states from central and eastern Europe. Our evidence suggests it has been the enforcement of EU standards for rights and liberties at the time of accession that was decisive. Once in the union, enforcement has proved more difficult, as shown by recent efforts to undermine a free press and an independent judiciary in Poland and Hungary.

We have offered a number of reforms that have the potential to improve each dimension of EU performance. We propose the adoption of a union-wide, experience-rated policy for temporary unemployment insurance and the completion of the EU's banking union to improve economic performance. To aid the direct participation of citizens in EU policy-making, we propose the direct election of the president of the commission. Finally, to protect the rights and liberties of EU citizens, we advocate the use of an independent oversight agency, the Copenhagen Commission, with the right to recommend fines or finally the expulsion of any member state found in violation of the union's Charter of Fundamental Rights.

We view a move toward a full political union as infeasible at this time. To be successful, a well-functioning political union will require EU citizens to view the tasks of governance not as citizens of their Member States but rather *as EU citizens* willing to trust their member states to decide policies in the collective interest of all union citizens. We see the best chances for a fully democratic political union arising only after a continued record of successful modest reforms, decided and implemented through the governance principles of Cooperative Federalism.

10

Mandela's Federal Democracy

A FRAGILE COMPACT

1. Introduction

South Africa's transition from apartheid to a truly multiracial democracy stands as one of the significant political events of the last century. The transition was peacefully negotiated and a new democracy put in place, and despite still significant inequities, the average South African resident, black or white, is economically better off today than he or she was under the last years of apartheid.[1] Though peaceful and mutually understood as essential for the long-run future of all South Africans, the constitutional negotiations were far from harmonious.[2] It took nearly four years, from the date of Nelson

1. Significant progress had been made in most dimensions of the economic life of South Africans from the fall of apartheid beginning in 1993 to 2011; see Levy, Hirsch, and Woolard (2015). Absolute poverty, measured by daily hunger, has fallen from 28 percent to 11 percent; access to electricity is up from 58 percent to 85 percent and to piped water from 56 percent to 91 percent; immunization coverage has increased from 58 percent to 98 percent; secondary-school enrollment has increased from 50 percent to 75 percent; and the number of qualified recipients of old age or child support or disability income grants has increased from 2.4 million to 15 million. Overall crime rates have fallen since 2004. Today South Africa's rate of four thousand property and personal crime offenses per one hundred thousand is comparable to that of most large U.S. cities. Income inequality and young adult unemployment remain significant concerns.

2. By late 1989, the National Party was suffering under the economic and cultural sanctions imposed by Western industrial nations begun in the mid-1970s. National economic growth of real income declined from 2.5 percent per year from 1950 to 1976 (the year of the Soweto Uprising) to 0 percent thereafter. Also by 1989, the African National Congress had lost its economic support with the fall of the Soviet Union. Both sides realized there was no path forward other than to create a democratic South Africa. As expressed by Chester Crocker, secretary of state

Mandela's release from Robben Island on February 11, 1990, until November 1993, before even an outline of a democratic constitution was accepted by the three relevant parties to the negotiations, the National Party (NP), representing the once-ruling whites; the African National Congress (ANC), representing the majority of blacks and Asian South Africans; and the Inkatha Freedom Party (IFP), representing the rural blacks of the historic Zulu nation.

The central stumbling block in the initial constitutional negotiations was finding a balance between the ANC's demand for significant income redistribution to redress decades of economic exploitation and the NP's demand for constitutional protections against expropriation of incomes and assets by the ANC political majority. The ANC leadership demanded a true democracy of "one person, one vote" and unitary governance with all fiscal policies set by the national government. The NP favored shared executive powers between majority and minority parties and federal governance with significant fiscal policies, particularly redistribution policies, set by provincial or local governments. Under the NP proposal, national policies would require the collective agreement of the provinces following the principles of Economic and Cooperative Federalism. After three years of stalemate, and under the pressure of an ANC-NP commitment to hold the first democratic elections for a parliament and president by the end of 1994, the three sides finally reached an agreement on November 18, 1993, for what became known as the Interim Constitution.[3] The Interim Constitution outlined an institutional structure closely approximating Democratic Federalism.

As specified in the Interim Constitution, representatives to the national parliament, called the National Assembly, would be elected by proportional representation from party lists. The elected majority party or a majority coalition of parties would then select a president for a five-year term. These provisions ensured the control of the national government by the ANC for at least the initial years of the new democracy. Second, upon the insistence of Mandela and as a central concession to the NP and IFP, the Interim Constitution created nine provinces, with the boundaries explicitly drawn so as to facilitate the likely control of at least one province by each of the three negotiating parties. Third, the Interim Constitution proposed a senate (renamed the National

---

for Africa at the time, "The reality was the white government and the opposition had checkmated each other" (quoted in Giliomee, 1995, p. 91).

3. See Waldmeir (1997, pt. 2) for a summary of the negotiations leading first to the Interim Constitution and then to the final constitution.

Council of Provinces in the final constitution) to be composed of ten representatives from each of the nine provinces, with the ten seats allocated by each party's share of votes for the provincial legislatures. Approval by the Senate was required for all national policies directly affecting the budgets or policies of the provinces. Finally, the Interim Constitution created a constitutional court that was responsible for ensuring that the final constitution followed the principles outlined in the interim agreement. Though not explicitly called a federal constitution, the Interim Constitution had established all the institutions required for Democratic Federalism. What was not specified was the allocation of policy responsibilities among the national, provincial, and local governments. That was the task of presidentially appointed constitutional commissions assigned to draft a final constitution for approval by the newly elected National Assembly.[4] The newly elected parliament assumed office on May 10, 1994, and chose Mandela as the first democratically elected president of South Africa. Negotiations for the final constitution for the Republic of South Africa took an additional two years. The Constitution was unanimously approved by the multiracial, multiparty National Assembly on October 11, 1996.

The Constitution's final assignment of policy responsibilities gave the national government responsibility for setting the taxation of income and capital and for the regulation of business but allocated to provincial and local governments a shared responsibility (known as concurrent powers) for the provision of education, health care, housing, and welfare services—the services of primary importance for lower-income families, who constitute the majority of ANC supporters. The financing of these services would be provided by a constitutionally guaranteed share of national tax revenues known as the "equitable share," as recommended by an independent commission known as the Financial and Fiscal Commission (FFC). The equitable share would be paid as intergovernmental grants to the provinces and municipalities so that sufficient funds were available to finance FFC-recommended levels of education, health care, housing, and welfare services. The provision of those services would be the administrative responsibility of the provinces and municipalities.

We argue in Section 2 that the final constitution's federal structure of national, provincial, and local governments, coupled with its assignment of significant policy responsibility for providing redistributive services to provinces

---

4. Though the ANC held more 60 percent of the seats in the new National Assembly, President Mandela appointed equal representation of ANC and NP members to each Commission so as ensure equal standing, at least symbolically, in the continuing negotiations.

and municipalities, created a "hostage game" in fiscal policies. Minority-controlled provinces have the potential to check the national party majority, then as now the ANC, from expropriating the incomes and assets of minority landowners and middle- and upper-income households. With the disastrous Zimbabwe economy just to the north, President Mandela and the ANC leadership were very aware of the economic minority's concerns over expropriation. At a 1994 press conference, Mandela stated, "The ANC is very much concerned to address the question of concerns to whites [when] they insist on *structural guarantees* to ensure that . . . majority rule does not result in the domination of whites by blacks. We understand that fear. The whites are our fellow South Africans. We want them to feel safe" (quoted in Waldmeir, 1997, p. 157; italics added).[5] To date, these structural guarantees in the form of federal institutions and decentralized policy assignments have offered protections for the incomes and assets of the Republic of South Africa's landowners and economic elites.

Section 3 details the fiscal performance of the new, democratic South Africa under federal governance and the ability of federal institutions to deliver on the original Mandela compact. Section 4 then provides estimates of the net economic benefits for South Africans from the transition; in the aggregate they are sizeable. While the transition from apartheid to democracy has been a success, the future is less certain. Section 5 outlines what will now be needed to consolidate South Africa's new democracy as a viable and ongoing democratic state. There are risks, as the presidency of Jacob Zuma has made clear. But here too the institutions of Democratic Federalism have made an important contribution toward ensuring a democratic South Africa. Section 6 provides a summary.

2. Federal Institutions and the Democratic Transition

The central issue for the design of South Africa's new constitution was how to credibly assure the NP leaders and their constituents—landowners, investors in South Africa's natural resources, and the professional elite—that their investments and incomes would be protected against full expropriation by the new ANC majority. South Africa's economic elite acknowledged early on in

---

5. One of the most important of the ANC leaders at the time of the negotiations, Joe Slovo, expressed a similar sentiment: "Clearly the enemy is not defeated. . . . We need a package that, while not compromising the interests of the people, will also adequately address the interests of the minorities" (quoted in Giliomee, 1995, p. 97).

the negotiations that additional taxes would be needed to correct for years of economic impoverishment of South Africa's black majority. The constitutional issue was how to choose those taxes. Observing the collapse of the Zimbabwean economy under the autocratic rule of President Robert Mugabe, both the NP and the ANC leadership recognized that institutional safeguards would be needed to check any similar excesses by an elected ANC majority. The 1996 Constitution establishing South Africa as a federal democracy was their solution, using a governance structure of Democratic Federalism.[6]

First, the structure of provincial governance outlined in the Interim Constitution was retained in the final constitution. The original nine provinces were created to ensure provincial majorities for each of the three negotiating parties to the transition. The ANC would be the likely majority in the provinces of Eastern Cape, Free State, Gauteng (including Johannesburg, Soweto, and Alexandria), Mpumalanga, Northern Province, and North West. The IFP, representing the Zula nation, would be the likely majority in the province of KwaZulu-Natal. Finally, the NP was expected to be the majority party in both the rural province of Northern Cape and the urban province of Western Cape (including Cape Town). During the negotiations, the borders of the provinces were explicitly drawn with this political outcome in mind.[7]

Second, Chapter 13 (Finance) of the final constitution assigned to the national government full responsibility for income, capital, and value-added taxation. Provincial and local taxation was limited to a provincial surcharge on the national income tax, but only with approval of the National Assembly. Property taxation, user fees, and charges can be assessed by provincial and local governments, provided their impacts do not conflict with national policies. Chapters 11 (Security Services) and 13 and Schedules 4 and 5 assigned exclusive spending and policy responsibilities for national defense, foreign policy, police services, business regulation, and monetary policy to the national government, and concurrent responsibilities for infrastructures, education, housing, public health, and welfare services for the poor and elderly to

---

6. The analysis here and in Sections 3 and 4 of South Africa's transition to democracy was first presented in Inman and Rubinfeld (2005) and developed more completely in Inman and Rubinfeld (2012, 2013). The analysis can be seen as a working example of the general framework presented in Acemoglu and Robinson (2006, chap. 6).

7. See Muthien and Khosa (1998). In the initial elections for Parliament in 1994, the ANC carried the Northern Cape as well, largely because of an election boycott by white farmers thought to be in support of the NP but angered by the NP's "capitulation" to the ANC.

the national government and the provinces. Though constitutionally the national government can at any time assume direct responsibility for providing a concurrent service, as now implemented, provinces are the primary direct provider of all important redistributive services.[8] Separately elected municipal governments are the responsibility of the provinces in both the financing and the administration of provincial policies.

While provincial governments are given primary responsibility for the provision of K–12 education, health care, and services for the poor and elderly, they have been assigned no significant revenues of their own. Rather, financing for these services comes from intergovernmental transfers from the national government to the provinces and municipalities. Grants are paid in two ways: first, as conditional transfers tied to explicit requirements for providing education, health care, and poverty services; and second, as general-purpose grants that can be allocated by the provinces for provincially and municipally decided services. Importantly, the aggregate amount of funding for provincial and locally elected governments is set by the National Assembly according to financing rules defined in the Constitution (Chapter 13, Section 214) to provide provinces and municipalities with an "equitable share" of national tax revenues. The Constitution requires that the equitable share be sufficient to provide the concurrent services provided by the provinces, while considering their relative fiscal capacities and the economic needs of their citizens.[9]

Third, to protect the institutional standing of the provinces in the federal structure and their constitutionally assigned equitable share of national revenues, the Constitution established an independently elected second legislative chamber, the National Council of Provinces (NCOP), to represent provincial interests in national policy and an independent commission of financial experts, the FFC, to recommend the equitable share for the financing of provincial and municipal services following constitutional guidelines. The NCOP is composed of ten representatives from each of the nine provinces, with the ten seats allocated by each party's share of votes for the provincial legislatures. Approval by the NCOP is required for all national policies directly affecting the budgets or policies of the provinces. Members of the FFC are to be appointed by the president for their professional qualifications as accountants, budgetary analysts, and fiscal policy experts. In setting its allocations across

8. See Simeon and Murray (2009).

9. As specified in Chapter 7 of the Constitution. And see our Chapter 7, Box 7.1 for how the equitable share might be specified to allow for fiscal capacities and economic needs.

the provinces, the commission recommendations are to be formula driven, based on provincial incomes and economic needs as measured by the number of school-age children, the number of elderly, the rate of poverty, and the cost of living. Provinces are free to spend their allocated share on their constitutionally required service responsibilities and, once met, on their own provincial and local policy objectives. The Constitutional Court is responsible for enforcing these protections of federal governance.

The objectives of this constitutional structure are threefold. First, to give the national government sole responsibility for *financing* national public goods, transfer incomes, and redistributive public services. Second, to give individual provincial governments primary responsibility for *providing* the assigned redistributive services, most importantly K–12 education, public health, and services for the elderly and the poor. And third, to insulate the financing and delivery of provincial services from national political interference. If held in place, the result is a federal political economy that closely approximates the efficient assignment of tax and spending responsibilities in a federal public economy, but with an important added benefit. The resulting federal institutions have the potential to protect elite incomes and assets against majority expropriation through an annual hostage game in fiscal politics. Each party would hold "hostage" something of value to the other. Here's how the hostage game might work for South Africa's fiscal politics.[10]

By South Africa's constitutional rules, all important taxing powers lie with the national government, which has been controlled by the ANC since its conception. As noted, the provinces have responsibility for providing all important redistributive services funded by the "equitable share" of national taxation. ANC constituents are lower-income citizens demanding education, health care, and redistributive services. Provincial boundaries were explicitly drawn with the possibility of minority party control. The province of KwaZulu-Natal was originally controlled by the IFP but is today an ANC province. Since

10. While there are constitutional provisions protecting property (Chapter 2, Section 25) and institutions protecting provinces as separate, politically independent jurisdictions (Chapter 6) with assigned responsibilities (Schedule 4), neither the Constitutional Court nor the NCOP alone will be sufficient to protect the economic incomes and wealth of the middle- and upper-income citizens of the Republic of South Africa from expropriation by the majority. The NCOP remains firmly in the control of the ANC through the ANC's control of provincial elections in all but the Western Cape. When the application of constitutional provisions has been at all uncertain, the Court has decided in favor of the national government, stressing national unity for the new democracy; see Steytler (2017).

the 1994 elections, however, the relatively wealthy and urban Western Cape has been controlled by, first, the NP and, more recently, by the Democratic Alliance (DA). While middle- and upper-income residents are a sufficient majority to elect the DA as the dominant political party in the Western Cape, the cape has a sizeable lower-income population that is dependent on provincially provided public education, health care, and lower-income transfers. Those lower-income residents are an important national constituency for the ANC.

As a result of this federal structure, provincial demographics, and national and provincial elections, each important constituency in the hostage game controls a fiscal policy important to the other. The majority poor, represented by the ANC, controls the national taxation of the elite. The minority economic elite, represented by the DA in the Western Cape, control redistributive services to a significant fraction of the poor. If the ANC taxes "too much," the DA can reallocate the Western Cape's equitable share of national revenues meant for the poor to middle-class services. If the DA ignores the Western Cape's poor and allocates its equitable share to middle-class services, the ANC can raise the national tax rate or bypass the province altogether and provide redistributive services nationally. As a result, the ANC's poor and the DA's economic elite each decide something of value to the other. The ANC poor controls elite after-tax incomes, and the DA elite controls redistributive services to a significant fraction of the ANC's poor. Each can therefore check the "excesses" of the other. It was this institutional structure, agreed to by Mandela in the Interim Constitution and codified in the final constitution, that provided the elite with the *structural guarantees* they needed to move forward to democracy.

But has it worked to control redistributive taxation? Two conditions must hold.[11] First, the economic elite must politically control fiscal policies in at least one province, and that province must be of sufficient size that a sizeable number, but not a majority, of residents are lower-income constituents of the ANC. We call this requirement for provincial control by the elite the *border constraint for Democratic Federalism*. Provincial borders were drawn to define a lower bound and an upper bound on the majority population within the elite-controlled province. The upper bound is set so that the elite retains political control of the province. The lower bound is set to ensure that there are enough lower-income constituents within the province so that a decision by

---

11. The full details of this fiscal game are outlined in Inman and Rubinfeld (2012). We provide a summary of the argument here.

the elite to withhold redistributive services is politically costly to the national ANC.[12] In today's South Africa, this province is the Western Cape. The NP won political control of the Western Cape in the first election, in 1994; and today the province is controlled by the DA, a wider and more inclusive middle class political party.

Second, the redistributive services assigned by the Constitution for provincial control must be services that are important to the welfare of the lower-income, ANC constituents. This is again the case for South Africa with the concurrent assignment for the delivery of K–12 education, health care, and lower-income transfers and services as provincial responsibilities. We call this constraint the *assignment constraint for Democratic Federalism*.[13] When both the border and assignment constraints are met, the elite-controlled province has a credible threat to withhold redistributive services and to influence ANC decisions in the setting of national tax rates.

Figure 10.1 illustrates how the ANC national majority and the DA elite controlling the Western Cape might play the hostage game. The majority has two strategies: either to set a "moderate" national tax rate on national income (τ_F) sufficient to fund national public goods and a "moderate" level of redistributive services (the cooperation strategy) or to set a "maximal" national tax rate (τ_U) defined by the peak of the national revenue hill (the defection strategy). The maximal tax rate is set by the economy and the work, investment, and mobility (leaving South Africa) decisions of the economic elite. The elite-controlled province has two strategies as well: either to provide the agreed-to (FFC-specified) level of redistributive services (q_F) (the cooperation strategy) or to reallocate national funding for redistributive services from poor residents to economic elite residents and provide only (q_D) services to the poor (the defection strategy). For example, the elite can use its equitable share of

12. The formal specification of the border constraint allows for the fact that lower-income citizens may move to other, ANC-controlled provinces to avoid the elite's effort to withhold redistributive services.

13. Assigning only street cleaning or parks and recreation to the provinces will not be sufficient to meet the assignment constraint for Democratic Federalism. Further, the elite province must have a comparative cost advantage in the provision of important services so that the majority-controlled national government (i.e., the ANC) cannot costlessly set up a parallel network of providers in the elite province. If so, then the elite threat to deny important services to the lower-income households will not be credible. This cost advantage for the elite has certainly been the case in South Africa. See Inman and Rubinfeld (2012) for the precise specification of the constraint.

	Majority cooperation τ_F	Majority defection τ_U
Elite cooperation q_F	(I) $U(\tau_F|q_F) = 17{,}100$ rand $y(q_F|\tau_F) = 73{,}000$ rand	(II) $U(\tau_U|q_F) = 17{,}800$ rand $y(q_F|\tau_U) = 70{,}300$ rand
Elite defection q_D	(III) $U(\tau_F|q_D) = 16{,}500$ rand $y(q_D|\tau_F) = 74{,}400$ rand	(IV) $U(\tau_U|q_D) = 17{,}000$ rand $y(q_D|\tau_U) = 71{.}900$ rand

Payoffs

$U(\tau_U|q_F) = 17{,}800$ rand $> U(\tau_F|q_F) = 17{,}100$ rand $> U(\tau_U|q_D) = 17{,}000$ rand $> U(\tau_F|q_D) = 16{,}500$ rand

$U(q_D|\tau_F) = 74{,}400$ rand $> y(q_F|\tau_F) = 73{,}000$ rand $> U(q_D|\tau_U) = 71{.}900$ rand $> y(q_F|\tau_U) = 70{,}300$ rand

FIGURE 10.1. The Hostage Game in Fiscal Policy

national revenues to fund elite public schools with entrance exams; supplement private health insurance premiums or locate clinics in rich neighborhoods; or establish high administrative hurdles for the receipt of welfare services, allocating savings to lowering local taxation. Each strategy and the resulting payoffs for the lower-income ANC majority and the middle- and upper-income residents controlling the Western Cape are shown in the figure.[14]

14. The exact values for the payoffs in the figure are given in Inman and Rubinfeld (2012, appendix). Majority resident welfare is estimated as the income (W) available to the majority resident, plus the income-equivalent value of the redistributive services (q) made available by provincial equitable share transfers: $U - W + [\alpha + \lambda \cdot \ln(q)]$. W is the income of the average majority resident, and q is the level of redistributive service inputs available to the average majority resident, where $[\alpha + \lambda \cdot \ln(q)]$ is the income-equivalent value placed on redistributive services by the political majority. Estimates for the level of redistributive inputs (q) are given in Table 10.1. Estimates of α and λ are provided in Inman and Rubinfeld (2012, appendix). Welfare for the average elite resident is specified by the after-tax income (y) of the average elite resident, where taxes equal the average national tax rate on personal income as chosen by the majority plus any income "captured back" by adoption of the provincial defect strategy. Estimates for elite after-tax incomes follow from estimates for the average tax rate as reported in

When both the ANC national government and the DA elite cooperate, their respective annual benefits will be (1) after-tax incomes for the elite when the national tax rate is τ_F and the elite province provides q_F in redistributive transfers, denoted as $y(q_F \mid \tau_F)$ in Quadrant I, and (2) utility for the majority when they receive q_F in services from revenues made possible by the choice of tax rate τ_F, denoted as $U(\tau_F \mid q_F)$. If the majority defects and adopts the maximal tax rate of τ_U but the elite province cooperates and provides q_F, then the payoffs will be $U(\tau_U \mid q_F)$ for the majority and $y(q_F \mid \tau_U)$ for the elite, as shown in Quadrant II. In this case, the level of services and thus utility will be significantly higher for the majority and the after-tax incomes significantly lower for the elite. Alternatively, in Quadrant III, if only the elite province defects, the elite's after-tax incomes will rise to $y(q_D \mid \tau_F)$, as it now captures back redistributive transfers paid to its province; welfare for the majority falls to $U(\tau_F \mid q_D)$, however, as it loses redistributive services. Finally, if both the elite and the majority defect from the cooperative federal agreement by adopting the maximal tax rate (τ_U) and no longer provide promised provincial services (q_D), the majority and elite payoffs will be $U(\tau_U \mid q_D)$ and $y(q_D \mid \tau_U)$, respectively, as shown in Quadrant IV.

It seems reasonable to assume, and the estimated payoffs in Figure 10.1 confirm, that the majority prefers to have a maximal tax rate and cooperative elite provinces $(\tau_U$ and $q_F)$ to the federal compromise $(\tau_F$ and $q_F)$, and both those outcomes are preferred to that with maximal tax rates and elite provinces that defect and allocate provincial resources to elite services or tax relief $(\tau_U$ and $q_D)$. Finally, each of these outcomes is preferred by the majority to being a "naive" cooperator, setting the national tax rate at τ_F and allowing the elite province to reallocate its equitable share revenues to elite services or tax relief $(\tau_F$ and $q_D)$. Thus, $U(\tau_U \mid q_F) > U(\tau_F \mid q_F) > U(\tau_U \mid q_D) > U(\tau_F \mid q_D)$. The elite province prefers the cooperative national tax rate (τ_F) coupled with its capture of redistributive revenues (q_D) to the full federal compromise $(\tau_F$ and $q_F)$, and it will prefer both of these outcomes to the outcome with a maximal tax rate and elite capture of redistributive revenues $(\tau_U$ and $q_D)$. Just as being a naive cooperator is the worst outcome for the majority, so too will it be for the elite, where not capturing back the province's equitable share when the national tax rate is maximal means very low elite incomes. Thus, $y(q_D \mid \tau_F) > y(q_F \mid \tau_F) > y(q_D \mid \tau_U) > y(q_F \mid \tau_U)$.

Table 10.1. Estimates for the maximal tax rate (τ_U) follow from assuming an elasticity of South Africa's national tax base with respect to the average elite tax rate of $-.50$ based on the work of Gruber and Saez (2002); again, see Inman and Rubinfeld (2012, appendix).

MANDELA'S FEDERAL DEMOCRACY 351

What is the likely outcome of this fiscal policy game? With this ranking of outcomes, the hostage game between the national government and elite-controlled provinces becomes a prisoner's dilemma. If played only once, or with no thought as to the future, the outcome will be Quadrant IV—the autocratic unitary state that the NP first feared when negotiating the transition. If the elite budgets for and provides redistributive services of q_F assuming a national of tax rate of τ_F, the majority can always impose an end-of-year tax surcharge setting national taxation at τ_U. If so, the outcome is Quadrant II, the worst outcome for the elite. Alternatively, if the majority naively collects τ_F in taxes, the elite province can always allocate equitable share transfers to elite services or give an end-of-year provincial tax rebate and provide only q_D in redistributive services. If so, the outcome is Quadrant III, the worst outcome for the majority. To avoid an outcome in Quadrant II, the elite allocates its transfers to elite services and provides q_D. To avoid an outcome in Quadrant III, the majority sets an end-of-year maximal tax rate of τ_U. The outcome in both cases is now Quadrant IV, a worse outcome for both the majority and the elite when compared with the cooperative outcome in Quadrant I. If played only once or by naive politicians, the hostage game created by the institutions of Democratic Federalism unravels into de facto unitary governance with maximal taxation and inefficient fiscal redistribution. Mandela's original hope for a federal compact is not ensured.

Fortunately, this worst outcome can be avoided if both the majority and the elite are sufficiently forward looking and each is willing to punish the other for any deviations from the cooperative federal agreement. While there are many possible punishment strategies for a deviation, the one with the strongest incentive to induce cooperation is to defect "forever" if the other party defects from federal cooperation. This is the strategy that shows the least trust of the other party, perhaps a good description of postapartheid South Africa's politics. Game theorists call this permanent defection from cooperation the "grim-trigger" punishment. There is nothing harsher, and if the grim-trigger punishment cannot enforce cooperation, nothing will.

Suppose, for example, that the majority were to defect from cooperation for one budget period, moving the payoffs to Quadrant II, and in response, the elite were then to defect from the federal agreement forever, forcing both parties into the payoffs of Quadrant IV forever. What are the long-run benefits for the majority of this one-time defection to maximal taxation, and how do those long-run benefits compare with those from remaining in the cooperative federal agreement forever? Here's the comparison.

The cooperative agreement will be preferred by the majority if

$$U(\tau_F \mid q_F) + [U(\tau_F \mid q_F)/r_M] > U(\tau_U \mid q_F) + [U(\tau_U \mid q_D)/r_M],$$

where the left-hand side of the inequality is the long-run benefits of being cooperative forever with annual benefits from Quadrant I discounted at the majority's rate of time preference, r_M. The right-hand side of the inequality represents the long-run benefits from grabbing one year of Quadrant II's most favorable outcome from the defection of $U(\tau_U \mid q_F)$, but then a future of worst outcomes $U(\tau_U \mid q_D)$ when the elite imposes the grim-trigger punishment and forces all future budget outcomes into Quadrant IV.[15] The inequality can be rearranged to give a lower bound on the majority's relative payoffs from cooperation or defection sufficient to sustain long-run cooperation:

$$[U(\tau_F \mid q_F) - U(\tau_U \mid q_D)]/[U(\tau_U \mid q_F) - U(\tau_F \mid q_F)] > r_M.$$

The expression $[U(\tau_F \mid q_F) - U(\tau_U \mid q_D)]$ is the majority's annual net benefits of being in the cooperative federal agreement of Quadrant I forever rather than the uncooperative outcome of Quadrant IV. The expression $[U(\tau_U \mid q_F) - U(\tau_F \mid q_F)]$ is the majority's one-time net benefit from its defection from Quadrant I to Quadrant II. This ratio of the two net benefits is the relative attractiveness of federal cooperation forever over the one-time gains from defection. From the estimated payoffs in Figure 10.1 for the average majority ANC resident at the time of the transition,

$$[U(\tau_F \mid q_F) - U(\tau_U \mid q_D)]/[U(\tau_U \mid q_F) - U(\tau_F \mid q_F)] =$$
$$[17,100 - 17,000]/[17,800 - 17,100] = .14 > r_M.$$

If the typical majority resident's annual rate of time preference is less than .14, then he or she will find remaining in the cooperative agreement of Democratic Federalism the preferred long-run outcome in the hostage game of fiscal politics.[16] A less patient majority resident with a rate of time preference greater

---

15. The initial ("today") budget outcomes from Quadrants I and II are not discounted, but the value of all future outcomes from Quadrant I, if there is joint cooperation; or Quadrant IV, if there is joint defection, must be discounted to give the present values in today's rands.

16. A citizen's discount rate, or rate of time preference, describes how much future income he or she must receive to compensate for giving up—that is, saving—one rand of consumption

than .14 will prefer the one time defection from the Mandela compromise in Quadrant I and a future of de facto unitary governance in Quadrant IV.

What about the elite? The cooperative agreement of Democratic Federalism will be preferred by the elite if

$$y(q_F \mid \tau_F) + [y(q_F \mid \tau_F)/r_E] > y(q_D \mid \tau_F) + [y(q_D \mid \tau_U)/r_E],$$

where the left-hand side of the inequality is the long-run benefits of being cooperative forever with annual benefits from Quadrant I discounted at the elite's rate of time preference, r_E, and the right-hand side of the inequality is the long-run benefits from grabbing one year of Quadrant III's most favorable outcome from defection of $y(q_D \mid \tau_F)$ but then a future of worst outcomes $y(q_D \mid \tau_U)$ when the majority forces all future budget outcomes into Quadrant IV. The inequality for the elite can also be rearranged to give an upper bound on the elite's rate of time preference sufficient to sustain long-run cooperation:

$$[y(q_F \mid \tau_F) - y(q_D \mid \tau_U)]/[y(q_D \mid \tau_F) - y(q_F \mid \tau_F)] > r_E.$$

The expression $[y(q_F \mid \tau_F) - y(q_D \mid \tau_U)]$ is the elite's annual net benefits of being in the cooperative federal agreement of Quadrant I forever rather than the uncooperative "unitary" outcome of Quadrant IV, while $[y(q_D \mid \tau_F) - y(q_F \mid \tau_F)]$ is the elite's one-time net benefit from their defection from Quadrant I to Quadrant III. Again, the ratio of these two net benefits is the relative attractiveness of federal cooperation forever over the one-time gains from defection, now for the economic elite. From the estimated payoffs for the average elite resident at the time of the transition,

$$[y(q_F \mid \tau_F) - y(q_D \mid \tau_U)]/[y(q_D \mid \tau_F) - y(q_F \mid \tau_F)] =$$
$$[73{,}000 - 71{,}900]/[74{,}400 - 73{,}000] = .79 > r_E.$$

If the typical elite resident's rate of time preference is less than .79, then he or she will find remaining in the cooperative agreement the preferred long-run outcome in the hostage game of fiscal politics. Even a relatively impatient elite

---

today. A discount rate of .14 implies that the average lower-income citizen will agree to give up one rand of consumption in return for 1.14 rands next year. A higher discount rate means the citizen would rather have that rand today than wait for 1.14 rands tomorrow. Patient, farsighted citizens can wait for future consumption and will therefore have low discount rates.

resident is likely to prefer the Mandela Compromise in Quadrant I to defection and Quadrant IV.

The cooperative fiscal compact promised by Mandela will be sustainable when both parties to Democratic Federalism's constitutional agreement are sufficiently farsighted—that is, have discount rates lower than .14 for a lower-income citizen and .79 for a middle- or upper-income citizen. This seems likely for the elite, but perhaps less so for the typical poor and perhaps unemployed majority citizen.

Section 3 summarizes what has actually happened to South Africa's fiscal policies since the transition. Political pressure for significantly greater income redistribution becomes evident in the budgets after 2009 with the presidency of Jacob Zuma.

3. The Fiscal Record of Democratic South Africa

Table 10.1 summarizes the time path of redistributive provincial fiscal policies in democratic South Africa from the first democratically approved budget of Nelson Mandela's presidency beginning in 1995, through the presidency of Mandela's chosen successor, Thabo Mbeki, to the recent budgets of Jacob Zuma. Intergovernmental revenues (g_F) allocated from national taxation as the constitutionally required equitable share are reported in Columns 1–3, first for the nation as a whole, then for the Western Cape, and finally for an average over the remaining eight ANC- or IFP-majority provinces. Columns 4 and 5 provide estimates for an index of what these provincial revenues can purchase as trained educational and health-care personnel per capita.[17] The index represents productive inputs per capita to provide redistributive public services in the elite and majority provinces, denoted q^E and q^M, respectively. The final three columns of Table 10.1 summarize the aggregate fiscal choices for South Africa's national budget. Column 6 reports the real (2000 rand) level of national taxation per capita, Column 7 the ratio of national taxation to national GDP as an estimate of the aggregate national tax rate on incomes, and Column

17. Provincial budgets per capita are divided by the national average salary for teachers and health-care personnel to give an estimate of "available personnel per capita." National labor negotiations for public employees ensure a common average salary across provinces. Available personnel per capita is then multiplied by an estimate of the average years of training for education and health-care employees in the elite Western Cape and in the average majority-controlled province; 17 years of schooling (university degree) in the elite province and an average of 14.6 years of schooling (associate's degree) in the majority-controlled provinces. See Inman and Rubinfeld (2012).

TABLE 10.1. Redistributive Fiscal Policies in South Africa: Real (2000) Rand per Capita

Fiscal year	President	g_F National average (1)	g_F Western Cape (2)	g_F Majority provinces (3)	q^E Western Cape (4)	q^M Majority provinces (5)	National taxes (6)	National taxes/ GDP (7)	National debt/ GDP (8)
1995/96	Mandela	2,189	2,923	2,119	.56	.44	4,237	.23	.49
1996/97	Mandela	2,030	2,587	1,978	.52	.44	3,938	.24	.48
1997/98[a]	Mandela	2,000	2,424	1,959	.49	.43	3,942	.24	.50
1998/99	Mandela	2,154	2,206	2,149	.55	.55	4,265	.24	.47
1999/2000	Mandela	2,108	2,097	2,110	.54	.54	4,093	.23	.42
2000/2001	Mbeki	2,242	2,185	2,247	.57	.58	6,636	.24	.42
2001/2	Mbeki	2,302	2,196	2,313	.59	.59	5,570	.24	.36
2002/3[b]	Mbeki	1,903	1,720	1,923	.53	.49	5,178	.23	.35
2003/4	Mbeki	2,151	1,896	2,180	.58	.55	5,630	.24	.34
2004/5	Mbeki	2,231	1,941	2,264	.60	.57	5,610	.26	.33
2005/6	Mbeki	2,327	2,011	2,363	.63	.61	5,962	.26	.31
2006/7	Mbeki	2,559	2,186	2,603	.69	.68	6,764	.27	.27
2007/8	Mbeki	2,735	2,293	2,787	.72	.72	7,760	.27	.26
2008/9	Mbeki[c]	3,005	2,522	3,063	.79	.79	7,182	.25	.30
2009/10	Zuma	3,213	2,710	3,273	.85	.85	6,549	.25	.35
2010/11	Zuma	3,514	2,592	3,626	.79	.98	6,828	.25	.38
2011/12	Zuma	3,547	2,785	3,643	.85	.97	7,020	.26	.41

Continued on next page

TABLE 10.1. (*continued*)

Fiscal year	President	g_F National average (1)	g_F Western Cape (2)	g_F Majority provinces (3)	q^E Western Cape (4)	q^M Majority provinces (5)	National taxes (6)	National taxes/ GDP (7)	National debt/ GDP (8)
2012/13	Zuma	3,605	2,976	3,684	.90	.96	7,198	.27	.44
2013/14	Zuma	3,639	3,026	3,717	.90	.95	7,504	.28	.47
2014/15	Zuma	3,603	3,037	3,676	.89	.92	7,687	.29	.49
2015/16	Zuma	3,538	3,131	3,589	.91	.87	7,632	.29	.52
2016/17	Zuma	3,539	3,234	3,578	.92	.86	7,624	.30	.53

Notes: g_F = total intergovernmental transfers per capita paid to the province(s), averaged over all provinces (national average), for the Western Cape, and for all other provinces excluding the Western Cape (average for other provinces); q^E and q^M are estimates of the redistributive service bundle provided in the elite (Western Cape) province and all other majority-run provinces. *National taxes* equals total revenues per capita raised by central government taxation. *National taxes/GDP* is total national taxation divided by GDP. *National debt/GDP* is outstanding national government debt divided by GDP.

[a] Data for fiscal year 1997/98 are based on projected grants provided in South Africa, Financial and Fiscal Commission (1997/98), table 6b. Fiscal years 1995/96–1997/98: South Africa, Financial and Fiscal Commission (1997/98) tables 2, 3, 6b. Fiscal years 1998/99–2016/17: Minister of Finance, *Division of Revenue Bill, Various Years*, Part 4: Provincial Allocations.

[b] Beginning with the fiscal year 2002/3 budget, the Finance Department adjusted the accounting procedures for funding of the provincial activity. All financial data from fiscal year 2002/3 onward are recorded on a consistent basis.

[c] The last Mbeki budget was negotiated with, and implemented by, the new ANC majority under the de facto leadership of Jacob Zuma, but with the presidency held by an interim president, Kgalema Motlanthe. Motlanthe served until May 2009.

8 the ratio of national debt outstanding to GDP. Increases in the national debt have been used to finance current-fiscal-year government services and transfers, thereby postponing the burden of the current budget on GDP. The debt-to-GDP ratio represents a future tax burden on the elite. The ratio of the national average level of intergovernmental transfers reported in Column 1 to national taxation reported in Column 6 is an estimate of the FFC's recommended equitable share. Consistent with the Constitution's commitment to federal governance, the provinces have received, on average, 42 percent of all national tax revenues and, in a few years, as much as 50 percent.[18]

The Mandela and Mbeki Budgets

The Mandela budget for provincial redistributive public services is significantly greater than what had been available under apartheid. Apartheid's homeland payments averaged about 525 rand per capita over the years 1977–1993; the average level of redistributive service inputs in the last years of apartheid was $q = .17$. In contrast, the equitable share from Mandela's first five budgets averaged 2,100 rand per capita in provincial aid, sufficient to finance a threefold increase in the level of redistributive services (q).[19] While showing a significant improvement in redistributive services for South Africa's poor majority, Mandela's budgets also kept his commitment to the economic elite to control elite taxation. The aggregate level of taxation never exceeded 4,300 rand per capita, or about 24 percent of GDP. The tax rate during the last years of apartheid was 21 percent of GDP.

At the end of his presidency, Mandela chose Mbeki as his successor to lead the ANC and, by default, serve as the next president. Mandela's first choice was Cyril Ramaphosa, a young union leader instrumental in organizing a

18. The aggregate equitable share is allocated across provinces, giving extra weight to the share of the province's population that is elderly, of school age, and of lower income; as a result, the wealthier Western Cape receives relatively fewer provincial transfers. The most important component of the formula, known as the "standards" grant, is to finance K–12 educational services and health care for all citizens. The remaining share, known as the "basic" grant, is to be allocated at the discretion of the elected provincial parliaments. Transfers from the national government directly to local governments are not included in the totals in Table 10.1.

19. The higher level of aid and thus redistributive services in the Western Cape in the first three Mandela budgets follows from a decision by the FFC to award "transitional" funding to the Western Cape, particularly for health services, to ease the consequences of the loss of the Western Cape's favored status under apartheid.

"second generation" of supporters for the ANC, but the older ANC leadership preferred Mbeki. Mbeki's presidency was problematic from the start. Corruption among ANC appointed officials was condoned or overlooked.[20] Mbeki denied the importance of the HIV/AIDS epidemic and promoted ineffective herbal treatments for those afflicted. The resulting delays in treatment were blamed for as many as 365,000 avoidable early deaths.[21] The one bright spot, at least initially, was fiscal policy. Mbeki reappointed Mandela's internationally respected minister of finance Trevor Manuel. Under Manuel's economic leadership, nation income grew at its highest rate in over thirty years. The resulting dividend in tax revenues allowed increases in provincial transfers and, particularly important to the international financial markets, a significant reduction in national debt as a share of GDP (Column 8).

Beginning in 2006, however, pressure from the left to significantly increase spending for redistributive services, particularly for public housing, forced Mbeki to deviate from his initial commitment to the Mandela budgets of moderate taxation and redistribution. The average national tax rate was increased from 24 percent to 27 percent used to fund a 30 percent increase in provincial grants for redistributive services.[22] It was not enough. A coalition of the largest private-sector union (Congress of South African Trade Unions, COSATU), the South African Communist Party, and the younger, radical ANC Youth League, led by Julius Malema, forced Mbeki to resign from the presidency of the ANC in 2007, to be replaced by Zuma.[23] In 2009, Zuma was elected president of South Africa. The importance of the political left to Zuma's initial election raised for the first time a serious political challenge to Mandela's fiscal compromise.

The Zuma Budgets

While President Mandela was able to achieve a compromise redistributive budget holding elite taxation at rates only slightly higher than those of the last apartheid budget, Zuma was not so accommodating. Pressure for significant

20. See Rotberg (2014).

21. Celia Duggar, "Study Cites Toll of AIDS Policy in South Africa," *New York Times*, November 25, 2008.

22. Finance Minister Manuel continued to repay national debt, however. In contrast to what was to come under the debt policies of the Zuma presidency, increased redistributive spending was paid for by increased taxation. Manuel resigned as minister of finance in 2009 when Mbeki resigned his presidency.

23. See Bassett and Clarke (2008).

income redistribution has always come from the rank and file of the ANC. The federal compromise of Quadrant I of Figure 10.1 depended on on both parties being sufficiently patient in waiting for the economic benefits of the postapartheid fiscal agreement. In particular, the implicit discount rate for a typical elite resident must be less than .79 and that for a typical majority resident less than .14. The fact that middle- and upper-income households are willing to save and invest in South African ten-year Treasury bonds paying as little as 8 percent suggests that elite residents are sufficiently patient. In contrast, recent studies of the savings behavior of lower-income South Africans suggest their discount rate may be as high as 2![24] While this may seem very high, discount rates of .25 or even .50 for lower-income, perhaps unemployed, South Africans seem reasonable and are certainly greater than what was required from our analysis of Figure 10.1 for continued ANC support of Quadrant I's federal compromise.

Lacking the status of President Mandela or proximity to the very repressive apartheid years for comparison, President Zuma felt significant pressure from within the ANC to transfer incomes and redistributive services to appease the rising impatience of the nation's poor majority. Zuma first official budget appeared in fiscal year (FY) 2009/10 and began an immediate increase in intergovernmental transfers to the provinces for redistributive spending. The average equitable share grant to provinces increased from 3,200 to 3,500 (real) rand per capita, and redistributive services were increased proportionally; see Table 10.1, Columns 1–5 after 2009/10. The increases favored the ANC-controlled provinces through the allocation of discretionary "basic grants." They were financed by an increase in the national average tax rate from 25 percent to 30 percent and, particularly, national debt as a share of GDP, which rose from 35 percent to 53 percent. Zuma's budgets marked the end of the Mandela fiscal compromise.

4. Federalism and the Economic Benefits of the Democratic Transition

South Africa's transition from apartheid to democracy has yielded sizeable economic returns for all citizens of South Africa. As they helped to facilitate this transition, the institutions of Democratic Federalism can rightly claim a

---

24. That is, to give up one rand today, the lower-income South African must be promised three rand next year; see Karlin and Zinman (2008).

TABLE 10.2. South African Economic Growth: 1950–2018

Independent variables	Growth rate (1950–2008) Mean = 1.64 (1)	Growth rate (1950–2008) Mean = 1.64 (2)	Growth rate (1950–2018) Mean = 1.62 (3)	Growth rate (1950–2018) Mean = 1.62 (4)
Constant	1.24	2.09	1.12	2.09
	(.32)*	(.37)*	(.53)*	(.35)*
Democracy	1.78	2.69	1.24	2.69
	(.67)*	(.96)*	(.31)*	(.90)*
COSATU	—	−1.76	—	−1.76
		(.76)*		(.72)*
Sanctions	—	−1.03	—	−1.03
		(.67)		(.62)*
Zuma	—	—	—	−1.30
				(.79)*
Financial crisis	—	—	—	−4.56
				(1.87)*
R^2(Adj)	.09	.26	.05	.27

Notes: The dependent variable is South Africa's annual real rate of growth of GDP per capita. Independent variables include Democracy (=1 for the years 1994–2018; 0 otherwise); COSATU (=1 for the years 1985–2018; 0 otherwise); Sanctions (=1 for the years 1976–1993; 0 otherwise); Zuma (=1, for the years 2011–2018, 0 otherwise); and Financial crisis (=1 for the year 2009; 0 otherwise).
Source: Growth rate is from the OECD, available from the Federal Reserve Bank of St. Louis.
*Significant at the 90 percent level of confidence; standard errors within parentheses.

share of the credit. Table 10.2 details the impact of the transition on the rate of economic growth for the years before the Zuma presidency (1950–2008) and then for all years before and after (1950–2018) his election. The Zuma "years" are for the calendar years 2011–2018, reflecting the years directly influenced by a Zuma budget, beginning with FY 2010. Also included in the full specifications for both the pre- and post-Zuma years are indicator variables for the potential influence of private union bargaining by COSATU beginning in 1985, the presence of political and economic sanctions on South Africa beginning in 1976 after the Soweto demonstrations and ending with the election of Mandela in 1994, and the 2009 world financial crisis. Controlling for exogenous political (sanctions), economic (COSATU), and financial (2009 financial crisis) events, the results in the table show South Africa's federal democracy to have made a significant difference for the growth of income, more than doubling the rate of real income growth from 1.24 percent per year under apartheid (democracy = 0) to 3.02 percent per year or more after the emergence of democratic governance (democracy = 1). Clearly too, the presidency

TABLE 10.3. Net Economic Gains from the Democratic Transition

	ΔV: 70 year horizon	Years until $\Delta V_t \geq 0$	Democracy's internal rate of return
Majority resident			
Unitary democracy	$\Delta V_M(U) = 154{,}300$ rand	0	∞
Federal democracy	$\Delta V_M(F) = 161{,}400$ rand	0	∞
Elite resident			
Unitary democracy	$\Delta V_E(U) = 396{,}000$ rand	4	.27
Federal democracy	$\Delta V_E(F) = 413{,}000$ rand	4	.28

Notes: ΔV: 70 year horizon is the difference between the estimated discounted present value of resident welfare under democracy and under apartheid, where $V = \sum U(q_t, y_t)/(1+r)^t$ for a majority resident and $V = \sum y_t/(1+r)^t$ for an elite resident specified for apartheid, a federal democracy, and a unitary democracy. The social discount rate used in the estimates is .05. The horizon is for $t = 1996$ to 2066. Years until $\Delta V_t \geq 0$ is the number of years until the net present-value gains in after-tax incomes or welfare in moving from apartheid to each form of democracy just exceed zero. Democracy's internal rate of return is the discount rate where net present value of after-tax incomes under democracy is just equal to the net present value of after-tax incomes under apartheid for the 70 year. Since majority welfare is larger under the first year of democracy onward, the internal rate of return is infinite for the majority.

of Zuma had a depressing effect on country growth, lowering the annual rate of growth in real incomes by 1.3 percent during the years of his presidency.[25]

The estimates for democracy's benefits to growth and for the impact of fiscal redistribution on the provision of redistributive services allow us to estimate the long-run economic benefits of the transition from apartheid to democracy for the average majority and elite resident; see Table 10.3. The table reports estimates of the present value for the economic gains from leaving apartheid for either a federal or a unitary democracy, both for majority and elite residents of South Africa, and based on the estimates for majority welfare and elite incomes as reported in Quadrant I of Figure 10.1 for the cooperative outcome under a federal democracy and in Quadrant IV for joint defection becoming a de facto unitary democracy. These initial transition benefits are then increased into perpetuity at the estimated increase in the country's

25. The estimates for the economic benefits of democracy are consistent with the international evidence generally and with the hopes of the ANC and NP leadership as the move to democracy was debated; see Acemoglu et al. (2019) and Waldmeir (1997, pp. 132–133). The strong negative effect of the Zuma presidency might be attributable to the growing reports of corruption in his administration; see South Africa, Development Indicators, (2016), table 3, and Fahad and Ahmed (2016). For the adverse impact of corruption on country growth more generally, see Olken and Pande (2012).

annual rate of growth of 1.8 percent under democracy rather than apartheid.[26] Net benefits for both majority and elite residents have been discounted at an assumed social discount rate of .05.

From the economics alone, the original majority residents gain unequivocally by the transition to democracy, as both their real incomes and their access to redistributive services increase significantly under democracy. Their increase in the discounted present value of economic welfare over that available under a continuation of apartheid is estimated as 161,400 real (2000) rand per majority resident with the adoption of democratic federalism and 154,300 real (2000) rand per majority resident had the new democracy been a unitary government. The slightly lower level of welfare under unitary democracy arises from the lower value of redistributive services under unitary governance following the (assumed) elite reallocation of intergovernmental aid away from redistributive services in the Western Cape. Finally, the majority receives its net benefits immediately, in the first year (1996) of the new democracy, so there is no cost to waiting or any direct financial loss from the transition.

The average elite resident also gains in the long run from the transition from apartheid to democracy. The discounted present value of the economic gains is 413,000 real (2000) rand per elite resident under federal governance and 396,000 real (2000) rand per elite resident under unitary democracy. The gains are lower under unitary governance because of higher taxes on elite residents. Gains are not immediate for the elite resident, however. While incomes increase immediately because of higher growth, taxes under the new democracy also increase. It takes four years before the future gains in income from improved growth offset the initial losses from the increase in taxes. After that, there is a net increase in after-tax incomes for the elite, and these later gains more than offset the initial fall in after-tax incomes. The resulting "internal rate of return" for an elite resident is positive and equals .28 with the adoption of a

---

26. Reestimating the growth equation for the full sample years and "assigning" the influence of COSATU and the international sanctions as part of the overall effect of the apartheid years gives the following effect for the democratic transition on growth as

$$\text{Growth} = 1.24 + 1.80 \cdot \text{DEMOCRACY} - 1.61 \cdot \text{ZUMA} - 4.58 \cdot \text{FINANCIAL CRISIS}$$
$$(.30)^* (.60)^* \qquad\qquad (.82)^* \qquad (2.07)^*$$

where all variables are defined as in Table 10.2 and an asterisk indicates significance at the 90 percent level of confidence; standard errors within parentheses.

federal democracy and .27 with the adoption of a unitary democracy.[27] For both the majority and the elite, democracy has been a "good investment."

Three comments seem in order. First, the estimated present value of welfare gains can be thought of as the increase in lifetime wealth for a majority or elite child born into a democracy in 1996, rather than into apartheid. The gains are driven almost entirely by the improved income growth following the adoption of democracy made possible by the federal compromise. Second, the lifetime economic gains under a federal democracy are greater than those available under a unitary democracy, but only 5 percent greater. The difference is due to the higher level of redistributive services for the majority and the lower national tax rate for the elite that results from federal rather than unitary governance—that is, from the Mandela compromise. Third, if the lifetime economic gains from federal over unitary governance are so modest, why was federal governance so essential to the original democratic agreement between the majority ANC and the elite NP? Why did the NP not agree immediately to a unitary democracy as first proposed by the ANC? The answer is that there was a lack of trust between ANC and NP negotiators and a fear that unitary governance could easily become a unitary autocracy, as in Zimbabwe. As stated by Mandela at the time, the need was for "structural guarantees." The institutions of Democratic Federalism as outlined in the Interim Constitution provided those assurances and allowed the transition to democracy to go forward. Whether these federal institutions can provide sufficient protection for the future of the new democracy is less certain.

5. Federalism and the Consolidation of South Africa's Democracy

Long-run stable democracies require both a *transition* from autocracy to democracy and then the *consolidation* of democracy as the preferred long-run form of governance. Consolidation is said to occur when citizens view

27. Much was made of a possible "peace dividend" from reduced military hostilities following the transition to democracy. While the military expenditures needed to contain the guerrilla war ceased with the transition, spending for police services has risen dramatically since 1995. The increase in police spending has exceeded the decline in military spending. By this comparison, the peace dividend is negative and lowers the net returns to the elite from the transition. Overall net benefits for the elite remain significantly positive, however. See Inman and Rubinfeld (2013).

democracy as "the only game in town."[28] From the perspective of the average citizen or that citizen's representatives, the long-run economic and social outcomes of all "other games" are viewed as inferior to those offered by democratic rule. While there may be short-run gains from seizing political control, there are no guarantees that one's opponents might not seize control back and then impose costs that more than outweigh any short-run gains the temporary control of the government may have offered. Democracy will be consolidated when all major factions within society share this long-run view.[29] Our comparison of the long-run economic benefits of a democratic South Africa with those of apartheid show that this may be the case for South Africa. Whether these long-run benefits are sufficient to hold the democratic compromise in place is not guaranteed.

Zuma's policies after his election in 2014 illustrate how fragile continued democratic governance may be. While his early budgets offered increases in redistributive spending, they failed to address one major consequence of the country's declining rate of economic growth: rising unemployment, particularly among young South Africans.[30] Beginning in 2016, rather than address unemployment directly, Zuma switched his spending strategy from service provision to one of building a political machine based on rising wage payments for public employees, particularly teachers and new hires in state-owned enterprises. Public employee wage increases came at the expense of redistributive service provision, as seen by the fall in available public service inputs in Table 10.1 beginning in 2016, particularly in the ANC-majority provinces. Rather than strengthen Mandela's federal compromise, Zuma's budgets centralized spending and moved decision-making toward a unitary state.

In the face of Zuma's challenge, even restored economic growth might not be sufficient to sustain democracy. What long-run, stable democracies require are regular elections, a realistic chance that the incumbent can lose, and a willingness on the part of the losing incumbent to leave office when that happens. Four institutions are necessary: (1) fixed terms of office with regularly scheduled and fair elections, (2) easy entry of competitive candidates, (3) a

28. Linz and Stepan (1996).

29. The formal analysis that shows when this condition will hold is presented in Weingast (1997) and Acemoglu and Robinson (2006, chap. 7).

30. Current (2019) national rates of unemployment are 55 percent for those less than twenty-four years of age, 31 percent for youths who have graduated from high school, and 27 percent for the economy as a whole.

free press to ensure informed and engaged voters, and (4) the independent enforcement of election outcomes.[31]

To this end, the institutions of Democratic Federalism can play a valuable supplemental role. Both Robert Dahl and Roger Myerson have argued for the importance of politically independent provincial or local governments as protectors of democratic governance. Dahl sees competitive local elections and inclusive local governance as laboratories for learning the ground rules of democracy and as the organizational basis for nationally competitive political parties.[32] Myerson (2006) sees local governments as the "testing grounds" for new political platforms and candidates for national office.[33] First, local governments are likely to have lower barriers to entry for competitive candidates, and second, if a candidate's local policies are successful, they can be mimicked by other candidates in other communities or provinces. From a base of successful local candidates with a common successful platform there might then arise a national candidate or party with a reputation for good governance capable of defeating an autocratic national incumbent. For both Dahl and

31. See Dahl (1998, chap. 8) and Przeworski et al. (2000, chap. 1). Chapter 2 of the South African Constitution explicitly requires conditions 1–3, while Chapter 5 provides for an independent Constitutional Court as needed by requirement 4. The Court's ability to enforce the ground rules of democratic governance will ultimately turn on citizen support. Steytler (2017) and Peekhaus (2014) provide reviews of the important Court decisions protecting free elections, a free press, and, particularly important for the role of federal governance, independent provinces and local governments. Former chief justice of the Constitutional Court Ismael Mohamed appreciated the source of Court support when he commented that the Court's "ultimate power must therefore rest on the esteem in which the judiciary is held within the psyche and soul of the nation" (quoted in Steytler, 2017, p. 345). The Constitutional Court seems to have such support, at least at the moment. Since 1999, the World Values Survey has asked the citizens of South Africa, "Do you have confidence in the justice system/courts?" and those responding a "good deal" or "quite a lot" has never been less than 50 percent and has been as high as 70 percent; see the World Value Survey, Wave 7, Table E069_17, for South Africa. Further, popular support for the Court has been greatest among lower-income households; see Boateng and Makin (2016).

32. See Dahl (1998, p. 88) and his presidential address to the American Political Science Association in Dahl (1967).

33. His argument turns on three assumptions. First, there must be politically and economically independent provincial or local governments. Second, citizens must be able to distinguish the performance of an honest politician from that of a corrupt politician (hence, a free press is essential). Third, and most importantly, there must be a "sufficient" supply of honest politicians with campaign resources, measured by the chance such a politician will run and win. Here the number of independent provincial local governments is important.

TABLE 10.4.

A: Local Efficiency and Local Voting

	Local DA Vote Share, 2016	
	ANC Provinces .16 (.13) (1)	Western Cape .54 (.11) (2)
Efficiency, 2015	.082 (.022)*	.269 (.153)*
DA Vote Share, 2011	.788 (.051)*	.735 (.189)*
Pop. Density	.021 (.015)	−.113 (.053)*
% > 65	.624 (.306)*	−.964 (.923)
% University	−.005 (.165)	.281 (.602)
% Owner	−.062 (.041)	.042 (.184)
Constant	.005 (.026)	−.036 (.149)
Sample Size	168	25
R² (Adj)	.82	.58

Note: Mean values (standard deviation) of the dependent variables are reported in each column. An * indicates statistical significance at the .90 level of confidence or higher with standard errors reported in parentheses.

B: Local Voting and National Elections

	Provincial DA Share, 2014 National Election .22 (.17)	Provincial DA Share, 2019 National Election .22 (.15)
DA Share, 2011 Local Election	.382 (.191)*	—
DA Share, 2009 National Election	.763 (.192)*	—
DA Share, 2016 Local Election	—	−.056 (.421)
DA Share, 2014 National Election	—	.916 (.367)*
Constant	.018 (.015)	.036 (.023)
Sample Size	9	9
R² (Adj)	.98	.96

Note: Mean values (standard deviation) of the dependent variables are reported in each column. An * indicates statistical significance at the .90 level of confidence or higher with standard errors reported in parentheses.

Myerson, politically independent and competitive local governments provide a stable foundation for a consolidated democratic state.[34]

The 2017 decision to replace Zuma as head of the ANC provides anecdotal evidence for the Dahl-Myerson argument. The growing electoral success of the Western Cape–based DA in the national elections of 2014 and that of the newly formed Economic Freedom Fighters and the DA in the municipal elections of 2016 demonstrated Zuma's inability to hold the ANC's political base with an approaching 2019 national election. Coupled with Zuma's pending indictments for corruption in a 1999 arms sale and for influence peddling with cabinet appointments, these local election successes were enough to force his resignation.[35] His replacement as head of the ANC was Cyril Ramaphosa. Ramaphosa had been a close and favored subordinate of Mandela's—indeed, Mandela's choice as his successor—and became a successful businessman after leaving politics following his loss to Mbeki in the election for head of the ANC. With the 2019 national elections approaching, the ANC leadership felt Ramaphosa could best hold together the established ANC coalition and counter the growing support among the middle class for the DA.

Table 10.4, Panels A and B, tests the Dahl-Myerson hypothesis more directly. Panel A seeks to understand the source of the DA's political success in the 168 municipalities in the ANC provinces and in the 25 municipalities of the Western Cape. Panel B then relates that local success to subsequent DA vote gains in the national elections for provincial party representation to the National Assembly. It will be that representation that elects the president.

Much of the DA's local election gains shown in Panel A have come from the DA's promise for efficient local governance and its ability to deliver on that promise. This is seen by the impact of an outside evaluation of each local government's relative efficiency in delivering local services (Efficiency, 2015) on the DA vote share in its 2016 local elections, conditional on the DA vote share in the last local election (DA vote share, 2011) and four community controls from the 2010 census: population density, the percentage of the population

---

34. Historical cross-national evidence provides support for their conclusion. Boix's (2003, pp. 162–169) study of democratic stability from 1850 to 1980 finds that federal governance leads to significantly lower rates of democratic "breakdown." Perhaps encouraging for South Africa is the fact that the effects of federal governance are strongest in nations with large rural populations.

35. See "In Family's Rise and Fall, a Tale Rift with Graft," *New York Times*, December 23, 2018.

over sixty-five years old, the percentage of the population that graduated from university, and the rate of home ownership.[36] Results are presented for local governments in ANC-controlled provinces and in the Western Cape. The DA has been rewarded with higher vote shares for improved local government efficiency in both sets of provinces, in the Western Cape where the DA typically has a local majority but also in the ANC provinces were the DA is in a local minority. A one-standard-deviation improvement in a community's efficiency ranking (say, from the median to the sixtieth percentile, or a .10 improvement in the ranking) increased the DA share of votes by about 1 percent in ANC controlled provinces ($= .1 \times .082$) and by 3 percent in the Western Cape ($= .1 \times .269$). In all provinces the gains in the DA vote shares came almost exclusively from losses by the ANC.[37]

While local politics rewards the DA for locally efficient service delivery, that local success has not always translated into significant improvements in national election performance; see Table 10.4, Panel B. Even large gains for the DA at the local level do not appear to be enough to significantly challenge the ANC's domination of national elections. At best we might expect each increment in the DA's province-wide vote share in local elections to translate into an equal increment in the DA's province-wide vote share in national elections. Panel B provides estimates for the effects of the share of DA votes in local elections in each of the nine provinces on each province's share of votes for the DA in a subsequent national election. Each regression includes lagged values of the DA share in the previous national election as a control. The

36. The measure of local government efficiency is the Good Governance Africa Government Performance Index for 2015. The index uses citizen evaluation to rank each municipality on fifteen separate indicators of performance in the broad categories of government administration (specifically, extent of local corruption), economic development, and service delivery. Municipalities are ranked nationally by their overall average score, which we have converted to an efficiency index with a score of 1.0 for the nationally most efficient local community and a score of 0 for the least efficient community. DA communities dominate the upper end of the overall efficiency ranking. ANC-controlled communities had an average efficiency ranking of .44, while the DA-controlled communities had an average index rank of .88. The index can be interpreted as either an ordinal or cardinal ranking. If ordinal, it will provide a basis for "yardstick competition" between governments. If cardinal, it can be interpreted as a direct measure of local government "output."

37. The Economic Freedom Fighters, as a third party, did draw votes from the ANC vote share in the ANC provinces, but that was only in a handful of communities and the overall share of votes gained was relatively small.

impact of local DA voting success on national outcomes is much less than one for one. In the 2014 election, each 1 percent gain in the DA's local vote earned the DA .38 percent gain in its party representation in the National Assembly. Even more discouraging for the DA are the 2019 results. Despite the ANC's public concern for the DA's growing success in the 2016 local elections, the DA's larger local vote in 2016 had no significant impact on aggregate support for the DA in the 2019 national election.

Two possible explanations suggest themselves for the inability of the DA to leverage its local success to national election success. First, organizing for national elections is more difficult than for local elections, and here the ANC has inherited significant advantages in both resources and voter loyalty. Overcoming the ANC's advantages will require the DA to become a truly national political party, one capable of tying together its local successes into a national political organization.[38] Second, national elections may be less about government efficiency—the DA's comparative advantage as revealed in local elections—and more about economic equity and jobs. In the 2019 elections, the Economic Freedom Fighters seized that advantage by championing land reform, industry nationalization, and job creation.[39] To be successful nationally, the DA's platform will need to appeal to South Africa's unemployed young adults while not alienating its middle-class base. One strategy playing to the DA's reputational strength for efficient governance might be to promise to move aggressively against inefficient and corrupt ANC-dominated state enterprises and then allocate those savings to training and job placement policies.[40] Addressing both the need for a national organization and a nationally attractive platform seem essential if the DA is to become a successful national political party capable of challenging the ANC in national elections. The long-run consolidation and future of South Africa's democracy may depend on it.

38. See Riker (1964, pp. 91–101) and Filippov, Ordeshook, and Shvetsova (2004, chap. 6). The early history of the U.S. Democratic Party provides an example for creating a national party from local organizations; see Aldrich (2011, chap. 5).

39. With their aggressive redistributive platform, the Economic Freedom Fighters' vote share rose from 6 percent in 2014 to 11 percent in 2019. All the gains came at the expense of the ANC, whose vote share fell from 62 percent in 2014 to 57 percent in 2019.

40. The World Bank (2019), in conjunction with South Africa's National Planning Commission and leaders from private industry and private unions, has developed an initial proposal incorporating such policies.

6. Summing Up

South Africa's successful transition from apartheid and autocratic rule to a functioning democracy stands as one of the most significant political achievements of the last century. The Constitution approved in 1996 remains firmly in place as the new democracy's guiding document. It is a federal constitution creating nine provincial governments with independently elected provincial parliaments and local governments, and it protects policy responsibility and fiscal resources of both levels of government.

The Constitution's federal structure was central to the original democratic agreement. It defined the rules for a policy game in which a (likely, ANC) national majority would hold power over elite after-tax incomes, while elite provincial and local governments would hold power over the provision of redistributive services important to the majority. As long as a sufficient number of majority citizens reside within elite-controlled provinces (the border constraint), and provincial services are economically important to the majority (the assignment constraint), then the majority and elite coalitions each have the ability to check the potential policy excesses of the other—the national government's temptation to set maximal tax rates and the elite provincial government's temptation to allocate assigned national revenues only to middle-class services or tax relief. The result has been a constitutionally created hostage game in fiscal policies that, at least to date, has supported a federal compromise with moderate national taxation and the relatively efficient provision of redistributive services to poor majority residents. In the end, both majority and elite residents have enjoyed significant economic benefits over what might have been available with the continuation of apartheid.

While still in place, the transition's negotiated federal compromise is a fragile compact. A small loss in the ability of elite-controlled provinces to be efficient providers of redistributive services or a small increase in the desire of the majority to tax elite resident incomes will undo the elite's ability to check the majority's temptation for maximal taxation. The Constitution's assignment of fiscal responsibilities and provincial boundaries—James Madison's "parchment barriers"—may no longer be enough to hold the federal compromise in place. If not, the predicted outcome will be de facto unitary governance, maximal income taxation, and the risk of confiscation of private property. South Africa will no longer be able to provide what Mandela had promised at the inception of the new democracy: federally created "structural guarantees" to reassure the economic elite that their property and civil rights will be protected. As Zuma's presidency made clear, it may not be a long step from a federal democracy to unitary governance and finally to autocracy. The removal of Zuma as head of the ANC has therefore been a promising sign for South Africa's democratic future. It was motivated by the growing political success of the DA in local elections generally, and the Western Cape specifically.

As the institutions of Democratic Federalism facilitated South Africa's transition to democracy, so too might they contribute to the democracy's consolidation. Politically independent provincial and local governments provide a training ground for being democratic, as argued by Robert Dahl, and a testing ground for honest and credible national candidates, as argued by Roger Myerson. The DA's success in fostering local public efficiency and the ability of that agenda to win growing local support for the DA provide evidence for Dahl's and Myerson's faith in local governance.[41] We should place less confidence in their hope that this local success will lead to competitive national politics. As yet, the DA's local success has generated neither the national political organization nor the compelling national platform needed to challenge the ANC's dominance of national politics.

Democratic Federalism made possible South Africa's transition to democracy. Whether Democratic Federalism can secure South Africa's democratic future is less certain.

---

41. And perhaps because of this performance, for a continued faith in democratic governance more generally, even in the face of Zuma's abuses. The most recent survey of citizen preferences for governance shows that a clear majority of South Africans prefer the current democratic rule to the alternatives of military rule (67 percent prefer democracy), one-party rule (72 percent prefer democracy), one-man rule (77 percent prefer democracy), or a return to apartheid (80 percent prefer democracy). See "Support for Democracy in South Africa Declines amid Rising Discontent with Implementation," *Afro Barometer*, Dispatch No. 71, February 9, 2016.

11

Epilogue

FEDERAL GOVERNANCE, with responsibilities and authority divided among a central government and a number of decentralized political units, has become the polity of choice both for emerging democracies and for established states undergoing economic and democratic reforms. Not only have the last century's new democracies in Argentina, Brazil, and South Africa chosen to use a federal form of government, but so too has the European Union as it seeks to unite and coordinate the long-run policy and diplomatic interests of the many independent European nations. Centralized political states as different as China and Norway are now discovering that the institutions of federal governance offer new channels for implementing major economic reforms. Our task here has been to understand exactly how federal governance might enhance the performance of the democratic state.

From Adam Smith, Montesquieu, and James Madison to today's prominent scholars, as exemplified by the writings of Wallace Oates, William Riker, and Akhil Reed Amar, economists, political scientists, and legal scholars have long appreciated the potential benefits of federal democratic governance. The anticipated benefits are a more efficient government for the provision of citizen-demanded goods and services, greater political and civic engagement when making government decisions, and finally, greater protections for individual rights and liberties. A valued by-product of a more efficient and respectful government is a more efficient and dynamic private economy. Chapter 1 presented evidence that these anticipated benefits are correlated with democratic federal governance for a sample of seventy-three countries for the period 1965–2000. While strongly suggestive of the benefits of federal governance, the empirical work itself does not establish a causal link between the institutions of what we have called Democratic Federalism and socially valued outcomes. Our theoretical analysis has pointed to two particularly important institutions that distinguish a federal democracy from its most important alternative, unitary democratic governance. The first is politically independent and democratically elected local and provincial governments with constitutionally protected policy and revenue responsibilities. The second is democratically elected local or provincial representation to the national legislature. A unitary democracy governed by a nationally elected president or legislature has neither. Our task here has been to understand how Democratic Federalism's two local institutions can improve the performance of democratic governance.

Efficiency in the provision of government services is potentially enhanced by both. What we have called Economic Federalism in Chapter 2 utilizes local governments. Chapter 2 showed that local and provincial governments can significantly improve the efficient provision of local public goods through fiscal competition when setting both the level of public services and local tax rates. What are not efficiently allocated by local or provincial governments are public services showing significant economies of scale and local public goods having spillovers between governments. Taking us a step further, Chapter 3 outlined the potential through Cooperative Federalism for affected local and provincial governments to jointly cooperate for the efficient provision of such public goods. Mutual agreements are not always possible, however, as bargaining governments have incentives both to conceal their true gains from cooperation and to disagree on how to fairly divide a potential agreement's costs and benefits. The most prominent example of Cooperative Federalism is the European Union, as illustrated in Chapter 9. To date, the EU's customs union has provided significant economic benefits to member states from the reductions in market regulations and trade barriers, both resulting in greater mobility of capital and labor across national borders and improved EU-wide rates of economic growth. Because of disagreements as to how to divide costs and benefits, however, the EU has been much less successful in addressing fiscal and financial spillovers between member states and the problem of ensuring a common border for immigration enforcement.

When unanimous agreements are not possible, perhaps majority rule is an effective alternative for the provision of large-scale public goods and for managing cross-community spillovers? The institutions of Democratic Federalism offer one such strategy. Chapters 4 and 5 considered how the representation of local and provincial governments to a majority-rule national legislature might better provide for national public goods and better manage wide-scale local spillovers. For the provision of goods and services such as national defense and monetary policy that affect all citizens equally, we expect to see little difference from what would be provided by a democratically elected unitary government. For both federal and unitary governance, such services will meet the demands of the country's median or majority voter. Local representation matters, however, for how the national legislature allocates divisible public services such as infrastructure or how it might differentially regulate the activities of local and provincial jurisdictions. On the one hand, local representation will improve the allocation of spillover services because collective actions can be enforced with decisions still responsive to local interests. But as noted in Chapter 4, local representation also creates incentives to abuse the national tax base through the inefficient overprovision of local public services without spillovers. Chapter 5 provides for federal safeguards against this local abuse through a more inclusive provincially elected senate, a nationally elected president, and nationally representative political parties. Together, the result is a more efficient and responsive national government.

Democratic Federalism's use of locally elected governments for the provision of local public services, and locally elected representation to the national government, also appears to encourage political participation and civic engagement. Through the local governments of Economic Federalism, citizens have higher rates of voter participation, are more knowledgeable about candidates and local issues, and show greater trust in their elected local officials. They are also more engaged in informal political activities. This is true in the United States and in Germany, Mexico, Sweden, Switzerland, Norway, and Denmark. Further, and particularly important for national minorities, local governance allows for the possibility of "majority-minority" electorates. As a result, government services in those communities are more equitably allocated. Through the representative institutions of Democratic Federalism, local representatives to the national legislature also provide, as James Madison had hoped, a voice for minorities in national politics. Minority representatives from majority-minority legislative districts can lead to more equitable allocations of divisible, national government services. Finally, the ability of citizens to directly contact their locally elected national representatives through the "personal vote" provides another responsive channel for democratic engagement. What local governance and local representation have not been able to do is ensure the franchise for the disenfranchised. But here again Democratic Federalism can call on a strong presidency and strong political parties for assistance.

Local governance and local representation may have their most important impacts on the protection of individual rights and liberties. The local economies of Economic Federalism provide workers, families, and mobile capital with protections against local exploitation. If exploited, residents and businesses can relocate to a more hospitable location. To illustrate, the exodus of African Americans from the South to the North after World War I increased significantly both their economic and political freedoms. Even without mobility, observing the benefits of increased rights for minorities has created demands for comparable freedoms among neighboring communities. Local U.S. communities and states have been the prime movers for increased personal liberties for members of the LGBTQ community.

Associations of local governments through Cooperative Federalism provide an additional layer of protection for property rights when providing national public goods or addressing spillovers. Citizens represented by a local government need not join an alliance unless the alliance provides economic benefits greater than the taxes taken to cover economic costs. As we have seen in Chapter 9, the European Union has leveraged the significant economic benefits from its alliance as a customs union to win human rights reforms from the former dictatorships of eastern Europe. Most recently, the threat of disenfranchisement or expulsion from the EU leveled against Poland following its recent interference with judicial appointments and policies has led to the partial restoration of Polish court independence.

Importantly, all these gains in rights through the institutions of Democratic Federalism have come voluntarily, without violence or by denying rights to initial oppressors. Perhaps the most dramatic example of the ability of federal institutions to peacefully advance human rights is the transition from apartheid to democracy in South Africa, as described in Chapter 10. South Africa adopted the institutions of Democratic Federalism to provide the assurances needed by whites and the economic elite that the new African majority would not nationalize white-owned industries or farms or set maximally redistributive tax rates. The federally enforced fiscal compromise first championed by Nelson Mandela has remained in place. As a result, the South African economy has enjoyed twenty-five years of peace and, for most South Africans, economic prosperity.

As we hope our analysis makes clear, Democratic Federalism's use of independent local governments and local representation to the national legislature has much to recommend it as a way to manage a democracy. Both institutions are important. Fully successful Democratic Federalism requires local governments and local representation to efficiently meet citizen demands for local goods, to encourage democratic participation, and to protect individuals' property and civil rights. That said, a nationally elected president, a more inclusive national senate, and nationally focused political parties will also be required to check, as for government efficiency, or to enhance, as for political participation and the protection of rights, the performance of federalism's local institutions. But in adding a national president, a senate, and national political parties, we may unwittingly undermine the ability of local governments and local representation to do their jobs. Given the policy advantages of national governments, not the least of which are an army and taxation, the institutions of national governance "may overawe," in William Riker's words (1964, p. 50), the institutions of local governance. If so, Democratic Federalism may evolve to a *de facto* unitary state.

The only effective response to this risk is to give national officials a vested interest in the benefits of local governance. To do so, those who vote for national officials must understand and value local governance. Chapters 6, 7, and 8 sought to provide a means to that understanding. Chapter 6, through the guidance of a Federalism Impact Statement, or FIST, outlined the steps required for an informed national conversation on how to balance the relative merits of local and national federal governance. Chapters 7 and 8 provided applications of FIST for debating and deciding the assignment of fiscal and regulatory policies to the separate tiers of government. Like an expanded principle of subsidiarity, FIST is meant to be an early warning beacon for when the local institutions of Democratic Federalism are at risk.

For all its virtues, Democratic Federalism need not be for everyone, a fact made most evident with the immediate dissolution of the once federal states of Yugoslavia, Czechoslovakia, and the Soviet Union when they were given the chance to design their own democratic constitutions. History provides other examples: the bloody efforts at secession by the eleven slave states of the U.S. South from the free North in 1861, the 1947 partitioning of once British India into the independent Hindu state of India and the Muslim state of Pakistan, and the secession of the Bengali Bangladesh from East Pakistan in 1971. More recently and after decades of civil war, the largely Christian South Sudan voted in 2011 to secede from the predominantly Muslim Sudan. The new democratic nation of Iraq, governed at least in principle by federal institutions, hopes to balance the competing interests of the Kurds in the north, the Sunni Muslims centered in and around Bagdad, and Shiites from the south; its future as a federal democracy remains uncertain. The common feature of each example is a long-standing and deep distrust of others whose cooperation is required for an effective federal democracy. Lacking an ability to cooperate, and perhaps fearing military domination by the largest common population, separation into independent nations may be preferable. At the other extreme will be nation-states whose citizens share nearly identical tastes and values and for whom the institutions of Democratic Federalism may be superfluous and an unnecessary expense. If we all agree, there may be little added economic or political value from using the local institutions of Democratic Federalism beyond what is possible from a well-run and honest national legislature and bureaucracy.

The case for Democratic Federalism will then be the most persuasive for new and evolving democratic states where citizen preferences for public goods and services vary but where there is sufficient goodwill and respect for such differences that compromise is possible. It will be for these societies that the local institutions that define Democratic Federalism might offer their greatest value. How to design, administer, and protect these institutions has been our agenda here.

BIBLIOGRAPHY

Acemoglu, Daron (2003), "Why Not a Political Coase Theorem? Social Conflict, Commitment, and Politics," *Journal of Comparative Economics*, 31 (December), 620–652.

Acemoglu, Daron (2005), "Constitutions, Politics, and Economics: A Review Essay on Persson and Tabellini's *The Economic Effects of Constitutions*," *Journal of Economic Literature*, 43 (December), 1025–1048.

Acemoglu, Daron, Simon Johnson, and James Robinson (2001), "The Colonial Origins of Comparative Development," *American Economic Review*, 91 (December), 1369–1401.

Acemoglu, Daron, Suresh Naidu, Pascual Restrepo, and James Robinson (2019), "Democracy Does Cause Growth," *Journal of Political Economy*, 127 (1), 47–100.

Acemoglu, Daron, and James Robinson (2006), *Economic Origins of Dictatorships and Democracy*, Cambridge University Press, New York.

Ackerman, Bruce (1991), *We the People: Foundations*, Harvard University Press, Cambridge, MA.

Ackerman, Bruce, and Ian Ayres (2002), *Voting with Dollars: A New Paradigm for Campaign Financing*, Yale University Press, New Haven, CT.

Adamolekun, Ladipo (2005), "The Nigerian Federation at the Crossroads: The Way Forward," *Publius: The Journal of Federalism*, 35 (Summer), 383–405.

Adler, E. Scott, and John Lapinski (1997), "Demand-Side Theory and Congressional Committee Composition: A Constituency Characteristics Approach," *American Journal of Political Science*, 41 (July), 895–918.

Aksoy, Deniz (2010), "Who Gets What, When, and How Revisited: Voting and Proposal Powers in the Allocation of the EU Budget," *European Union Politics*, 11 (June), 171–194.

Aksoy, Deniz (2012), "Institutional Arrangements and Logrolling: Evidence from the European Union," *American Journal of Political Science*, 56 (July), 538–552.

Albouy, David (2012), "Evaluating the Efficiency and Equity of Federal Fiscal Equalization," *Journal of Public Economics*, 96 (October), 824–839.

Albouy, David (2013), "Partisan Representation in Congress and the Geographic Distribution of Federal Funds," *Review of Economics and Statistics*, 95 (March), 127–141.

Aldrich, John (2011), *Why Parties? A Second Look*, University of Chicago Press, Chicago.

Alesina, Alberto, and Enrico Spolaore (2005), *The Size of Nations*, MIT Press, Cambridge, MA.

Alesina, Alberto, Guido Tabellini, and Francesco Trebbi (2017), "Is Europe an Optimal Political Area?," *Brookings Papers on Economic Activity*, Spring, 169–234.

Allen, Chris, Michael Gasiorek, and Alasdair Smith (1998), "European Single Market: How the Program Has Fostered Competition," *Economic Policy*, 11 (October), 441–486.

Allen, Franklin, and Douglas Gale (2007), *Understanding Financial Crises*, Oxford University Press, New York.

Alston, Philip, and Joseph H. Weiler (1998), "An 'Ever Closer Union' in Need of a Human Rights Policy," *European Journal of International Law*, 9 (4), 658–723.

Amar, Akhil Reed (1987), "Of Sovereignty and Federalism," *Yale Law Journal*, 96 (June), 1425–1520.

Anderson, Karen (2010), *Little Rock: Race and Resistance at Central High School*, Princeton University Press, Princeton, NJ.

Andrews, Matthew, William Duncombe, and John Yinger (2002), "Revisiting Economics of Size in American Education: Are We Any Closer to a Consensus?," *Economics of Education Review*, 21 (June), 245–262.

Andriamananjara, Soamiely (2011), "Customs Unions," in Jean-Pierre Chauffour and Jean-Christophe Maur (eds.), *Preferential Trade Agreement Policies for Development: A Handbook*, World Bank, Washington, DC, 111–120.

Ansolabehere, Stephen, Alan Gerber, and James Snyder (2002), "Equal Votes, Equal Money: Court-Ordered Redistricting and Public Expenditures in the American States," *American Political Science Review*, 96 (December), 767–777.

Ansolabehere, Stephen, James Snyder, and Charles Stewart (2001), "The Effects of Party and Preferences on Congressional Roll-Call Voting," *Legislative Studies Quarterly*, 26 (November), 533–572.

Ardagna, Silvia, and Francesco Caselli (2014), "The Political Economy of the Greek Debt Crisis: A Tale of Two Bailouts," *American Economic Journal: Macroeconomics*, 6 (October), 291–323.

Aristotle (1958), *The Politics of Aristotle*, edited by Ernest Barker, Oxford University Press, Oxford.

Armingeon, Klaus, and Lucio Baccaro (2012), "The Sorrows of Young Euro: The Sovereign Debt Crisis of Ireland and Southern Europe," in Nancy Bermeo and Jonas Pontusson (eds.), *Coping with Crisis: Government Reactions to the Great Recession*, Russell Sage Foundation, New York, 162–197.

Arnott, Richard, and Ronald Grieson (1981), "Optimal Fiscal Policy for a State and Local Government," *Journal of Urban Economics*, 9 (January), 21–48.

Arpaia, Alfonso, and Karl Pichelmann (2007), "Nominal and Real Wage Flexibility in EMU," *International Economics and Economic Policy*, 4 (November), 299–325.

Arrow, Kenneth (1951), *Social Choice and Individual Values*, Yale University Press, New Haven, CT.

Ash, Timothy (2012), "The Crisis in Europe: How the Union Came Together and Why It's Falling Apart," *Foreign Affairs*, 91 (October), 2–15.

Asplund, Marcus, Richard Friberg, and Fredrik Wilander (2007), "Demand and Distance: Evidence on Cross-Border Shopping," *Journal of Public Economics*, 91 (February), 141–157.

Atkeson, Lonna Rae, and Randall W. Partin (1995), "Economic and Referendum Voting: A Comparison of Gubernatorial and Senatorial Elections," *American Political Science Review*, 89 (1) (March), 99–10.

Atlas, Cary, Thomas Gilligan, Robert Hendershott, and Mark Zupan (1995), "Slicing the Federal Government New Spending Pie: Who Wins, Who Loses, and Why," *American Economic Review*, 85 (June), 624–629.

Auerbach, Alan, and Yuriy Gorodnichenko (2013), "Output Spillovers from Fiscal Policy," *American Economic Review: Papers and Proceedings*, 103 (May), 141–146.

Auerbach, Alan, and Laurence Kotlikoff (1987), *Dynamic Fiscal Policy*, Cambridge University Press, New York.

Auerbach, Alan, and Joel Slemrod (1997), "The Economic Effects of the Tax Reform Act of 1986," *Journal of Economic Literature*, 35 (June), 589–632.

Baerg, Nicole, and Mark Hallerberg (2016), "Explaining Instability in the Stability and Growth Pact: The Contribution of Member State Power and Euroskepticism to the Euro Crisis," *Comparative Political Studies*, 49 (June), 968–1009.

Bagchi, Sutirtha (2017), "Do Unfunded Pension Obligations Get Capitalized into House Prices?," working paper, Villanova University, Department of Economics, Villanova, PA.

Bagwell, Kyle, and Robert Staiger (2005), "Enforcement, Private Political Pressure, and the General Agreement on Tariffs, and Trade/World Trade Organization Escape Clause," *Journal of Legal Studies*, 34 (June), 471–513.

Bagwell, Kyle, and Robert Staiger (2010), "The World Trade Organization: Theory and Practice," *Annual Review of Economics*, 2010, 223–256.

Baicker, Katherine (2005), "The Spillover Effects of State Spending," *Journal of Public Economics*, 89 (February), 529–544.

Baird, Zoe (1986), "State Empowerment after Garcia," *The Urban Lawyer*, 18 (Summer), 491–517.

Baker, Lynn, and Ernest Young (2001), "Federalism and the Double Standard of Judicial Review," *Duke Law Journal*, 51 (October), 75–164.

Baldwin, Richard, Joseph Francois, and Richard Portes (1997), "The Costs and Benefits of Eastern Enlargement: The Impact on the EU and Central Europe," *Economic Policy*, 42 (April), 127–176.

Baldwin, Richard, and Charles Wyplosz (2004), *The Economics of Integration*, 4th ed., McGraw Hill, Boston.

Baqir, Reza (2002), "Districting and Government Overspending," *Journal of Political Economy*, 110 (December), 1318–1354.

Barankay, Iwan, and Ben Lockwood (2007), "Decentralization and the Productive Efficiency of Government: Evidence from Swiss Cantons," *Journal of Public Economics*, 91 (June), 1197–1218.

Bardhan, Pranab, and Dilip Mookherjee (eds.) (2006), *Decentralization and Local Governance in Developing Economies: A Comparative Perspective*, MIT Press, Cambridge, MA.

Baron, David (1990), "Distributive Politics and the Persistence of Amtrak," *Journal of Politics*, 52 (August), 883–913.

Baron, David, and John Ferejohn (1989), "Bargaining in Legislatures," *American Political Science Review*, 83 (December), 1181–1206.

Barrell, Ray, Sylvia Gottschalk, Dawn Holland, Ehsan Khoman, Iana Liadze, and Olga Pomerantz (2008), "The Impact of EMU on Growth and Employment," working paper, National Institute of Economic and Social Research, London, March.

Barrett, Scott (1994), "Self-Enforcing International Environmental Agreements," *Oxford Economic Papers*, 46 (October), 878–894.

Barro, Robert (1979), "On the Determination of the Public Debt," *Journal of Political Economy*, 87 (October), 940–971.

Barro, Robert, and Jong-Wha Lee (2001), "International Data on Educational Attainment: Updates and Implications," *Oxford Economic Papers*, 53 (July), 541–563.

Barseghyan, Levon, and Stephen Coate (2016), "Property Taxation, Zoning, and Efficiency: A Dynamic Analysis," *American Economic Journal: Policy*, 8 (February), 1–38.

Bartels, Larry M. (2000), "Partisanship and Voting Behavior, 1952–1996," *American Journal of Political Science*, 44 (January), 35–50.

Bartels, Larry, Joshua Clinton, and John Greer (2014), "Representation," in Richard Valelly, Suzanne Mettler, and Robert Lieberman (eds.), *The Oxford Handbook of American Political Development*, Oxford University Press, New York, 399–424.

Bassett, Carolyn, and Marlea Clarke (2008), "The Zuma Affair, Labour and the Future of Democracy in South Africa," *Third World Quarterly*, 29 (4), 787–803.

Bayer, Patrick, and Robert McMillan (2012), "Tiebout Sorting and Neighborhood Stratification," *Journal of Public Economics*, 96 (11), 1129–1143.

Bayoumi, Tamim, and Paul Masson (1995), "Fiscal Flows in the United States and Canada: Lessons for Monetary Union in Europe," *European Economic Review*, 39 (February), 253–274.

Bebchuk, Lucian (1992), "Federalism and the Corporation: The Desirable Limits on State Competition in Corporate Law," *Harvard Law Review*, 105 (May), 1435–1510.

Becker, Sascha, Peter Egger, and Maximilian von Ehrlich (2018), "Effects of EU Regional Policy: 1989–2013," *Regional Science and Urban Economics*, 69 (March), 143–152.

Becker, Sascha, Thiemo Fetzer, and Dennis Novy (2017), "Who Voted for Brexit? A Comprehensive District-Level Analysis," *Economic Policy*, 32 (October), 601–650.

Bednar, Jenna (2009), *The Robust Federation: Principles of Design*, Cambridge University Press, New York.

Beer, Samuel (1976), "Adoption of General Revenue Sharing: A Case Study in Public Sector Politics," *Public Policy*, 24 (Spring), 127–195.

Beer, Samuel (1978), "Federalism, Nationalism, and Democracy in America," *American Political Science Review*, 72 (March), 9–21.

Beer, Samuel (1993), *To Make a Nation: The Rediscovery of American Federalism*, Harvard University Press, Cambridge, MA.

Beetsma, Roel, and Massimo Giuliodori (2011), "The Effects of Government Purchases Shocks: Review and Estimates for the EU," *Economic Journal*, 121 (February), F4–F32.

Berglöf, Erik, Barry Eichengreen, Gerard Roland, Guido Tabellini, and Charles Wyplosz (2003), *Built to Last: A Political Architecture for Europe*, Centre for Economic Policy Research, London.

Bergstrom, Ted (1979), "When Does Majority Rule Supply Public Goods Efficiently?," *Scandinavian Journal of Economics*, 81 (February), 216–226.

Bergstrom, Theodore, Judith Roberts, Daniel L. Rubinfeld, and Perry Shapiro (1988), "A Test for Efficiency in the Supply of Public Education," *Journal of Public Economics*, 35 (April), 289–307.

Berlin, Isaiah (1969), "Two Concepts of Liberty," in I. Berlin, *Four Essays on Liberty*, Oxford University Press.

Bermann, George (1994), "Taking Subsidiarity Seriously: Federalism in the European Community and the United States," *Columbia Law Review*, 94 (March), 331–456.

Bermann, George (1999), "Judicial Enforcement of Federalism Principles," in M. Kloper and I. Pernice (eds.), *Entwicklungsperspektiven der europaischen Verfassung im Lichte des Vertags von Amsterdam*, Nomos Verlagsgesellschaft, Baden-Baden, Germany, 64–75.

Besley, Timothy (1988), "A Simple Model for Merit Good Arguments," *Journal of Public Economics*, 35 (April), 371–383.

Besley, Timothy, and Anne C. Case (1995), "Incumbent Behavior, Vote Seeking, Tax Setting, and Yardstick Competition," *American Economic Review*, 85 (March), 25–45.

Besley, Timothy, and Stephen Coate (1997), "An Economic Model of Representative Democracy," *Quarterly Journal of Economics*, 112 (February), 85–116.

Besley, Timothy, and Stephen Coate (1998), Sources of Inefficiency in a Representative Democracy: A Dynamic Analysis," *American Economic Review*, 88 (March), 139–156.

Besley, Timothy, and Stephen Coate (2003a), "Centralized versus Decentralized Provision of Local Public Goods: A Political Economy Approach," *Journal of Public Economics*, 87 (December), 3611–2637.

Besley, Timothy, and Stephen Coate (2003b), "Elected vs. Appointed Regulators: Theory and Evidence," *Journal of the European Economic Association*, 1 (September), 1176–1205.

Besley, Timothy, and Stephen Coate (2008), "Issue Unbundling via Citizen Initiatives," *Quarterly Journal of Political Science*, 3 (November), 379–397.

Besley, Timothy, Ian Preston, and Michael Ridge (1997), "Fiscal Anarchy in the UK: Modeling Poll Tax Noncompliance," *Journal of Public Economics*, 64 (May), 137–152.

Besley, Timothy, and Harvey Rosen (1998), "Vertical Externalities in Tax Setting: Evidence from Gasoline and Cigarettes," *Journal of Public Economics*, 70 (December), 383–398.

Bettendorf, Leon, Michael Devereux, Albert van der Horst, Simon Loretz, and Ruud A. De Mooij (2010), "Corporate Tax Harmonization in the EU," *Economic Policy*, 25 (July), 537–590.

Bickers, Kenneth, and Robert Stein (1996), "The Electoral Dynamics of the Federal Pork Barrel," *American Journal of Political Science*, 40 (November), 1300–1326.

Bird, Richard (1986), *Federal Finance in a Comparative Perspective*, Canadian Tax Foundation, Toronto.

Bird, Richard M., Robert Ebel, and Christine Wallich (1995), *Decentralization of the Socialist State: Intergovernmental Finance in Transition Economies*, World Bank, Washington, DC.

Bird, Richard, and Pierre-Pascal Gendron (2000), "CVAT, VIVAT, and Dual VAT: Vertical 'Sharing' and Interstate Trade," *International Tax and Public Finance*, 7 (December), 753–761.

Birnbaum, Jeffrey, and Alan Murray (1987), *Showdown at Gucci Gulch: Lawmakers, Lobbyists, and the Unlikely Triumph of Tax Reform*, Random House, New York.

Bitler, Marianne, and Hillary Hoynes (2016), "The More Things Change, the More They Stay the Same? The Safety Net and Poverty in the Great Recession," *Journal of Labor Economics*, 34 (January), S403–S444.

Black, Sandra (1999), "Do Better Schools Matter? Parental Valuation of Elementary Education," *Quarterly Journal of Economics*, 114 (May), 577–600.

Blanchard, Olivier, and Lawrence Katz (1992), "Regional Evolutions," *Brookings Papers on Economic Activity*, 1992 (1), 1–75.

Blank, Rebecca (2002), "Evaluating Welfare Reform in the US," *Journal of Economic Literature*, 40 (December), 1105–1166.

Bloom, David, and Jeffrey Sachs (1998), "Geography, Demography, and Economic Growth in Africa," *Brookings Papers on Economic Activity*, 1998 (2), 207–273.

Blue Ribbon Commission on America's Nuclear Future (2012), *Report to the Secretary of Energy*, Department of Energy, Washington, DC.

Blumstein, James (1994), "Federalism and Civil Rights: Complementary and Competing Paradigms," *Vanderbilt Law Review*, 47 (October), 1251–1301.

Boadway, Robin, and Frank Flatters (1982), "Efficiency and Equalization Payments in a Federal System of Government: A Synthesis and Extension of Recent Results," *Canadian Journal of Economics*, 15 (November), 613–633.

Boadway, Robin, Isao Horiba, and Raghbendra Jha (1999), "The Provision of Public Services by Government Funded Decentralized Agencies," *Public Choice*, 100 (September), 157–184.

Boadway, Robin, and Anwar Shah (2009), *Fiscal Federalism: Principles and Practice of Multiorder Governance*, Cambridge University Press, New York.

Boadway, Robin, and David Wildasin (1989), "A Median Voter Model of Social Security," *International Economic Review*, 30 (May), 307–328.

Boateng, Francis, and David Makin (2016), "Where Do We Stand? An Exploratory Analysis of Confidence in African Court Systems," *International Journal for Crime, Justice, and Social Democracy*, 5 (Fall), 132–153.

Bohn, Henning (1992), "Budget Deficits and Government Accounting," *Carnegie Rochester Conference Series on Public Policy* 37 (December), 1–84.

Bohn, Henning, and Robert Inman (1996), "Balanced Budget Rules and Public Deficits: Evidence from US States," *Carnegie-Rochester Conference Series on Public Policy*, 45 (November), 13–76.

Boix, Carles (2003), *Democracy and Redistribution*, Cambridge University Press, New York.

Boldrin, Michele, and Fabio Canova (2001), "Inequality and Convergence in Europe's Regions: Reconsidering European Regional Policies," *Economic Policy*, 16 (April), 207–253.

Bolton, Patrick, and Mathias Dewatripont (2005), *Contract Theory*, MIT Press, Cambridge, MA.

Bordignon, Massimo, Paolo Manasse, and Guido Tabellini (2001), "Optimal Regional Redistribution under Asymmetric Information," *American Economic Review*, 91 (June), 709–721.

Boustan, Leah (2016), *Competition in the Promised Land: Black Migration in Northern Cities and Labor Markets*, Princeton University Press, Princeton, NJ.

Bradbury, Charles, and Mark Crain (2001), "Legislative Organization and Government Spending," *Journal of Public Economics*, 82 (December), 309–325.

Bradbury, Charles, and Frank Stephenson (2003), "Local Government Structure and Public Expenditures," *Public Choice*, 115 (April), 185–198.

Bredemeier, Christian (2014), "Imperfect Information and the Meltzer-Richard Hypothesis," *Public Choice*, 159 (June), 561–576.

Brennan, Geoffrey, and James Buchanan (1980), *The Power to Tax: Analytical Foundations of a Fiscal Constitution*, Cambridge University Press, New York.

Breyer, Stephen (2005), *Active Liberty: Interpreting Our Democratic Constitution*, Random House, New York.

Brinkley, Douglas (2009), *The Wilderness Warrior: Theodore Roosevelt and the Crusade for America*, New York, HarperCollins.

Brøchner, Jens, Jesper Jensen, Patrik Svensson, and Peter Birch Sørenson (2007), "The Dilemmas of Tax Coordination in the Enlarged European Union," *CESifo Economic Studies*, 53 (November), 561–595.

Brown-Dean, Khalilah, Zoltan Hajnal, Christina Rivers, and Ismail White (2015), "50 Years of the Voting Rights Act: The State of Race in Politics," Joint Center of Political and Economic Studies, Washington, DC.

Brülhart, Marius, and Mario Jametti (2006), "Vertical versus Horizontal Tax Externalities: An Empirical Test," *Journal of Public Economics* 90 (November), 2027–2062.

Buccirossi, Paolo, Lorenzo Ciari, Tomaso Duso, Giancarol Spagnolo, and Cristiana Vitale (2011), "Measuring the Deterrence Properties of Competition Policy: The Competition Policy Indices," *Journal of Competition Law and Economics*, 7 (January), 165–204.

Buchanan, James M. (1965), "An Economic Theory of Clubs," *Economica*, 32 (February), 1–14.

Bucovetsky, Sam, and John D. Wilson (1991), "Tax Competition with Two Tax Instruments," *Regional Science and Urban Economics*, 21 (November), 331–350.

Buettner, Thiess (2003), "Tax Base Effects and Fiscal Externalities of Local Capital Taxation: Evidence from a Panel of German Jurisdictions," *Journal of Urban Economics*, 54 (July), 110–128.

Buiter, Willem (1985), "A Guide to Public Sector Debt and Deficits," *Economic Policy*, 1 (November), 13–79.

Burns, Charlotte, Anne Rasmussen, and Christine Reh (2013), "Legislative Codecision and Its Impact on the Political System of the European Union," *Journal of European Public Policy*, 20 (7), 941–952.

Butler, Henry, and Larry Ribstein (2008), "A Jurisdictional Competition Approach to Reforming Insurance Regulation," Searle Research Symposium on Insurance Markets and Regulation, Northwestern University Law School.

Button, James (1989), *Blacks and Social Change: Impact of the Civil Rights Movement in Southern Communities*, Princeton University Press, Princeton, NJ.

Cain, Bruce, John Ferejohn, and Morris Fiorina (1987), *The Personal Vote*, Harvard University Press, Cambridge, MA.

Calabrese, Stephen, Dennis Epple, and Richard Romano (2012), "Inefficiencies from Metropolitan Political and Fiscal Decentralization: Failures of Tiebout Competition," *Review of Economic Studies*, 79 (July), 1081–1111.

California Retail Liquor Dealers Association v. Midcal Aluminum, 445 U.S. 97 (1980).

Callander, Steven (2005), "Electoral Competition in Heterogeneous Districts," *Journal of Political Economy*, 113 (5), 1116–1145.

Callander, Steven, and Bard Harstad (2015), "Experimentation in Federal Systems," *Quarterly Journal of Economics*, 130 (May), 915–1002.

Calvert, Randall L., and Richard F. Fenno (1994), "Strategy and Sophisticated Voting in the Senate," *Journal of Politics*, 56 (May), 349–376.

Cameron, Charles (2000), *Veto Bargaining: Presidents and Politics of Negative Power*, Cambridge University Press, New York.

Cameron, Charles, David Epstein, and Sharyn O'Halloran (1996), "Do Majority-Minority Districts Maximize Substantive Black Representation?," *American Political Science Review*, 90 (December), 794–812.

Cameron, David (2012), "European Fiscal Responses to the Great Recession," in Nancy Bermeo and Jonas Pontusson (eds.), *Coping with Crisis: Government Reactions to the Great Recession*, Russell Sage Foundation, New York, 91–129.

Campos, Nauro, Fabrizio Coricelli, and Luigi Moretti (2014), "Economic Growth and Political Integration: Estimating the Benefits from Membership in the European Union Using the Synthetic Counterfactuals Method," Working Paper No. 8162, IZA, Bonn, Germany.

Carlino, Gerald, and Robert Inman (2013), "Local Deficits and Local Jobs: Can US States Stabilize Their Own Economies?," *Journal of Monetary Economics*, 60 (July), 517–530.

Carlino, Gerald, and Robert Inman (2016), "Fiscal Stimulus in Economic Unions: What Role for States?," *Tax Policy and the Economy*, 30, 1–50.

Carman, Katherine G, Christine Eibner, and Susan M. Paddock (2015), "Trends in Health Insurance Enrollment, 2013–15, *Health Affairs*, 34 (June), 1044–1048.

Carrubba, Clifford, Matthew Gabel, and Charles Hankla (2008), "Judicial Behavior under Political Constraints: Evidence from the European Court of Justices," *American Political Science Review*, 102 (November), 435–452.

Carruthers, Bruce, and Naomi Lamoreaux (2015), "Regulatory Races: The Effects of Jurisdictional Competition on Regulatory Standards," *Journal of Economic Literature*, 54 (September), 52–97.

Carson, Richard (2012), "Contingent Valuation: A Practical Alternative When Prices Aren't Available," *Journal of Economic Perspectives*, 26 (Fall), 27–42.

Cary, William L. (1974), "Federalism and Corporate Law: Reflections upon Delaware," *Yale Law Journal*, 83 (March), 663–707.

Cascio, Elizabeth, and Ebonya Washington (2014), "Valuing the Vote: The Redistribution of Voting Rights and State Funds following the Voting Rights Act of 1965," *Quarterly Journal of Economics*, 129 (February), 379–433.

Chamberlain, John (1974), "Provision of Collective Goods as a Function of Group Size," *American Political Science Review*, 68 (June), 707–716.

Charles, Guy-Uriel, and Luis Fuentes-Rohwer (2015), "Race, Federalism, and Voting Rights," *University of Chicago Legal Forum*, 2015, 113–152.

Cheibub, Jose Antonio (2006), "Presidentialism, Electoral Identifiability, and Budget Balances in Democratic Systems," *American Political Science Review*, 100 (August), 353–368.

Chen, Cuicui, and Richard Zeckhauser (2018), "Collective Action in an Asymmetric World," *Journal of Public Economics*, 158 (February), 103–112.

Chen, Jowei, and Neil Malhotra (2007), "The Law of k/n: the Effect of Chamber Size on Government Spending," *American Political Science Review*, 101 (November), 657–676.

Chernick, Howard (1979), "An Economic Model of the Distribution of Project Grants," in Peter Mieszkowski and William Oakland (eds.), *Fiscal Federalism and Grants-in-Aid*, Urban Institute Press, Washington, DC.

Chernick, Howard (1998), "Fiscal Effects of Block Grants for the Needy: An Interpretation of the Evidence," *International Tax and Public Finance*, 5 (2), 205–233.

Chernow, Ron (2004), *Alexander Hamilton*, Penguin Books, New York.

Chodorow-Reich, Gabriel, Laua Feiveson, Zachary Liscow, and William Gui Woolston (2012), "Does State Fiscal Relief during Recessions Increase Employment? Evidence from the American Recovery and Reinvestment Act," *American Economic Journal: Economic Policy*, 4 (August), 118–145.

Choi, Jay Pil (1998), "Brand Extension as Informational Leverage," *Review of Economic Studies*, 65 (October), 655–669.

Choper, Jesse (1980), *Judicial Review and the National Political Process: A Functional Reconsideration of the Role of the Supreme Court*, University of Chicago Press, Chicago.

Christafore, David, and J. Susane Leguizamon (2012), "The Influence of Gay and Lesbian Households on House Prices and Conservative and Liberal Households," *Journal of Urban Economics*, 71 (2), 258–267.

Christiansen, Vidar (1994), "Cross-Border Shopping and the Optimum Commodity Tax in a Competitive and Monopoly Market," *Scandinavian Journal of Economics*, 96 (3), 329–341.

Cion, Richard (1966), "Accommodation Par Excellence: The Lakewood Plan," in Michael Danielson (ed.), *Metropolitan Politics: A Reader*, Little, Brown, Boston, 272–280.

Citizens United v. FEC, 558 U.S. 210 (2010).

Clausing, Kimberly (2016), "The US State Experience under Formulary Apportionment: Are There Lessons for International Reform?," *National Tax Journal*, 69 (June), 353–386.

Coase, Ronald (1960), "The Problem of Social Cost," *Journal of Law and Economics*, 3 (1), 1–44.

Coate, Stephen, and Michael Conlin (2004), "A Group Rule–Utilitarian Approach to Voter Turnout: Theory and Evidence," *American Economic Review*, 94 (December), 1476–1504.

Coates, Dennis, Victoria Heid, and Michael Munger (1994), "Not Equitable, Not Efficient: U.S. Policy on Low-Level Radioactive Waste Disposal," *Journal of Public Policy and Management*, 13 (Summer), 526–538.

Coenen Günter, Roland Staub, and Mathias Trabandt (2012), "Fiscal Policy and the Great Recession in the Euro Area," *American Economic Review*, 102 (May), 71–76.

Colantone, Italo, and Piero Stanig (2018), "Global Competition and Brexit," *American Political Science Review*, 112 (March), 201–218.

Cole, Harold, and Lee Ohanian (2004), "New Deal Policies and the Persistence of the Great Depression: A General Equilibrium Analysis," *Journal of Political Economy*, 112 (December), 779–816.

Collie, Melissa (1988), "Universalism and the Parties in the U.S. House of Representatives, 1921–1980," *American Journal of Political Science*, 32 (November), 865–883.

Collins, John N., and Bryan T. Downes (1977), "The Effects of Size on the Provision of Public Services: The Case of Solid Waste Collection in Smaller Cities," *Urban Affairs Review*, 12 (March), 333–347.

Congleton, Roger, and William Shughart (1990), "The Growth of Social Security: Electoral Push or Political Pull?," *Economic Inquiry*, 28 (January), 109–132.

Conlan, Timothy, and Paul Posner (2011), "Inflection Point? Federalism and the Obama Administration," *Publius: The Journal of Federalism*, 41 (Summer), 421–446.

Conlan, Timothy J., James D. Riggle, and Donna E. Schwartz (1995), "Deregulating Federalism? The Politics of Mandate Reform in the 104th Congress," *Publius: The Journal of Federalism*, 25 (Summer), 23–39.

Cooley, Thomas, and Jorge Soares (1996), "Will Social Security Survive the Baby Boom?," *Carnegie-Rochester Conference Series on Public Policy*, 45, 89–121.

Coons, John, William Clune, and Stephen Sugarman (1970), *Private Wealth and Public Education*, Harvard University Press, Cambridge, MA.

Cooper, Ian (2006), "The Watchdogs of Subsidiarity: National Parliaments and the Logic of Arguing in the EU," *Journal of Common Market Studies*, 44 (June), 281–304.

Cooter, Robert (1982), "The Cost of Coase," *Journal of Legal Studies*, 11 (January), 1–33.

Cooter, Robert, and Neil Siegel (2011), "Collective Action Federalism: A General Theory of Article I, Section 8," *Stanford Law Review*, 63 (December), 115–185.

Cornes, Richard, and Todd Sandler (1986), *The Theory of Externalities, Public Goods and Club Goods*, Cambridge University Press, Cambridge.

Corwin, Edward S. (1950), "The Passing of Dual Federalism," *Virginia Law Review*, 36 (February), 1–24.

Cosgrove, Michael H., and Leroy J. Hushak (1972), *Costs and Quality of Water in Ohio Cities, Columbus, Ohio,* Research Bulletin 1052, Ohio Agricultural Research and Development Center, Wooster, OH.

Costello, Rory, and Robert Thomson (2013), "The Distribution of Power among EU Institutions: Who Wins Under Co-decision and Why?," *Journal of European Public Policy*, 20 (7), 1025–1039.

Courant, Paul N., and Daniel L. Rubinfeld (1978), "On the Measurement of Benefits in an Urban Context: Some General Equilibrium Issues," *Journal of Urban Economics*, 5 (July), 346–356.

Cox, Gary (1997), *Making Votes Count: Strategic Coordination in the World's Electoral Systems*, Cambridge University Press, Cambridge.

Cox, Gary, and Mathew McCubbins (2007), *Legislative Leviathan: Party Government in the House*, 2nd ed., Cambridge University Press, New York.

Cremer, Jacques (1986), "Cooperation in Ongoing Organizations," *Quarterly Journal of Economics*, 101 (1), 33–49.

Dahl, Robert (1967), "The City in the Future of Democracy," *American Political Science Review*, 61 (December), 953–970.

Dahl, Robert (1994), "A Democratic Dilemma: System Effectiveness versus Citizen Participation," *Political Science Quarterly*, 109 (Spring), 23–34.

Dahl, Robert (1998), *On Democracy*, Yale University Press, New Haven, CT.

Dahl, Robert, and Edward Tufte (1973), *Size and Democracy*, Stanford University Press, Stanford, CA.

Dahlby, Bev (1996), "Fiscal Externalities and the Design of Intergovernmental Grants," *International Tax and Public Finance*, 3 (July), 397–411.

Dahlby, Bev (2008), *The Marginal Costs of Public Funds: Theory and Applications*, MIT Press, Cambridge, MA.

Daines, Robert (2001), "Does Delaware Law Improve Firm Value?," *Journal of Financial Economics*, 62 (December), 525–558.

Dawson, Mark (2017), *The Governance of EU Fundamental Rights*, Cambridge University Press, New York.

Deaton, Angus, and John Muellbauer (1980), *Economics and Consumer Behavior*, Cambridge University Press, New York.

DeBoer, Larry (1992), "Economies of Scale and Input Substitution in Public Libraries," *Journal of Urban Economics*, 32 (September), 257–268.

Dee, Thomas (2004), "Are There Civic Returns to Education?," *Journal of Public Economics*, 88 (August), 1697–1720.

Dee, Thomas, and Brian Jacob (2010), "The Impact of No Child Left Behind on Students, Teachers, and Schools," *Brookings Papers on Economic Activity*, Fall, 149–194.

De Figueiredo, Rui, Tonia Jacobi, and Barry Weingast (2006), "The New Separation of Powers Approach to American Politics," in Barry Weingast and Donald Wittman (eds.), *The Oxford Handbook of Political Economy*, Oxford University Press, New York, 199–222.

De Figueiredo, Rui, and Barry Weingast (2005), "Self-Enforcing Federalism," *Journal of Law, Economics, and Organizations*, 21 (April), 103–135.

De Grauwe, Paul (1992), *The Economics of Monetary Integration*, Oxford University Press, Oxford.

De Grauwe, Paul (2013), "The Political Economy of the Euro," *Annual Review of Political Science*, 13, 153–170.

Delli Carpini, Michael, Fay Cook, and Lawrence Jacobs (2004), "Public Deliberation, Discursive Participation, and Citizen Engagement," *Annual Review of Political Science*, 7, 315–344.

DelRossi, Alison, and Robert Inman (1999), "Changing the Price of Pork: The Impact of Local Cost Sharing on Legislators' Demands for Distributive Public Goods," *Journal of Public Economics*, 71 (February), 247–273.

Derthick, Martha (1974), *Between State and Nation: Regional Organizations and the United States*, Brookings Institution, Washington, DC.

De Tocqueville, Alexis (1969), *Democracy in America*, edited by J. P. Mayer, Anchor Books, Garden City, NY.

Dettrey, Bryan, and Leslie Schwindt-Bayer (2009), "Voter Turnout in Presidential Elections," *Comparative Political Studies*, 42 (October), 1317–1338.

Devereux, Michael, Ben Lockwood, and Michela Redoano (2008), "Do Country Compete over Corporate Tax Rates?," *Journal of Public Economics*, 92 (June), 1210–1235.

De Visser, Jaap, and Zemelak Ayele (2014), "Intergovernmental Fiscal Relations in South Africa and the Role of the Financial and Fiscal Commission: 20 Year Review," *Community Law Center*, July, 2014.

Dhingra, Swati, Hanwei Huang, Gianmarco Ottaviano, João Paulo Pessoa, Thomas Sampson, and John van Reenen (2017), "The Costs and Benefits of Leaving the EU: Trade Effects," CEP Discussion Paper 1478, Centre for Economic Performance, London School of Economics and Political Science, April.

Diamond, Martin (1961), "The Federalist's View of Federalism." *Essays on Federalism* (1961), in George Benson (ed.), Institute for Studies on Federalism, Claremont, CA, 21–64.

Diamond, Martin (1977), "The Federalist on Federalism: Neither a National Nor a Federal Constitution, but a Composition of Both," *Yale Law Journal*, 86 (May), 1273–1285.

Diamond, Peter, and James Mirrlees (1971), "Optimal Taxation and Public Production I: Production Efficiency," *American Economic Review*, 61 (March), 8–27.

Diaz-Cayeros, Alberto (2006), *Federalism, Fiscal Authority, and Centralization in Latin America*, Cambridge University Press, New York.

Dilger, Robert Jay, and Richard S. Beth (2016), *Unfunded Mandates Reform Act: History, Impact, and Issues*, R40957, Congressional Research Service, Washington, DC, January.

Dinan, John (2004), "Strengthening the Political Safeguards of Federalism: The Fate of the Recent Federalism Legislation in the U.S. Congress," *Publius: The Journal of Federalism*, 34 (Summer), 55–84.

Dinan, John (2011), "Shaping Health Reform: State Government Influence in the Patient Protection and Affordable Care Act," *Publius: The Journal of Federalism*, 41 (Summer), 395–420.

Dinan, Terry M., Maureen L. Cropper, and Paul R. Portney (1999), "Environmental Federalism: Welfare Losses from Uniform National Drinking Water Standards," in Arvind Panagariya, Paul R. Portney, and Robert M. Schwab (eds.), *Environmental and Public Economics: Essays in Honor of Wallace E. Oates*, Edward Elgar, Cheltenham, UK, 13–31.

Dixit, Avanash (1996), *The Making of Economic Policy*, MIT Press, Cambridge, MA.

Dixit, Avinash, and Mancur Olson (2000), "Does Voluntary Participation Undermine the Coase Theorem?," *Journal of Public Economics*, 76 (June), 309–335.

Dorf, Michael (2005), "The Coherentism of Democracy and Distrust," *Yale Law Journal*, 114 (April), 1237–1278.

Dougherty, Keith (2001), *Collective Action under the Articles of Confederation*, Cambridge University Press, New York.

Douglas, Morris, and Luther Tweeten (1971), "The Cost of Controlling Crime: A Study in Economies of City Life," *Annals of Regional Science*, 5, 33–49.

Downes, Alexander (2004), "The Problem with Negotiated Settlements to Ethnic Civil Wars," *Security Studies*, 13 (Summer), 230–279.

Drautzburg, Thorsten, and Harald Uhlig (2015), "Fiscal Stimulus and Distortionary Taxation," *Review of Economic Dynamics*, 18 (October), 894–920.

Drew, Elizabeth (1996), *Showdown: The Struggle between the Gingrich Congress and the Clinton White House*, Simon and Schuster, New York.

Duval, Romain, and Davide Furceri (2018), "The Effects of Labor and Product Market Reforms: The Role of Macroeconomic Conditions and Policies," *IMF Economic Review*, 66 (March), 31–69.

Dworkin, Ronald (1986), *Law's Empire*, Harvard University Press, Cambridge, MA.

Easterbrook, Frank (1983), "Antitrust and the Economics of Federalism," *Journal of Law and Economics*, 23 (April), 23–50.

Ebrahim, Hassen, and Laurel Miller (2010), "Creating the Birth Certificate of a New South Africa: Constitution Making after Apartheid," in Laurel Miller (ed.), *Framing the State in Times of Transition: Case Studies in Constitution Making*, United States Institute of Peace Press, Washington, DC, 111–158.

EEOC v. Wyoming, 460 U.S. 226 (1983).

Eichengreen, Barry (1990), "One Money for Europe? Lessons from the U.S. Currency and Customs Union," *Economic Policy*, 5 (April), 117–187.

Eichengreen, Barry (2018a), "Euro Malaise: From Remission to Cure," *Milken Institute Review*, January.

Eichengreen, Barry (2018b), *The Populist Temptation: Economic Grievance and Political Reaction in the Modern Era*, Oxford University Press, Oxford.

Eichengreen, Barry, and Charles Wyplosz (1998), "Stability Pact: More than a Minor Nuisance?," *Economic Policy*, 13 (April), 66–113.

Elazar, Daniel (1968), "Federalism," in David Sills (ed.), *International Encyclopedia of the Social Sciences*, Macmillan, New York, 353–367.

Elliott, Donald, Bruce Ackerman, and John Millian (1985), "Toward a Theory of Statutory Evolution: The Federalization of Environmental Law," *Journal of Law, Economics, and Organization*, 1 (Fall), 313–340.

Ely, John Hart (1980), *Democracy and Distrust: A Theory of Judicial Review*, Harvard University Press, Cambridge, MA.

Environmental Planning: Politics and Space (2002), 20 (December), 793–869.

Epple, Dennis (1987), "Hedonic Prices and Implicit Markets: Estimating Demand and Supply Functions for Differentiated Products," *Journal of Political Economy*, 95 (February) 59–80.

Epple, Dennis, and Glenn Platt (1998), "Equilibrium and Local Redistribution in an Urban Economy When Households Differ in Both Preferences and Incomes," *Journal of Urban Economics*, 43 (January), 23–51.

Epple, Dennis, and Michael Riordan (1987), "Cooperation and Punishment under Repeated Majority Rule," *Public Choice*, 55 (September), 41–73.

Epple, Dennis, and Katherine Schipper (1981), "Municipal Pension Funding: A Theory and Some Evidence," *Public Choice*, 37 (January), 141–178.

Epple, Dennis, and Holger Sieg (1999), "Estimating Equilibrium Models of Local Jurisdictions," *Journal of Political Economy*, 107 (August), 645–681.

Epple, Dennis, and Allan Zelenitz (1981), "The Implications of Competition among Jurisdictions: Does Tiebout Need Politics?," *Journal of Political Economy*, 89 (December), 1197–1217.

Epstein, David, and Sharyn O'Halloran (1999), *Delegating Powers: A Transaction Cost Politics Approach to Policy Making Under Separate Powers*, Cambridge University Press, Cambridge.

Eraslan, Hulya (2002), "Uniqueness of Stationary Equilibrium Payoffs in Baron-Ferejohn Model," *Journal of Economic Theory*, 103 (March), 11–30.

Eskridge, William, and John Ferejohn (1994), "The Elastic Commerce Clause: A Political Theory of American Federalism," *Vanderbilt Law Review*, 47 (October), 1355–1400.

Esteller-Moré, Alejandro, and Albert Solé-Ollé (2001), "Vertical Income Tax Externalities and Fiscal Interdependence: Evidence from the US," *Regional Science and Urban Economics*, 31 (April), 247–272.

Esteller-Moré, Alejandro, and Albert Solé-Ollé (2002), "Tax Setting in a Federal System: The Case of Personal Income Taxation in Canada," *International Tax and Public Finance*, 9 (May), 235–257.

Fahad, Aysar, and Mazen Ahmed (2016), "The Impact of Corruption on Foreign Direct Investment (FDI) in Post-Conflict Countries: A Panel Causality Test," *Journal of Advanced Social Research*, 6 (March), 1–12.

Fahcy, Bridget (forthcoming.), "Federalism by Contract," *Yale Law Journal*. 129.

Farhi, Emmanuel, and Ivan Werning (2017), "Fiscal Unions," *American Economic Review*, 107 (December), 3788–3834.

Feddersen, Timothy (2004), "Rational Choice Theory and the Paradox of Not Voting," *Journal of Economic Perspectives*, 18 (Winter), 99–112.

Feeley, Malcolm, and Edward Rubin (2008), *Federalism: Political Identity and Tragic Compromise*, University of Michigan Press, Ann Arbor.

Feldstein, Martin, and Marian Vaillant Wrobel (1998), "Can State Taxes Redistribute Income?" *Journal of Public Economics*, 68 (June), 369–396.

FERC v. Mississippi, 456 U.S. 742 (1982).

Ferejohn, John (1974), *Pork Barrel Politics: Rivers and Harbors Legislation, 1947–1968*, Stanford University Press, Stanford, CA.

Ferejohn, John (1986), "Logrolling in an Institutional Context: A Case Study of Food Stamp Legislation," in Gerald C. Wright Jr., Leroy N. Rieselbach, and Lawrence C. Dodd (eds.), *Congress and Policy Change*, Agathon, New York, 223–256.

Ferguson, Christopher (2009), "An Effect Size Primer: A Guide for Clinicians and Researchers," *Professional Psychology: Research and Practice*, 40 (5), 532–538.

Fernandez, Raquel, and Richard Rogerson (1996), "Income Distribution, Communities, and the Quality of Public Education," *Quarterly Journal of Economics*, 111 (February), 135–164.

Feyrer, J., and Bruce Sacerdote (2011), "Did The Stimulus Stimulate? Real Time Estimates of the Effects of the American Recovery and Reinvestment Act," NBER Working Paper No. 16759, National Bureau of Economic Research, Cambridge, MA.

Filippov, Mikhail, Peter Ordeshook, and Olga Shvetsova (2004), *Designing Federalism: A Theory of Self-Sustainable Federal Institutions*, Cambridge University Press, New York.

Finkel, Steven (1985), "Reciprocal Effects of Participation and Political Efficacy: A Panel Analysis," *American Journal of Political Science*, 29 (November), 891–913.

Fischel, William (1975), "Fiscal and Environmental Considerations in the Location of Firms in Suburban Communities," in Edwin Mills and Wallace Oates (eds.), *Fiscal Zoning and Land Use Controls*, D. C. Heath, Lexington, MA, 119–173.

Fischel, William (2001), "Homevoters, Municipal Corporate Governance, and the Benefit View of the Property Tax," *National Tax Journal*, 54 (March), 157–174.

Fitts, Michael, and Robert Inman (1992), "Controlling Congress: Presidential Influence in Domestic Fiscal Policy," *Georgetown Law Journal*, 80 (June), 1737–1785.

Foner, Eric (1993), *Freedom's Lawmakers*, Oxford University Press, Oxford.

Frankel, Jeffrey, and Jesse Schreger (2012), "Over-optimistic Official Forecasts in the Eurozone and Fiscal Rules," *Review of World Economics*, 149 (June), 247–272.

Freedom House (2018), *Freedom in the World, 2018*, Freedom House, Washington, DC.

Freeman, Richard (1988), "Labour Market Institutions and Economic Performance," *Economic Policy*, 3 (April), 63–80.

Friedlaender, Ann (1965), *Interstate Highway System: A Study in Public Investment*, North Holland Publishing, Amsterdam.

Friedman, Barry, and Erin Delaney (2011), "Becoming Supreme: The Federal Foundation of Judicial Supremacy," *Columbia Law Journal*, 111 (October), 1137–1193.

Friedman, Milton, and Anna J. Schwartz (1963), *A Monetary History of the United States, 1867–1960*, Princeton University Press, Princeton, NJ.

Frug, Gerald (1999), *City Making: Building Communities without Building Walls*, Princeton University Press, Princeton, NJ.

Fujiwara, Thomas (2011), "A Regression Discontinuity Test for Strategic Voting and Duverger's Law," *Quarterly Journal of Political Science*, 6 (November), 197–233.

Gamm, Gerald, and Kenneth Shepsle (1989), "Emergence of Legislative Institutions: Standing Committees in the House and Senate, 1810–1825," *Legislative Studies Quarterly*, 14 (February), 39–66.

Garcia v. San Antonio Metropolitan Transit Authority, 469 U.S. 528 (1985).

Gardbaum, Stephen (1996), "Rethinking Constitutional Federalism," *Texas Law Review*, 74 (March), 795–838.

Garrett, Geoffrey (1995), "From the Luxembourg Compromise to Codecision: Decision Making in the European Union," *Electoral Studies*, 14 (September), 289–308.

Gaustad, Edwin, and Philip Barlow (2001), *New Historical Atlas of Religion in America*, Oxford University Press, New York.

Gehring, Kai, and Stephan Schneider (2018), "Towards the Greater Good? EU Commissioners' Nationality and Budget Allocation in the European Union," *American Economic Journal: Policy*, 10 (February), 214–239.

Gelbach, Jonah (2004), "Migration, the Life Cycle, and State Benefits: How Low Is the Bottom?," *Journal of Political Economy*, 112 (October), 1091–1130.

Gelbach, Jonah (2016), "Uncontrolled Experiments from Laboratories of Democracy: Traditional Cash Welfare, Federalism, and Welfare Reform," Public Law and Legal Theory Research Paper Series, Paper No. 16–37, University of Pennsylvania Law School.

Gentzkow, Matthew, and Jesse Shapiro (2008), "Competition and Truth in Market for News," *Journal of Economic Perspectives*, 22 (Spring), 133–154.

Gerber, Alan (1998), "Estimating the Effect of Campaign Spending on Senate Election Outcomes Using Instrumental Variables," *American Political Science Review*, 92 (June), 401–411.

Gerber, Elisabeth R., and Jeffrey B. Lewis (2004), "Beyond the Median: Voter Preferences, District Heterogeneity, and Political Representation," *Journal of Political Economy*, 112 (December), 1364–1383.

Gerken, Heather (2010). "Federalism All the Way Down," *Harvard Law Review*, 124 (November), pp. 4–74.

Gerken, Heather (2012), "A New Progressive Federalism," *Democracy Journal*, 24 (Spring) 37–48.

Gerken, Heather (2014a), "Federalism as the New Nationalism: An Overview," *Yale Law Journal*, 123 (April), 1889–1918.

Gerken, Heather (2014b), "Slipping the Bonds of Federalism," *Harvard Law Review*, 128 (November), 85–123.

Germanis, Peter (2016), "TANF in Michigan: Did We Really 'Fix' Welfare in 1996? A Cautionary Tale for Speaker Ryan," *Center for Budget and Policy Priorities*, May 25.

Gienapp, William (2002), *Abraham Lincoln and Civil War America*, Oxford University Press, New York.

Giles v. Harris, 189 U.S. 475 (1903).

Giliomee, Hermann (1995), "Democratization in South Africa," *Political Science Quarterly*, 110 (Spring), 83–104.

Gilligan, Thomas, and Keith Krehbiel (1990), "Organization of Informative Committees by a Rational Legislature," *American Journal of Political Science*, 34 (May), 531–564.

Gilligan, Thomas, and John Matsusaka (1995), "Deviations from Constituent Interests: The Role of Legislative Structure and Political Parties in the States," *Economic Inquiry*, 33 (July), 383–401.

Gilligan, Thomas, and John Matsusaka (2001), "Fiscal Policy, Legislative Size, and Political Parties: Evidence from the First Half of the Twentieth Century," *National Tax Journal*, 54 (March), 57–82.

Glencross, Andrew (2009), "Altiero Spinelli and the Ideas of the US Constitution as a Model for Europe: The Promises and Pitfalls of an Analogy," *Journal of Common Market Studies*, 47 (March), 287–307.

Glotz, Gustave (1929), *The Greek City and Its Institutions*, K. Paul, Trench, Trubner, London.

Gokhale, Jagadeesh, and Kent Smetters (2003), *Fiscal and Generational Imbalances: New Budget Measures for New Budget Priorities*, American Enterprise Institute Press, Washington, DC.

Golden, Miriam, and Brian Min (2013), "Distributive Politics around the World," *Annual Review of Political Science*, 16, 73–99.

Goolsbee, Austan, and Edward Maydew (2000), "Coveting Thy Neighbor's Manufacturing: The Dilemma of State Income Apportionment," *Journal of Public Economics*, 75 (January), 125–143.

Gordon, Roger (1983), "An Optimal Taxation Approach to Fiscal Federalism," *Quarterly Journal of Economics*, 98 (November), 567–586.

Gordon, Roger, and John Wilson (1986), "An Examination of Multijurisdictional Corporate Income Taxation under Formula Apportionment," *Econometrica*, 54 (November), 1357–1373.

Gould, Robert (2014), "Roma Rights and Roma Expulsions in France: Official Discourse and EU Responses," *Critical Social Policy*, 35 (1), 24–44.

Goulder, Lawrence (2013), "Markets for Pollution Allowances: What Are the (New) Lessons?" *Journal of Economic Perspectives*, 27 (Winter), 87–102.

Gourinchas, Pierre-Olivier, Thomas Philippon, and Dimtri Vayanos (2017), "The Analytics of the Greek Crisis," in Martin Eichenbaum and Jonathan Parker (eds.), *The NBER Macroeconomics Annual, 2016*, University of Chicago Press, Chicago, 1–81.

Gouveia, Miguel (1997), "Majority Rule and the Public Provision of a Private Good," *Public Choice*, 93 (December), 221–224.

Goyal, Rishi, Petra Koava Brooks, Mahmood Pradhan, Thierry Tressel, Giovanni Dell'Ariccia, Ross Leckow, Ceyla Pazarbasioglu, and IMF Staff Team (2013), "A Banking Union for the Euro Area," IMF Staff Discussion Note SDN/13/01.

Gramlich, Edward (1976), "The New City Fiscal Crisis: What Happened and What Is to Be Done?," *American Economic Review*, 66 (May), 415–429.

Gramlich, Edward (1987), "Subnational Fiscal Policy," *Perspectives on Local Public Finance and Public Policy*, 3, 3–27.

Gramlich, Edward M., and Daniel L. Rubinfeld (1982), "Micro Estimates of Public Spending Demand Functions and Tests of the Tiebout and Median Voter Hypotheses," *Journal of Political Economy*, 90 (June), 536–560.

Grandmont, Jean-Michel (1978), "Intermediate Preferences and the Majority Rule," *Econometrica*, 46 (2), 317–330.

Gray, Virginia (1973), "Innovation in the States: A Diffusion Study," *American Political Science Review*, 67 (December), 1174–1185.

Gregory v. Ashcroft, 501 U.S. 452 (1991).

Griffiths, Ann, and Karl Nerenberg (eds.) (2002), *Handbook of Federal Countries, 2002*, McGill-Queens University Press, Montreal.

Grogger, Jeffrey, and Lynn Karoly (2005), *Welfare Reform: Effects of a Decade of Change*, Harvard University Press, Cambridge, MA.

Grossman, Margaret Rosso (1996), "Environmental Federalism in Agriculture: The Case of Pesticide Regulation in the United States," in John S. Braden, Henk Folmer, and Thomas S. Ulen (eds.), *Environmental Policy with Political and Economic Integration: The European Union and the United States*, Edward Elgar, Cheltenham, UK, 274–304.

Grossman, Sanford, and Joseph Stiglitz (1980), "On the Impossibility of Informationally Efficient Markets," *American Economic Review*, 70 (June), 393–408.

Gruber, John (2008), "Covering the Uninsured in the United States," *Journal of Economic Literature*, 46 (3), 571–606.

Gruber, John, and Emmanuel Saez (2002), "The Elasticity of Taxable Income: Evidence and Implications," *Journal of Public Economics*, 84 (April), 1–32.

Guinier, Lani (1994), *The Tyranny of the Majority: Fundamental Fairness in Representative Democracy*, Free Press, New York.

Gupta, Sanjay, and Lillian Mills (2003), "The Effect of State Income Tax Apportionment and Tax Incentives on New Capital Expenditures," *Journal of the American Taxation Association*, 25 (Supplement), 1–25.

Guth, Werner, Rolf Schmittberger, and Bernt Schwarze (1982), "An Experimental Analysis of Ultimatum Bargaining," *Journal of Economic Behavior and Organization*, 3 (December), 367–388.

Gutiérrez, Germàn, and Thomas Philippon (2018), "How EU Markets Became More Competitive than US Markets: A Study in Institutional Drift," NBER Working Paper No. 24700, National Bureau of Economic Research, Cambridge, MA.

Gutmann, Amy, and Dennis Thompson (2004), *Why Deliberative Democracy?*, Princeton University Press, Princeton, NJ.

Gyourko, Joseph, and Joseph Tracy (1989), "On the Political Economy of Land Value Capitalization and Local Public Sector Rent Seeking in a Tiebout Model," *Journal of Urban Economics*, 26 (September), 152–173.

Häge, Frank (2012), "Coalition Building and the Consensus in the Council of the European Union," *British Journal of Political Science*, 43 (3), 481–504.

Hall, Robert, and Charles Jones (1999), "Why Do Some Countries Produce So Much More Output per Worker?," *Quarterly Journal of Economics*, 114 (February), 83–116.

Hamilton, Alexander, James Madison, and John Jay (1982), *The Federalist Papers*, edited by Garry Wills, Bantam Books, New York.

Hamilton, Bruce (1975), "Zoning and Property Taxation in a System of Local Governments," *Urban Studies*, 12, 205–211.

Hamilton, Bruce, and Ailsa Röell (1982), "Wasteful Commuting," *Journal of Political Economy*, 90 (October), 1035–1053.

Hanemann, W. Michael (1991), "Willingness to Pay and Willingness to Accept: How Much Can They Differ?" *American Economic Review*, 81 (June), 635–647.

Hankla, Charles (2013), "Fragmented Legislatures and the Budget: Analyzing Presidential Democracies," *Economics and Politics*, 25 (July), 200–228.

Harrington, Joseph (1990), "The Power of the Proposal-Maker in a Model of Endogenous Agenda Formation," *Public Choice*, 64 (January), 1–20.

Hatfield, John (2015), "Federalism, Taxation, and Economic Growth," *Journal of Urban Economics*, 87 (May), 114–125.

Haughwout, Andrew, and Robert Inman (2002), "Should Suburbs Help Their Central City?," *Brookings-Wharton Papers on Urban Affairs*, 2002, 45–94.

Haughwout, Andrew, Robert Inman, Steven Craig, and Thomas Luce (2004), "Local Revenue Hills: Evidence from Four US Cities," *Review of Economics and Statistics*, 86 (May), 570–585.

Hebous, Shafik, and Tom Zimmermann (2013), "Estimating the Effects of Coordinated Fiscal Actions in the Euro Area," *European Economic Review*, 58 (February), 110–121.

Heikkila, Eric (1996), "Are Municipalities Tieboutian Clubs?," *Regional Science and Urban Economics*, 26 (April), 203–226.

Heinz, Ferdinand and Desislava Rusinova (2011), "How Flexible Are Real Wages in EU Countries? A Panel Investigation," Working Paper Series, No. 1360, European Central Bank, Frankfurt am Main, Germany.

Helms, L. Jay (1985), "The Effect of State and Local Taxes on Economic Growth: A Time-Series, Cross-Section Approach," *Review of Economics and Statistics*, 67 (November), 574–582.

Henkel, Christoph (2002), "The Allocation of Powers in the European Union: A Closer Look at the Principle of Subsidiarity," *Berkeley Journal of International Law*, 20 (2), 359–386.

Hill, Sarah A., and D. Roderick Kiewiet (2015), "The Impact of State Supreme Court Decisions on Public School Finance," *Journal of Law, Economics and Organization*, 31 (March), 61–92.

Hills, Roderick (1998), "The Political Economy of Cooperative Federalism: Why State Autonomy Makes Sense and 'Dual Sovereignty' Doesn't," *Michigan Law Review*, 96 (February), 813–944.

Hills, Roderick (2007), "Against Preemption: How Federalism Can Improve the National Legislative Process," *New York University Law Review*, 82 (April), 1–68.

Hitzhusen, Frederick J. (1973), "Some Measurement Criteria for Community Service Output and Costs: The Case of Fire Protection in Texas," *Southern Journal of Agricultural Economics*, 5 (July), 1–9.

Hix, Simon (2006), "The European Union as a Polity," in Knud Erik Jørgensen, Mark Pollack, and Ben Rosamond (eds.), *Handbook of European Union Politics*, Sage, Thousand Oaks, CA, 141–158.

Hix, Simon (2008), *What's Wrong with the European Union and How to Fix It*, Polity, Malden, MA.

Hix, Simon, and Bjørn Høyland (2013), "Empowerment of the European Parliament," *Annual Review of Political Science*, 16, 171–189.

Hix, Simon, and Michael Marsh (2007), "Punishment or Protest? Understanding European Parliament Elections," *Journal of Politics*, 69 (May), 495–510.

Hodel v. Virginia Surface Mining and Reclamation Ass'n, 452 U.S. 264 (1981).

Holm-Hadulla, Fédéric, Kishore Kamath, Ana Lame, Javier Pérez, and Ludger Schuknecht (2010), "Public Wages in the Euro Area: Towards Securing Stability and Competitiveness," *European Central Bank*, Occasional Paper Series, No. 112, June 2010.

House, Christopher, and Linda Tesar (2015), "Greek Budget Realities: No Easy Option," *Brookings Papers on Economic Activity*, Fall, 329–347.

Hovenkamp, Herbert, and John MacKerron (1985), "Municipal Regulation and Federal Antitrust Policy," *UCLA Law Review*, 32 (April), 719–783.

Hoxby, Caroline M. (2000), "Does Competition among Public Schools Benefit Students and Taxpayers?," *American Economic*, 90 (December), 1209–1238.

Hoxby, Caroline M. (2007), "Does Competition among Public Schools Benefit Students and Taxpayers? Reply," *American Economic Review*, 97 (December), 2038–2055.

Inman, Robert (1978), "Optimal Fiscal Reform of Metropolitan Schools: Some Simulation Results," *American Economic Review*, 68 (March), 107–122.

Inman, Robert P. (1979), "Fiscal Performance of Local Governments," in Peter Mieszkowski and Mahlon Straszheim (eds.), *Current Issues in Urban Economics*, Johns Hopkins University Press, Baltimore, 270–321.

Inman, Robert P. (1982), "Public Employee Pensions and the Local Labor Budget," *Journal of Public Economics*, 19 (October), 49–71.

Inman, Robert (1987), "Markets, Governments, and the 'New' Political Economy," in Alan Auerbach and Martin Feldstein (eds.), *Handbook of Public Economics*, vol. II, North-Holland, New York, 647–777.

Inman, Robert (1988), "Federal Assistance and Local Services in the United States: The Evolution of a New Federal Fiscal Order," in Harvey Rosen (ed.), *Fiscal Federalism: Quantitative Studies*, University of Chicago Press, Chicago, 33–74.

Inman, Robert (1993), "Local Interests, Central Leadership, and the Passage of TRA86," *Journal of Policy Analysis and Management*, 12 (Winter), 156–180.

Inman, Robert (1995), "How to Have a Fiscal Crisis," *American Economic Review*, 85 (May), 378–383.

Inman, Robert (1997), "Do Balanced Budget Rules Work? US Experience and Possible Lessons for the EMU," in Horst Siebert (ed.), *Quo Vadis Europe?*, JCB Mohr, Tübingen, Germany, 307–332.

Inman, Robert (2003), "Transfers and Bailouts: Enforcing Local Fiscal Discipline with Lessons from U.S. Federalism," in Jonathan Rodden (ed.), *Enforcing a Hard Budget Constraint*, MIT Press, Cambridge, MA, 3–83.

Inman (2007). "Federalism's Values and the Value of Federalism," *CESifo Economic Studies*, 53 (December), 522–560.

Inman, Robert (2010), "States in Fiscal Distress," *Regional Economic Development*, 6 (1), 65–80.

Inman, Robert (2013), "Managing Country Debts in the European Union: Stronger Rules or Stronger Union?," in Franklin Allen, Elena Carletti, and Joanna Gray (eds.), *Political, Fiscal, and Banking Union in the Eurozone?*, FIC Press, Philadelphia, 79–102.

Inman, Robert, and Michael Fitts (1990), "Political Institutions and Fiscal Policy: Evidence from the U.S. Historical Record," *Journal of Law, Economics, and Organizations*, 6 (Special Issue), 79–132.

Inman, Robert, and Daniel Rubinfeld (1979), "Judicial Pursuit of Local Fiscal Equity," *Harvard Law Review*, 92 (June), 1662–1750.

Inman, Robert P., and Daniel L. Rubinfeld (1996), "Designing Tax Policy in Federal Economies: An Overview," *Journal of Public Economics*, 60 (June), 307–334.

Inman, Robert, and Daniel L. Rubinfeld (1997), "Making Sense of the Antitrust State-Action Doctrine: Balancing Political Participation and Economic Efficiency in Regulatory Federalism," *Texas Law Review*, 75 (May), 1203–1299.

Inman, Robert P., and Daniel L. Rubinfeld (1998), "Subsidiarity and the European Union," in Peter Newman (ed.), *The New Palgrave Dictionary of Economics and Law*, Macmillan Reference Ltd., London, 545–551.

Inman, Robert P., and Daniel L. Rubinfeld (2001), "Can We Decentralize Our Unemployment Policies? Evidence from the United States," *Kyklos*, 54 (May), 287–308.

Inman, Robert, and Daniel Rubinfeld (2005), "Federalism and the Democratic Transition: Lessons from South Africa," *American Economic Review*, 95 (May), 39–43.

Inman, Robert P., and Daniel L. Rubinfeld (2012), "Federal Institutions and the Democratic Transition: Learning from South Africa," *Journal of Law, Economics, and Organization*, 28 (October), 783–817.

Inman, Robert P., and Daniel L. Rubinfeld (2013), "Understanding the Democratic Transition in South Africa," *American Law and Economics Review*, 17 (Spring), 1–38.

In re City of Bridgeport, 129 B.R. 332 (Ba74nkr. D. Conn. 1991).

International Monetary Fund (2015), "Greece: An Update of the IMF's Staff's Preliminary Public Debt Sustainability Analysis," Country Report no 15/186, Washington, DC.

Jack, Brian (2013), "Article 260(2) TFEU: An Effective Judicial Procedure for Enforcement of Judgments?," *European Law Journal*, 19 (May), 404–421.

Jackson, Vicki (1998), "Federalism and the Uses and Limits of Law: Printz and Principle,? *Harvard Law Review*, 111 (June), 2186–2259.

Jacob, Johanna, and Douglas Lundin (2005), "A Median Voter Model of Health Insurance with Ex-Post Moral Hazard," *Journal of Health Economics*, 24 (March), 407–426.

Jéhiel, Phillippe (1997), "Bargaining between Benevolent Jurisdictions or When Delegation Induces Inefficiencies," *Journal of Public Economics*, 65 (July), 61–74.

Jenkins, Shannon, and Douglas Roscoe (2014), "Parties as the Political Safeguards of Federalism: The Impact of Local Political Party Activity on National Elections," *Publius: The Journal of Federalism*, 44 (Summer), 519–540.

Jin, Hehui, Yingyi Qian, and Barry Weingast (2005), "Regional Decentralization and Fiscal Incentives: Federalism, Chinese Style," *Journal of Public Economics*, 89 (September), 1719–1742.

Johansen, Lief (1963), "Some Notes on the Lindahl Theory of Determination of Public Expenditures," *International Economic Review*, 4 (September), 346–358.

Johnson, Erica (2010), "Financing of Public Education," PhD dissertation, Wharton School, University of Pennsylvania.

Jones, Mark, Osvaldo Meloni, and Mariano Tommasi (2012), "Voters as Fiscal Liberals: Incentives and Accountability in Federal Systems," *Economics and Politics*, 24 (July), 135–156.

Joyce, Phillip (2011), *The Congressional Budget Office*, Georgetown University Press, Washington, DC.

Kahanec, Martin, and Klaus Zimmerman (eds.) (2010), *EU Labor Markets after Post-enlargement*, Springer-Verlag, Berlin.

Kahanec, Martin, and Klaus Zimmerman (2016), "Post-enlargement Migration and the Great Recession in the E(M)U: Lessons and Policy Implications," Working Paper 2016–2066, United Nations University–MERIT, Maastricht, Netherlands.

Kam, Christopher (2014), "Party Discipline," in K. Strom and S. Martin (eds.), *Oxford Handbook of Legislative Politics*, Oxford University Press, New York, 399–417.

Karlin, David, and Jonathan Zinman (2008), "Credit Elasticities in Less-Developed Economies: Implications for Microfinance," *American Economic Review*, 98 (3), 1040–1068.

Katz, Michael (1996), *In the Shadow of the Poorhouse: A Social History of Welfare in America*, Harvard University Press, Cambridge, MA.

Kauppi, Heikki, and Mika Widgrén (2004), "What Determines UE-Making? Needs, Power, or Both?," *Economic Policy*, 19 (July), 221–266.

Keech, William (1968), *The Impact of Negro Voting: The Role of the Vote in the Quest for Equality*, Rand McNally, Chicago.

Keen, Michael (1998), "Vertical Tax Externalities in the Theory of Fiscal Federalism," *IMF Staff Papers*, 45 (September), 454–485.

Keen, Michael, and Christo Kotsogiannis (2002), "Does Federalism Lead to Excessively High Taxes?," *American Economic Review*, 92 (March), 363–370.

Keen, Michael, and Stephen Smith (1996), "VIVAT: An Alternative VAT for the EU," *Economic Policy*, 11 (October), 373–411.

Kelemen, R. Daniel (2016), "The Court of Justice of the European Union in the Twenty-First Century," *Law and Contemporary Problems*, 79 (1), 117–140.

Kelley, John J. (2000), *Freedom in the Church: A Documented History of the Principle of Subsidiary Function*, Peter Li, Dayton.

Kenen, Peter B. (1998), "Monetary Policy in Stage Three: A Review of the Framework Proposed by the European Monetary Institute," *International Journal of Finance and Economics*, 3 (January), 3–12.

Kessler, Anke (2014), "Communication in Federal Politics: Universalism, Policy Uniformity, and Optimal Allocation of Fiscal Authority," *Journal of Political Economy*, 122 (August), 766–805.

Keyssar, Alexander (2009), *The Right to Vote: The Contested History of Democracy in the United States*, Basic Books, New York.

Kim, Jinyoung, and John D. Wilson (1997), "Capital Mobility and Environmental Standards: Racing to the Bottom with Multiple Tax Instruments," *Japan and the World Economy*, 9 (December), 537–551.

Knack, Stephen, and Philip Keefer (1997), "Does Social Capital Have an Economic Payoff? A Cross-Country Investigation," *Quarterly Journal of Economics*, 112 (November), 1251–1288.

Knight, Brian (2004), "Parochial Interests and the Centralized Provision of Local Public Goods: Evidence from Congressional Voting on Transportation Projects," *Journal of Public Economics*, 88 (3), 845–866.

Knight, Brian (2013), "State Gun Policy and Cross State Externalities: Evidence from Crime Gun Tracing," *American Economic Journal: Economic Policy*, 5 (November), 200–229.

Kolstad, Charles (2007), "Systematic Uncertainty in Self-Enforcing International Environmental Agreements," *Journal of Environmental Economics and Management*, 53 (January), 68–79.

Kolstad, Charles, and Frank Wolak (1983), "Competition in Interregional Taxation: The Case of Western Coal," *Journal of Political Economy*, 91 (June), 443–459.

Kolstad, Charles, and Frank Wolak (1985), "Strategy and Market Structure in Western Coal Taxation," *Review of Economics and Statistics*, 67 (May), 23–249.

Kontopoulos, Yianos, and Roberto Perotti (1999), "Government Fragmentation and Fiscal Policy in OECD and EU Countries," in James Poterba and Jurgen von Hagen (eds.), *Fiscal Institutions and Fiscal Performance*, University of Chicago Press, Chicago, 81–102.

Kramer, Larry (1994), "Understanding Federalism," *Vanderbilt Law Review*, 47 (October), 1485–1561.

Kramer, Larry (2000), "Putting the Politics Back into the Political Safeguards of Federalism," *Columbia Law Review*, 100 (January), 215–293.

Krehbiel, Keith (1992), *Information and Legislative Organization*, University of Michigan Press, Ann Arbor.

Krehbiel, Keith (2006), "Pivots," in Barry Weingast and Donald Wittman (eds.), *The Oxford Handbook of Political Economy*, Oxford University Press, New York, 223–246.

Krusell, Per, and José-Victor Ríos-Rull (1999), "On the Size of the US Government: Political Economy in the Neoclassical Growth Model," *American Economic Review*, 89 (December), 1156–1181.

Kydland, Finn, and Edward Prescott (1977), "Rules Rather than Discretion: The Inconsistency of Optimal Plans," *Journal of Political Economy*, 85 (3), 473–491.

Ladd, Helen (1975), "Local Education Expenditures, Fiscal Capacity, and the Composition of the Property Tax Base," *National Tax Journal*, 28 (June), 146–158.

Lambert, Frank (2003), *The Founding Fathers and the Place of Religion in America*, Princeton University Press, Princeton, NJ.

Landes, William, and Richard Posner (1976), "Legal Precedent: A Theoretical and Empirical Analysis," *Journal of Law and Economics*, 19 (August), 249–307.

Lane, Philip (2012), "The European Sovereign Debt Crisis," *Journal of Economic Perspectives*, 26 (Summer), 49–68.

Le Breton, Michel, and Shlomo Weber (2003), "The Art of Making Everybody Happy: How to Prevent a Secession," *IMF Staff Papers*, 50 (3), 400–435.

Lee, Frances (1998), "Representation and Public Policy: The Consequences of Senate Apportionment for the Geographic Distribution of Federal Funds," *Journal of Politics*, 60 (February), 34–62.

Leeds, Michael (1985), "Property Values and Pension Underfunding in the Local Public Sector," *Journal of Urban Economics*, 18 (July), 34–46.

Leone, Robert, and John Jackson (1981), "The Political Economy of Federal Regulatory Activity: The Case of Water Pollution Controls," in Gary Fromm (ed.), *Studies in Public Regulation*, MIT Press, Cambridge, MA, 231–276.

Lessig, Larry (2011), *Republic Lost: How Money Corrupts Congress*, Hachette, New York.

Levinson, Arik (2003), "Environmental Regulatory Competition: A Status Report and Some New Evidence," *National Tax Journal*, 56 (March), 91–106.

Levitt, Steven (1994), "Using Repeat Challengers to Estimate the Effect of Campaign Spending on Election Outcomes in the U.S House," *Journal of Political Economy*, 102 (August), 777–798.

Levitt, Steven, and James Snyder (1997), "The Impact of Federal Spending on House Election Outcomes," *Journal of Political Economy*, 105 (February), 30–53.

Levy, Brian, Alan Hirsch, and Ingrid Woolard (2015), "Governance and Inequality: Benchmarking and Interpreting South Africa's Evolving Political Settlement," ESID Working Paper No. 51, Effective States and Inclusive Development Research Centre, University of Manchester, July.

Lijphart, Arend (1997), "Unequal Participation: Democracy's Unresolved Dilemma," *American Political Science Review*, 91 (March), 1–14.

Lindahl, Erik (1958), "Just Taxation: A Positive Solution," reprinted in R. Musgrave and A. Peacock (eds.), *Classics in the Theory of Public Finance*, St. Martin's Press, New York.

Linz, Juan, and Alfred Stepan (1996), "Towards Consolidated Democracies," *Journal of Democracy*, 7 (April), 14–30.

Lockwood, Ben (1999), "Inter-regional Insurance," *Journal of Public Economics*, 72 (April), 1–37.

Loevy, Robert (1997), *The Civil Rights Act of 1964: The Passage of the Law That Ended Racial Segregation*, State University of New York Press, Albany.

Lohmann, Susanne (1994), "The Dynamic of Informational Cascades: The Monday Demonstrations in Leipzig, East Germany, 1981–91," *World Politics*, 47 (1), 42–101.

Londregan, John, and James Snyder (1994), "Comparing Committees and Floor Preferences," *Legislative Studies Quarterly*, 19 (May), 233–266.

Lowenberg, Anton (1992), "A Post-apartheid Constitution for South Africa: Lessons from Public Choice," *Cato Journal*, 12 (Fall), 297–319.

MacKay, Robert C. (2014), "Implicit Debt Capitalization in Local Housing Prices: An Example of Unfunded Pension Liabilities," *National Tax Journal*, 67 (March), pp. 77–122.

MacKay, Robert, and Carolyn Weaver (1981), "Agenda Control by Budget Maximizers in a Multi-bureau Setting," *Public Choice*, 37 (January), 447–472.

MacLaughlin, Andrew (1918), "The Background of American Federalism," *American Political Science Review*, 12 (May), 215–240.

Mackil, Emily (2008), "The Greek *Koinon*," in P. Bang and W. Scheidel (eds.), *The Oxford Handbook of Ancient States*, Oxford University Press, New York, 469–491.

Maggs, Gregory (2017), "A Concise Guide to the Articles of Confederation as a Source for Determining the Meaning of the Constitution," *George Washington Law Review*, 85 (March), 397–450.

Majone, Giandomenico (1992), "Regulatory Federalism in the European Community," *Environment and Planning: Government and Policy*, 10 (September), 299–316.

Marmor, Theodore (2000), *The Politics of Medicare*, 2nd ed., Aldine De Gruyter, New York.

Martin, Isaac (2006), "Does School Finance Litigation Cause Taxpayer Revolts? *Serrano* and Proposition 13," *Law and Society Review*, 40 (September), 525–557.

Matsusaka, John (2005), "Direct Democracy Works," *Journal of Economic Perspectives*, 19 (Spring), 185–206.

Mattila, Mikko, and Jan-Erik Lane (2001), "Why Unanimity in the Council?," *European Union Politics*, 2 (1), 31–52.

Mayer, Kenneth, Timothy Werner, and Amanda Williams (2006), "Do Public Funding Programs Enhance Electoral Competition?," in Michael McDonald and John Samples (eds.), *The Marketplace for Democracy: Electoral Competition and American Politics*, Brookings Institution Press, Washington, DC, 245–267.

Mayhew, David R. (1974), *Congress and the Electoral Connection*, Yale University Press, New Haven, CT.

Mayhew, David R. (1986), *Placing Parties in American Politics*, Princeton University Press, Princeton, NJ.

McCarty, Nolan (2000), "Presidential Pork: Executive Veto Power and Distributive Politics," *American Political Science Review*, 94 (March), 117–129.

McConnell, Michael (1987), "Review: Federalism: Evaluating the Founders' Design," *University of Chicago Law Review*, 54 (Autumn), 1484–1512.

McConnell, Michael (1990), "The Origins and Historical Understanding of Free Exercise of Religion," *Harvard Law Review*, 103 (May), 1409–1519.

McConnell, Michael, and Randal Picker (1993), "A Conceptual Introduction to Municipal Bankruptcy," *University of Chicago Law Review*, 60 (Spring), 425–495.

McCubbins, Mathew, Roger Noll, and Barry Weingast (1987), "Administrative Procedures as Instruments of Political Control," *Journal of Law, Economics, and Organization*, 3 (Autumn), 243–277.

McCubbins, Matthew, Roger Noll, and Barry Weingast (1989), "Structure and Process, Politics and Policy: Administrative Arrangements and the Political Control of Agencies," *Virginia Law Review*, 75 (March), 431–482.

McCubbins, Mathew, and Thomas Schwartz (1984), "Congressional Oversight Overlooked: Police Patrols vs. Fire Alarms," *American Journal of Political Science*, 28 (February), 165–179.

McDowell, Bruce D. (1997), "Advisory Commission on Intergovernmental Relations in 1996: The End of an Era," *Publius: The Journal of Federalism*, 27 (Spring), 111–128.

McGarry, Aidan (2012), "The Dilemma of the European Union's Roma Policy," *Critical Social Policy*, 32 (1), 126–136.

McGarry, John (2002), "Federal Political Systems, and Accommodation of National Minorities," in Ann Griffiths (ed.), *Handbook of Federal Countries, 2002*, McGill-Queens University Press, Montreal, 416–447.

McGinnis, John O., and Ilya Somin (2004), "Federalism vs. States' Rights: A Defense of Judicial Review in a Federal System," *Northwestern University Law Review*, 99 (Fall), 89–130.

McGowan, Francis (2000), "Competition Policy: The Limits of the European Regulatory State," in Helen Wallace and William Wallace (eds.), *Policy-Making in the European Union*, Oxford University Press, New York, 115–176.

McKelvey, Richard (1976), "Intransitivities in Multidimensional Voting Models and Some Implications for Agenda Control," *Journal of Economic Theory*, 12 (June), 472–482.

McKinney, Matthew, John Parr, and Ethan Seltzer (2004), "Working across Boundaries: A Framework for Regional Collaboration," *Land Lines*, 16 (3), July.

McLure, Charles (1981), "Market Dominance and the Exporting of State Taxes," *National Tax Journal*, 34 (December), 483–485.

McLure, Charles (2000), "Implementing Subnational Value Added Taxes on Internal Trade: The Compensating VAT (CVAT)," *International Tax and Public Finance*, 7 (December), 723–740.

Mélitz, Jacques, and Frédéric Zumer (2002), "Regional Redistribution and Stabilization by the Center in Canada, France, the UK and the US: A Reassessment and New Tests," *Journal of Public Economics*, 86 (November), 263–286.

Meltzer, Allan (2003), *The History of the Federal Reserve*, vol. 1, 1913–1951, University of Chicago Press, Chicago.

Meltzer, Allan, and Scott Richard (1981), "A Rational Theory of the Size of Government," *Journal of Political Economy*, 89 (October), 914–927.

Mendelson, Nina (2004), "Chevron and Preemptions," *Michigan Law Review*, 102 (March), 737–798.

Mendelson, Nina (2008a), "The California Greenhouse Gas Waiver Decision and Agency Interpretation: A Response to Professors Galle and Seidenfeld," *Duke Law Journal*, 57 (May), 2158–2175.

Mendelson, Nina (2008b), "A Presumption against Agency Preemption," *Northwestern Law Review*, 102 (2), 695–725.

Mendoza, Enrique, and Linda Telsar (2005), "Why Hasn't Tax Competition Triggered a Race to the Bottom? Some Quantitative Lessons from the EU," *Journal of Monetary Economics*, 52 (January), 163–204.

Merlingen, Michael, Cas Mudde, and Ulrich Sedelmeier (2001), "The Right and the Righteous? European Norms, Domestic Politics and Sanction against Austria," *Journal of Common Market Studies*, 39 (1), 59–72.

Merritt, Deborah (1988), "The Guarantee Clause and State Autonomy: Federalism for a Third Century," *Columbia Law Review*, 88 (January), 1–78.

Metzger, Gillian (2007), "Congress, Article IV, and Interstate Relations," *Harvard Law Review*, 120 (April), 1468–1542.

Metzger, Gillian (2008), "Administrative Law as the New Federalism," *Duke Law Journal*, 57 (May), 2023–2109.

Metzger, Gillian (2011), "Federalism under Obama," *William and Mary Law Review*, 53 (November), 567–619.

Michelman, Frank (1977), "States' Rights and States' Roles: Permutations of 'Sovereignty' in *National League of Cities v. Usery*," *Yale Law Journal*, 86 (May), 1165–1195.

Michelman, Frank (1988), "Law's Republic," *Yale Law Journal*, 97 (July), 1493–1537.

Miller, John C. (1951), *Crisis in Freedom: The Alien and Sedition Acts*, Little, Brown, Boston.

Milligan, Kevin, Enrico Moretti, and Philip Oreopoulos (2004), "Does Education Improve Citizenship? Evidence from the United States and the United Kingdom," *Journal of Public Economics*, 88 (August), 1667–1695.

Mintz, Jack, and Michael Smart (2004), "Income Shifting, Investment, and Tax Competition: Theory and Evidence from Provincial Taxation in Canada," *Journal of Public Economics*, 88 (June), 1149–1168.

Mirrlees, James (1971), "An Exploration in the Theory of Optimum Income Taxation," *Review of Economic Studies*, 38 (April), 175–208.

Moe, Terry M., and Scott A. Wilson (1994), "Presidents and the Politics of Structure," *Law and Contemporary Problems*, 57 (Spring), 1–44.

Moens, Gabriel, and John Trone (2015), "The Principle of Subsidiarity in EU Judicial and Legislative Practice: Panacea or Placebo?," *Journal of Legislation*, 41(July), 65–102.

Moffitt, Robert (1990), "Have State Redistribution Policies Grown More Conservative?," *National Tax Journal*, 43 (June), 123–142.

Moffitt, Robert (1999), "Explaining Welfare Reform: Public Choice and the Labor Market," *International Tax and Public Finance*, 6 (August), 289–315.

Moffitt, Robert, David Ribar, and Mark Wilhelm (1998), "The Decline of Welfare Benefits in the US: The Role of Wage Inequality," *Journal of Public Economics*, 68 (June), 421–452.

Monras, Joan (2016), "Economic Shocks and Internal Migration," working paper, Sciences Po, Paris.

Montinola, Gabriella, Yingyi Qian, and Barry R. Weingast (1995), "Federalism, Chinese Style: The Political Basis for Economic Success in China," *World Politics*, 48 (October), 60–81

Moorman Mfg. Co. v. Bair, 437 U.S. 267 (1978).

Moravcsik, Andrew (2008), "The Myth of Europe's 'Democratic Deficit,'" *Intereconomics*, November/December, 331–340.

Morris, Charles (1980), *The Costs of Good Intentions*, W. W. Norton, New York.

Morrow, James (1994), *Game Theory for Political Scientists*, Princeton University Press, Princeton, NJ.

Mueller, Dennis (2003), *Public Choice III*, Cambridge University Press, New York.

Mulligan, Casey B. and Charles G. Hunter (2003), "The Empirical Frequency of a Pivotal Vote," *Public Choice*, 116 (1–2, July), 31–54.

Müller, Jan-Werner (2015), "Should the EU protect Democracy and the Rule of Law Inside Member States?", *European Law Journal*, 21 (March), 141–160.

Murdoch, James, and Todd Sandler (1997), "The Voluntary Provision of a Pure Public Good: The Case of Reduced CFC Emissions and the Montreal Protocol," *Journal of Public Economics*, 63 (February), 331–349.

Murray, Sheila, William Evans, and Robert Schwab (1998), "Education-Finance Reform and the Distribution of Education Resources," *American Economic Review*, 88 (September), 789–812.

Musgrave, Richard (1959), *The Theory of Public Finance*, McGraw-Hill, New York.

Musgrave, Richard, and Tun Thin (1948), "Income Tax Progression," *Journal of Political Economy*, 56 (December), 498–514.

Muthien, Yvonne, and Meshack Khosa (1998), "Demarcating the New Provinces: A Critical Reflection on the Process," in Y. Muthien and M. Khosa (eds.), *Regionalism in the New South Africa*, Ashgate, Brookfield, VT, 23–56.

Myerson, Roger (2006), "Federalism and Incentives for Success of Democracy," *Quarterly Journal of Political Science*, 1 (January), 3–23.

Myerson, Roger, and Mark Satterthwaite (1983), "Efficient Mechanisms for Bilateral Trading," *Journal of Economic Theory*, 29 (April), 265–281.

Myles, Gareth (1995), *Public Economics*, Cambridge University Press, New York.

Nagel, Jack (1987), *Participation*, Prentice-Hall, Englewood Cliffs, NJ.

National League of Cities v. Usery, 426 U.S. 833 (1976).

New York v. United States, 505 U.S. 144 (1992).

Niou, Emerson, and Peter Ordeshook (1985), "Universalism in Congress," *American Journal of Political Science*, 29 (May), 246–258.

North Carolina State Board of Examiners v. FTC, 135 S. Ct. 1101 (2015).

Noury, Abdul G., and Gerard Roland (2002), "More Power to the European Parliament?," *Economic Policy*, 17 (35), 279–319.

Novy-Marx, Robert, and Joshua Rauh (2011), "Public Pension Promises: How Big Are They and What Are They Worth?," *Journal of Finance*, 66 (August), 1211–1249.

Nozick, Robert (1974), *Anarchy, State, and Utopia*, Basic Books, New York.

Oates, Wallace (1972), *Fiscal Federalism*, Harcourt, Brace, Jovanovich, New York.

Oates, Wallace (1999), "An Essay on Fiscal Federalism," *Journal of Economic Literature*, 30 (September), 1120–1199.

Oates, Wallace E., and Robert M. Schwab (1988), "Economic Competition among Jurisdictions: Efficiency Enhancing or Distortion Inducing?," *Journal of Public Economics*, 35 (April), 333–354.

Oates, Wallace, and Robert Schwab (1997), "Impact of Urban Land Taxation: The Pittsburgh Experience," *National Tax Journal*, 50 (March), 1–21.

Obstfeld, Maurice, and Giovanni Peri (1998), "EMU: Ready or Not?," *Essays in International Finance No. 209*, International Finance Section, Department of Economics, Princeton University, Princeton, NJ.

Odom, Thomas (1987), "The Tenth Amendment after *Garcia*: Process-Based Procedural Protections," *University of Pennsylvania Law Review*, 135 (July), 1657–1694.

O'Leary, Brendan, Ian Lustick, and Thomas Callaghy (eds.) (2001), *Right-Sizing the State: The Politics of Moving Borders*, Oxford University Press, New York.

Oliver, Eric (2000), "City Size and Civic Involvement in Metropolitan America," *American Political Science Review*, 94 (June), 361–373.

Oliver, Eric (2012), *Local Elections and the Politics of Small-Scale Democracy*, Princeton University Press, Princeton, NJ.

Oliver, Eric, and Shang Ha (2007), "Vote Choice in Suburban Elections," *American Political Science Review*, 101 (August), 393–408.

Olken, Benjamin, and Rohini Pande (2012), "Corruption in Developing Countries," *Annual Review of Economics*, 4, 479–510.

Olson, Mancur (1965), *The Logic of Collective Action*, Harvard University Press, Cambridge, MA.

Olson, Mancur (1969), "The Principle of 'Fiscal Equivalence': The Division of Responsibilities among Different Levels of Government," *American Economic Review*, 59 (May), 479–487.

Ordeshook, Peter, and Olga Shvetsova (1997), "Federalism and Constitutional Design," *Journal of Democracy*, 8 (January), 27–42.

Ostrom, Elinor (1990), *Governing the Commons: The Evolution of Institutions for Collective Action*, Cambridge University Press, New York.

Overby, L. Marvin, and Kenneth M. Cosgrove (1996), "Unintended Consequences? Racial Redistricting and the Representation of Minority Interests," *Journal of Politics*, 58 (May), 540–550.

Pack, Howard, and Janet Pack (1978), "Metropolitan Fragmentation and Local Public Expenditures," *National Tax Journal*, 31 (December), 349–362.

Palfrey, Thomas, and Howard Rosenthal (1984), "Participation and the Provision of Discrete Public Goods: A Strategic Analysis," *Journal of Public Economics*, 24 (July), 171–193.

Panagariya, Arvind, Paul R. Portney, and Robert M. Schwab (eds.) (1999), *Environmental and Public Economics: Essays in Honor of Wallace Oates*, Edward Elgar, Cheltenham, UK.

Pande, Rohini (2003), "Can Mandated Political Representation Increase Policy Influence of Disadvantaged Minorities? Theory and Evidence from India," *American Economic Review*, 93 (September), 1132–1151.

Panning, William (1985), "Formal Models of Legislative Processes," in Gerhard Lowenberg, Samuel C. Patterson, and Malcolm Jewell (eds.), *Handbook of Legislative Research*, Harvard University Press, Cambridge, MA, 669–697.

Parker v. Brown, 317 U.S. 341 (1943).

Pateman, Carole (1970), *Participation and Democratic Theory*, Cambridge University Press, New York.

Patterson, James (1981), *America's Struggle against Poverty, 1900–1980*, Harvard University Press, Cambridge, MA.

Pauly, Mark (1967), "Clubs, Commonality, and the Core: An Integration of Game Theory and the Theory of Public Goods," *Economica*, 34 (April), 314–324.

Pauly, Mark (1970), "Optimality, 'Public' Goods, and Local Governments: A General Theoretical Analysis," *Journal of Political Economy*, 78 (June), 572–586.

Pauly, Mark (1973), "Income Redistribution as a Local Public Good," *Journal of Public Economics*, 2 (February), 35–58.

Peekhaus, Wilhelm (2014), "South Africa's *Promotion of Access to Information Act*: An Analysis of Relevant Jurisprudence," *Journal of Information Policy*, 4 (January), 570–596.

Penner, Rudolph, and Alan Abramson (1988), *Broken Purse Strings: Congressional Budgeting, 1974 to 1988*, Urban Institute Press, Washington, DC.

Persson, Torsten, Gerard Roland, and Guido Tabellini (2007), "How Do Electoral Rules Shape Party Structures, Government Coalitions, and Economic Policies?," *Quarterly Journal of Political Science*, 2 (May), 155–188.

Persson, Torsten, and Guido Tabellini (1996), "Federal Fiscal Constitution: Risk Sharing and Moral Hazard," *Econometrica*, 64 (May), 623–646.

Persson, Torsten, and Guido Tabellini (1999), "The Size and Scope of Government: Comparative Politics with Rational Politicians," *European Economic Review*, 43 (April), 699–735.

Persson, Torsten, and Guido Tabellini (2003), *Economic Effects of Constitutions*, MIT Press, Cambridge, MA.

Persson, Torsten, and Guido Tabellini (2004), "Constitutional Rules and Fiscal Policy Outcomes," *American Economic Review*, 94 (January), 25–46.

Pettit, Philip (1997), *Republicanism: A Theory of Freedom and Government*, Oxford University Press, New York.

Pindyck, Robert S., and Daniel L. Rubinfeld (2018), *Microeconomics*, 9th ed., Pearson, New York.

Pisani-Ferry, Jean (2011), *The Euro Crisis and Its Aftermath*, Oxford University Press, New York.

Plato (1970), *The Laws*, edited by Trevor J. Saunders, Penguin Classics, London.

Plott, Charles (1967), "A Notion of Equilibrium and Its Possibility under Majority Rule," *American Economic Review*, 57 (September), 787–806.

Poole, Keith, and Howard Rosenthal (1997), *Congress: A Political-Economic History of Role Call Voting*, Oxford University Press, New York.

Powell, G. Bingham (1986), "American Voter Turnout in a Comparative Perspective," *American Political Science Review*, 80 (March), 17–43.

Pradhan, Menno, Daniel Suryadarma, Amanda Bratty, Maisy Wong, Arya Gaduh, Armida Alisjahbana, and Rima Prama Artha (2014), "Improving Education Quality Through Enhancing Community Participation: Results from a Randomized Field Experiment in Indonesia," *American Economic Journal: Applied Economics*, 6 (April), 105–126.

Preuhs, Robert (2006), "The Conditional Effects of Minority Descriptive Representation: Black Legislators and Policy Influence in the American States," *Journal of Politics*, 68 (August), 585–599.

Primo, David (2006), "Stop Us before We Spend Again: Institutional Constraints on Government Spending," *Economics and Politics*, 18 (November), 269–312.

Primo, David, and James Snyder (2008), "Distributive Politics and the Law of 1/n," *Journal of Politics*, 70 (April), 477–486.

Printz v. United States, 521 U.S. 898 (1997).

Przeworski, Adam, Michael Alvarez, José Antonio Cheibub, and Fernando Limongi (1990), *Democracy and Development: Political Institutions and Material Well-Being in the World, 1950–1990*, Cambridge University Press, New York.

Przeworkski, Adam, Michael Alvarez, José Cheibub, and Fernando Limongi (2000), *Democracy and Development: Political Institutions and Material Well-Being in the World: 1950–1990*, Cambridge University Press, New York.

Rakove, Jack (1979), *The Beginnings of National Politics: An Interpretive History of the Continental Congress*, Alfred A. Knopf, New York.

Rakove, Jack (1996), *Original Meanings: Politics and Ideas in the Making of the Constitution*, Alfred A. Knopf, New York.

Ramey, Valerie (2011), "Can Governments Purchases Stimulate the Economy?," *Journal of Economic Literature*, 49 (September), 673–685.

Rao, Govinda, and Nirvikar Singh (2006), "The Political Economy of India's Fiscal Federal System and Its Reform," *Publius: The Journal of Federalism*, 37 (January), 26–44.

Rapaczynski, Andrzej (1985), "From Sovereignty to Process: The Jurisprudence of Federalism After Garcia," *Supreme Court Review*, 1985, 341–419.

Rawls, John (1971), *A Theory of Justice*, Harvard University Press, Cambridge, MA.

Reinhart, Carmen, and Kenneth Rogoff (2014), "Recovery from Financial Crises: Evidence from 100 Episodes," *American Economic Review*, 104 (May), 50–55.

Reinhart, Carmen, and Christoph Trebesch (2015), "The Pitfalls of External Debt Dependence: Greece, 1829–2015," *Brookings Papers on Economic Activity*, Fall, 307–328.

Reinikka, Ritva, and Jakob Svensson (2004), "Local Capture: Evidence from a Central Government Transfer Program in Uganda," *Quarterly Journal of Economics*, 119 (May), 679–709.

Revesz, Richard (1992), "Rehabilitating Interstate Competition: Rethinking the 'Race to the Bottom' Rationale for Federal Environmental Regulation," *New York University Law Review*, 67 (December), 1210–1254.

Revesz, Richard (1996). "Federalism and Interstate Environmental Externalities," *University of Pennsylvania Law Review*, 144 (June), 2341–2416.

Revesz, Richard (2000), "Federalism and Environmental Regulation: An Overview," in Richard Revesz, Philippe Sands, and Richard Stewart (eds.), *Environmental Law, the Economy, and Sustainable Development: The United States, the European Union, and the International Community*, Cambridge University Press, New York, 37–79.

Revesz, Richard L. (2001). "Federalism and Environmental Regulation: A Public Choice Analysis," *Harvard Law Review*, 115 (December), 555–641.

Revesz, Richard, and Michael Livermore (2008), *Retaking Rationality: How Cost-Benefit Analysis Can Better Protect the Environment and Our Health*, Oxford University Press, New York.

Rhode, Paul, and Koleman Strumpf (2003), "Assessing the Importance of Tiebout Sorting: Local Heterogeneity from 1850 to 1990," *American Economic Review*, 93 (December), 1648–1677.

Riker, William (1955), "The Senate and American Federalism," *American Political Science Review*, 49 (June), 452–469.

Riker, William (1964), *Federalism: Origin, Operation, Significance*, Little, Brown, Boston.

Riker, William (1980), "Implications from the Disequilibrium of Majority Rule for the Study of Institutions," *American Political Science Review*, 74 (June), 432–446.

Riker, William (1987), "The Lessons of 1787," *Public Choice*, 55 (February), 5–34.

Riker, William, and Peter Ordeshook (1973), *An Introduction to Positive Political Theory*, Prentice-Hall, Englewood Cliffs, NJ.

Rodden, Jonathan (2003), "Federalism and Bailouts in Brazil," in Jonathan Rodden, Gunnar S. Eskeland, and Jennie Litvack (eds.), *Fiscal Decentralization and the Challenge of Hard Budget Constraints*, MIT Press, Cambridge, MA, 213–248.

Rodden, Jonathan (2006), *Hamilton's Paradox: The Promise and Peril of Fiscal Federalism*, Cambridge University Press, New York.

Rodden, Jonathan, Gunnar S. Eskeland, and Jennie Litvack (eds.) (2003), *Fiscal Decentralization and the Challenge of Hard Budget Constraints*, MIT Press, Cambridge, MA.

Rodgers, Harrell, Glenn Beamer, and Lee Payne (2008), "No Race in Any Direction: State Welfare and Income Regimes," *Policy Studies Journal*, 36 (November), 525–543.

Roe, Mark (2003), "Delaware's Competition," *Harvard Law Review*, 117 (December), 588–646.

Roe, Mark (2005), "Delaware's Politics," *Harvard Law Review*, 118 (June), 2491–2543.

Roemer, John, Rolk Aaberge, Ugo Colombino, Johan Fritzell, Stephen Jenkins, Arnaud Lefranc, et al. (2003), "To What Extent Do Fiscal Regimes Equalize Opportunities for Income Acquisition Among Citizens," *Journal of Public Economics*, 87 (March), 539–565.

Romano, Roberta (1985) "Law as a Product: Some Pieces of the Incorporation Puzzle," *Journal of Law, Economics, and Organization*, 1 (Autumn), 225–283.

Romano, Roberta (1993), *The Genius of American Corporate Law*, AEI Press, Washington, DC.

Romano, Roberta (2002), *The Advantage of Competitive Federalism for Securities Regulation*, AEI Press, Washington, DC.

Romer, Thomas, and Howard Rosenthal (1979), "Bureaucrats vs. Voters: On the Political Economy of Resource Allocation in a Direct Democracy," *Quarterly Journal of Economics*, 93 (November), 562–587.

Romer, Thomas, Howard Rosenthal, and Vincent Munley (1992), "Economic Incentives and Political Institutions: Spending and Voting in School Budget Referenda," *Journal of Public Economics*, 49 (October), 1–33.

Rose, Mark H. (1990), *Interstate: Express Highway Politics, 1939–1989*, University of Tennessee Press, Knoxville.

Rosenberg, Gerald (2008), *The Hollow Hope: Can Courts Bring About Social Change?*, University of Chicago Press, Chicago.

Ross, Stephen, and John Yinger (1999), "Sorting and Voting: A Review of the Literature on Urban Public Finance," in Paul Cheshire and Edwin S. Mills (eds.), *Handbook of Regional and Urban Economics*, vol. 3, *Applied Urban Economics*, North-Holland, Amsterdam, 2001–2060.

Rossiter, Clinton (1966), *1787: The Grand Convention*, Macmillan, New York.

Rotberg, Robert (2014), "The Need for Strengthened Political Leadership," *Annals of the American Academy of Political and Social Sciences*, 652 (March), 238–256.

Roth, Alvin E. (1985), "Towards a Focal Point Theory of Bargaining," in A. E. Roth (ed.), *Game-Theoretic Models of Bargaining*, Cambridge University Press, Cambridge, 259–268.

Rothstein, Jesse (2007), "Does Competition among Public Schools Benefit Students and Taxpayers? Comment," *American Economic Review*, 97 (5), 2026–2037.

Roubini, Nouriel, and Jeffrey Sachs (1989a), "Government Spending and Budget Deficits in Industrial Countries," *Economic Policy*, 4 (April), 99–132.

Roubini, Nouriel, and Jeffrey Sachs (1989b), "Political and Economic Determinants of Budget Deficits in Industrial Democracies," *European Economic Review*, 33 (May), 903–918.

Rubinfeld, Daniel L. (1973), "Credit Ratings and the Market for General Obligation Bonds," *National Tax Journal*, 26 (March), 17–27.

Rubinfeld, Daniel L. (2019), "Antitrust Enforcement in the U.S. and the EU: A Comparison of the Two Federal Systems," in Damien Gerard and Ioannis Lianos (eds.), *Reconciling*

Efficiency and Equity: A Global Challenge for Competition Policy, Cambridge University Press, Cambridge, chapter 18.

Ryan, Erin (2011), "Negotiating Federalism," *Boston College Law Review*, 52 (January), 1–136.

Saari, Donald (2006), "A Tool Kit for Voting Theory," in Barry Weingast and Donald Wittman (eds.), *The Oxford Handbook of Political Economy*, Oxford University Press, New York, 390–407.

Saenz v. Roe, 526 U.S. 489 (1999).

Saez, Emmanuel, and Stefanie Stantcheva (2016), "Generalized Social Marginal Welfare Weights for Optimal Tax Theory," *American Economic Review*, 106 (January), 24–45.

Samuelson, Paul (1954), "The Pure Theory of Public Expenditure," *Review of Economics and Statistics*, 36 (November), 387–389.

San Antonio Independent School District v. Rodriguez, 411 U.S. 1 (1973).

Sandler, Todd, and James Murdoch (1990), "Nash-Cournot or Lindahl Behavior: An Empirical Test for the NATO Allies," *Quarterly Journal of Economics*, 105 (November), 875–894.

Scalia, Anthony (1982), "Two Faces of Federalism," *Harvard Journal of Law and Public Policy*, 6 (Special Issue), 19–22.

Schapiro, Robert (2009), *Polyphonic Federalism: Toward the Protection of Fundamental Rights*, University of Chicago Press, Chicago.

Scheiber, Harry (1978), "American Federalism and the Diffusion of Power: Historical and Contemporary Perspective," *Toledo Law Review*, 9 (Summer), 619–680.

Scheingold, Stuart (1974), *The Politics of Rights*, Yale University Press, New Haven, CT.

Schelling, Thomas (1960), *The Strategy of Conflict*, Harvard University Press, Cambridge, MA.

Scheppele, Kim Lane (2016), "Enforcing the Basic Principles of EU Law through Systemic Infringement Procedures," in Dimitry Kochenov and Carlos Closa (eds.), *Reinforcing the Rule of Law Oversight in the European Union*, Cambridge University Press, New York, 105–132.

Schick, Allen (1980), *Congress and Money: Spending, Taxing, Budgeting*, Urban Institute, Washington, DC.

Schlesinger, Arthur, Jr. (1945), *The Age of Jackson*, Little, Brown, Boston.

Schlesinger, Arthur (1958), *The Coming of the New Deal: 1933–35*, vol. 2 of *The Age of Roosevelt*, Houghton Mifflin, Boston.

Schlesinger, Joseph (1984), "On the Theory of Party Organization," *Journal of Politics*, 46 (May), 369–400.

Schneider, Christina (2013), "Globalizing Electoral Politics: Political Competence and Distributional Bargaining in the European Union," *World Politics*, 65 (July), 452–490.

Scotchmer, Suzanne (1997), "On Price-Taking Equilibria in Club Economies with Nonanonymous Crowding," *Journal of Public Economics*, 65 (July), 75–88.

Semuels, Alana (2016), "The End of Welfare As We Know It," *The Atlantic*, April 1, 2016.

Sen, Amartya (1973), *On Economic Inequality*, Clarendon Press, Oxford, UK.

Sen, Amartya (1999), *Development as Freedom*, Random House, New York.

Serrano v. Priest, 487 P.2d 1241 (Cal. 1971).

Shapiro, David (1995), *Federalism: A Dialogue*, Northwestern University Press, Evanston, IL.

Shapiro v. Thompson, 394 U.S. 618 (1969).

Sharkey, Catherine (2007), "Preemption by Preamble: Federal Agencies and the Federalization of Tort Law," *DePaul Law Review*, 56 (April), 227–260.

Sharkey, Catherine (2009), "Federalism Accountability: 'Agency-Forcing' Measures," *Duke Law Journal*, 58 (May), 2125–2192.

Sharkey Catherine (2012), "Inside Agency Preemption," *Michigan Law Review* 110 (February), 522–595.

Shaviro, Daniel (1993), *Federalism in Taxation: The Case for Greater Uniformity*, AEI Press, Washington, DC.

Shelby County v. Holder, 570 U.S. 529 (2013).

Shepsle, Kenneth (1978), *The Giant Jigsaw Puzzle: Democratic Committee Assignments in the Modern House*, University of Chicago Press, Chicago.

Shepsle, Kenneth (1979), "Institutional Arrangements and Equilibrium in Multidimensional Voting Models," *American Journal of Political Science*, 28 (February), 49–74.

Shepsle, Kenneth (1994), "Positive Theories of Congressional Institutions," *Legislative Studies Quarterly*, 19 (May), 149–179.

Shepsle, Kenneth (2006), "Old Questions and New Answers about Institutions: The Riker Objection Revisited," in Barry Weingast and Donald Wittman (eds.), *The Oxford Handbook of Political Economy*, Oxford University Press, New York, 1031–1049.

Shepsle, Kenneth and Barry Weingast (1981), "Structure-Induced Equilibrium and Legislative Choice," *Public Choice*, 37 (January), 503–519.

Shliefer, Andre (1985), "A Theory of Yardstick Competition," *Rand Journal of Economics*, 16 (Autumn), 319–327.

Sigman, Hilary (2002), "International Spillovers and Water Quality in Rivers: Do Countries Free Ride?" *American Economic Review*, 92 (September), 1152–1159.

Sigman, Hilary (2005), "Transboundary Spillovers and Decentralization of Environmental Policies," *Journal of Environmental Economics and Management*, 50 (July), 82–101.

Sigman, Hilary (2014), "Decentralization and Environmental Quality: An International Analysis of Water Pollution Levels and Variation," *Land Economics*, 90 (February), 114–130.

Simeon, Richard, and Christina Murray (2009), "Reforming Multi-level Government in South Africa," *Canadian Journal of African Studies*, 43 (3), 536–571.

Small, Kenneth, and Shunfeng Song (1992), "Wasteful Commuting: A Resolution," *Journal of Political Economy*, 100 (August), 888–898.

Small, Kenneth, Clifford Whinston, and Carol Evans (1989), *Road Work: A New Highway Pricing and Investment Policy*, Brookings Institution, Washington, DC.

Smart, Michael (1998), "Taxation and Deadweight Loss in a System of Intergovernmental Transfers," *Canadian Journal of Economics*, 31 (February), 189–206.

Smith, Adam (1976), *An Inquiry into the Wealth of Nations*, edited by R. H. Campbell and A. S. Skinner, Liberty Classic Edition, Clarendon, Oxford.

Smith, James Morton (1956), *Freedom's Fetters: The Alien and Sedition Laws and American Civil Liberties*, Cornell University Press, Ithaca, NY.

Snyder, James (1989), "Election Goals and the Allocation of Campaign Resources," *Econometrica*, 57 (May), 637–660.

Snyder, James (1990), "Campaign Contributions as Investments: The US House of Representatives, 1980–1986, *Journal of Political Economy*, 98 (December), 1195–1227.

Snyder, James (1991), "On Buying Legislatures," *Economics and Politics*, 3 (July), 93–109.

Snyder, James (1993), "The Market for Campaign Contributions: Evidence from the US Senate: 1980–1986," *Economic and Politics*, 5 (November), 219–240.

Snyder, James, and Timothy Groseclose (2000), "Estimating Party Influence in Congressional Roll Call Voting," *American Journal of Political Science*, 44 (April), 187–205.

Snyder, James, and Gerald Kramer (1988), "Fairness, Self-Interest, and the Politics of the Progressive Income Tax," *Journal of Public Economics*, 36 (July), 197–230.

Snyder, James, and Michael Ting (2002), "An Informational Rationale for Political Parties," *American Journal of Political Science*, 46 (January), 90–110.

Soltani, Mohammad, and Sayed Saghaian (2012), "Export Demand Function Estimation for U.S. Raisins," paper presented at the Southern Agriculture Economics Association Annual Meetings, Birmingham, AL, February 4–7.

Sorensen, Bent, Lisa Wu, and Oved Yosha (2001), "Output Fluctuations and Fiscal Policy: U.S. State and Local Governments, 1978–1994," *European Economic Review*, 45 (June), 1271–1310.

South Africa, Department of Planning, Monitoring, and Evaluation (2016), *Development Indicators (2016)*.

South Africa, Financial and Fiscal Commission (Various Years), *The Allocation of Financial Resources Between the National and Provincial Governments, FY 1997/98–FY 2016/17*.

South Africa, Financial and Fiscal Commission (1996/97), "The Financial and Fiscal Commission's Recommendations for the Allocation of Financial Resources to the National Government and the Provincial Governments for the 1997/98 Financial Year."

South Africa, Minister of Finance, *Division of Revenue Bill, Various Years: Part 4: Provincial Allocations, FY 2000/01–FY 2016/2017*.

South Dakota v. Dole, 483 U.S. 203 (1987).

Southwick, Lawrence (2005), "Economies of Scale and Market Power in Policing," *Managerial and Decision Economics*, 26 (8), 461–473.

Southwick, Lawrence (2012), "Economies of Scale in Local Government: General Government Spending," *iBusiness*, 4 (September), 265–278.

Spolaore, Enrico (2013), "What Is European Integration Really About? A Political Guide for Economists," *Journal of Economic Perspectives*, 27 (Summer), 125–144.

Stark, Kirk, and Jonathan Zasloff (2003), "Tiebout and the Tax Revolt: Did Serrano *Really* Cause Proposition 13?," *UCLA Law Review*, 50 (February), 801–858.

Stavins, Robert (2019), "The Future of US Carbon-Pricing Policy," paper presented at "Environmental and Energy Policy and the Economy," National Bureau of Economic Research conference, National Press Club, Washington, DC, March 4.

Stein, Ernesto, Ernesto Talvi, and Alejandro Grisanti (1999), "Institutional Arrangements and Fiscal Performance: The Latin American Experience," in James Poterba and Jurgen von Hagen (eds.), *Fiscal Institutions and Fiscal Performance*, University of Chicago Press, Chicago, 103–134.

Stein, Robert, and Kenneth Bickers (1995), *Perpetuating the Pork Barrel: Policy Subsystems and American Democracy*, Cambridge University Press, New York.

Stephenson, Matthew (2004), "Court of Public Opinion: Government Accountability and Judicial Independence," *Journal of Law, Economics, and Organization*, 20 (October), 379–399.

Stevens, Barbara J. (1978), "Scale, Market Structure, and the Cost of Refuse Collection," *Review of Economics and Statistics*, 60 (August), 438–448.

Stevens, L. Nye (1999), "Testimony: Federalism Implementation of Executive Order 12612 in Rulemaking Process," *United States General Accounting Office*, GAO/T-GGD-99-93, Washington, DC.

Stewart, Richard (1986), "Reconstitutive Law," *Maryland Law Review*, 46 (Fall), 86–114.

Steytler, Nico (2017), "The Constitutional Court of South Africa: Reinforcing and Hourglass System of Multi-level Government," in Nicholas Aroney and John Kincaid (eds.), *Courts in Federal Countries*, University of Toronto Press, Toronto, 328–366.

Stockman, David (1975), "The Social Pork Barrel," *Public Interest*, 39 (Spring), 3–30.

Storing, Herbert (1981), *What the Anti-Federalists Were For: The Political Thought of the Opponents of the Constitution*, University of Chicago Press, Chicago.

Stratmann, Thomas (2005), "Some Talk: Money in Politics. A (Partial) Review of the Literature," *Public Choice*, 124 (July), 135–156.

Stratmann, Thomas, and Francisco Aparicio-Castillo (2006), "Competition Policy for Elections: Do Campaign Contribution Limits Matter?," *Public Choice*, 127 (April), 177–206.

Stratmann, Thomas, and Francisco Aparicio-Castillo (2007), " Campaign Finance Reform and Electoral Competition: Comment," *Public Choice*, 133 (October), 107–110.

Strumpf, Koleman (2002), "Does Government Decentralization Increase Policy Innovation?," *Journal of Public Economic Theory*, 4 (April), 207–241.

Suárez Serrato, Juan Carlos, and Owen Zidar (2016), "Who Benefits from State Corporate Tax Cuts? A Local Labor Markets Approach with Heterogeneous Firms," *American Economic Review*, 106 (September), 2582–2624.

Suberu, Rotimi (2001), *Federalism and Ethnic Conflict in Nigeria*, United States Institute for Peace Press, Washington.

Sunstein, Cass (1987), "Constitutionalism after the New Deal," *Harvard Law Review*, 101 (December), 421–510.

Sunstein, Cass (1988), "Beyond the Republican Revival," *Yale Law Journal*, 97 (July), 1539–1590.

Sunstein, Cass (2016), "The Most Knowledgeable Branch," *University of Pennsylvania Law Review*, 164 (June), 1607–1648.

Swinton, Katherine (1992), "Federalism under Fire: The Role of the Supreme Court in Canada," *Law and Contemporary Problems*, 55 (Winter), 121–145.

Tavares, Jose, and Romain Wacziarg (2001), "How Democracy Affects Growth," *European Economic Review*, 45 (8), 1341–1378.

Teske, Paul (2004), *Regulation in the States*, Brookings Institution Press, Washington, DC.

Thimann, Christian (2015), "The Microeconomic Dimensions of the Eurozone Crisis and Why European Politics Cannot Solve Them," *Journal of Economic Perspectives*, 29 (Summer), 141–161.

Thompson, Earl (1968), "The Perfectly Competitive Production of Collective Goods," *Review of Economics and Statistics*, 50 (February), 1–12.

Thompson, Robert (2011), *Resolving Controversy in the European Union*, Cambridge University Press, New York.

Tiebout, Charles (1956), "A Pure Theory of Local Expenditures," *Journal of Political Economy*, 64 (October), 416–424.

Treisman, Daniel (2007), *The Architecture of Government: Rethinking Political Decentralization*, Cambridge University Press, New York.

United States Department of Justice and Federal Trade Commission (2010), *Horizontal Merger Guidelines*, Washington, DC.

United States v. Darby Lumber, 312 U.S. 100 (1941).

United States v. Lopez, 514 U.S. 549 (1995).

United States v. Morrison, 529 U.S. 598 (2000).

United Transportation Union v. Long Island R.R., 455 U.S. 678 (1982).

Valelly, Richard (2004), *The Two Reconstructions: The Struggle for Black Enfranchisement*, University of Chicago Press, Chicago.

Van den Bergh, Roger (2000), "Economic Criteria for Applying the Subsidiarity Principle in European Environmental Law," in Richard Revesz, Philippe Sands, and Richard Stewart (eds.), *Environmental Law, the Economy, and Sustainable Development: The United States, the European Union, and the International Community*, Cambridge University Press, New York, 80–95.

Vandenbruwaene, Werner (2014), "The Legal Enforcement of the Principles of Subsidiarity," *Perspectives on Federalism*, 6 (2), E45-E73.

Velasco, Andrés (2000), "Debts and Deficits with Fragmented Fiscal Policymaking," *Journal of Public Economics*, 76 (April), 105–125.

Volden, Craig (2006), "States as Policy Laboratories: Emulating Success in the Children's Health Insurance Program," *American Journal of Political Science*, 50 (April), 294–312.

Waldmeir, Patti (1997), *Anatomy of a Miracle: The End of Apartheid and Birth of the New South Africa*, W. W. Norton, New York.

Walker, J. Samuel (2009), *The Road to Yucca Mountain: Development of Radioactive Waste Policy in the United States*, University of California Press, Berkeley.

Watts, Ronald (1999), *Comparing Federal Systems*, McGill-Queen's University Press, Montreal.

Weaver, Kent (2000), *Ending Welfare as We Know It*, Brookings Institution, Washington, DC.

Webb, Stephen (2003), "Argentina: Hardening the Provincial Budget Constraint," in Jonathan Rodden, Gunnar S. Eskeland, and Jennie Litvack (eds.), *Fiscal Decentralization and the Challenge of Hard Budget Constraints*, MIT Press, Cambridge, MA, 189–211.

Wechsler, Herbert (1954), "The Political Safeguards of Federalism: The Role of the States in the Composition and Selection of the National Government," *Columbia Law Review*, 54 (April), 543–560.

Weingast, Barry (1979), "A Rational Choice Perspective on Congressional Norms," *American Journal of Political Science*, 23 (May), 245–262.

Weingast, Barry (1995), "The Economic Role of Political Institutions: Market-Preserving Federalism and Economic Development," *Journal of Law, Economics, and Organization*, 11 (April), 1–31.

Weingast, Barry (1997), "The Political Foundations of Democracy and the Rule of Law," *American Political Science Review*, 90 (June), 245–263.

Weingast, Barry (2005), "The Constitutional Dilemma of Economic Liberty," *Journal of Economic Perspectives*, 19 (3), (Summer), 89–108.

Weingast, Barry (2009), "Second Generation Fiscal Federalism: Implications for Decentralized Democratic Governance and Economic Development," *Journal of Urban Economics*, 65 (November), 279–293.

Weingast, Barry, and William Marshall (1988), "The Industrial Organization of Congress," *Journal of Political Economy*, 96 (April), 132–163.

Weiser, Philip J. (2001), "Federal Common Law, Cooperative Federalism, and the Enforcement of the Telecom Act," *New York University Law Review*, 76 (December), 1692–1767.

Weitzman, Martin (1974), "Prices vs. Quantities," *Review of Economic Studies*, 41 (December), 477–491.

Wellisch, Dietmar (2000), *Theory of Public Finance in a Federal State*, Cambridge University Press, New York.

Wheare, Kenneth Clinton (1964), *Federal Government*, Oxford University Press, New York.

White, Lawrence (2013), "Credit Rating Agencies: An Overview," *Annual Review of Financial Economics*, 5, 93–122.

White, Michelle (1975), "Firm Location in a Zoned Metropolitan Area," in Edwin Mills and Wallace Oates (eds.), *Fiscal Zoning and Land Use Controls*, D. C. Heath, Lexington, MA, 175–202.

White, Michelle (1988), "Urban Commuting Journeys Are Not 'Wasteful,'" *Journal of Political Economy*, 96 (October), 1097–1110.

Whittington, Keith (1998), "Dismantling the Modern State? The Changing Structural Foundations of Federalism," *Hastings Constitutional Law Quarterly*, 25 (Spring), 483–527.

Wicksell, Knut (1958), "A New Principle of Just Taxation," reprinted in R. Musgrave and A. Peacock (eds.), *Classics in the Theory of Public Finance*, Macmillan, London, 72–118.

Wildasin, David (1989), "Interjurisdictional Capital Mobility: Fiscal Externality and a Corrective Subsidy," *Journal of Urban Economics*, 25 (March), 193–212.

Wildasin, David (1991), "Income Redistribution in a Common Labor Market," *American Economic Review*, 81 (September), 757–774.

Wildasin, David (1999), "Public Pensions in the EU: Migration Incentives and Impacts," in Arvind Panagariya, Paul R. Portney, and Robert M. Schwab (eds.), *Environmental and Public Economics: Essays in Honor of Wallace E. Oates*, Edward Elgar, Cheltenham, UK, 253–282.

Williams, Andrew (2015), "Human Rights in the EU," in Damian Chalmers and Anthony Arnull (eds.), *Oxford Handbook of European Union Law*, Oxford University Press, New York, pp. 1–24.

Willig, Bobby (1976), "Consumer Surplus without Apology," *American Economic Review*, 66 (September), 589–597.

Wilson, John D. (1995), "Mobile Labor, Multiple Tax Instruments, and Tax Competition," *Journal of Urban Economics*, 38 (November), 333–356.

Wilson, Rick (1986), "An Empirical Test of Preferences for the Political Pork Barrel: District Level Appropriations for River and Harbor Legislation, 1899–1913," *American Journal of Political Science*, 30 (August), 729–754.

Winter, Ralph K. (1977), "State Law, Shareholder Protection, and the Theory of the Corporation," *Journal of Legal Studies*, 6 (June), 251–292.

Wittman, Donald (1989), "Why Democracies Produce Efficient Results," *Journal of Political Economy*, 97 (December), 1395–1424.

Wong, Kenneth, and Gail Sunderman (2007), "Education Accountability as a Presidential Priority: No Child Left Behind and the Bush Presidency," *Publius: The Journal of Federalism*, 37 (Summer), 333–350.

Wong, Ho Lun, Yu Wang, Benfu Luo, Linxiu Zhang, and Scott Rozelle (2017), "Local Governance and the Quality of Local Infrastructure: Evidence from Village Road Projects in Rural China," *Journal of Public Economics*, 152 (August), 119–132.

World Bank (2005), *World Development Report, 2005: A Better Investment Climate for Everyone*, Washington, DC.

World Bank (2019), "Measuring Business Regulations," *Doing Business 2020*, Washington, D.C.

Young, Ernest (2001), "Two Cheers for Process Federalism," *Villanova Law Review*, 46 (5), 1349–1395.

Zax, Jeffrey (1989), "Is There a Leviathan in Your Neighborhood?," *American Economic Review*, 79 (June), 560–567.

Zetland, David (2009), "The End of Abundance: How Water Bureaucrats Created and Destroyed the Southern California Oasis," *Water Alternatives*, 2 (3), 350–369.

Zettelmeyer, Jeromin, Christoph Trebesch, and Mitu Gulati (2013), "The Greek Debt Restructuring: An Autopsy," *Economic Policy*, 28 (July), 513–563.

Zhao, Bo (2014), "Saving for a Rainy Day: Estimating the Appropriate Size of the US State Budget Stabilization Funds," Working Paper No. 14–12, Federal Reserve Bank of Boston.

Ziliak, James (2016), "Temporary Assistance for Needy Families," in Robert Moffitt (ed.), *The Economics of Means-Tested Transfer Programs in the United States*, University of Chicago Press, Chicago, 1:303–393.

Zodrow, George (2010), "Capital Mobility and Capital Tax Competition," *National Tax Journal*, 63 (December), 865–901.

Zodrow, George, and Peter Mieszkowski (1986), "Pigou, Tiebout, Property Taxation, and the Underprovision of Local Public Goods," *Journal of Urban Economics*, 19 (May), 356–370.

NAME INDEX

Acemoglu, Daron, 15n20, 167n37, 181n2, 344n6, 361n, 364n29
Ackerman, Bruce, 4n, 67, 167n39, 183, 188, 196n25
Adamolekun, Ladipo, 68n
Adler, E. Scott, 118n36
Aksoy, Deniz, 313n21
Albouy, David, 163n35
Aldrich, John, 171n44, 369n38
Alesina, Alberto, 7n8, 251n74, 333
Allen, Chris, 309n11
Allen, Franklin, 318n33
Alston, Philip, 324n45
Amar, Akil Reed, 4n, 5n6, 67, 68–69, 372
Anderson, Karen, 70n
Andrews, Matthew, 39n
Andriamananjara, Soamiely, 308n9
Ansolabehere, Stephen, 147n6, 163n33
Ardagna, Silvia, 320 (note e)
Armingeon, Klaus, 324n43
Arnott, Richard, 234n36
Arpaia, Alfonso, 317n27
Arrow, Kenneth, 23, 100
Ash, Timothy, 333n
Asplund, Marcus, 235n41
Atkeson, Lonna Rae, 116n30
Atlas, Cary, 147n6
Auerbach, Alan, 63n, 134n63, 243n54, 317n29
Ayres, Ian, 167n39

Baerg, Nicole, 322n41
Bagwell, Kyle, 79n9, 92n23
Baicker, Katherine, 226n19, 238

Baird, Zoe, 185n13
Baker, Lynn, 157n19
Baldwin, Richard, 305n6, 313n20
Baqir, Reza, 119n39
Barankay, Iwan, 47n13
Bardhan, Pranab, 31, 223n14
Baron, David, 107, 108n16, 111, 118n33
Barrell, Ray, 316n26
Barrett, Scott, 89n19
Barro, Robert, 19n, 243n53
Barseghyan, Levon, 54n
Bartels, Larry, 135n66, 162n
Bassett, Carolyn, 358n23
Bayer, Patrick, 44n7
Bayoumi, Tamim, 216n
Bebchuk, Lucian, 275, 276, 279n36
Becker, Sascha, 307 (notes a, b), 315n24
Bednar, Jenna, 29–30, 113n25, 122n44, 139, 156n15
Beer, Samuel, 2nn2–3, 5nn6–7, 20n, 67n36, 76n1, 131n52, 133n60, 147n4, 147n7, 153n14, 205n44
Beetsma, Roel, 243n54, 317n29
Berglöf, Erik, 333n, 336n55
Bergstrom, Theodore (Ted), 41, 61n30
Berlin, Isiah, 70–71
Bermann, George, 156n15, 185nn11–12
Besley, Timothy, 43n, 49, 58, 61, 113n25, 127n, 168n40, 198n, 231n33
Bettendorf, Leon, 240n
Bickers, Kenneth, 119n38
Bird, Richard, 11n, 31, 236n46
Birnbaum, Jeffrey, 62–63n, 152

417

SUBJECT INDEX

Page numbers in *italics* refer to figures and tables.

A NOTE ON THE TYPE

This book has been composed in Arno, an Old-style serif typeface in the classic Venetian tradition, designed by Robert Slimbach at Adobe.